THE EGO AND HIS OWN

The Case of the Individual Against Authority

MAX STIRNER

Translated from the German by
Steven T. Byington

Edited, with Annotations and an Introduction, by
James J. Martin

DOVER PUBLICATIONS, INC.
Mineola, New York

Bibliographical Note

This Dover edition, first published in 2005, is an unabridged republication of the work first published by the Libertarian Book Club, New York, in 1963 and first republished by Dover Publications, Inc., in 1973.

International Standard Book Number: 0-486-44581-X

Manufactured in the United States of America
Dover Publications, Inc., 31 East 2nd Street, Mineola, N.Y. 11501

Contents

EDITOR'S INTRODUCTION vii

TRANSLATOR'S PREFACE xvii

ALL THINGS ARE NOTHING TO ME 3

Part First: MAN

I. A HUMAN LIFE 9

II. MEN OF THE OLD TIME AND THE NEW 15

   A. The Ancients 15

   B. The Moderns 24

      1. The Spirit 27

      2. The Possessed 34

      3. The Hierarchy 67

   C. The Free 98

      1. Political Liberalism 98

      2. Social Liberalism 116

      3. Humane Liberalism 123

Part Second: I

III. OWNNESS 155

IV. THE OWNER 173

   A. My Power 186

   B. My Intercourse 210

   C. My Self-Enjoyment 319

V. THE UNIQUE ONE 362

Editor's Introduction

"**F**IFTY years sooner or later can make little difference in the case of a book so revolutionary as this." This was the opening sentence of James L. Walker's introduction to the first English language issuance of Max Stirner's *Der Einzige und sein Eigentum* by Benjamin R. Tucker in 1907. It is probably as succinct and concise a summarization of the significance of the book as has ever been uttered. But Walker has not been the only one to speak of Stirner in this manner. Two years later James Huneker, in his famous evaluation, referred to the book as "the most revolutionary ever written." "He has left behind him a veritable breviary of destruction, a striking and dangerous book," Huneker declared; "it is dangerous in every sense of the word—to socialism, to politicians, to hypocrisy."[1]

There is little doubt that *The Ego and His Own* is one of the most formidable assaults on authoritarianism ever launched. It may even belong in the first position as such. It is at once a historical document, a pamphlet of the intellectual disturbance of the mid-nineteenth century, and a timeless classic. Its persistent reappearance in one language or another in the last hundred years testifies to the latter.

However, the attention to Stirner has not been smooth and steady, but, rather, irregular and spasmodic. Its appearance in English for the first time was a product of one of these surges of interest, largely ignited by the great impact of Friedrich Nietzsche, especially between 1885 and 1910. As a consequence Stirner was attached to the tail of Nietzsche's comet as a "precursor" though he had been a comet in his own right before Nietzsche had even been old enough to learn to walk.[2]

---

1. Huneker, "Max Stirner," in *Egoists* (New York, 1909), p. 371.
2. The only biography of Stirner is John Henry Mackay, *Max Stirner: sein Leben und sein Werke* (Berlin, 1898); it has not been translated into English. It remains the only significant source on Stirner. Paul Lauterbach, in his introduction to the 1892 Reclam edition of *Der Einzige,* thought it was ironic that Stirner dedicated his book to his second wife, Marie

It is not of prime significance that Max Stirner's life be stressed here, though a few items of substance may be mentioned. He was born Johann Kaspar Schmidt in Bayreuth, Germany on October 25, 1806. The name he adopted as a pseudonym was originally a nickname from student days, a reference to his broad, high forehead. His career prior to the writing of his first, and major, book was obscure, though it included education in three universities, and half a dozen years' experience in teaching. His first wife died in childbirth in 1838, and he remarried in 1843, which also appears to be the date when he began to draw together his thoughts and material into the book which was to shock and outrage a goodly portion of intellectual Germany the year after, and subsequently the whole Western world.

From internal evidence it appears that he completed *Der Einzige* sometime in February or March, 1844. A rather expert job of book production followed, for, although the book bore the date 1845, it was actually in the hands of readers in November, 1844. The Leipzig house of Otto Wigand issued it in an octavo volume of about 500 pages.[3]

Stirner's book came out at a stormy time in Western and Central European affairs. France, Italy and the whole German world were in furious distress caused by the pressure of Liberalism upon the monarchical structure of politics in these lands, clamoring for a voice in the making of public policy and the running of affairs. And in the background and the underground boiled the propaganda of socialism, supervised by a score or more expert tenders of mainly French and German origin. The philosophical proponents of the powerful national secular State had also made their appearance, and the polished thought of Johann Gottlieb Fichte and Georg Wilhelm Friedrich Hegel, in particular

---

Dähnhardt, whose education, background and interests hardly suggested she was capable of grasping more than a very scant portion of it. Lauterbach recalled the old Spanish saying, "da Dios almendras al que no tiene muelas" ("God gives almonds to him who has no teeth"). Lauterbach, "Kurze Einführung zum *'Einzige und sein Eigentum,'*" Reclam edition, p. 10.

3. Hermann Schultheiss, *Stirner: Grundlagen zum Verständnis des Werkes* "Der Einzige und sein Eigentum," (2nd ed., Leipzig, 1922), p. 9.

the latter, had made a deep impression on the thinkers of the whole political spectrum of the time. In a way, Stirner was both a product and a victim of these factors. His book came out of them, and it was buried in the avalanche of the revolutions of March 1848 and thereafter. But in the interval between its publication and the uprising of the '48ers, a lively intellectual conflict spread. Few books have aroused such hostility and general disparagement as Stirner's, though it was not the author's intent to avoid a battle, by any means.[4] His spirited polemics against the principal figures among the so-called Left Hegelians, the *Junghegelianer,* particularly Ludwig Feuerbach and Bruno Bauer, invited reprisal, let alone his equally rousing tilt with the socialists, especially Wilhelm Weitling and Moses Hess. Stirner represented a "third force" in these agitated times, neither a defender of the theological or monarchical State, nor a protagonist of the secular models advanced by the Liberals and socialists. His views were as shocking and repellent to the latter as to the former. And Stirner went into almost total eclipse in the following forty years, while the modern secular State took shape, with its distinctive homogenization of the new nationalism and socialism, and the surviving but mutated strains of the earlier divine right and ecclesiastical authority, plus the ingredients consisting of the enfranchised and compulsorily armed masses which the French Revolution contributed.

Stirner's principal intellectual and social company had been the Berliners of Hegelian inspiration and tendencies whom he had encountered at Hippel's restaurant, who were known as "Die Freien," in some circles. These "bold spirits" included Ludwig Buhl, C.F. Köppen, Arthur Müller, and the brothers Bruno, Edgar and Egbert Bauer. And there were others. It was assumed Stirner was one of them, and the largest part of the critics in the subsequent half-century generally lumped him in the Hegelian Left. But Stirner's book is *the* Anti-Hegel, as Victor Basch

---

4. Critics such as Kuno Fischer insisted that the proper antecedent of Stirner was the French philosopher of the Enlightenment, Claude Adrien Helvétius (1712-1771), especially in his work *De l'Esprit* (1758), which in one sense produced the same sensation in its time as *Der Einzige.*

elaborated nearly sixty years ago.[5] And in an important sense a thorough reading and understanding of Hegel is necessary to understand Stirner. The assault on the master was not an explicit one, however. Hegel is mentioned sparingly, though significantly, in a direct sense. It is through his younger exponents that Stirner propels his critique of their State and its related personifications and generalized ideas.

It was in the company of these persons that such previews of Stirner as exist made their appearance. He published a few articles in the *Hallische Jahrbücher* and the *Deutsche Jahrbücher,* ephemeral journals edited by Arnold Ruge[6] in the years just previous. They were largely ignored at the time, and not made generally available for over half a century. It is in these that the germs of his anti-Hegelian revolt are first discerned.[7]

The history of *Der Einzige und sein Eigentum* is worthy of a glance. After its first appearance, it sank out of sight for nearly four decades. The original publishing house of Wigand brought out a second edition in 1882, and a third in 1901.[8] These latter two were separated chronologically by the 1892 Universal-Bibliotek edition of Philipp Reclam, Jr., also of Leipzig, in the famous "Miniatur-Ausgaben" series, which found Stirner in the company of world-famous literature. The publication of a full-scale biography of Stirner by John Henry Mackay in 1893 preceded two

5. Basch, *L'Individualisme Anarchiste Max Stirner* (Paris, 1904).

6. Ruge, long active in German literary affairs, edited the *Hallische Jahrbücher für deutsche Wissenschaft und Kunst* from 1838 until mid-1841. From that time until the end of 1842 it was titled the *Deutsche Jahrbücher für Wissenschaft und Kunst,* and was suspended after the issue of December, 1842. Ruge's collaboration with Karl Marx in publishing the equally-shortlived *Deutsch-französische Jahrbücher* in Paris in 1844 is discussed in another context. Early pieces by Stirner appear in the first two of these.

7. On these fugitive fragments of Stirner see Mackay (ed.), *Max Stirners kleinere Schriften und sein Entgegnungen auf die Kritik seines Werkes* (2nd ed., Berlin, 1914); Anselm Ruest, *Stirnerbrevier: die Stärke des Einsamen Max Stirners Individualismus und Egoismus* (Berlin, 1906); same author, *Max Stirner: Leben — Weltanschauung — Vermächtnis* (Berlin, 1906); Stirner, *Das unwahre Prinzip unserer Erziehung* (with foreword "In Memoriam Max Stirner" by Willy Storrer) (Basel, 1926).

8. Schultheiss, *Stirner,* p. 37.

translations in French which were published one after the other in Paris in 1900 under the title *L'Unique et sa Propriété*. These set the stage for the English translation and publication.

The first American to dwell at length on Stirner was James L. Walker, a Texas newspaperman and later physician, and an associate of Tucker. Walker brought Stirner's "egoism" into the pages of Tucker's world-famous anarchist weekly, *Liberty*, with increasing frequency during the 1890's, and himself prepared a strongly Stirner-influenced book, *The Philosophy of Egoism*,[9] published posthumously, Walker having died in Mexico in 1904. His introduction to the Tucker edition of Stirner was written in 1902 or 1903, evidence that Tucker planned to release the book in that time, though some unknown circumstance delayed its issuance. In a publishing career which went back to 1875, Tucker insisted that making Stirner available in English was his most important contribution in the entire time.[10]

After Tucker's property was burned out in the fire of January, 1908 his work ended,[11] but apparently the plates of this book were salvaged, because editions in the identical format with that of 1907 came out in London and New York in 1913-15 under different auspices, and a third by still another publisher was produced in New York in 1918.[12] The history of Stirner's book in languages other than those examined above is obscure; there were Italian and Russian translations, and possibly in a Scandinavian language, as Stirner was very familiar to Henrik Ibsen and the Danish critic Georg Brandes,[13] the latter having written at some length on Stirnerism.

Huneker declared that the translation, by the erudite philologist Steven T. Byington, was "admirable," which is indeed a fact.

9. Denver, 1905.

10. *Liberty*, vol. 16 (April, 1907), p. 1.

11. See the editor's preface to Paul Eltzbacher, *Anarchism* (New York: Libertarian Book Club, 1960), pp. xii-xiv, for an account of this event and related matters.

12. The 1913-15 editions were by E. C. Walker in New York and A. C. Fifield in London; Boni and Liveright issued the book three years later in the Modern Library series.

13. See Max Messer, *Max Stirner* (Berlin, 1907), a brief appreciative study edited by Brandes.

He was aided in his work by Walker and by Emma Heller Schumm and George Schumm, all expert in German, so in one sense it was a cooperative project. Byington did the greater part of the work, however. His preface to the original edition is preserved here in order to illuminate some of the difficulties encountered in Stirner's frequently diffuse style, and his etymological references are preserved throughout the book in the original footnotes. His choice of the English title, *The Ego and His Own,* is specially felicitous.

Friedrich Nietzsche was a few months old when Stirner's book was published, but no other thinker has been compared more to Stirner than Nietzsche, and perhaps with less evidence for it. A critical controversy raged among philosophers and academic people over this issue, in particular between 1890 and the first World War, and a literature of large enough scope exists on this subject alone to warrant a substantial book. Albert Lévy, in his careful study *Stirner et Nietzsche,*[14] points out that Stirner is not mentioned in either the works or the correspondence of Nietzsche at any time, and with the exception of a single instance, Nietzsche appears not to have been aware of him at all. In the case of every writer who has tried to establish such relationship, the method has consisted of dependence on inference and the coincidental similarities which can be established by superficial content analysis. This is the approach of a considerable number of over-simplifiers, of whom Paul Carus is one of the best examples.[15]

Stirner was an uncommonly keen student of classical antiquity, the French Revolution, and the Bible, in particular. The latter is his most quoted source by a wide margin. In one sense this appears incomprehensible, considering Stirner's position on religion. Of this, more will be said shortly. An attempt has

14. Paris, 1904. Lévy appended an exhaustive list of all the books Nietzsche had charged out of the university library at Basel between 1869 and 1879 as evidence that he had not taken out Stirner's book during this important period, as well as giving a thorough look at the literary influences on Nietzsche.

15. See Carus, *Nietzsche and Other Exponents of Individualism* (Chicago, 1914).

been made to annotate as many of Stirner's literary references and allusions as seems practicable, in view of their number and his careless documentation. The latter in particular suggests the contemporary polemic part of his book; the sources are thrown about carelessly like so much spare lumber, and the overall impression conveyed is that his readers are fully aware of their nature or have read them.[16]

The Ego and His Own is a piece of fierce writing, in an "icy, relentless, epigrammatic style," as Huneker describes it. Nothing distracts Stirner from his pursuit of the exposition of freedom; he is for freedom for everyone, not just himself. And he is consistent in not shrinking from the consequences of this pursuit. It may very well be that the largest number of mid-twentieth century individualists does not have the stamina to stick with Stirner to the bitter logical end. The various libertarians are free to decamp at that point of the journey beyond where they no longer care to proceed. But it is their responsibility to know whence individualism stems and where its logic goes. No one has surpassed Stirner in dealing with these two aspects of the problem. There are uncanny portions of this work; one might cite in particular his discussion of the semantics of "freedom" and compare them with the similar dissertations by George Orwell in *Nineteen Eight-four* and Eugen Zamyatin in *We,* those most exquisitely anti-Stirner worlds. Stirner in a sense was a pioneer in the area of general semantics.

Stirner wanted all to be free; he was not arguing just for himself or for a special segment of mankind. But he stressed over and over the part the one desirous of freedom had to play; freedom was not something someone else *gave* you. All freedom is essentially self-liberation, says Stirner. His concern is with the individual rebel, not the revolution. It is as such that he respected Jesus, a rebel who concerned himself not a whit with the politics and the State of his time. But for organized Christianity, and for all other organized religions, Stirner had particularly

16. NOTE: Stirner's original footnotes have been reproduced and stand without enclosures. Byington's notes are enclosed in parentheses, while the editor's annotations are enclosed in brackets.

harsh words. Personal insurrection rather than general revolution was his message; he recognized the futility of meeting the authorities at street barricades with broom handles at a time when the Romantics were still enamored with this concept. The age of automatic arms and instantaneous communication was just around the corner. The general revolution brought either "Socialism or a tyrant," in his view; the revolutionist merely exchanged masters, often for the worse.

There are only five chapters in Stirner, three very short ones, separated by two very long ones, and it is in the latter that he has packed the very largest part of his message. Though he assaults religion, philosophy, morals, every source of inspiration for authority, as for his principal target Victor Basch remarks, "L'État, voilà le grand ennemi, voilà l'éternel tyran du Moi."[17] All authority materials end up as arms and nutriment for the State, and Hegel and his chief disciples were the agents of his time who appeared to be doing the most thorough job of preparing the world for the new secular Leviathan. Stirner was scornful of the German national unity fervor of the 1840's. He was almost completely untouched by one of the most uproarious political fermentations in the history of Central Europe. In his view, unity would just be the superimposing of a far more grim and ferocious monster for the existing thirty-eight separate weaker ones of the existing states. He saw no net gain in replacing the ecclesiastic or monarchical State with the new secular product in the making; in fact, he was sure that the latter had immeasurably superior means and capabilities for oppressiveness.

But if Stirner was appalled by the Hegelians, he was equally appalled by the communists. *The Ego and His Own* was a pitiless attack on communism well before the *Communist Manifesto* was published, and it is at the same time one of the most original and unanswerable critiques of coercive collectivism. A social associate of Friedrich Engels, published in one of the journals edited by Karl Marx, Stirner's socialist antagonists were Weitling and Hess and the French propounders of the same ideology, all more prominent at that moment. Stirner saw clearly

17. Basch, *Max Stirner*, p. 84.

through the communist appeals of the 1840's (the seedbed of the *Manifesto*), in particular the talk of the necessity of eliminating the State. He reiterated that communism would produce instead a State far more onerous than the royal, ecclesiastic or bourgeois models communists fulminated against so tirelessly.

Yet Stirner does not talk of future societies, or blueprints for them, himself. For the most part he avoids all soothsaying; the structure of the free "union" is beyond his ken, and he felt it was a futile field for prediction in the first place. As he says in one place of the slave, and the speculations as to his likely behavior once his servitude is ended, one cannot know what he will do until he actually gets free.

The century coinciding roughly with the end of the Second World War may be described ideologically as the Age of Marx, during which Marxism was presumed to be victorious over Stirner and all other antagonists. The fact that Marx devoted such an immense part of his ponderous *Die Deutsche Ideologie* to an attack on Stirner was conceded to be the principal *prima facie* evidence of the former's triumph. A generation ago Sidney Hook in two widely-acclaimed books calmly reaffirmed that Marx demolished *Der Einzige und sein Eigentum*, it being nothing but a "social defense mechanism of a petty bourgeois soul."[18] Marxists long tended to display this cavalier attitude toward Stirner, generally without reading a line of his work. In fact, Marxist literary and intellectual influence for a time all but brought about Stirner's consignment to the "Memory Hole" of *1984* fame.

But there is plentiful evidence that he, Proudhon, Bakunin and the others against whom Marx tilted never lost their validity during this period. The last two decades in particular have seen the repeated reappearance of their works in various forms. As

18. Hook, *Towards the Understanding of Karl Marx: A Revolutionary Interpretation* (New York, 1933), pp. 66, 148-150. There is a further elaboration by Hook in his *From Hegel to Marx* (New York, 1936). It is instructive to note Hook in the first title above spelled the title of Stirner's book *Das Einzige und sein Eigentum*.

Herbert Read declared in his masterful essay[19] commemorating the centennial of Stirner's book, "After a sleep of a hundred years the giants whom Marx thought he had slain show signs of coming to life again," and indeed they have returned. "Marx's criticism" of Stirner, Read advanced in a famous second-thought, "would need drastic revision to be convincing today." As for critics of Stirnerite egoism such as Berdyaev, Read was of the view that Stirner could have handled him capably with a single sentence. Concerning Stirner's examination of love and his consistent plea in behalf of the "integration of personality," Read concludes with several impressive observations. He finds many "modern" views in such areas as held by Erich Fromm, Jung, Martin Buber and even the existentialists in very close rapport with, if not dependent on, Max Stirner.

The fashionable day for *ad hominem* attacks on Stirner seems past. *The Ego and His Own* has demonstrated survival value; it deserves to be read in the same spirit and in the same way one reads *The Prince*.

JAMES J. MARTIN

Malibu, California
September 8, 1962

19. Read, "Max Stirner," reprinted in his *The Tenth Muse: Essays in Criticism* (New York, 1958), pp. 74-82.

Translator's Preface

IF the style of this book is found unattractive, it will show that I have done my work ill and not represented the author truly; but, if it is found odd, I beg that I may not bear all the blame. I have simply tried to reproduce the author's own mixture of colloquialisms and technicalities, and his preference for the precise expression of his thought rather than the word conventionally expected.

One especial feature of the style, however, gives the reason why this preface should exist. It is characteristic of Stirner's writing that the thread of thought is carried on largely by the repetition of the same word in a modified form or sense. That connection of ideas which has guided popular instinct in the formation of words is made to suggest the line of thought which the writer wishes to follow. If this echoing of words is missed, the bearing of the statements on each other is in a measure lost; and, where the ideas are very new, one cannot afford to throw away any help in following their connection. Therefore, where a useful echo (and there are few useless ones in the book) could not be reproduced in English, I have generally called attention to it in a note. My notes are distinguished from the author's by being enclosed in parentheses.

One or two of such coincidents of language, occurring in words which are prominent throughout the book, should be borne constantly in mind as a sort of *Keri perpetuum;* for instance, the identity in the original of the words "spirit" and "mind," and of the phrases "supreme being" and "highest essence." In such cases I have repeated the note where it seemed that such repetition might be absolutely necessary, but have trusted the reader to carry it in his head where a failure of his memory would not be ruinous or likely.

For the same reason—that is, in order not to miss any indication of the drift of the thought—I have followed the original in the very liberal use of italics, and in the occasional eccentric use of a punctuation mark, as I might not have done in translating a work of a different nature.

I have set my face as a flint against the temptation to add notes that were not part of the translation. There is no telling how much I might have enlarged the book if I had put a note at every sentence which deserved to have its truth brought out by fuller elucidation—or even at every one which I thought needed correction. It might have been within my province, if I had been able, to explain all the allusions to contemporary events, but I doubt whether any one could do that properly without having access to the files of three or four well-chosen German newspapers of Stirner's time. The allusions are clear enough, without names and dates, to give a vivid picture of certain aspects of German life then. The tone of some of them is explained by the fact that the book was published under censorship.

I have usually preferred, for the sake of the connection, to translate Biblical quotations somewhat as they stand in the German, rather than conform them altogether to the English Bible. I am sometimes quite as near the original Greek as if I had followed the current translation.

Where German books are referred to, the pages cited are those of the German editions even when (usually because of some allusions in the text) the titles of the books are translated.

STEVEN T. BYINGTON

TO MY SWEETHEART

MARIE DÄHNHARDT

Pencil sketch of Max Stirner
Drawn after his death from memory by Engels

All Things Are Nothing To Me [1]

WHAT is not supposed to be my concern! [2] First and foremost, the Good Cause, [3] then God's cause, the cause of mankind, of truth, of freedom, of humanity, of justice; further, the cause of my people, my prince, my fatherland; finally, even the cause of Mind, and a thousand other causes. Only *my* cause is never to be my concern. "Shame on the egoist who thinks only of himself!"

Let us look and see, then, how they manage *their* concerns —they for whose cause we are to labor, devote ourselves, and grow enthusiastic.

You have much profound information to give about God, and have for thousands of years "searched the depths of the Godhead," and looked into its heart, so that you can doubtless tell us how God himself attends to "God's cause," which we are called to serve. And you do not conceal the Lord's doings, either. Now, what is his cause? Has he, as is demanded of us, made an alien cause, the cause of truth or love, his own? You are shocked by this misunderstanding, and you instruct us that God's cause is indeed the cause of truth and love, but that this cause cannot be called alien to him, because God is himself truth and love; you are shocked by the assumption that God could be like us poor worms in furthering an alien cause as his own. "Should God take up the cause of truth if he were not himself truth?" He cares only for *his* cause, but, because he is all in all, therefore all is *his* cause! But we, we are not all in all, and our cause is altogether little and contemptible; therefore we must "serve a higher cause."—Now it is clear, God cares

1. (*Ich hab' Mein' Sach' auf Nichts gestellt,* first line of Goethe's poem, *Vanitas! Vanitatum Vanitas!* Literal translation: "I have set my affair on nothing.")
2. (*Sache*)
3. (*Sache*)

3

only for what is his, busies himself only with himself, thinks only of himself, and has only himself before his eyes; woe to all that is not well-pleasing to him! He serves no higher person, and satisfies only himself. His cause is—a purely egoistic cause.

How is it with mankind, whose cause we are to make our own? Is its cause that of another, and does mankind serve a higher cause? No, mankind looks only at itself, mankind will promote the interests of mankind only, mankind is its own cause. That it may develop, it causes nations and individuals to wear themselves out in its service, and, when they have accomplished what mankind needs, it throws them on the dung-heap of history in gratitude. Is not mankind's cause—a purely egoistic cause?

I have no need to take up each thing that wants to throw its cause on us and show that it is occupied only with itself, not with us, only with its good, not with ours. Look at the rest for yourselves. Do truth, freedom, humanity, justice, desire anything else than that you grow enthusiastic and serve them?

They all have an admirable time of it when they receive zealous homage. Just observe the nation that is defended by devoted patriots. The patriots fall in bloody battle or in the fight with hunger and want; what does the nation care for that? By the manure of their corpses the nation comes to "its bloom!" The individuals have died "for the great cause of the nation," and the nation sends some words of thanks after them and—has the profit of it. I call that a paying kind of egoism.

But only look at that Sultan who cares so lovingly for his people. Is he not pure unselfishness itself, and does he not hourly sacrifice himself for his people? Oh, yes, for "his people." Just try it; show yourself not as his, but as your own; for breaking away from his egoism you will take a trip to jail. The Sultan has set his cause on nothing but himself; he is to himself all in all, he is to himself the only one, and tolerates nobody who would dare not to be one of "his people."

And will you not learn by these brilliant examples that the egoist gets on best? I for my part take a lesson from them, and propose, instead of further unselfishly serving those great egoists, rather to be the egoist myself.

God and mankind have concerned themselves for nothing,

for nothing but themselves. Let me then likewise concern myself for *myself*, who am equally with God the nothing of all others, who am my all, who am the only one.[4]

If God, if mankind, as you affirm, have substance enough in themselves to be all in all to themselves, then I feel that *I* shall still less lack that, and that I shall have no complaint to make of my "emptiness." I am not nothing in the sense of emptiness, but I am the creative nothing, the nothing out of which I myself as creator create everything.

Away, then, with every concern that is not altogether my concern! You think at least the "good cause" must be my concern? What's good, what's bad? Why, I myself am my concern, and I am neither good nor bad. Neither has meaning for me.

The divine is God's concern; the human, man's. My concern is neither the divine nor the human, not the true, good, just, free, etc., but solely what is *mine*, and it is not a general one, but is—unique,[5] as I am unique.

Nothing is more to me than myself!

4. (*der Einzige*)
5. (*einzig*)

Transvaluation of values

PART FIRST

MAN

Man is to man the supreme being, says Feuerbach.
Man has just been discovered, says Bruno Bauer.

Then let us take a more careful look at this supreme being and this new discovery.

I

A Human Life

FROM the moment when he catches sight of the light of the world a man seeks to find out *himself* and get hold of *himself* out of its confusion, in which he, with everything else, is tossed about in motley mixture.

But everything that comes in contact with the child defends itself in turn against his attacks, and asserts its own persistence.

Accordingly, because each thing *cares for itself* and at the same time comes into constant collision with other things, the *combat* of self-assertion is unavoidable.

Victory or defeat—between the two alternatives the fate of the combat wavers. The victor becomes the *lord*, the vanquished one the *subject*: the former exercises *supremacy* and "rights of supremacy," the latter fulfills in awe and deference the "duties of a subject."

But both remain *enemies*, and always lie in wait: they watch for each other's *weaknesses*—children for those of their parents and parents for those of their children (their fear, for example); either the stick conquers the man, or the man conquers the stick.

In childhood liberation takes the direction of trying to get to the bottom of things, to get at what is "back of" things; therefore we spy out the weak points of everybody, for which, it is well known, children have a sure instinct; therefore we like to smash things, like to rummage through hidden corners, pry after what is covered up or out of the way, and try what we can do with everything. When we once get at what is back of the things, we know we are safe; when we have got at the fact that the rod is too weak against our obduracy, then we no longer fear it, "have outgrown it."

Back of the rod, mightier than it, stands our—obduracy, our obdurate courage. By degrees we get at what is back of everything that was mysterious and uncanny to us, the mysterious-

9

ly-dreaded might of the rod, the father's stern look, etc., and back of all we find our ataraxia—our imperturbability, intrepidity, our counter forces, our odds of strength, our invincibility. Before that which formerly inspired in us fear and deference we no longer retreat shyly, but take *courage*. Back of everything we find our *courage*, our superiority; back of the sharp command of parents and authorities stands, after all, our courageous choice or our outwitting shrewdness. And the more we feel ourselves, the smaller appears that which before seemed invincible. And what is our trickery, shrewdness, courage, obduracy? What else but—*mind!*[1]

Through a considerable time we are spared a fight that is so exhausting later—the fight against *reason*. The fairest part of childhood passes without the necessity of coming to blows with reason. We care nothing at all about it, do not meddle with it, admit no reason. We are not to be persuaded to anything by *conviction,* and are deaf to good arguments and principles; on the other hand, coaxing, punishment, and the like are hard for us to resist. This stern life-and-death combat with *reason* enters later, and begins a new phase; in childhood we scamper about without racking our brains much.

Mind is the name of the *first* self-discovery, the first un-deification of the divine; that is, of the uncanny, the spooks, the "powers above." Our fresh feeling of youth, this feeling of self, now defers to nothing; the world is discredited, for we are above it, we are *mind*. Now for the first time we see that hitherto we have not looked at the world *intelligently* at all, but only stared at it.

We exercise the beginnings of our strength on *natural powers*. We defer to parents as a natural power; later we say: Father and mother are to be forsaken, all natural power to be counted as riven. They are vanquished. For the rational, the "intel-lectual" man, there is no family as a natural power; a renunciation of parents, brothers, etc., makes its appearance. If these are

1. (*Geist.* This word will be translated sometimes "mind" and sometimes "spirit" in the following pages.)

"born again" as *intellectual, rational powers,* they are no longer at all what they were before.

And not only parents, but *men in general,* are conquered by the young man; they are no hindrance to him, and are no longer regarded; for now he says: One must obey God rather than men.

From this high standpoint everything *"earthly"* recedes into contemptible remoteness; for the standpoint is—the *heavenly.*

The attitude is now altogether reversed; the youth takes up an *intellectual* position, while the boy, who did not yet feel himself as mind, grew up on mindless learning. The former does not try to get hold of *things* (for instance, to get into his head the *data* of history), but of the *thoughts* that lie hidden in things, and so, therefore, of the *spirit* of history. On the other hand, the boy understands *connections* no doubt, but not ideas, the spirit; therefore he strings together whatever can be learned, without proceeding *a priori* and theoretically, without looking for ideas.

As in childhood one had to overcome the resistance of the *laws of the world,* so now in everything that he proposes he is met by an objection of the mind, of reason, of his *own conscience.* "That is unreasonable, unchristian, unpatriotic," and the like, cries conscience to us, and—frightens us away from it. Not the might of the avenging Eumenides, not Poseidon's wrath, not God, far as he sees the hidden, not the father's rod of punishment, do we fear, but—*conscience.*

We "run after our thoughts" now, and follow their commands just as before we followed parental, human ones. Our course of action is determined by our thoughts (ideas, conceptions, *faith*) as it is in childhood by the commands of our parents.

For all that, we were already thinking when we were children, only our thoughts were not fleshless, abstract, *absolute,* that is, NOTHING BUT THOUGHTS, a heaven in themselves, a pure world of thought, *logical* thoughts.

On the contrary, they had been only thoughts that we had about a *thing;* we thought of the thing so or so. Thus we may have thought "God made the world that we see there," but we did not think of ("search") the "depths of the Godhead itself";

we may have thought "that is the truth about the matter," but we do not think of Truth itself, nor unite into one sentence "God is truth." The "depths of the Godhead, who is truth," we did not touch. Over such purely logical (theological) questions, "What is truth?" Pilate does not stop, though he does not therefore hesitate to ascertain in an individual case "what truth there is in the thing," whether the *thing* is true.

Any thought bound to a *thing* is not yet *nothing but a thought,* absolute thought.

To bring to light the *pure thought,* or to be of its party, is the delight of youth; and all the shapes of light in the world of thought, like truth, freedom, humanity, Man, illumine and inspire the youthful soul.

But, when the spirit is recognized as the essential thing, it still makes a difference whether the spirit is poor or rich, and therefore one seeks to become rich in spirit; the spirit wants to spread out so as to found its empire—an empire that is not of this world, the world just conquered. Thus, then, it longs to become all in all to itself; for, although I am spirit, I am not yet *perfected* spirit, and must first seek the complete spirit.

But with that I, who had just now found myself as spirit, lose myself again at once, bowing before the complete spirit as one not my own but *supernal,* and feeling my emptiness.

Spirit is the essential point for everything, to be sure; but then is every spirit the "right" spirit? The right and true spirit is the ideal of spirit, the "Holy Spirit." It is not my or your spirit, but just—an ideal, supernal one, it is "God." "God is spirit." And this supernal "Father in heaven gives it to those that pray to him."[2]

The man is distinguished from the youth by the fact that he takes the world as it is, instead of everywhere fancying it amiss and wanting to improve it, model it after his ideal; in him the view that one must deal with the world according to his *interest,* not according to his *ideals,* becomes confirmed.

So long as one knows himself only as *spirit,* and feels that all the value of his existence consists in being spirit (it becomes

2. Luke 11. 13.

easy for the youth to give his life, the "bodily life," for a nothing, for the silliest point of honor), so long it is only *thoughts* that one has, ideas that he hopes to be able to realize some day when he has found a sphere of action; thus one has meanwhile only *ideals,* unexecuted ideas or thoughts.

Not till one has fallen in love with his *corporeal* self, and takes a pleasure in himself as a living flesh-and-blood person— but it is in mature years, in the man, that we find it so—not till then has one a personal or *egoistic* interest, an interest not only of our spirit, for instance, but of total satisfaction, satisfaction of the whole chap, a *selfish* interest. Just compare a man with a youth, and see if he will not appear to you harder, less magnanimous, more selfish. Is he therefore worse? No, you say; he has only become more definite, or, as you also call it, more "practical." But the main point is this, that he makes *himself* more the centre than does the youth, who is infatuated about other things, for example, God, fatherland, and so on.

Therefore the man shows a *second* self-discovery. The youth found himself as *spirit* and lost himself again in the *general spirit,* the complete, holy spirit, Man, mankind—in short, all ideals; the man finds himself as *embodied* spirit.

Boys had only *unintellectual* interests (those interests devoid of thoughts and ideas), youths only *intellectual* ones; the man has bodily, personal, egoistic interests.

If the child has not an *object* that it can occupy itself with, it feels *ennui;* for it does not yet know how to occupy itself with *itself.* The youth, on the contrary, throws the object aside, because for him *thoughts* arose out of the object; he occupies himself with his *thoughts,* his dreams, occupies himself intellectually, or "his mind is occupied."

The young man includes everything not intellectual under the contemptuous name of "externalities." If he nevertheless sticks to the most trivial externalities (such as the customs of students' clubs and other formalities), it is because, and when, he discovers *mind* in them, when they are *symbols* to him.

As I find myself back of things, and that as mind, so I must later find *myself* also back of *thoughts*—to wit, as their creator and *owner.* In the time of spirits thoughts grew till they overtopped my head, whose offspring they yet were; they hovered about me and convulsed me like fever-phantasies—an awful power. The thoughts had become *corporeal* on their own account, were ghosts, such as God, Emperor, Pope, Fatherland, etc. If I destroy their corporeity, then I take them back into mine, and say: "I alone am corporeal." And now I take the world as what it is to me, as *mine,* as my property; I refer all to myself.

If as spirit I had thrust away the world in the deepest contempt, so as owner I thrust spirits or ideas away into their "vanity." They have no longer any power over me, as no "earthly might" has power over the spirit.

The child was realistic, taken up with the things of this world, till little by little he succeeded in getting at what was back of these very things; the youth was idealistic, inspired by thoughts, till he worked his way up to where he became the man, the egoistic man, who deals with things and thoughts according to his heart's pleasure, and sets his personal interest above everything. Finally, the old man? When I become one, there will still be time enough to speak of that.

II

Men of The Old Time and The New

HOW each of us developed himself, what he strove for, attained, or missed, what objects he formerly pursued and what plans and wishes his heart is now set on, what transformation his views have experienced, what perturbations his principles —in short, how he has to-day become what yesterday or years ago he was not—this he brings out again from his memory with more or less ease, and he feels with especial vividness what changes have taken place in himself when he has before his eyes the unrolling of another's life.

Let us therefore look into the activities our forefathers busied themselves with.

A.—THE ANCIENTS

CUSTOM having once given the name of "the ancients" to our pre-Christian ancestors, we will not throw it up against them that, in comparison with us experienced people, they ought properly to be called children, but will rather continue to honor them as our good old fathers. But how have they come to be antiquated, and who could displace them through his pretended newness?

We know, of course, the revolutionary innovator and disrespectful heir, who even took away the sanctity of the fathers' sabbath to hallow his Sunday, and interrupted the course of time to begin at himself with a new chronology; we know him, and know that it is—the Christian. But does he remain forever young, and is he to-day still the new man, or will he too be superseded, as he has superseded the "ancients"?

The fathers must doubtless have themselves begotten the young one who entombed them. Let us then peep at this act of generation.

"To the ancients the world was a truth," says Feuerbach,[1]

but he forgets to make the important addition, "a truth whose untruth they tried to get back of, and at last really did." What is meant by those words of Feuerbach will be easily recognized if they are put alongside the Christian thesis of the "vanity and transitoriness of the world." For, as the Christian can never convince himself of the vanity of the divine word, but believes in its eternal and unshakable truth, which, the more its depths are searched, must all the more brilliantly come to light and triumph, so the ancients on their side lived in the feeling that the world and mundane relations (such as the natural ties of blood) were the truth before which their powerless "I" must bow. The very thing on which the ancients set the highest value is spurned by Christians as the valueless, and what they recognized as truth these brand as idle lies; the high significance of the fatherland disappears, and the Christian must regard himself as "a stranger on earth";[2] the sanctity of funeral rites, from which sprang a work of art like the Antigone of Sophocles, is designated as a paltry thing ("Let the dead bury their dead"); the infrangible truth of family ties is represented as an untruth which one cannot promptly enough get clear of;[3] and so in everything.

If we now see that to the two sides opposite things appear as truth, to one the natural, to the other the intellectual, to one earthly things and relations, to the other heavenly (the heavenly fatherland, "Jerusalem that is above," etc.), it still remains to be considered how the new time and that undeniable reversal could come out of antiquity. But the ancients themselves worked toward making their truth a lie.

Let us plunge at once into the midst of the most brilliant years of the ancients, into the Periclean century. Then the Sophistic culture was spreading, and Greece made a pastime of what had hitherto been to her a monstrously serious matter.

1. [Ludwig Andreas Feuerbach (1804-1872), probably the outstanding of the young Hegelians, had abandoned the master and moved into front rank himself as a philosopher with the publication of *Das Wesen des Christentums* (Leipzig, 1841).]

2. Heb. 11. 13.

3. Mark 10. 29.

The fathers had been enslaved by the undisturbed power of existing things too long for the posterity not to have to learn by bitter experience to *feel themselves.* Therefore the Sophists, with courageous sauciness, pronounce the reassuring words, "Don't be bluffed!" and diffuse the rationalistic doctrine, "Use your understanding, your wit, your mind, against everything; it is by having a good and well-drilled understanding that one gets through the world best, provides for himself the best lot, the pleasantest *life."* Thus they recognize in *mind* man's true weapon against the world. This is why they lay such stress on dialectic skill, command of language, the art of disputation, etc. They announce that mind is to be used against everything; but they are still far removed from the holiness of the Spirit, for to them it is a *means,* a weapon, as trickery and defiance serve children for the same purpose; their mind is the unbribable *understanding.*

To-day we should call that a one-sided culture of the understanding, and add the warning, "Cultivate not only your understanding, but also, and especially, your heart." Socrates did the same. For, if the heart did not become free from its natural impulses, but remained filled with the most fortuitous contents and, as an uncriticized *avidity,* altogether in the power of things, nothing but a vessel of the most various *appetites*— then it was unavoidable that the free understanding must serve the "bad heart" and was ready to justify everything that the wicked heart desired.

Therefore Socrates says that it is not enough for one to use his understanding in all things, but it is a question of what *cause* one exerts it for. We should now say, one must serve the "good cause." But serving the good cause is—being moral. Hence Socrates is the founder of ethics.

Certainly the principle of the Sophistic doctrine must lead to the possibility that the blindest and most dependent slave of his desires might yet be an excellent sophist, and, with keen understanding, trim and expound everything in favor of his coarse heart. What could there be for which a "good reason" might not be found, or which might not be defended through thick and thin?

Therefore Socrates says: "You must be 'pure-hearted' if your

shrewdness is to be valued." At this point begins the second
period of Greek liberation of the mind, the period of *purity of
heart*. For the first was brought to a close by the Sophists in
their proclaiming the omnipotence of the understanding. But
the heart remained *worldly-minded,* remained a servant of the
world, always affected by worldly wishes. This coarse heart
was to be cultivated from now on—the era of *culture of the heart*.
But how is the heart to be cultivated? What the understanding,
this one side of the mind, has reached—to wit, the capability
of playing freely with and over every concern—awaits the heart
also; everything *worldly* must come to grief before it, so that
at last family, commonwealth, fatherland, and the like, are given
up for the sake of the heart, that is, *of blessedness,* the heart's
blessedness.

Daily experience confirms the truth that the understanding
may have renounced a thing many years before the heart has
ceased to beat for it. So the Sophistic understanding too had
so far become master over the dominant, ancient powers that
they now needed only to be driven out of the heart, in which
they dwelt unmolested, to have at last no part at all left in
man. This war is opened by Socrates, and not till the dying
day of the old world does it end in peace.

The examination of the heart takes its start with Socrates,
and all the contents of the heart are sifted. In their last and
extremest struggles the ancients threw all contents out of the
heart and let it no longer beat for anything; this was the deed
of the Skeptics. The same purgation of the heart was now
achieved in the Skeptical age, as the understanding had succeeded
in establishing in the Sophistic age.

The Sophistic culture has brought it to pass that one's
understanding no longer *stands still* before anything, and the
Skeptical, that his heart is no longer *moved* by anything.

So long as man is entangled in the movements of the world
and embarrassed by relations to the world—and he is so till the
end of antiquity, because his heart still has to struggle for independence from the worldly—so long he is not yet spirit; for
spirit is without body, and has no relations to the world and
corporeality; for it the world does not exist, nor natural bonds,

That's why Agnostics rarely became Atheists

but only the spiritual, and spiritual bonds. Therefore man must first become so completely unconcerned and reckless, so altogether without relations, as the Skeptical culture presents him— so altogether indifferent to the world that even its falling in ruins would not move him—before he could feel himself as worldless; that is, as spirit. And this is the result of the gigantic work of the ancients: that man knows himself as a being without relations and without a world, as *spirit*.

Only now, after all worldly care has left him, is he all in all to himself, is he only for himself, is he spirit for the spirit, or, in plainer language, he cares only for the spiritual.

In the Christian wisdom of serpents and innocence of doves the two sides—understanding and heart—of the ancient liberation of mind are so completed that they appear young and new again, and neither the one nor the other lets itself be bluffed any longer by the worldly and natural.

Thus the ancients mounted to *spirit,* and strove to become *spiritual.* But a man who wishes to be active as spirit is drawn to quite other tasks than he was able to set himself formerly: to tasks which really give something to do to the spirit and not to mere sense or acuteness,[4] which exerts itself only to become master *of things.* The spirit busies itself solely about the spiritual, and seeks out the "traces of mind" in everything; to the *believing* spirit "everything comes from God," and interests him only to the extent that it reveals this origin; to the *philosophic* spirit everything appears with the stamp of reason, and interests him only so far as he is able to discover in it reason, that is, spiritual content.

Not the spirit, then, which has to do with absolutely nothing unspiritual, with no *thing,* but only with the essence which exists behind and above things, with *thoughts*—not that did the ancients exert, for they did not yet have it; no, they had only reached the point of struggling and longing for it, and therefore sharpened it against their too-powerful foe, the world of sense (but what would not have been sensuous for them, since Jehovah or the

---

4. (Italicized in the original for the sake of its etymology, *Scharfsinn* ="sharp sense." Compare next paragraph.)

gods of the heathen were yet far removed from the conception "God is *spirit*," since the "heavenly fatherland" had not yet stepped into the place of the sensuous, etc.?)—they sharpened against the world of sense their *sense,* their acuteness. To this day the Jews, those precocious children of antiquity, have got no farther; and with all the subtlety and strength of their prudence and understanding, which easily becomes master of things and forces them to obey it, they cannot discover *spirit,* which *takes no account whatever of things.*

The Christian has spiritual interests, because he allows himself to be a *spiritual* man; the Jew does not even understand these interests in their purity, because he does not allow himself to assign *no value* to things. He does not arrive at pure *spirituality,* a spirituality such as is religiously expressed, for instance, in the *faith* of Christians, which alone (without works) justifies. Their *unspirituality* sets Jews forever apart from Christians; for the spiritual man is incomprehensible to the unspiritual, as the unspiritual is contemptible to the spiritual. But the Jews have only "the spirit of this world."

The ancient acuteness and profundity lies as far from the spirit and the spirituality of the Christian world as earth from heaven.

He who feels himself as free spirit is not oppressed and made anxious by the things of this world, because he does not care for them; if one is still to feel their burden, he must be narrow enough to attach *weight* to them—as is evidently the case, for instance, when one is still concerned for his "dear life." He to whom everything centers in knowing and conducting himself as a free spirit gives little heed to how scantily he is supplied meanwhile, and does not reflect at all on how he must make his arrangements to have a thoroughly free or enjoyable *life.* He is not disturbed by the inconveniences of the life that depends on things, because he lives only spiritually and on spiritual food, while aside from this he only gulps things down like a beast, hardly knowing it, and dies bodily, to be sure, when his fodder gives out, but knows himself immortal as spirit, and closes his eyes with an adoration or a thought. His life is occupation with the spiritual, is—*thinking;* the rest does not bother him; let him busy himself with the spiritual in any way that he can and chooses —in devotion, in contemplation, or in philosophic cognition— his doing is always thinking; and therefore Descartes, to whom this had at last become quite clear, could lay down the proposition: "I think, that is—I am." This means, my thinking is my being or my life; only when I live spiritually do I live; only as spirit am I really, or—I am spirit through and through and nothing but spirit. Unlucky Peter Schlemihl,[5] who has lost his shadow, is the portrait of this man become a spirit; for the spirit's body is shadowless.—Over against this, how different among the ancients! Stoutly and manfully as they might bear themselves against the might of things, they must yet acknowledge the might itself, and got no farther than to protect their *life* against it as well as possible. Only at a late hour did they recognize that their "true life" was not that which they led in the fight against the things of the world, but the "spiritual life," "turned away" from these things; and, when they saw this, they became Christians, the moderns, and innovators upon the ancients. But the life turned away from things, the spiritual life, no longer draws any nourishment from nature, but "lives only on thoughts," and therefore is no longer "life," but—*thinking.*

Yet it must not be supposed now that the ancients were *without thoughts,* just as the most spiritual man is not to be conceived of as if he could be without life. Rather, they had their thoughts about everything, about the world, man, the gods, etc., and showed themselves keenly active in bringing all this to their consciousness. But they did not know *thought,* even though they thought of all sorts of things and "worried themselves with their thoughts." Compare with their position the Christian saying, "My thoughts are not your thoughts; as the heaven is higher than the earth, so are my thoughts higher than your thoughts," and remember what was said above about our child-thoughts.

5. [The reference is to the famous work of the German writer Adelbert von Chamisso (1781-1838), *Peter Schlemihls wundersame Geschichte,* published in 1814, a fantasy built around a man who sold his shadow; reprinted many times. An English translation appeared in London in 1845 titled, *The Shadowless Man; or, the Wonderful History of Peter Schlemihl.*]

What is antiquity seeking, then? The true *enjoyment of life!* You will find that at bottom it is all the same as "the true life."

The Greek poet Simonides[6] sings: "Health is the noblest good for mortal man, the next to this is beauty, the third riches acquired without guile, the fourth the enjoyment of social pleasures in the company of young friends." These are all *good things of life,* pleasures of life. What else was Diogenes of Sinope seeking for than the true enjoyment of life, which he discovered in having the least possible wants? What else Aristippus,[7] who found it in a cheery temper under all circumstances? They are seeking for cheery, unclouded *life-courage,* for *cheeriness;* they are seeking to "be of good *cheer.*"

The Stoics want to realize the *wise man,* the man with *practical philosophy,* the man who *knows how to live*—a wise life, therefore; they find him in contempt for the world, in a life without development, without spreading out, without friendly relations with the world, thus in the *isolated life,* in life as life, not in life with others; only the Stoic *lives,* all else is dead for him. The Epicureans, on the contrary, demand a moving life.

The ancients, as they want to be of good cheer, desire *good living* (the Jews especially a long life, blessed with children and goods), *eudaemonia,* well-being in the most various forms. Democritus, for example, praises as such the "calm of the soul" in which one "*lives* smoothly, without fear and without excitement."

So what he thinks is that with this he gets on best, provides for himself the best lot, and gets through the world best. But as he cannot get rid of the world—and in fact cannot for the very reason that his whole activity is taken up in the effort to get rid of it, that is, in *repelling the world* (for which it is yet necessary that what can be and is repelled should remain existing, otherwise there would be no longer anything to repel)—he reaches at most an extreme degree of liberation, and is distinguish-

6. [A Greek lyric poet, probable dates 556-468 B.C. Only scattered portions of his work survive.]

7. [Founder of a hedonistic school of philosophy at Cyrene, a Greek city in North Africa; his probable dates 435-356 B.C.]

able only in degree from the less liberated. If he even got as far as the deadening of the earthly sense, which at last admits only the monotonous whisper of the word "Brahm,"[8] he nevertheless would not be essentially distinguishable from the *sensual* man.

Even the stoic attitude and manly virtue amounts only to this —that one must maintain and assert himself against the world; and the ethics of the Stoics (their only science, since they could tell nothing about the spirit but how it should behave toward the world, and of nature (physics) only this, that the wise man must assert himself against it) is not a doctrine of the spirit, but only a doctrine of the repelling of the world and of self-assertion against the world. And this consists in "imperturbability and equanimity of life," and so in the most explicit Roman virtue.

The Romans too (Horace, Cicero, and others) went no further than this *practical philosophy*.

The *comfort* (hedone) of the Epicureans is the same *practical philosophy* the Stoics teach, only trickier, more deceitful. They teach only another *behavior* toward the world, exhort us only to take a shrewd attitude toward the world; the world must be deceived, for it is my enemy.

The break with the world is completely carried through by the Skeptics. My entire relation to the world is "worthless and truthless." Timon[9] says, "The feelings and thoughts which we draw from the world contain no truth." "What is truth?" cries Pilate. According to Pyrrho's[10] doctrine the world is neither good nor bad, neither beautiful nor ugly, but these are predicates which I give it. Timon says that "in itself nothing is either good or bad, but man only *thinks* of it thus or thus"; to face the world only *ataraxia* (unmovedness) and *aphasia* (speechlessness—or, in other words, isolated *inwardness*) are left. There is "no longer

8. [Presumably a reference to the impersonal theological Absolute in early Hindu philosophy.]

9. [An Athenian philosopher and moralist of the latter half of the fifth century B.C., usually associated with the famed general and politician Alcibiades.]

10. [Founder of a Greek school of extreme skeptic philosophy, probable dates 365-275 B.C.]

early relativism

any truth to be recognized" in the world; things contradict themselves; thoughts about things are without distinction (good and bad are all the same, so that what one calls good another finds bad); here the recognition of "truth" is at an end, and only the *man without power of recognition,* the *man* who finds in the world nothing to recognize, is left, and this man just leaves the truth-vacant world where it is and takes no account of it.

So antiquity gets through with the *world of things,* the order of the world, the world as a whole; but to the order of the world, or the things of this world, belong not only nature, but all relations in which man sees himself placed by nature, as in the family, the community—in short, the so-called "natural bonds." With the *world of the spirit* Christianity then begins. The man who still faces the world *armed* is the ancient, the—*heathen* (to which class the Jew, too, as non-Christian, belongs); the man who has come to be led by nothing but his "heart's pleasure," the interest he takes, his fellow-feeling, his—*spirit,* is the modern, the—Christian.

As the ancients worked toward the *conquest of the world* and strove to release man from the heavy trammels of connection with *other things,* at last they came also to the dissolution of the State and giving preference to everything private. Of course community, family, and so forth, as *natural* relations, are burdensome hindrances which diminish my *spiritual freedom.*

B.—THE MODERNS

"IF any man be in Christ, he is a *new creature;* the old is passed away, behold, all is become *new.*"[11]

As it was said above, "To the ancients the world was a truth," we must say here, "To the moderns the spirit was a truth"; but here, as there, we must not omit the supplement, "a truth whose untruth they tried to get back of, and at last they really do."

A course similar to that which antiquity took may be demon-

11. 2 Cor. 5. 17. (The words "new" and "modern" are the same in German.)

strated in Christianity also, in that the *understanding* was held
a prisoner under the dominion of the Christian dogmas up to
the time preparatory to the Reformation, but in the pre-
Reformation century asserted itself *sophistically* and played hereti-
cal pranks with all tenets of the faith. And the talk then was,
especially in Italy and at the Roman court, "If only the heart
remains Christian-minded, the understanding may go right on
taking its pleasure."

Long before the Reformation, people were so thoroughly
accustomed to fine-spun "wranglings" that the pope, and most
others, looked on Luther's appearance too as a mere "wrangling
of monks" at first. Humanism corresponds to Sophisticism, and,
as in the time of the Sophists Greek life stood in its fullest bloom
(the Periclean age), so the most brilliant things happened in the
time of Humanism, or, as one might perhaps also say, of
Machiavellianism (printing, the New World, etc.). At this time
the heart was still far from wanting to relieve itself of its Christian
contents.

But finally the Reformation, like Socrates, took hold seriously
of the *heart* itself, and since then hearts have kept growing
visibly—more unchristian. As with Luther people began to take
the matter to heart, the outcome of this step of the Reformation
must be that the heart also gets lightened of the heavy burden
of Christian faith. The heart, from day to day more unchristian,
loses the contents with which it had busied itself, till at last
nothing but empty *warmheartedness* is left it, the quite general
love of men, the love of *Man,* the consciousness of freedom,
"self-consciousness."

Only so is Christianity complete, because it has become
bald, withered, and void of contents. There are now no contents
whatever against which the heart does not mutiny, unless indeed
the heart unconsciously or without "self-consciousness" lets them
slip in. The heart *criticizes* to death with *hard-hearted* mercilessness everything that wants to make its way in, and is capable
(except, as before, unconsciously or taken by surprise) of no
friendship, no love. What could there be in men to love, since
they are all alike "egoists," none of them *man* as such, none

are *spirit only?* The Christian loves only the spirit; but where could one be found who should be really nothing but spirit?

To have a liking for the corporeal man with hide and hair —why, that would no longer be a "spiritual" warm-heartedness, it would be treason against "pure" warm-heartedness, the "theoretical regard." For pure warm-heartedness is by no means to be conceived as like that kindliness that gives everybody a friendly hand-shake; on the contrary, pure warm-heartedness is warm-hearted toward nobody, it is only a theoretical interest, concern for man as man, not as a person. The person is repulsive to it because of being "egoistic," because of not being that abstraction, Man. But it is only for the abstraction that one can have a theoretical regard. To pure warm-heartedness or pure theory men exist only to be criticized, scoffed at, and thoroughly despised; to it, no less than to the fanatical parson, they are only "filth" and other such nice things.

[margin note: most philanthropists]

Pushed to this extremity of disinterested warm-heartedness, we must finally become conscious that the spirit, which alone the Christian loves, is nothing; in other words, that the spirit is—a lie.

What has here been set down roughly, summarily, and doubtless as yet incomprehensibly, will, it is to be hoped, become clear as we go on.

Let us take up the inheritance left by the ancients, and, as active workmen, do with it as much as—can be done with it! The world lies despised at our feet, far beneath us and our heaven, into which its mighty arms are no longer thrust and its stupefying breath does not come. Seductively as it may pose, it can delude nothing but our *sense;* it cannot lead astray the spirit—and spirit alone, after all, we really are. Having once got *back of* things, the spirit has also got *above* them, and become free from their bonds, emancipated, supernal, free. So speaks "spiritual freedom."

To the spirit which, after long toil, has got rid of the world, the worldless spirit, nothing is left after the loss of the world and the worldly but—the spirit and the spiritual.

Yet, as it has only moved away from the world and made of itself a being *free from the world,* without being able really to annihilate the world, this remains to it a stumbling-block that cannot be cleared away, a discredited existence; and, as, on the other hand, it knows and recognizes nothing but the spirit and the spiritual, it must perpetually carry about with it the longing to spiritualize the world, to redeem it from the "black list." Therefore, like a youth, it goes about with plans for the redemption or improvement of the world.

The ancients, we saw, served the natural, the worldly, the natural order of the world, but they incessantly asked themselves of this service; and, when they had tired themselves to death in ever-renewed attempts at revolt, then, among their last sighs, was born to them the *God,* the "conqueror of the world." All their doing had been nothing but *wisdom of the world,* an effort to get back of the world and above it. And what is the wisdom of the many following centuries? What did the moderns try to get back of? No longer to get back of the world, for the ancients had accomplished that; but back of the God whom the ancients bequeathed to them, back of the God who "is spirit," back of everything that is the spirit's, the spiritual. But the activity of the spirit, which "searches even the depths of the Godhead," is *theology.* If the ancients have nothing to show but wisdom of the world, the moderns never did nor do make their way further than to theology. We shall see later that even the newest revolts against God are nothing but the extremest efforts of "theology," that is, theological insurrections.

1.—THE SPIRIT

THE realm of spirits is monstrously great, there is an infinite deal of the spiritual; yet let us look and see what the spirit, this bequest of the ancients, properly is.

Out of their birth-pangs it came forth, but they themselves could not utter themselves as spirit; they could give birth to it, it itself must speak. The "born God, the Son of Man," is the first to utter the word that the spirit, he, God, has to do with nothing earthly and no earthly relationship, but solely with the spirit and spiritual relationships.

Is my courage, indestructible under all the world's blows, my inflexibility and my obduracy, perchance already spirit in the full sense, because the world cannot touch it? Why, then it would not yet be at enmity with the world, and all its action would consist merely in not succumbing to the world! No, so long as it does not busy itself with itself alone, so long as it does not have to do with *its* world, the spiritual, alone, it is not *free* spirit, but only the "spirit of this world," the spirit fettered to it. The spirit is free spirit, that is, really spirit, only in a world of *its own;* in "this," the earthly world, it is a stranger. Only through a spiritual world is the spirit really spirit, for "this" world does not understand it and does not know how to keep "the maiden from a foreign land"[12] from departing.

But where is it to get this spiritual world? Where but out of itself? It must reveal itself; and the words that it speaks, the revelations in which it unveils itself, these are *its* world. As a visionary lives and has *his* world only in the visionary pictures that he himself creates, as a crazy man generates for himself his own dream-world, without which he could not be crazy, so the spirit must create for itself its spirit world, and is not spirit till it creates it.

Thus its creations make it spirit, and by its creatures we know it, the creator; in them it lives, they are its world.

Now, what is the spirit? It is the creator of a spiritual world! Even in you and me people do not recognize spirit till they see that we have appropriated to ourselves something spiritual; though thoughts may have been set before us, we have at least brought them to live in ourselves; for, as long as we were children, the most edifying thoughts might have been laid before us without our wishing, or being able, to reproduce them in ourselves. So the spirit also exists only when it creates something spiritual; it is real only together with the spiritual, its creature.

As, then, we know it by its works, the question is what these works are. But the works or children of the spirit are nothing else but—spirits.

If I had before me Jews, Jews of the true metal, I should have to stop here and leave them standing before this mystery

12. [Title of a poem by the celebrated Johann Christoph-Friedrich Schiller (1759-1805).]

as for almost two thousand years they have remained standing before it, unbelieving and without knowledge. But, as you, my dear reader, are at least not a full-blooded Jew—for such a one will not go astray as far as this—we will still go along a bit of road together, till perhaps you too turn your back on me because I laugh in your face.

If somebody told you you were altogether spirit, you would take hold of your body and not believe him, but answer: "I *have* a spirit, no doubt, but do not exist only as spirit, but as a man with a body." You would still distinguish *yourself* from "your spirit." "But," replies he, "it is your destiny, even though now you are yet going about in the fetters of the body, to be one day a 'blessed spirit,' and, however you may conceive of the future aspect of your spirit, so much is yet certain, that in death you will put off this body and yet keep yourself, your spirit, for all eternity; accordingly your spirit is the eternal and true in you, the body only a dwelling here below, which you may leave and perhaps exchange for another."

Now you believe him! For the present, indeed, *you* are not spirit only; but, when you emigrate from the mortal body, as one day you must, then you will have to help yourself without the body, and therefore it is needful that you be prudent and care in time for your proper self. "What should it profit a man if he gained the whole world and yet suffered damage in his soul?"

But, even granted that doubts, raised in the course of time against the tenets of the Christian faith, have long since robbed you of faith in the immortality of your spirit, you have nevertheless left one tenet undisturbed, and still ingenuously adhere to the one truth, that the spirit is your better part, and that the spiritual has greater claims on you than anything else. Despite all your atheism, in zeal against *egoism* you concur with the believers in immortality.

But whom do you think of under the name of egoist? A man who, instead of living to an idea, that is, a spiritual thing, and sacrificing to it his personal advantage, serves the latter. A good patriot brings his sacrifice to the altar of the fatherland; but it cannot be disputed that the fatherland is an idea, since for beasts incapable of mind,[13] or children as yet without mind, there is no fatherland and no patriotism. Now, if any one does not approve himself as a good patriot, he betrays his egoism with reference to the fatherland. And so the matter stands in innumerable other cases: he who in human society takes the benefit of a prerogative sins egoistically against the idea of equality; he who exercises dominion is blamed as an egoist against the idea of liberty, and so on.

You despise the egoist because he puts the spiritual in the background as compared with the personal, and has his eyes on himself where you would like to see him act to favor an idea. The distinction between you is that he makes himself the central point, but you the spirit; or that you cut your identity in two and exalt your "proper self," the spirit, to be ruler of the paltrier remainder, while he will hear nothing of this cutting in two, and pursues spiritual and material interests just *as he pleases*. You think, to be sure, that you are falling foul of those only who enter into no spiritual interest at all, but in fact you curse at everybody who does not look on the spiritual interest as his "true and highest" interest. You carry your knightly service for this beauty so far that you affirm her to be the only beauty of the world. You live not to *yourself*, but to your *spirit* and to what is the spirit's, that is, ideas.

As the spirit exists only in its creating of the spiritual, let us take a look about us for its first creation. If only it has accomplished this, there follows thenceforth a natural propagation of creations, as according to the myth only the first human beings needed to be created, the rest of the race propagating of itself. The first creation, on the other hand, must come forth "out of nothing"—the spirit has toward its realization nothing but itself, or rather it has not yet even itself, but must create itself; hence its first creation is itself, *the spirit*. Mystical as this sounds, we

13. (The reader will remember (it is to be hoped he has never forgotten) that "mind" and "spirit" are one and the same word in German. For several pages back the connection of the discourse has seemed to require the almost exclusive use of the translation "spirit," but to complete the sense it has often been necessary that the reader recall the thought of its identity with "mind," as stated in a previous note.)

yet go through it as an every-day experience. Are you a thinking being before you think? In creating the first thought you create yourself, the thinking one; for you do not think before you think a thought, or have a thought. Is it not your singing that first makes you a singer, your talking that makes you a talker? Now, so too it is the production of the spiritual that first makes you a spirit.

Meantime, as you distinguish *yourself* from the thinker, singer, and talker, so you no less distinguish yourself from the spirit, and feel very clearly that you are something beside spirit. But, as in the thinking ego hearing and sight easily vanish in the enthusiasm of thought, so you also have been seized by the spirit-enthusiasm, and you now long with all your might to become wholly spirit and to be dissolved in spirit. The spirit is your *ideal,* the unattained, the other-worldly; spirit is the name of your—god, "God is spirit."

Against all that is not spirit you are a zealot, and therefore you play the zealot against *yourself* who cannot get rid of a remainder of the non-spiritual. Instead of saying, "I am *more* than spirit," you say with contrition, "I am less than spirit; and spirit, pure spirit, or the spirit that is nothing but spirit, I can only think of, but am not; and, since I am not it, it is another, exists as another, whom I call 'God'."

It lies in the nature of the case that the spirit that is to exist as pure spirit must be an otherworldly one, for, since I am not it, it follows that it can only be *outside* me; since in any case a human being is not fully comprehended in the concept "spirit," it follows that the pure spirit, the spirit as such, can only be outside of men, beyond the human world—not earthly, but heavenly.

Only from this disunion in which I and the spirit lie; only because "I" and "spirit" are not names for one and the same thing, but different names for completely different things; only because I am not spirit and spirit not I—only from this do we get a quite tautological explanation of the necessity that the spirit dwells in the other world, that is, is God.

But from this it also appears how thoroughly theological is

the liberation that Feuerbach[14] is laboring to give us. What he says is that we had only mistaken our own essence, and therefore looked for it in the other world, but that now, when we see that God was only our human essence, we must recognize it again as ours and move it back out of the other world into this. To God, who is spirit, Feuerbach gives the name "Our Essence." Can we put up with this, that "Our Essence" is brought into opposition to *us*—that we are split into an essential and an unessential self? Do we not therewith go back into the dreary misery of seeing ourselves banished out of ourselves?

What have we gained, then, when for a variation we have transferred into ourselves the divine outside us? *Are we* that which is in us? As little as we are that which is outside us. I am as little my heart as I am my sweetheart, this "other self" of mine. Just because we are not the spirit that dwells in us, just for that reason we had to take it and set it outside us; it was not we, did not coincide with us, and therefore we could not think of it as existing otherwise than outside us, on the other side from us, in the other world.

With the strength of *despair* Feuerbach clutches at the total substance of Christianity, not to throw it away, no, to drag it to himself, to draw it, the long-yearned-for, ever-distant, out of its heaven with a last effort, and keep it by him forever. Is not that a clutch of the uttermost despair, a clutch for life or death, and is it not at the same time the Christian yearning and hungering for the other world? The hero wants not to go into the other world, but to draw the other world to him, and compel it to become this world! And since then has not all the world, with more or less consciousness, been crying that "this world" is the vital point, and heaven must come down on earth and be experienced even here?

Let us, in brief, set Feuerbach's theological view and our contradiction over against each other! "The essence of man is man's supreme being;[15] now by religion, to be sure, the *supreme*

14. *Essence of Christianity.* [Byington's translation of Feuerbach's *Das Wesen des Christentums.*]

15. (Or, "highest essence." The word *Wesen*, which means both "essence" and "being," will be translated now one way and now the other

being is called *God* and regarded as an objective essence, but in truth it is only man's own essence; and therefore the turning point of the world's history is that henceforth no longer *God,* but man, is to appear to man as God."[16]

To this we reply: The supreme being is indeed the essence of man, but, just because it is his *essence* and not he himself, it remains quite immaterial whether we see it outside him and view it as "God," or find it in him and call it "Essence of Man" or "Man." I am neither God nor *Man,*[17] neither the supreme essence nor my essence, and therefore it is all one in the main whether I think of the essence as in me or outside me. Nay, we really do always think of the supreme being as in both kinds of otherworldliness, the inward and outward, at once; for the "Spirit of God" is, according to the Christian view, also "our spirit," and "dwells in us."[18] It dwells in heaven and dwells in us; we poor things are just its "dwelling," and, if Feuerbach goes on to destroy its heavenly dwelling and force it to move to us bag and baggage, then we, its earthly apartments, will be badly overcrowded.

But after this digression (which, if we were at all proposing to work by line and level, we should have had to save for later pages in order to avoid repetition) we return to the spirit's first creation, the spirit itself.

The spirit it something other than myself. But this other, what is it?

in the following pages. The reader must bear in mind that these two words are identical in German; and so are "supreme" and "highest.")

16. *Essence of Christianity,* p. 402.

17. (That is, the abstract conception of man, as in the preceding sentence.)

18. For instance, Rom. 8. 9; 1 Cor. 3. 16; John 20. 22 and innumerable other passages.

2.—THE POSSESSED

HAVE you ever seen a spirit? "No, not I, but my grand-mother." Now, you see, it's just so with me too; I myself haven't seen any, but my grandmother had them running between her feet all sorts of ways, and out of confidence in our grand-mothers' honesty we believe in the existence of spirits.

But had we no grandfathers then, and did they not shrug their shoulders every time our grandmothers told about their ghosts? Yes, those were unbelieving men who have harmed our good religion much, those rationalists! We shall feel that! What else lies at the bottom of this warm faith in ghosts, if not the faith in "the existence of spiritual beings in general," and is not this latter itself disastrously unsettled if saucy men of the under-standing may disturb the former? The Romanticists were quite conscious what a blow the very belief in God suffered by the laying aside of the belief in spirits or ghosts, and they tried to help us out of the baleful consequences not only by their re-awakened fairy world, but at last, and especially, by the "intrusion of a higher world," by their somnambulists of Prévorst,[19] etc. The good believers and fathers of the church did not suspect that with the belief in ghosts the foundation of religion was withdrawn, and that since then it had been floating in the air. He who no longer believes in any ghost needs only to travel on consistently in his unbelief to see that there is no separate being at all con-cealed behind things, no ghost or—what is naively reckoned as synonymous even in our use of words—no "*spirit*."

"Spirits exist!" Look about in the world, and say for your-self whether a spirit does not gaze upon you out of everything. Out of the lovely little flower there speaks to you the spirit of the Creator, who has shaped it so wonderfully; the stars proclaim the spirit that established their order; from the mountain-tops a spirit of sublimity breathes down; out of the waters a spirit of yearning murmurs up; and—out of men millions of spirits speak.

19. [Friederike Hauffe (1801-1829), known as the "Visionary of Prévorst," a young woman native to this small town in Württemberg. Her trances and visions made her one of the celebrated cases involving mag-netism and somnambulism which excited wide attention in Europe.]

The mountains may sink, the flowers fade, the world of stars fall in ruins, the men die—what matters the wreck of these visible bodies? The spirit, the "invisible spirit," abides eternally!

Yes, the whole world is haunted! Only *is* haunted? Nay, it itself "walks," it is uncanny through and through, it is the wandering seeming-body of a spirit, it is a spook. What else should a ghost be, then, than an apparent body, but real spirit? Well, the world is "empty," is "naught," is only glamorous "semblance"; its truth is the spirit alone; it is the seeming-body of a spirit.

Look out near or far, a *ghostly* world surrounds you everywhere; you are always having "apparitions" or visions. Everything that appears to you is only the phantasm of an indwelling spirit, is a ghostly "apparition"; the world is to you only a "world of appearances," behind which the spirit walks. You "see spirits."

Are you perchance thinking of comparing yourself with the ancients, who saw gods everywhere? Gods, my dear modern, are not spirits; gods do not degrade the world to a semblance, and do not spiritualize it.

But to you the whole world is spiritualized, and has become an enigmatical ghost; therefore do not wonder if you likewise find in yourself nothing but a spook. Is not your body haunted by your spirit, and is not the latter alone the true and real, the former only the "transitory, naught" or a "semblance"? Are we not all ghosts, uncanny beings that wait for "deliverance"—to wit, "spirits"?

Since the spirit appeared in the world, since "the Word became flesh," since then the world has been spiritualized, enchanted, a spook.

You have spirit, for you have thoughts. What are your thoughts? "Spiritual entities." Not things, then? "No, but the spirit of things, the main point in all things, the inmost in them, their—idea." Consequently what you think is not only your thought? "On the contrary, it is that in the world which is most real, that which is properly to be called true; it is the truth itself; if I only think truly, I think the truth. I may, to be sure, err with regard to the truth, and *fail to recognize* it; but, if I *recognize* truly, the object of my cognition is the truth." So, I suppose, you strive at all times to recognize the truth? "To me the truth is sacred. It may well happen that I find a truth incomplete and replace it with a better, but *the* truth I cannot abrogate. I *believe* in the truth, therefore I search in it; nothing transcends it, it is eternal."

Sacred, eternal is the truth; it is the Sacred, the Eternal. But you, who let yourself be filled and led by this sacred thing, are yourself hallowed. Further, the sacred is not for your senses—and you never as a sensual man discover its trace—but for your faith, or, more definitely still, for your *spirit;* for it itself, you know, is a spiritual thing, a spirit—is spirit for the spirit.

The sacred is by no means so easily to be set aside as many at present affirm, who no longer take this "unsuitable" word into their mouths. If even in a single respect I am still *upbraided* as an "egoist," there is left the thought of something else which I should serve more than myself, and which must be to me more important than everything; in short, somewhat in which I should have to seek my true welfare,[20] something—"sacred."[21] However human this sacred thing may look, though it be the Human itself, that does not take away its sacredness, but at most changes it from an unearthly to an earthly sacred thing, from a divine one to a human.

Sacred things exist only for the egoist who does not acknowledge himself, the *involuntary egoist,* for him who is always looking after his own and yet does not count himself as the highest being, who serves only himself and at the same time always thinks he is serving a higher being, who knows nothing higher than himself and yet is infatuated about something higher; in short, for the egoist who would like not to be an egoist, and abases himself (combats his egoism), but at the same time abases himself only for the sake of "being exalted," and therefore of gratifying his egoism. Because he would like to cease to be an egoist, he looks about in heaven and earth for higher beings to serve and sacrifice himself to; but, however much he shakes and disciplines himself,

20. (*Heil*)
21. (*heiling*)

in the end he does all for his own sake, and the disreputable egoism will not come off him. On this account I call him the involuntary egoist.

His toil and care to get away from himself is nothing but the misunderstood impulse to self-dissolution. If you are bound to your past hour, if you must babble to-day because you babbled yesterday,[22] if you cannot transform yourself each instant, you feel yourself fettered to slavery and benumbed. ⁻ Therefore over each minute of your existence a fresh minute of the future beckons to you, and, developing yourself, you get away "from yourself," that is, from the self that was at that moment. As you are at each instant, you are your own creature, and in this very "creature" you do not wish to lose yourself, the creator. You are yourself a higher being than you are, and surpass yourself. But that *you* are the one who is higher than you, that is, that you are not only creature, but likewise your creator—just this, as an involuntary egoist, you fail to recognize; and therefore the "higher essence" is to you—an alien[23] essence. Every higher essence, such as truth, mankind, and so on, is an essence *over* us.

Alienness is a criterion of the "sacred." In everything sacred there lies something "uncanny," strange,[24] such as we are not quite familiar and at home in. What is sacred to me is *not my own;* and if, for instance, the property of others was not sacred to me, I should look on it as *mine,* which I should take to myself when occasion offered. Or, on the other side, if I regard the face of the Chinese emperor as sacred, it remains strange to my eye, which I close at its appearance.

Why is an incontrovertible mathematical truth, which might even be called eternal according to the common understanding

22. (How the priests tinkle! how important they
   Would make it out, that men should come their way
   And babble, just as yesterday, to-day!
   Oh, blame them not! They know man's need, I say!
   For he takes all his happiness this way,
   To babble just to-morrow as to-day.
                   — Translated from Goethe's *Venetian Epigrams.*)
23. (*fremd*)
24. (*fremd*)

of words, not—sacred? Because it is not revealed, or not the revelation of a higher being. If by revealed we understand only the so-called religious truths, we go far astray, and entirely fail to recognize the breadth of the concept "higher being." Atheists keep up their scoffing at the higher being, which was also honored under the name of the "highest" or *être suprême,* and trample in the dust one "proof of his existence" after another, without noticing that they themselves, out of need for a higher being, only annihilate the old to make room for a new. Is "Man" perchance not a higher essence than an individual man, and must not the truths, rights, and ideas which result from the concept of him be honored and—counted sacred, as revelations of this very concept? For, even though we should abrogate again many a truth that seemed to be made manifest by this concept, yet this would only evince a misunderstanding on our part, without in the least degree harming the sacred concept itself or taking their sacredness from those truths that must "rightly" be looked upon as its revelations. *Man* reaches beyond every individual man, and yet—though he be "his essence"—is not in fact *his* essence (which rather would be as single[25] as he the individual himself), but a general and "higher," yes, for atheists "the highest essence."[26] And, as the divine revelations were not written down by God with his own hand, but made public through "the Lord's instruments," so also the new highest essence does not write out its revelations itself, but lets them come to our knowledge through "true men." Only the new essence betrays, in fact, a more spiritual style of conception than the old God, because the latter was still represented in a sort of embodiedness or form, while the undimmed spirituality of the new is retained, and no special material body is fancied for it. And withal it does not lack corporeity, which even takes on a yet more seductive appearance because it looks more natural and mundane and consists in nothing less than in every bodily man—yes, or outright in "humanity" or "all men." Thereby the spectralness of the spirit in a seeming-body has once again become really solid and popular.

25. (*einzig*)
26. (The supreme being.)

Sacred, then, is the highest essence and everything in which this highest essence reveals or will reveal itself; but hallowed are they who recognize this highest essence together with its own, together with its revelations. The sacred hallows in turn its reverer, who by his worship becomes himself a saint, as likewise what he does is saintly, a saintly walk, saintly thoughts and actions, imaginations and aspirations.

It is easily understood that the conflict over what is revered as the highest essence can be significant only so long as even the most embittered opponents concede to each other the main point —that there is a highest essence to which worship or service is due. If one should smile compassionately at the whole struggle over a highest essence, as a Christian might at the war of words between a Shiite and a Sunnite or between a Brahman and a Buddhist,[27] then the hypothesis of a highest essence would be null in his eyes, and the conflict on this basis an idle play. Whether then the one God or the three in one, whether the Lutheran God or the *être suprême* or not God at all, but "Man," may represent the highest essence, that makes no difference at all for him who denies the highest essence itself, for in his eyes those servants of a highest essence are one and all—pious people, the most raging atheist not less than the most faith-filled Christian.

In the foremost place of the sacred,[28] then, stands the highest essence and the faith in this essence, our "holy[29] faith."

THE SPOOK

With ghosts we arrive in the spirit-realm, in the realm of *essences.*

What haunts the universe, and has its occult, "incomprehensible" being there, is precisely the mysterious spook that we call highest essence. And to get to the bottom of this *spook,* to comprehend it, to discover *reality* in it (to prove "the existence of God") — this task men set to themselves for thousands of

27. [The two major divisions of the religious world of the Muslim and Hindu communities, respectively.]

28. (*heilig*)

29. (*heilig*)

years; with the horrible impossibility, the endless Danaid-labor,[30] of transforming the spook into a non-spook, the unreal into something real, the *spirit* into an entire and *corporeal* person — with this they tormented themselves to death. Behind the existing world they sought the "thing in itself," the essence; behind the *thing* they sought the *un-thing*.

When one looks to the *bottom* of anything, searches out its *essence,* one often discovers something quite other than what it *seems* to be; honeyed speech and a lying heart, pompous words and beggarly thoughts, and so on. By bringing the essence into prominence one degrades the hitherto misapprehended appearance to a bare *semblance,* a deception. The essence of the world, so attractive and splendid, is for him who looks to the bottom of it—emptiness; emptiness is = world's essence (world's doings). Now, he who is religious does not occupy himself with the deceitful semblance, with the empty appearances, but looks upon the essence, and in the essence has—the truth.

The essences which are deduced from some appearances are the evil essences, and conversely from others the good. The essence of human feeling, for instance, is love; the essence of human will is the good; that of one's thinking, the true, and so on.

What at first passed for existence, such as the world and its like, appears now as bare semblance, and the *truly existent* is much rather the essence, whose realm is filled with gods, spirits, demons, with good or bad essences. Only this inverted world, the world of essences, truly exists now. The human heart may be loveless, but its essence exists, God, "who is love"; human thought may wander in error, but its essence, truth, exists; "God is truth," and the like.

To know and acknowledge essences alone and nothing but essences, that is religion; its realm is a realm of essences, spooks, and ghosts.

30. [The fate of the Danaides in Hades has traditionally been a figure of speech for endless labor; in Greek mythology, the fifty daughters of the king Danaüs who killed their husbands on their wedding night and were condemned, in one account or another, forever to raise water from a well with a perforated vessel, or pour it into a receptacle of similar construction.]

The longing to make the spook comprehensible, or to realize *non-sense,* has brought about a *corporeal ghost,* a ghost or spirit with a real body, an embodied ghost. How the strongest and most talented Christians have tortured themselves to get a conception of this ghostly apparition! But there always remained the contradiction of two natures, the divine and human, the ghostly and sensual; there remained the most wondrous spook, a thing that was not a thing. Never yet was a ghost more soul torturing, and no shaman, who pricks himself to raving fury and nerve-lacerating cramps to conjure a ghost, can endure such soul-torment as Christians suffered from that most incomprehensible ghost.

But through Christ the truth of the matter had at the same time come to light, that the veritable spirit or ghost is—man. The *corporeal* or embodied spirit is just man; he himself is the ghostly being and at the same time the being's appearance and existence. Henceforth man no longer, in typical cases, shudders at ghosts *outside* him, but at himself; he is terrified at himself. In the depth of his breast dwells the *spirit of sin;* even the faintest thought (and this is itself a spirit, you know) may be a *devil,* etc. — The ghost has put on a body, God has become man, but now man is himself the gruesome spook which he seeks to get back of, to exorcise, to fathom, to bring to reality and to speech; man is — *spirit.* What matter if the body wither, if only the spirit is saved? Everything rests on the spirit, and the spirit's or "soul's" welfare becomes the exclusive goal. Man has become to himself a ghost, an uncanny spook, to which there is even assigned a distinct seat in the body (dispute over the seat of the soul, whether in the head, etc.).

You are not to me, and I am not to you, a higher essence. Nevertheless a higher essence may be hidden in each of us, and call forth a mutual reverence. To take at once the most general, Man lives in you and me. If I did not see Man in you, what occasion should I have to respect you? To be sure, you are not Man and his true and adequate form, but only a mortal veil of his, from which he can withdraw without himself ceasing; but yet for the present this general and higher essence is housed in you, and you present before me (because an imperishable spirit has in you assumed a perishable body, so that really your form is only an "assumed" one) a spirit that appears, appears in you, without being bound to your body and to this particular mode of appearance—therefore a spook. Hence I do not regard you as a higher essence, but only respect that higher essence which "walks" in you; I "respect Man in you." The ancients did not observe anything of this sort in their slaves, and the higher essence "Man" found as yet little response. To make up for this, they saw in each other ghosts of another sort. The People is a higher essence than an individual, and, like Man or the Spirit of Man, a spirit haunting the individual—the Spirit of the People. For this reason they revered this spirit, and only so far as he served this or else a spirit related to it (as in the Spirit of the Family) could the individual appear significant; only for the sake of the higher essence, the People, was consideration allowed to the "member of the people." As you are hallowed to us by "Man" who haunts you, so at every time men have been hallowed by some higher essence or other, like People, Family, and such. Only for the sake of a higher essence has any one been honored from of old, only as a ghost has he been regarded in the light of a hallowed, a protected and recognized person. If I cherish you because I hold you dear, because in you my heart finds nourishment, my need satisfaction, then it is not done for the sake of a higher essence whose hallowed body you are, not on account of my beholding in you a ghost, an appearing spirit, but from egoistic pleasure; you yourself with *your* essence are valuable to me, for your essence is not a higher one, is not higher and more general than you, is unique[31] like you yourself, because it is you.

But it is not only man that "haunts"; so does everything. The higher essence, the spirit, that walks in everything, is at the same time bound to nothing, and only—"appears" in it. Ghosts in every corner!

Here would be the place to pass the haunting spirits in review, if they were not to come before us again further on in order to vanish before egoism. Hence let only a few of them be

31. (*einzig*)

particularized by way of example, in order to bring us at once
to our attitude toward them.

Sacred above all is the "holy Spirit," sacred the truth, sacred
are right, law, a good cause, majesty, marriage, the common
good, order, the fatherland, and son on.

WHEELS IN THE HEAD

Man, your head is haunted; you have wheels in your head!
You imagine great things, and depict to yourself a whole world
of gods that has an existence for you, a spirit-realm to which you
suppose yourself to be called, an ideal that beckons to you.
You have a fixed idea!

Do not think that I am jesting or speaking figuratively when
I regard those persons who cling to the Higher, and (because
the vast majority belongs under this head) almost the whole
world of men, as veritable fools, fools in a madhouse. What is
it, then, that is called a "fixed idea"? An idea that has subjected
the man to itself. When you recognize, with regard to such a
fixed idea, that it is a folly, you shut its slave up in an asylum.
And is the truth of the faith, say, which we are not to doubt;
the majesty of the people, which we are not to strike at (he who
does is guilty of—lese-majesty); virtue, against which the censor
is not to let a word pass, that morality may be kept pure;—are
these not "fixed ideas"? Is not all the stupid chatter of most of
our newspapers the babble of fools who suffer from the fixed
idea of morality, legality, Christianity, and so forth, and only
seem to go about free because the madhouse in which they walk
takes in so broad a space? Touch the fixed idea of such a fool,
and you will at once have to guard your back against the lunatic's
stealthy malice. For these great lunatics are like the little so-
called lunatics in this point too—that they assail by stealth him
who touches their fixed idea. They first steal his weapon, steal
free speech from him, and then they fall upon him with their
nails. Every day now lays bare the cowardice and vindictiveness
of these maniacs, and the stupid populace hurrahs for their crazy
measures. One must read the journals of this period, and must

hear the Philistines[32] talk, to get the horrible conviction that one is shut up in a house with fools. "Thou shalt not call thy brother a fool; if thou dost—etc." But I do not fear the curse, and I say, my brothers are arch-fools. Whether a poor fool of the insane asylum is possessed by the fancy that he is God the Father, Emperor of Japan, the Holy Spirit, or whatnot, or whether a citizen in comfortable circumstances conceives that it is his mission to be a good Christian, a faithful Protestant, a loyal citizen, a virtuous man—both these are one and the same "fixed idea." He who has never tried and dared not to be a good Christian, a faithful Protestant, a virtuous man, and the like, is *possessed* and prepossessed[33] by faith, virtuousness, etc. Just as the schoolmen philosophized only *inside* the belief of the church; as Pope Benedict XIV[34] wrote fat books *inside* the papist superstition, without ever throwing a doubt upon this belief; as authors fill whole folios on the State without calling in question the fixed idea of the State itself; as our newspapers are crammed with politics because they are conjured into the fancy that man was created to be a *zoon politicon*—so also subjects vegetate in subjection, virtuous people in virtue, liberals in humanity, without ever putting to these fixed ideas of theirs the searching knife of criticism. Undislodgeable, like a madman's delusion, those thoughts stand on a firm footing, and he who doubts them—lays hands on the *sacred!* Yes, the "fixed idea," that is the truly sacred!

Is it perchance only people possessed by the devil that meet

32. [Stirner is referring in the above passage to the furious controversy involving press censorship in the early 1840s and various legal proceedings which stemmed from these actions. There may be some debate as to whether Byington has translated the German *Philister* correctly. Originally the word was used by German university students to mean the townspeople, although it may be argued that Germans gave it the same meaning attributed to Matthew Arnold (1822-1888), the British man of letters, "Philistine" meaning a rude and uncultured materialist of a low sort.]

33. (*gefangen und befangen,* literally "imprisoned and prepossessed.")

34. [Prospero Lambertini (1675-1758), Pope Benedict XIV from 1740 to 1758, a very learned, intellectual and many-sided pope who came under the influence of eighteenth century Enlightenment.]

us, or do we as often come upon people *possessed* in the contrary way—possessed by "the good," by virtue, morality, the law, or some "principle" or other? Possessions of the devil are not the only ones. God works on us, and the devil does; the former "workings of grace," the latter "workings of the devil." Possessed[35] people are set[36] in their opinions.

If the word "possession" displeases you, then call it prepossession; yes, since the spirit possesses you, and all "inspirations" come from it, call it—inspiration and enthusiasm. I add that complete enthusiasm—for we cannot stop with the sluggish, half-way kind—is called fanaticism.

It is precisely among cultured people that *fanaticism* is at home; for man is cultured so far as he takes an interest in spiritual things, and interest in spiritual things, when it is alive, is and must be *fanaticism;* it is a fanatical interest in the sacred (*fanum*). Observe our liberals, look into the *Sächsischen Vaterlandsblätter*,[37] hear what Schlosser says:[38] "Holbach's company constituted a regular plot against the traditional doctrine and the existing system, and its members were as fanatical on behalf of their unbelief as monks and priests, Jesuits and Pietists, Methodists, missionary and Bible societies, commonly are for mechanical worship and orthodoxy."

Take notice how a "moral man" behaves, who today often thinks he is through with God and throws off Christianity as a bygone thing. If you ask him whether he has ever doubted that the copulation of brother and sister is incest, that monogamy is the truth of marriage, that filial piety is a sacred duty, then a moral shudder will come over him at the conception of one's being allowed to touch his sister as wife also. And whence this

35. (*besessene*)
36. (*versessen*)
37. [A weekly published in Dresden beginning in 1841.]
38. [Stirner cited page 519 from the second volume of *Geschichte des achtzenten Jahrhunderts* of Friedrich Christoph Schlosser (1776-1861), historian and professor at Heidelberg, whose book was published in that city in 1842. The reference is to the rationalists and the writers of the Enlightenment, Holbach, d'Alembert, Diderot and others, and their part in undermining the beliefs of the period prior to the French Revolution.]

shudder? Because he *believes* in those moral commandments. This moral *faith* is deeply rooted in his breast. Much as he rages against the *pious* Christians, he himself has nevertheless as thoroughly remained a Christian—to wit, a *moral* Christian. In the form of morality Christianity holds him a prisoner, and a prisoner under *faith*. Monogamy is to be something sacred, and he who may live in bigamy is punished as a *criminal;* he who commits incest suffers as a *criminal*. Those who are always crying that religion is not to be regarded in the State, and the Jew is to be a citizen equally with the Christian, show themselves in accord with this. Is not this of incest and monogamy a *dogma of faith?* Touch it, and you will learn by experience how this moral man is a *hero of faith* too, not less than Krummacher,[39] not less than Philip II.[40] These fight for the faith of the Church, he for the faith of the State, or the moral laws of the State; for articles of faith, both condemn him who acts otherwise than *their faith* will allow. The brand of "crime" is stamped upon him, and he may languish in reformatories, in jails. Moral faith is as fanatical as religious faith! They call that "liberty of faith" then, when brother and sister, on account of a relation that they should have settled with their "conscience," are thrown into prison. "But they set a pernicious example." Yes, indeed: others might have taken the notion that the State had no business to meddle with their relation, and thereupon "purity of morals" would go to ruin. So then the religious heroes of faith are zealous for the "sacred God," the moral ones for the "sacred good."

Those who are zealous for something sacred often look very little like each other. How the strictly orthodox or old-style believers differ from the fighters for "truth, light, and justice,"

39. [It is not clear from the context which member of this formidable family of fierce defenders of orthodox German Protestantism Stirner is referring to; Friedrich Adolf Krummacher (1768-1845), his brother Gottfried Daniel (1774-1837) and his son Friedrich Wilhelm (1796-1868) all had reputations as theologians. The latter's strong attacks on rationalists in various books suggest that he is the referent.]

40. [King of Spain (1556-1598), noted throughout the Western world for his strong devotion to advancing the fortunes of the Roman Catholic faith.]

from the Philalethes, the Friends of Light, the Rationalists, and others. And yet, how utterly unessential is this difference! If one buffets single traditional truths (miracles, unlimited power of princes), then the Rationalists buffet them too, and only the old-style believers wail. But, if one buffets truth itself, he immediately has both, as *believers,* for opponents. So with moralities; the strict believers are relentless, the clearer heads are more tolerant. But he who attacks morality itself gets both to deal with. "Truth, morality, justice, light, etc.," are to be and remain "sacred." What any one finds to censure in Christianity is simply supposed to be "unchristian" according to the view of these rationalists; but Christianity must remain a "fixture," to buffet it is outrageous, "an outrage." To be sure, the heretic against pure faith no longer exposes himself to the earlier fury of persecution, but so much the more does it now fall upon the heretic against pure morals.

*　　*　　*

Piety has for a century received so many blows, and had to hear its superhuman essence reviled as an "inhuman" one so often, that one cannot feel tempted to draw the sword against it again. And yet it has almost always been only moral opponents that have appeared in the arena, to assail the supreme essence in favor of—another supreme essence. So Proudhon, unabashed, says:[41] "Man is destined to live without religion, but the moral law is eternal and absolute. Who would dare to-day to attack morality?" Moral people skimmed off the best fat from religion, ate it themselves, and are now having a tough job to get rid of the resulting scrofula. If, therefore, we point out that religion has not by any means been hurt in its inmost part so long as people reproach it only with its superhuman essence, and that it takes its final appeal to the "spirit" alone (for God is spirit), then we have sufficiently indicated its final accord with morality, and can leave its stubborn conflict with the latter lying behind us. It is a question of a supreme essence with both, and whether

41. [Stirner quoted from page 36 of Pierre Joseph Proudhon's *De la Création de l'Ordre dans l'Humanité, ou Principes d'Organization politique* (Paris, 1843). Stirner did not recognize in Proudhon a holder of congenial tendencies.]

this is a superhuman or a human one can make (since it is in any case an essence over me, a super-mine one, so to speak) but little difference to me. In the end the relation to the human essence, or to "Man," as soon as ever it has shed the snake-skin of the old religion, will yet wear a religious snake-skin again.

So Feuerbach instructs us that, "if one only *inverts* speculative philosophy, always makes the predicate the subject, and so makes the subject the object and principle, one has the undraped truth, pure and clean."[42] Herewith, to be sure, we lost the narrow religious standpoint, lost the *God,* who from this standpoint is subject; but we take in exchange for it the other side of the religious standpoint, the *moral* standpoint. Thus we no longer say "God is love," but "Love is divine." If we further put in place of the predicate "divine" the equivalent "sacred," then, as far as concerns the sense, all the old comes back again. According to this, love is to be the *good* in man, his divineness, that which does him honor, his true *humanity* (it "makes him Man for the first time," makes for the first time a man out of him). So then it would be more accurately worded thus: Love is what is *human* in man, and what is inhuman is the loveless egoist. But precisely all that which Christianity and with it speculative philosophy (i.e., theology) offers as the good, the absolute, is to self-ownership simply not the good (or, what means the same, it is *only the good*). Consequently, by the transformation of the predicate into the subject, the Christian *essence* (and it is the predicate that contains the essence, you know) would only be fixed yet more oppressively. God and the divine would entwine themselves all the more inextricably with me. To expel God from his heaven and to rob him of his *"transcendence"* cannot yet support a claim of complete victory, if therein he is only chased into the human breast and gifted with indelible *immanence.* Now they say, "The divine is the truly human!"

The same people who oppose Christianity as the basis of

42. [This was cited from page 64 of the second volume of *Anekdota zur neuesten deutschen Philosophie und Publicistik von Bruno Bauer, Ludwig Feuerbach, Friedrich Köppen, Karl Nauwerck, Arnold Ruge,* published in Zurich and Mannheim in 1843.]

the State, who oppose the so-called Christian State, do not tire
of repeating that morality is "the fundamental pillar of social life
and of the State." As if the dominion of morality were not a
complete dominion of the sacred, a "hierarchy."

So we may here mention by the way that rationalist movement which, after theologians had long insisted that only faith
was capable of grasping religious truths, that only to believers
did God reveal himself, and that therefore only the heart, the
feelings, the believing fancy was religious, broke out with the
assertion that the "natural understanding," human reason, was
also capable of discerning God. What does that mean but that
the reason laid claim to be the same visionary as the fancy?[43]
In this sense Reimarus[44] wrote his *Most Notable Truths of
Natural Religion*. It had to come to this—that the *whole* man
with all his faculties was found to be *religious;* heart and affections,
understanding and reason, feeling, knowledge, and will—in short,
everything in man—appeared religious. Hegel has shown that
even philosophy is religious. And what is not called religion
to-day? The "religion of love," the "religion of freedom," "political religion"—in short, every enthusiasm. So it is, too, in
fact.

To this day we use the Romance word "religion," which
expresses the concept of a condition of being *bound*. To be sure,
we remain bound, so far as religion takes possession of our
inward parts; but is the mind also bound? On the contrary,
that is free, is sole lord, is not our mind, but absolute. Therefore
the correct affirmative translation of the word religion would be
"freedom of mind"! In whomsoever the mind is free, he is religious in just the same way as he in whom the senses have free
course is called a sensual man. The mind binds the former,
the desires the latter. Religion, therefore, is boundness or *religio*
with reference to me—I am bound; it is freedom with reference

43. (*dieselbe Phantastin wie die Phantasie.*)
44. [Hermann Samuel Reimarus (1694-1767), a German of impressive
erudition in many diverse fields, lifelong resident of Hamburg. His
Abhandlung von die vornehmsten Wahrheiten der natürlichen Religion
was first published in Hamburg in 1754, and was in its sixth edition
in 1791.]

to the mind—the mind is free, or has freedom of mind. Many know from experience how hard it is on *us* when the desires run away with us, free and unbridled; but that the free mind, splendid intellectuality, enthusiasm for intellectual interests, or however this jewel may in the most various phrase be named, brings *us* into yet more grievous straits than even the wildest impropriety, people will not perceive; nor can they perceive it without being consciously egoists.

Reimarus, and all who have shown that our reason, our heart, etc., also lead to God, have therewithal shown that we are possessed through and through. To be sure, they vexed the theologians, from whom they took away the prerogative of religious exaltation; but for religion, for freedom of mind, they thereby conquered yet more ground. For, when the mind is no longer limited to feeling or faith, but also, as understanding, reason, and thought in general, belongs to itself the mind—when, therefore, it may take part in the spiritual[45] and heavenly truths in the form of understanding, as well as in its other forms— then the whole mind is occupied only with spiritual things, that is, with itself, and is therefore free. Now we are so through-and-through religious that "jurors," "sworn men," condemn us to death, and every policeman, as a good Christian, takes us to the lock-up by virtue of an "oath of office."

Morality could not come into opposition with piety till after the time when in general the boisterous hate of everything that looked like an "order" (decrees, commandments, etc.) spoke out in revolt, and the personal "absolute lord" was scoffed at and persecuted; consequently it could arrive at independence only through liberalism, whose first form acquired significance in the world's history as "citizenship," and weakened the specifically religious powers (see "Liberalism" below). For, when morality not merely goes alongside of piety, but stands on feet of its own, then its principle lies no longer in the divine commandments, but in the law of reason, from which the commandments, so far as they are still to remain valid, must first await justification for

45. (The same word as "intellectual," as "mind" and "spirit" are the same.)

their validity. In the law of reason man determines himself out of himself, for "Man" is rational, and out of the "essence of Man" those laws follow of necessity. Piety and morality part company in this—that the former makes God the lawgiver, the latter Man.

From a certain standpoint of morality people reason about as follows: Either man is led by his sensuality, and is, following it, *immoral,* or he is led by the good, which, taken up into the will, is called moral sentiment (sentiment and prepossession in favor of the good); then he shows himself *moral.* From this point of view how, for instance, can Sand's act against Kotzebue be called immoral?[46] What is commonly understood by unselfish it certainly was, in the same measure as (among other things) St. Crispin's[47] thieveries in favor of the poor. "He should not have murdered, for it stands written, Thou shalt not murder!" Then to serve the good, the welfare of the people, as Sand at least intended, or the welfare of the poor, like Crispin—is moral; but murder and theft are immoral; the purpose moral, the means immoral. Why? "Because murder, assassination, is something absolutely bad." When the Guerrillas[48] enticed the enemies of the country into ravines and shot them down unseen from the bushes, do you suppose that was assassination? According to the principle of morality, which commands us to serve the good, you could really ask only whether murder could never in any case be a realization of the good, and would have to endorse that murder which realized the good. You cannot condemn Sand's deed at all; it was moral, because in the service of the good, because unselfish; it was an act of punishment, which the individual inflicted, an—*execution* inflicted at the risk of the

46. [The assassination of August Friedrich Ferdinand de Kotzebue (1761-1819) by Karl-Ludwig Sand (1795-1820). Kotzebue, a defender of the older political order, ridiculed the new German nationalism which grew out of the struggle against Napoleon. He was called a "traitor" and was stabbed to death by Sand, an extremely zealous younger exponent of this sentiment.]

47. [The patron saint of shoemakers.]

48. [A reference to the irregular forces fighting in Spain against Napoleon during the Peninsular Wars, 1808-1814.]

executioner's life. What else had his scheme been, after all, but that he wanted to suppress writings by brute force? Are you not acquainted with the same procedure as a "legal" and sanctioned one? And what can be objected against it from your principle of morality?—"But it was an illegal execution." So the immoral thing in it was the illegality, the disobedience to law? Then you admit that the good is nothing else than—law, morality nothing else than *loyalty*. And to this externality of "loyalty" your morality must sink, to this righteousness of works in the fulfillment of the law, only that the latter is at once more tyrannical and more revolting than the old-time righteousness of works. For in the latter only the *act* is needed, but you require the *disposition* too; one must carry *in himself* the law, the statute; and he who is most legally disposed is the most moral. Even the last vestige of cheerfulness in Catholic life must perish in this Protestant legality. Here at last the domination of the law is for the first time complete. "Not I live, but the law lives in me." Thus I have really come so far to be only the "vessel of its glory." "Every Prussian carries his *gendarme* in his breast," says a high Prussian officer.

Why do certain *opposition parties* fail to flourish? Solely for the reason that they refuse to forsake the path of morality or legality. Hence the measureless hypocrisy of devotion, love, etc., from whose repulsiveness one may daily get the most thorough nausea at this rotten and hypocritical relation of a "lawful opposition."—In the *moral* relation of love and fidelity a divided or opposed will cannot have place; the beautiful relation is disturbed if the one wills this and the other the reverse. But now, according to the practice hitherto and the old prejudice of the opposition, the moral relation is to be preserved above all. What is then left to the opposition? Perhaps the will to have a liberty, if the beloved one sees fit to deny it? Not a bit! It may not *will* to have the freedom, it can only *wish* for it, "petition" for it, lisp a "Please, please!" What would come of it, if the opposition really *willed,* willed with the full energy of the will? No, it must renounce *will* in order to live to *love,* renounce liberty—for love of morality. It may never "claim as a right" what it is permitted only to "beg as a favor." Love, devotion,

etc., demand with undeviating definiteness that there be only
one will to which the others devote themselves, which they serve,
follow, love. Whether this will is regarded as reasonable or as
unreasonable, in both cases one acts morally when one follows
it, and immorally when one breaks away from it. The will that
commands the censorship seems to many unreasonable; but he
who in a land of censorship evades the censoring of his book
acts immorally, and he who submits it to the censorship acts
morally. If some one let his moral judgment go, and set up
a secret press, one would have to call him immoral, and im-
prudent in the bargain if he let himself be caught; but will such
a man lay claim to a value in the eyes of the "moral"? Perhaps!
—That is, if he fancied he was serving a "higher morality."

The web of the hypocrisy of to-day hangs on the frontiers
of two domains, between which our time swings back and forth,
attaching its fine threads of deception and self-deception. No
longer vigorous enough to serve *morality* without doubt or weak-
ening, not yet reckless enough to live wholly to egoism, it
trembles now toward the one and now toward the other in the
spider-web of hypocrisy, and, crippled by the curse of *halfness,*
catches only miserable, stupid flies. If one has once dared to
make a "free" motion, immediately one waters it again with
assurances of love, and—*shams resignation;* if, on the other side,
they have had the face to reject the free motion with *moral*
appeals to confidence, immediately the moral courage also sinks,
and they assure one how they hear the free words with special
pleasure; they—*sham approval.* In short, people would like to
have the one, but not go without the other; they would like to
have a *free* will, but not for their lives lack the *moral will.*
Just come in contact with a servile loyalist, you Liberals.[49] You
will sweeten every word of freedom with a look of the most
loyal confidence, and he will clothe his servilism in the most
flattering phrases of freedom. Then you go apart, and he, like

49. [Stirner is speaking here to the reformers of the 1840s in
Germany, exponents of stronger national unity, constitutional rule, more
widespread participation in government, and civil and political rights
established by law.]

you, thinks "I know you, fox!" He scents the devil in you as
much as you do the dark old Lord God in him.

A Nero is a "bad" man only in the eyes of the "good";
in mine he is nothing but a *possessed* man, as are the good too.
The good see in him an arch-villain, and relegate him to hell.
Why did nothing hinder him in his arbitrary course? Why did
people put up with so much? Do you suppose the tame Romans,
who let all their will be bound by such a tyrant, were a hair the
better? In old Rome they would have put him to death instantly,
would never have been his slaves. But the contemporary "good"
among the Romans opposed to him only moral demands, not
their *will;* they sighed that their emperor did not do homage to
morality, like them; they themselves remained "moral subjects,"
till at last one found courage to give up "moral, obedient subjection." And then the same "good Romans" who, as "obedient
subjects," had borne all the ignominy of having no will, hurrahed
over the nefarious, immoral act of the rebel. Where then in the
"good" was the courage for the *revolution,* that courage which
they now praised, after another had mustered it up? The good
could not have this courage, for a revolution, and an insurrection
into the bargain, is always something "immoral," which one
can resolve upon only when one ceases to be "good" and becomes
either "bad" or—neither of the two. Nero was no viler than
his time, in which one could only be one of the two, good or
bad. The judgment of his time on him had to be that he was
bad, and this in the highest degree: not a milksop, but an arch-
scoundrel. All moral people can pronounce only this judgment on
him. Rascals such as he was are still living here and there to-day
(see for example the *Memoirs* of Ritter von Lang[50]) in the midst
of the moral. It is not convenient to live among them certainly,
as one is not sure of his life for a moment; but can you say that it
is more convenient to live among the moral? One is just as little
sure of his life there, only that one is hanged "in the way of

50. [Karl Heinrich, Ritters von Lang (1764-1835); Jean Bourdeau, in
his *Poètes et Humoristes de l'Allemagne* (Paris, 1906), referred to von
Lang as "A German Gil Blas." *Memorien des Karl Heinrich Ritters
von Lang; Skizzen aus meinem Leben und Wirken, meinen Reisen und
meiner Zeit* had been published in Brunswick in 1841-1842.]

justice," but least of all is one sure of his honor, and the national cockade is gone before you can say Jack Robinson. The hard fist of morality treats the noble nature of egoism altogether without compassion.

"But surely one cannot put a rascal and an honest man on the same level!" Now, no human being does that oftener than you judges of morals; yes, still more than that, you imprison as a criminal an honest man who speaks openly against the existing constitution, against the hallowed institutions, and you entrust portfolios and still more important things to a crafty rascal. So *in praxi* you have nothing to reproach me with. "But in theory!" Now there I do put both on the same level, as two opposite poles—to wit, both on the level of the moral law. Both have meaning only in the "moral world, just as in the pre-Christian time a Jew who kept the law and one who broke it had meaning and significance only in respect to the Jewish law; before Jesus Christ, on the contrary, the Pharisee was no more than the "sinner and publican." So before self-ownership the moral Pharisee amounts to as much as the immoral sinner.

Nero became very inconvenient by his possessedness. But a self-owning man would not sillily oppose to him the "sacred," and whine if the tyrant does not regard the sacred; he would oppose to him his will. How often the sacredness of the inalienable rights of man has been held up to their foes, and some liberty or other shown and demonstrated to be a "sacred right of man!" Those who do that deserve to be laughed out of court— as they actually are—were it not that in truth they do, even though unconsciously, take the road that leads to the goal. They have a presentiment that, if only the majority is once won for that liberty, it will also will the liberty, and will then take what it *will* have. The sacredness of the liberty, and all possible proofs of this sacredness, will never procure it; lamenting and petitioning only shows beggars.

The moral man is necessarily narrow in that he knows no other enemy than the "immoral" man. "He who is not moral is immoral!" and accordingly reprobate, despicable, etc. Therefore the moral man can never comprehend the egoist. Is not unwedded cohabitation an immorality? The moral man may turn as he

pleases, he will have to stand by this verdict; Emilia Galotti[51] gave
up her life for this moral truth. And it is true, it is an immorality.
A virtuous girl may become an old maid; a virtuous man may
pass the time in fighting his natural impulses till he has perhaps
dulled them, he may castrate himself for the sake of virtue as
St. Origen[52] did for the sake of heaven: he thereby honors sacred
wedlock, sacred chastity, as inviolable; he is—moral. Unchastity
can never become a moral act. However indulgently the moral
man may judge and excuse him who committed it, it remains a
transgression, a sin against a moral commandment; there clings
to it an indelible stain. As chastity once belonged to the monastic
vow, so it does to moral conduct. Chastity is a—good.—For
the egoist, on the contrary, even chastity is not a good without
which he could not get along; he cares nothing at all about it.
What now follows from this for the judgment of the moral man?
This: that he throws the egoist into the only class of men that
he knows besides moral men, into that of the—immoral. He cannot do otherwise; he must find the egoist immoral in everything
in which the egoist disregards morality. If he did not find him
so, then he would already have become an apostate from morality
without confessing it to himself, he would already no longer be
a truly moral man. One should not let himself be led astray by
such phenomena, which at the present day are certainly no longer
to be classed as rare, but should reflect that he who yields any
point of morality can as little be counted among the truly moral
as Lessing was a pious Christian when, in the well-known parable,
he compared the Christian religion, as well as the Mohammedan
and Jewish, to a "counterfeit ring." Often people are already
further than they venture to confess to themselves. For Socrates,
because in culture he stood on the level of morality, it would
have been an immorality if he had been willing to follow Crito's
seductive incitement and escape from the dungeon; to remain
was the only moral thing. But it was solely because Socrates was—

51. [The heroine of the famous dramatic work of the same name by
Gotthold Ephraim Lessing (1728-1781); this had been reprinted in 1841
and again in 1844.]
52. [One of the Fathers and Doctors of the Christian Church, resident
of Alexandria, probable dates 182-185/251-254 A.D.]

a moral man. The "unprincipled, sacrilegious" men of the Revolution, on the contrary, had sworn fidelity to Louis XVI,[53] and decreed his deposition, yes, his death; but the act was an immoral one, at which moral persons will be horrified to all eternity.

Yet all this applies, more or less, only to "civic morality," on which the freer look down with contempt. For it (like civism, its native ground, in general) is still too little removed and free from the religious heaven not to transplant the latter's laws without criticism or further consideration to its domain instead of producing independent doctrines of its own. Morality cuts a quite different figure when it arrives at the consciousness of its dignity, and raises its principle, the essence of man, or "Man," to be the only regulative power. Those who have worked their way through to such a decided consciousness break entirely with religion, whose God no longer finds any place alongside their "Man," and, as they (see below) themselves scuttle the ship of State, so too they crumble away that "morality" which flourishes only in the State, and logically have no right to use even its name any further. For what this "critical" party calls morality is very positively distinguished from the so-called "civic or political morality," and must appear to the citizen like an "insensate and unbridled liberty." But at bottom it has only the advantage of the "purity of the principle," which, freed from its defilement with the religious, has now reached universal power in its clarified definiteness as "humanity."

Therefore one should not wonder that the name "morality" is retained along with others, like freedom, benevolence, self-consciousness, and is only garnished now and then with the addition, a "free" morality—just as, though the civic State is abused, yet the State is to arise again as a "free State," or, if not even so, yet as a "free society."

Because this morality completed into humanity has fully settled its accounts with the religion out of which it historically came forth, nothing hinders it from becoming a religion on its own account. For a distinction prevails between religion and morality

53. [King of France from 1774 until his deposition by the revolutionaries in 1792, and guillotined the following year.]

only so long as our dealings with the world of men are regulated
and hallowed by our relation to a superhuman being, or so long
as our doing is a doing "for God's sake." If, on the other hand,
it comes to the point that "man is to man the supreme being,"
then that distinction vanishes, and morality, being removed from
its subordinate position, is completed into—religion. For then
the higher being who had hitherto been subordinated to the
highest, Man, has ascended to absolute height, and we are related
to him as one is related to the highest being, religiously. Morality
and piety are now as synonymous as in the beginning of Christianity, and it is only because the supreme being has come to be
a different one that a holy walk is no longer called a "holy" one,
but a "human" one. If morality has conquered, then a complete—
change of masters has taken place.

After the annihilation of faith Feuerbach thinks to put in
to the supposedly safe harbor of love. "The first and highest
law must be the love of man to man. Homo homini Deus est—
this is the supreme practical maxim, this is the turning point of
the world's history."[54] But, properly speaking, only the god is
changed—the deus; love has remained: there love to the superhuman God, here love to the human God, to homo as Deus.
Therefore man is to me—sacred. And everything "truly human"
is to me—sacred! "Marriage is sacred of itself. And so it is
with all moral relations. Friendship is and must be sacred for
you, and property, and marriage, and the good of every man, but
sacred in and of itself."[55] Haven't we the priest again there? Who
is his God? Man with a great M! What is the divine? The human!
Then the predicate has indeed only been changed into the subject,
and, instead of the sentence "God is love," they say "love is
divine"; instead of "God has become man," "Man has become
God," etc. It is nothing more or less than a new—religion. "All
moral relations are ethical, are cultivated with a moral mind, only
where of themselves (without religious consecration by the
priest's blessing) they are counted religious." Feuerbach's propo-

54. Essence of Christianity, second edition [1843], p. 402.
55. [Work cited above], p. 403.

sition, "Theology is anthropology," means only "religion must
be ethics, ethics alone is religion."

Altogether Feuerbach accomplishes only a transposition
of subject and predicate, a giving of preference to the latter. But,
since he himself says, "Love is not (and has never been considered
by men) sacred through being a predicate of God, but it is a
predicate of God because it is divine in and of itself," he might
judge that the fight against the predicates themselves, against
love and all sanctities, must be commenced. How could he hope
to turn men away from God when he left them the divine? And
if, as Feuerbach says, God himself has never been the main thing
to them, but only his predicates, then he might have gone on
leaving them the tinsel longer yet, since the doll, the real kernel,
was left at any rate. He recognizes, too, that with him it is "only
a matter of annihilating an illusion";[56] he thinks, however, that
the effect of the illusion on men is "downright ruinous, since
even love, in itself the truest, most inward sentiment, becomes an
obscure, illusory one through religiousness, since religious love
loves man[57] only for God's sake, therefore loves man only
apparently, but in truth God only." Is this different with moral
love? Does it love the man, *this* man for *this* man's sake, or for
morality's sake, and so—for *homo homini Deus*—for God's sake?

The wheels in the head have a number of other formal
aspects, some of which it may be useful to indicate here.

Thus *self-renunciation* is common to the holy with the unholy,
to the pure and the impure. The impure man *renounces* all "better
feelings," all shame, even natural timidity, and follows only the
appetite that rules him. The pure man renounces his natural
relation to the world ("renounces the world") and follows only
the "desire" which rules him. Driven by the thirst for money,
the avaricious man renounces all admonitions of conscience, all
feeling of honor, all gentleness and all compassion; he puts all
considerations out of sight; the appetite drags him along. The
holy man behaves similarly. He makes himself the "laughing-stock

56. [Work cited above], p. 408.
57. (Literally "the man.")

of the world," is hard-hearted and "strictly just"; for the desire drags him along. As the unholy man renounces *himself* before Mammon, so the holy man renounces *himself* before God and the divine laws. We are now living in a time when the *shameless-ness* of the holy is every day more and more felt and uncovered, whereby it is at the same time compelled to unveil itself, and lay itself bare, more and more every day. Have not the shameless-ness and stupidity of the reasons with which men antagonize the "progress of the age" long surpassed all measure and all expectation? But it must be so. The self-renouncers must, as holy men, take the same course that they do so as unholy men; as the latter little by little sink to the fullest measure of self-renouncing vulgarity and *lowness,* so the former must ascend to the most dishonorable *exaltation.* The mammon of the earth and the *God* of heaven both demand exactly the same degree of—self-renunci-ation. The low man, like the exalted one, reaches out for a "good"—the former for the material good, the latter for the ideal, the so-called "supreme good"; and at last both complete each other again too, as the "materially-minded" man sacrifices everything to an ideal phantasm, his *vanity,* and the "spiritually-minded" man to a material gratification, the *life of enjoyment.*

Those who exhort men to "unselfishness"[58] think they are saying an uncommon deal. What do they understand by it? Probably something like what they understand by "self-renunci-ation." But who is this self that is to be renounced and to have no benefit? It seems that *you* yourself are supposed to be it. And for whose benefit is unselfish self-renunciation recommended to you? Again for *your* benefit and behoof, only that through unselfishness you are procuring your "true benefit."

You are to benefit *yourself,* and yet you are not to seek *your* benefit.

People regard as unselfish the *benefactor* of men, a Francke[59] who founded the orphan asylum, an O'Connell[60] who works

58. (*uneigennuetzigkeit,* literally "un-self-benefitingness.")
59. [August Hermann Francke (1663-1727), the founder of pietism in Halle, professor and theologian, established an orphanage in Halle in 1698.]
60. [Daniel O'Connell (1775-1847), Irish political leader, member

tirelessly for his Irish people; but also the *fanatic* who, like St. Boniface,[61] hazards his life for the conversion of the heathen, or, like Robespierre,[62] sacrifices everything to virtue—like Körner,[63] dies for God, king, and fatherland. Hence, among others, O'Connell's opponents try to trump up against him some selfishness or mercenariness, for which the O'Connell fund seemed to give them a foundation; for, if they were successful in casting suspicion on his "unselfishness," they would easily separate him from his adherents.

Yet what could they show further than that O'Connell was working for another *end* than the ostensible one? But, whether he may aim at making money or at liberating the people, it still remains certain, in one case as in the other, that he is striving for an end, and that *his* end; selfishness here as there, only that his national self-interest would be beneficial to *others too,* and so would be for the *common* interest.

Now, do you suppose unselfishness is unreal and nowhere extant? On the contrary, nothing is more ordinary! One may even call it an article of fashion in the civilized world, which is considered so indispensable that, if it costs too much in solid material, people at least adorn themselves with its tinsel counterfeit and feign it. Where does unselfishness begin? Right where an end ceases to be *our* end and our *property,* which we, as owners, can dispose of at pleasure; where it becomes a fixed end or a— fixed idea; where it begins to inspire, enthuse, fanaticize us; in short, where it passes into our *stubbornness* and becomes our— master. One is not unselfish so long as he retains the end in his power; one becomes so only at that "Here I stand, I cannot do otherwise," the fundamental maxim of all the possessed; one

of Parliament and important figure in the emancipation of the Irish from religious discrimination in political life.]

61. [The English monk who became a Christian missionary in Germany and is credited with undermining paganism there; probable dates 680-755.]

62. See note 76.

63. [Karl-Theodore Körner (1791-1813), soldier and poet of German independence, killed in action near Hamburg in August, 1813.]

becomes so in the case of a *sacred* end, through the corresponding sacred zeal.

I am not unselfish so long as the end remains my *own,* and I, instead of giving myself up to be the blind means of its fulfillment, leave it always an open question. My zeal need not on that account be slacker than the most fanatical, but at the same time I remain toward it frostily cold, unbelieving, and its most irreconcilable enemy; I remain its *judge,* because I am its owner.

Unselfishness grows rank as far as possessedness reaches, as much on possessions of the devil as on those of a good spirit; there vice, folly, and the like; here humility, devotion, and so forth.

Where could one look without meeting victims of self-renunciation? There sits a girl opposite me, who perhaps has been making bloody sacrifices to her soul for ten years already. Over the buxom form droops a deathly-tired head, and pale cheeks betray the slow bleeding away of her youth. Poor child, how often the passions may have beaten at your heart, and the rich powers of youth have demanded their right! When your head rolled in the soft pillow, how awakening nature quivered through your limbs, the blood swelled your veins, and fiery fancies poured the gleam of voluptousness into your eyes! Then appeared the ghost of the soul and its external bliss. You were terrified, your hands folded themselves, your tormented eyes turned its look upward, you—prayed. The storms of nature were hushed, a calm glided over the ocean of your appetites. Slowly the weary eyelids sank over the life extinguished under them, the tension crept out unperceived from the rounded limbs, the boisterous waves dried up in the heart, the folded hands themselves rested a powerless weight on the unresisting bosom, one last faint "Oh dear!" moaned itself away, and—*the soul was at rest.* You fell asleep, to awake in the morning to a new combat and a new— prayer. Now the habit of renunciation cools the heat of your desire, and the roses of your youth are growing pale in the— chlorosis of your heavenliness. The soul is saved, the body may

perish!   O Lais, O Ninon,[64] how well you did to scorn this pale
virtue!   One free *grisette* against a thousand virgins grown gray
in virtue!

The fixed idea may also be perceived as "maxim," "principle,"
"standpoint," and the like.   Archimedes, to move the earth, asked
for a standpoint *outside* it.   Men sought continually for this
standpoint, and every one seized upon it as well as he was able.
This foreign standpoint is the *world of mind,* of ideas, thoughts,
concepts, essences; it is *heaven.*   Heaven is the "standpoint" from
which the earth is moved, earthly doings surveyed and—despised.
To assure to themselves heaven, to occupy the heavenly standpoint
firmly and for ever—how painfully and tirelessly humanity struggled for this!

Christianity has aimed to deliver us from a life determined
by nature, from the appetites as actuating us, and so has meant
that man should not let himself be determined by his appetites.
This does not involve the idea that *he* was not to have appetites,
but that the appetites were not to have him, that they were not
to become *fixed,* uncontrollable, indissoluble.   Now, could not
what Christianity (religion) contrived against the appetites be
applied by us to its own precept that *mind* (thought, conceptions,
ideas, faith) must determine us; could we not ask that neither
should mind, or the conception, the idea, be allowed to determine
us, to become fixed and inviolable or "sacred"?   Then it would
end in the *dissolution of mind,* the dissolution of all thoughts,
of all conceptions.   As we there had to say, "We are indeed to
have appetites, but the appetites are not to have us," so we
should now say, "We are indeed to have *mind,* but mind is not to
have us."   If the latter seems lacking in sense, think of the fact
that with so many a man a thought becomes a "maxim," whereby
he himself is made prisoner to it, so that it is not he that has
the maxim, but rather it that has him.   And with the maxim
he has a "permanent standpoint" again.   The doctrines of the
catechism become our *principles* before we find it out, and no

[handwritten marginalia: A foolish consistency is the hobgoblin of little minds (which is also a MAXIM!)]

64. [A reference to the beauteous Greek courtesan made famous by
Demosthenes, and to Ninon de Lenclos (1620-1705), the worldly French
beauty, known among other things for her many amatory liasons.]

plus we are flesh,
corporeal — our "mind" is
BRAIN — physical & *brain*

longer brook rejection. Their thought, or—mind, has the sole
power, and no protest of the "flesh" is further listened to.
Nevertheless it is only through the "flesh" that I can break the
tyranny of mind; for it is only when a man hears his flesh along
with the rest of him that he hears himself wholly, and it is only
when he wholly hears *himself* that he is a hearing or rational[65]
being. The Christian does not hear the agony of his enthralled
nature, but lives in "humility"; therefore he does not grumble
at the wrong which befalls his *person*; he thinks himself satisfied
with the "freedom of the spirit." But, if the flesh once takes
the floor, and its tone is "passionate," "indecorous," "not well-
disposed," "spiteful" (as it cannot be otherwise), then he thinks
he hears voices of devils, voices *against* the *spirit* (for decorum,
passionlessness, kindly disposition, and the like, is—spirit), and
is justly zealous against them. He could not be a Christian if
he were willing to endure them. He listens only to morality,
and slaps unmorality in the mouth; he listens only to legality,
and gags the lawless word. The *spirit* of morality and legality
holds him a prisoner; a rigid, unbending *master*. They call that
the "mastery of the spirit"—it is at the same time the *standpoint*
of the spirit.

And now whom do the ordinary liberal gentlemen mean to
make free? Whose freedom is it that they cry out and thirst
for? The *spirit's!* That of the spirit of morality, legality, piety,
the fear of God. That is what the anti-liberal gentlemen also
want, and the whole contention between the two turns on a
matter of advantage—whether the latter are to be the only speakers, or the former are to receive a "share in the enjoyment of
the same advantage." The *spirit* remains the absolute *lord* for
both, and their only quarrel is over who shall occupy the hier-
archical throne that pertains to the "Vicegerent of the Lord."
The best of it is that one can calmly look upon the stir with
the certainty that the wild beasts of history will tear each other
to pieces just like those of nature; their putrefying corpses fertilize
the ground for—our crops.

We shall come back later to many another wheel in the

65. (*vernuenftig*, derived from *vernehmen*, to hear.)

head—for instance, those of vocation, truthfulness, love, and the like.

When one's own is contrasted with what is *imparted* to him, there is no use in objecting that we cannot have anything isolated, but receive everything as a part of the universal order, and therefore through the impression of what is around us, and that consequently we have it as something "imparted"; for there is a great difference between the feelings and thoughts which are *aroused* in me by other things and those which are *given* to me. God, immortality, freedom, humanity, are drilled into us from childhood as thoughts and feelings which move our inner being more or less strongly, either ruling us without our knowing it, or sometimes in richer natures manifesting themselves in systems and works of art; but are always not aroused, but imparted, feelings, because we must believe in them and cling to them. That an Absolute existed, and that it must be taken in, felt, and thought by us, was settled as a faith in the minds of those who spent all the strength of their mind on recognizing it and setting it forth. The *feeling* for the Absolute exists there as an imparted one, and thenceforth results only in the most manifold revelations of its own self. So in Klopstock[66] the religious feeling was an imparted one, which in the *Messiad* simply found artistic expression. If, on the other hand, the religion with which he was confronted had been for him only an incitation to feeling and thought, and if he had known how to take an attitude completely *his own* toward it, then there would have resulted, instead of religious inspiration, a dissolution and consumption of the religion itself. Instead of that, he only continued in mature years his childish feelings received in childhood, and squandered the powers of his manhood in decking out his childish trifles.

The difference is, then, whether feelings are imparted to me

66. [Friedrich Gottlieb Klopstock (1724-1803), one of the important 18th century German poets; *Der Messias* drew enthusiastic acclaim the world over. Several multi-volume editions of his works appeared in the 1820s and 1830s.]

or only aroused. Those which are aroused are my own, egoistic, because they are not *as feelings* drilled into me, dictated to me, and pressed upon me; but those which are imparted to me I receive, with open arms—I cherish them in me as a heritage, cultivate them, and am *possessed* by them. Who is there that has never, more or less consciously, noticed that our whole education is calculated to produce *feelings* in us, impart them to us, instead of leaving their production to ourselves however they may turn out? If we hear the name of God, we are to feel veneration; if we hear that of the prince's majesty, it is to be received with reverence, deference, submission; if we hear that of morality, we are to think that we hear something inviolable; if we hear of the Evil One or evil ones, we are to shudder. The intention is directed to these *feelings,* and he who should hear with pleasure the deeds of the "bad" would have to be "taught what's what" with the rod of discipline. Thus stuffed with *imparted feelings,* we appear before the bar of majority and are "pronounced of age." Our equipment consists of "elevating feelings, lofty thoughts, inspiring maxims, eternal principles." The young are of age when they twitter like the old; they are driven through school to learn the old song, and, when they have this by heart, they are declared of age.

We *must not* feel at every thing and every name that comes before us what we could and would like to feel thereat; at the name of God we must think of nothing laughable, feel nothing disrespectful, it being prescribed and imparted to us what and how we are to feel and think at mention of that name.

That is the meaning of the *care of souls*—that my soul or my mind be tuned as others think right, not as I myself would like it. How much trouble does it not cost one, finally to secure to oneself a feeling of one's *own* at the mention of at least this or that name, and to laugh in the face of many who expect from us a holy face and a composed expression at their speeches. What is imparted is *alien* to us, is not our own, and therefore is "sacred," and it is hard work to lay aside the "sacred dread of it."

To-day one again hears "seriousness" praised, "seriousness

in the presence of highly important subjects and discussions,"
"German seriousness," and so on. This sort of seriousness pro-
claims clearly how old and grave lunacy and possession have
already become. For there is nothing more serious than a
lunatic when he comes to the central point of his lunacy; then
his great earnestness incapacitates him for taking a joke. (See
madhouses.)

3.—THE HIERARCHY

THE historical reflections on our Mongolism which I propose
to insert episodically at this place are not given with the
claim of thoroughness, or even of approved soundness, but solely
because it seems to me that they may contribute toward making
the rest clear.

The history of the world, whose shaping properly belongs
altogether to the Caucasian race, seems till now to have run
through two Caucasian ages, in the first of which we had to
work out and work off our innate *negroidity;* this was followed
in the second by *Mongoloidity* (Chineseness), which must likewise
be terribly made an end of. Negroidity represents *antiquity,*
the time of dependence on *things* (on cocks' eating, birds' flight,
on sneezing, on thunder and lightning, on the rustling of sacred
trees, and so forth); Mongoloidity the time of dependence on
thoughts, the *Christian* time. Reserved for the future are the
words, "I am owner of the world of things, and I am owner
of the world of mind."

In the negroid age fall the campaigns of Sesostris[67] and the
importance of Egypt and of northern Africa in general. To the
Mongoloid age belong the invasions of the Huns and Mongols,
up to the Russians.

The value of *me* cannot possibly be rated high so long as
the hard diamond of the *not-me* bears so enormous a price as
was the case both with God and with the world. The not-me

67. [Stirner did not specify which of the two Egyptian pharaohs who
bore this name during the Twelfth Dynasty he was thinking of, but
presumably it was Sesostris III (1887-1849 B.C.), who conquered Nubia.]

is still too stony and indomitable to be consumed and absorbed by me; rather, men only creep about with extraordinary *bustle* on this *immovable* entity, on this *substance,* like parasitic animals on a body from whose juices they draw nourishment, yet without consuming it. It is the bustle of vermin, the assiduity of Mongolians. Among the Chinese, we know, everything remains as it used to be, and nothing "essential" or "substantial" suffers a change; all the more actively do they work away *at* that which remains, which bears the name of the "old," "ancestors," and the like.

Accordingly, in our Mongolian age all change has been only reformatory or ameliorative, not destructive or consuming and annihilating. The substance, the object, *remains.* All our assiduity was only the activity of ants and the hopping of fleas, jugglers' tricks on the immovable tight-rope of the objective, *corvée*-service under the leadership of the unchangeable or "eternal." The Chinese are doubtless the most *positive* nation, because totally buried in precepts; but neither has the Christian age come out from the *positive,* from "limited freedom," freedom "within certain limits." In the most advanced stage of civilization this activity earns the name of *scientific* activity, of working on a motionless presupposition, a *hypothesis* that is not to be upset.

In its first and most unintelligible form morality shows itself as *habit.* To act according to the habit and usage (*mores*) of one's country—is to be moral there. Therefore pure moral action, clear, unadulterated morality, is most straightforwardly practiced in China; they keep to the old habit and usage, and hate each innovation as a crime worthy of death. For *innovation* is the deadly enemy of *habit,* of the *old,* of *permanence.* In fact, too, it admits of no doubt that through habit man secures himself against the obtrusiveness of things, of the world, and founds a world of his own in which alone he is and feels at home, builds himself a *heaven.* Why, heaven has no other meaning than that it is man's proper home, in which nothing alien regulates and rules him any longer, no influence of the earthly any longer makes him himself alien; in short, in which the dross of the earthly is thrown off, and the combat against the world has found an end—in which, therefore, nothing is any longer *denied* him. Heaven is the end of *abnegation*, it is *free enjoyment*. There man no longer denies himself anything, because nothing is any longer alien and hostile to him. But now habit is a "second nature," which detaches and frees man from his first and original natural condition, in securing him against every casualty of it. The fully elaborated habit of the Chinese has provided for all emergencies, and everything is "looked out for"; whatever may come, the Chinaman always knows how he has to behave, and does not need to decide first according to the circumstances; no unforeseen case throws him down from the heaven of his rest. The morally habituated and inured Chinaman is not surprised and taken off his guard; he behaves with equanimity (that is, with equal spirit or temper) toward everything, because his temper, protected by the precaution of his traditional usage, does not lose its balance. Hence, on the ladder of culture or civilization humanity mounts the first round through habit; and, as it conceives that, in climbing to culture, it is at the same time climbing to heaven, the realm of culture or second nature, it really mounts the first round of the—ladder to heaven.

If Mongoldom has settled the existence of spiritual beings —if it has created a world of spirits, a heaven—the Caucasians have wrestled for thousands of years with these spiritual beings, to get to the bottom of them. What were they doing, then, but building on Mongolian ground? They have not built on sand, but in the air; they have wrestled with Mongolism, stormed the Mongolian heaven, Tien. When will they at last annihilate this heaven? When will they at last become *really Caucasians,* and find themselves? When will the "immortality of the soul," which in these latter days thought it was giving itself still more security if it presented itself as "immortality of mind," at last change to the *mortality of mind*?

It was when, in the industrious struggle of the Mongolian race, men had *built a heaven,* that those of the Caucasian race, since in their Mongolian complexion they have to do with heaven, took upon themselves the opposite task, the task of storming

that heaven of custom, *heaven-storming*[68] activity. To dig under
all human ordinance, in order to set up a new and—better one
on the cleared site, to wreck all customs in order to put new
and—better customs in their place—their act is limited to this.
But is it thus already purely and really what it aspires to be,
and does it reach its final aim? No, in this creation of a*"better"*
it is tainted with Mongolism. It storms heaven only to make
a heaven again, it overthrows an old power only to legitimate a
new power, it only—*improves.* Nevertheless the point aimed
at, often as it may vanish from the eyes at every new attempt,
is the real, complete downfall of heaven, customs—in short,
of man secured only against the world, of the *isolation* or
inwardness of man. Through the heaven of culture man seeks
to isolate himself from the world, to break its hostile power.
But this isolation of heaven must likewise be broken, and the
true end of heaven-storming is the—downfall of heaven, the
annihilation of heaven. *Improving* and *reforming* is the Mongolism of the Caucasian, because thereby he is always getting
up again what already existed—to wit, a *precept,* a generality,
a heaven. He harbors the most irreconcilable enmity to heaven,
and yet builds new heavens daily; piling heaven on heaven, he
only crushes one by another; the Jews' heaven destroys the
Greeks', the Christians' the Jews', the Protestants' the Catholics'.
—If the *heaven-storming* men of Caucasian blood throw off
their Mongolian skin, they will bury the emotional man under
the ruins of the monstrous world of emotion, the isolated man
under his isolated world, the paradisaical man under his heaven.
And heaven is the *realm of spirits,* the realm *of freedom of the
spirit.*

The realm of heaven, the realm of spirits and ghosts, has
found its right standing in the speculative philosophy. Here
it was stated as the realm of thoughts, concepts, and ideas;
heaven is peopled with thoughts and ideas, and this "realm of
spirits" is then the true reality.

To want to win freedom for the *spirit* is Mongolism; freedom

68. (A German idiom for destructive radicalism.)

of the spirit is Mongolian freedom, freedom of feeling, moral freedom, and so forth.

We may find the word "morality" taken as synonymous with spontaneity, self-determination. But that is not involved in it; rather has the Caucasian shown himself spontaneous only *in spite* of his Mongolian morality. The Mongolian heaven, or morals,[69] remained the strong castle, and only by storming incessantly at this castle did the Caucasian show himself moral; if he had not had to do with morals at all any longer, if he had not had therein his indomitable, continual enemy, the relation to morals would cease, and consequently morality would cease. That his spontaneity is still a moral spontaneity, therefore, is just the Mongoloidity of it—is a sign that in it he has not arrived at himself. "Moral spontaneity" corresponds entirely with "religious and orthodox philosophy," "constitutional monarchy," "the Christian State," "freedom within certain limits," "the limited freedom of the press," or, in a figure, to the hero fettered to a sick-bed.

Man has not really vanquished Shamanism and its spooks till he possesses the strength to lay aside not only the belief in ghosts or in spirits, but also the belief in the spirit.

He who believes in a spook no more assumes the "introduction of a higher world" than he who believes in the spirit, and both seek behind the sensual world a supersensual one; in short, they produce and believe *another* world, and this other *world, the product of their mind,* is a spiritual world; for their senses grasp and know nothing of another, a non-sensual world, only their spirit lives in it. Going on from this Mongolian belief in the *existence of spiritual beings* to the point that the *proper being* of man too is his *spirit,* and that all care must be directed to this alone, to the "welfare of his soul," is not hard. Influence on the spirit, so-called "moral influence," is hereby assured.

Hence it is manifest that Mongolism represents utter absence of any rights of the sensuous, represents non-sensuousness and

69. (The same word that has been translated "custom" several times in this section.)

unnature, and that sin and the consciousness of sin was our Mongolian torment that lasted thousands of years.

But who, then, will dissolve the spirit into its *nothing*? He who by means of the spirit set forth nature as the *null*, finite, transitory, he alone can bring down the spirit too to like nullity. I can; each one among you can, who does his will as an absolute I; in a word, the *egoist* can.

Before the sacred, people lose all sense of power and all confidence; they occupy a *powerless* and *humble* attitude toward it. And yet no thing is sacred of itself, but by my *declaring it sacred,* by my declaration, my judgment, my bending the knee; in short, by my—conscience.

Sacred is everything which for the egoist is to be unapproachable, not to be touched, outside his *power*—above *him;* sacred, in a word, is every *matter of conscience,* for "this is a matter of conscience to me" means simply, "I hold this sacred."

For little children, just as for animals, nothing sacred exists, because, in order to make room for this conception, one must already have progressed so far in understanding that he can make distinctions like "good and bad," "warranted and unwarranted"; only at such a level of reflection or intelligence—the proper standpoint of religion—can unnatural (that is, brought into existence by thinking) *reverence,* "sacred dread," step into the place of natural fear. To this sacred dread belongs holding something outside oneself for mightier, greater, better warranted, better; the attitude in which one acknowledges the might of something alien—not merely feels it, then, but expressly acknowledges it, admits it, yields, surrenders, lets himself be tied (devotion, humility, servility, submission). Here walks the whole ghostly troop of the "Christian virtues."

Everything toward which you cherish any respect or reverence deserves the name of sacred; you yourselves, too, say that you would feel a *"sacred dread"* of laying hands on it. And you give this tinge even to the unholy (gallows, crime, etc.). You have a horror of touching it. There lies in it something uncanny, that is, unfamiliar or *not your own.*

"If something or other did not rank as sacred in a man's mind, why, then all bars would be let down to self-will, to unlimited subjectivity!" Fear makes the beginning, and one can make himself fearful to the coarsest man; already, therefore, a barrier against his insolence. But in fear there always remains the attempt to liberate oneself from what is feared, by guile, deception, tricks, etc. In reverence,[70] on the contrary, it is quite otherwise. Here something is not only feared,[71] but also honored:[72] what is feared has become an inward power which I can no longer get clear of; I honor it, am captivated by it and devoted to it, belong to it; by the honor which I pay it I am completely in its power, and do not even attempt liberation any longer. Now I am attached to it with all the strength of faith; I *believe*. I and what I fear are one; "not I live, but the respected lives in me!" Because the spirit, the infinite, does not allow of coming to any end, therefore it is stationary; it fears *dying,* it cannot let go its dear Jesus, the greatness of finiteness is no longer recognized by its blinded eye; the object of fear, now raised to veneration, may no longer be handled; reverence is made eternal, the respected is deified. The man is now no longer employed in creating, but in *learning* (knowing, investigating),occupied with a fixed *object,* losing himself in its depths, without return to himself. The relation to this object is that of knowing, fathoming, basing, not that of *dissolution* (abrogation). "Man is to be religious," that is settled; therefore people busy themselves only with the question how this is to be attained, what is the right meaning of religiousness, etc. Quite otherwise when one makes the axiom itself doubtful and calls it in question, even though it should go to smash. Morality too is such a sacred conception; one must be moral, and must look only for the right "how," the right way to be so. One dares not go at morality itself with the question whether it is not itself an illusion; it remains exalted above all doubt, unchangeable. And so we

70. (*Ehrfurcht*)
71. (*gefuerchtet*)
72. (*geehrt*)

go on with the sacred, grade after grade, from the "holy" to the "holy of holies."

Men are sometimes divided into two classes: *cultured* and *uncultured.* The former, so far as they were worthy of their name, occupied themselves with thoughts, with mind, and (because in the time since Christ, of which the very principle is thought, they were the ruling ones) demanded a servile respect for the thoughts recognized by them. State, emperor, church, God, morality, order, are such thoughts or spirits, that exist only for the mind. A merely living being, an animal, cares as little for them as a child. But the uncultured are really nothing but children, and he who attends only to the necessities of his life is indifferent to those spirits; but, because he is also weak before them, he succumbs to their power, and is ruled by—thoughts. This is the meaning of hierarchy.

Hierarchy is dominion of thoughts, dominion of mind!

We are hierarchic to this day, kept down by those who are supported by thoughts. Thoughts are the sacred.

But the two are always clashing, now one and now the other giving the offense; and this clash occurs, not only in the collision of two men, but in one and the same man. For no cultured man is so cultured as not to find enjoyment in things too, and so be uncultured; and no uncultured man is totally without thoughts. In Hegel it comes to light at last what a longing for things even the most cultured man has, and what a horror of every "hollow theory" he harbors. With him reality, the world of things, is altogether to correspond to the thought, and no concept is to be without reality. This caused Hegel's system to be known as the most objective, as if in it thought and thing celebrated their union. But this was simply the extremest case of violence on the part of thought, its highest pitch of despotism and sole dominion, the triumph of mind, and with it the triumph of *philosophy.* Philosophy cannot hereafter achieve anything higher, for its highest is the *omnipotence of mind,* the almightiness of mind.[73]

---

73. Rousseau, the Philanthropists, and others were hostile to culture

Spiritual men have *taken into their head* something that is to be realized. They have *concepts* of love, goodness, and the like, which they would like to see *realized;* therefore they want to set up a kingdom of love on earth, in which no one any longer acts from selfishness, but each one "from love." Love is to *rule*. What they have taken into their head, what shall we call it but—*fixed idea?* Why, "their head is *haunted.*" The most oppressive spook is *Man*. Think of the proverb, "The road to ruin is paved with good intentions." The intention to realize humanity altogether in oneself, to become altogether man, is of such ruinous kind; here belong the intentions to become good, noble, loving, and so forth.

In the sixth part of the *Denkwürdigkeiten*,[74] p. 7, Bruno Bauer says: "That middle class, which was to receive such a terrible importance for modern history, is capable of no self-sacrificing action, no enthusiasm for an idea, no exaltation; it devotes itself to nothing but the interests of its mediocrity; i.e. it remains always limited to itself, and conquers at last only through its bulk, with which it has succeeded in tiring out the efforts of passion, enthusiasm, consistency—through its surface, into which it absorbs a part of the new ideas." And (p. 6) "It has turned the revolutionary ideas, for which not it, but unselfish or impassioned men sacrificed themselves, solely to its own profit, has turned spirit into money.—That is, to be sure, after it had taken away from those ideas their point, their consistency, their destructive seriousness, fanatical against all egoism." These people, then, are not self-sacrificing, not enthusiastic, not idealistic, not consistent, not zealots; they are egoists in the usual sense, selfish people, looking out for their advantage, sober, calculating.

---

and intelligence, but they overlooked the fact that this is present in *all* men of the Christian type, and assailed only learned and refined culture.

74. [A work in twelve parts bearing the full title *Denkwürdigkeiten zur Geschichte der neueren Zeit seit der französische Revolution; Nach den Quellen und Original-Memoiren bearbeiten und herausgeben von Bruno und Edgar Bauer* (Charlottenburg, 1843-1844). Bruno Bauer (1809-1882) was one of the most frequently-cited figures in Stirner's book, one of the outstanding of the *Junghegelianer* and a serious student of the French Revolution.]

Who, then, is "self-sacrificing?"[75] In the full sense, surely, he who ventures everything else for *one thing,* one object, one will, one passion. Is not the lover self-sacrificing who forsakes father and mother, endures all dangers and privations, to reach his goal? Or the ambitious man, who offers up all his desires, wishes, and satisfactions to the single passion, or the avaricious man who denies himself everything to gather treasures, or the pleasure-seeker? He is ruled by a passion to which he brings the rest as sacrifices.

And are these self-sacrificing people perchance not selfish, not egoist? As they have only one ruling passion, so they provide for only one satisfaction, but for this the more strenuously; they are wholly absorbed in it. Their entire activity is egoistic, but it is a one-sided, unopened, narrow egoism; it is possessedness.

"Why, those are petty passions, by which, on the contrary, man must not let himself be enthralled. Man must make sacrifices for a great idea, a great cause!" A "great idea," a "good cause," is, it may be, the honor of God, for which innumerable people have met death; Christianity, which has found its willing martyrs; the Holy Catholic Church, which has greedily demanded sacrifices of heretics; liberty and equality, which were waited on by bloody guillotines.

He who lives for a great idea, a good cause, a doctrine, a system, a lofty calling, may not let any worldly lusts, any self-seeking interest, spring up in him. Here we have the concept of *clericalism,* or, as it may also be called in its pedagogic activity, school-masterliness; for the idealists play the schoolmaster over us. The clergyman is especially called to live to the idea and to work for the idea, the truly good cause. Therefore the people feel how little it befits him to show worldly haughtiness, to desire good living, to join in such pleasures as dancing and gaming— in short, to have any other than a "sacred interest." Hence, too, doubtless, is derived the scanty salary of teachers, who are to feel themselves repaid by the sacredness of their calling alone, and to "renounce" other enjoyments.

75. (Literally, "sacrificing"; the German word has not the prefix "self.")

Even a directory of the sacred ideas, one or more of which man is to look upon as his calling, is not lacking. Family, fatherland, science, etc., may find in me a servant faithful to his calling.

Here we come upon the old, old craze of the world, which has not yet learned to do without clericalism—that to live and work *for an idea* is man's calling, and according to the faithfulness of its fulfilment his *human* worth is measured.

This is the dominion of the idea; in other words, it is clericalism. Thus Robespierre and St. Just were priests through and through, inspired by the idea, enthusiasts, consistent instruments of this idea, idealistic men.[76] So St. Just exclaims in a speech, "There is something terrible in the sacred love of country; it is so exclusive that it sacrifices everything to the public interest without mercy, without fear, without human consideration. It hurls Manlius down the precipice; it sacrifices its private inclinations; it leads Regulus to Carthage, throws a Roman into the chasm, and sets Marat, as a victim of his devotion, in the Pantheon."

Now, over against these representatives of ideal or sacred interests stands a world of innumerable "personal" profane interests. No idea, no system, no sacred cause is so great as never to be outrivaled and modified by these personal interests. Even if they are silent momentarily, and in times of rage and fanaticism, yet they soon come uppermost again through "the sound sense of the people." Those ideas do not completely conquer till they are no longer hostile to personal interests, till they satisfy egoism.

The man who is just now crying herrings in front of my window has a personal interest in good sales, and, if his wife or anybody else wishes him the like, this remains a personal interest all the same. If, on the other hand, a thief deprived him of his basket, then there would at once arise an interest of many, of the whole city, of the whole country, or ,in a word, of

76. [Maximilien François Robespierre (1758-1794) and Louis Antoine Leon de Saint-Just (1767-1794), two major leaders of the French Revolution who bear responsibility for the Reign of Terror and who were both victims of the reaction against it.]

all who abhor theft; an interest in which the herring-seller's person would become indifferent, and in its place the category of the "robbed man" would come into the foreground. But even here all might yet resolve itself into a personal interest, each of the partakers reflecting that he must concur in the punishment of the thief because unpunished stealing might otherwise become general and cause him too to lose his own. Such a calculation, however, can hardly be assumed on the part of many, and we shall rather hear the cry that the thief is a "criminal." Here we have before us a judgment, the thief's action receiving its expression in the concept "crime." Now the matter stands thus: even if a crime did not cause the slightest damage either to me or to any of those in whom I take an interest, I should nevertheless denounce it. Why? Because I am enthusiastic for *morality*, filled with the *idea* of morality; what is hostile to it I everywhere assail. Because in his mind theft ranks as abominable without any question, Proudhon, for instance, thinks that with the sentence "Property is theft" he has at once put a brand on property. In the sense of the priestly, theft is always a *crime*, or at least a misdeed.

Here the personal interest is at an end. This particular person who has stolen the basket is perfectly indifferent to my person; it is only the thief, this concept of which that person presents a specimen, that I take an interest in. The thief and man are in my mind irreconcilable opposites; for one is not truly man when one is a thief; one degrades *Man* or "humanity" in himself when one steals. Dropping out of personal concern, one gets into *philanthropism*, friendliness to man, which is usually misunderstood as if it was a love to men, to each individual, while it is nothing but a love of *Man*, the unreal concept, the spook. It is not τοὺς ἀνθρώπους, men, but τὸν ἄνθρωπον, Man, that the philanthropist carries in his heart. To be sure, he cares for each individual, but only because he wants to see his beloved ideal realized everywhere.

So there is nothing said here of care for me, you, us; that would be personal interest, and belongs under the head of "worldly love." Philanthropism is a heavenly, spiritual, a—priestly love. *Man* must be restored in us, even if thereby we poor devils should come to grief. It is the same priestly principle as that famous *fiat justitia, pereat mundus;* man and justice are ideas, ghosts, for love of which everything is sacrificed; therefore, the priestly spirits are the "self-sacrificing" ones.

He who is infatuated with *Man* leaves persons out of account so far as that infatuation extends, and floats in an ideal, sacred interest. *Man,* you see, is not a person, but an ideal, a spook.

Now, things as different as possible can belong to *Man* and be so regarded. If one finds Man's chief requirement in piety, there arises religious clericalism; if one sees it in morality, then moral clericalism raises its head. On this account the priestly spirits of our day want to make a "religion" of everything, a "religion of liberty," "religion of equality," etc., and for them every idea becomes a "sacred cause," even citizenship, politics, publicity, freedom of the press, trial by jury.

Now, what does "unselfishness" mean in this sense? Having only an ideal interest, before which no respect of persons avails!

The stiff head of the worldly man opposes this, but for centuries has always been worsted at least so far as to have to bend the unruly neck and "honor the higher power"; clericalism pressed it down. When the worldly egoist had shaken off a higher power (such as the Old Testament law, the Roman pope), then at once a seven times higher one was over him again, such as faith in the place of the law, the transformation of all laymen into divines in place of the limited body of clergy, and so on. His experience was like that of the possessed man into whom seven devils passed when he thought he had freed himself from one.

In the passage quoted above, all ideality is denied to the middle class. It certainly schemed against the ideal consistency with which Robespierre wanted to carry out the principle. The instinct of its interest told it that this consistency harmonized too little with what its mind was set on, and that it would be acting against itself if it were willing to further the enthusiasm for principle. Was it to behave so unselfishly as to abandon all its aims in order to bring a harsh theory to its triumph? It suits the priests admirably, to be sure, when people listen to their summons, "Cast away everything and follow me," or "Sell all that thou hast and give to the poor, and thou shalt have treasure

in heaven; and come, follow me." Some decided idealists obey
this call; but most act like Ananias and Sapphira, maintaining
a behavior half clerical or religious and half worldly, serving
God and Mammon.

I do not blame the middle class for not wanting to let its
aims be frustrated by Robespierre, for inquiring of its egoism
how far it might give the revolutionary idea a chance. But one
might blame (if blame were in place here anyhow) those who
let their own interests be frustrated by the interests of the middle
class. However, will not they likewise sooner or later learn to
understand what is to their advantage? August Becker says:[77]
"To win the producers (proletarians) a negation of the traditional
conception of right is by no means enough. Folks unfortunately
care little for the theoretical victory of the idea. One must
demonstrate to them *ad oculos* how this victory can be practically
utilized in life." And (p. 32): "You must get hold of folks by
their real interests if you want to work upon them." Immediately
after this he shows how a fine looseness of morals is already
spreading among our peasants, because they prefer to follow
their real interests rather than the commands of morality.

Because the revolutionary priests or schoolmasters served
Man, they cut off the heads of *men*. The revolutionary laymen,
those outside the sacred circle, did not feel any greater horror
of cutting off heads, but were less anxious about the rights
of Man than about their own.

How comes it, though, that the egoism of those who affirm
personal interest, and always inquire of it, is nevertheless forever
succumbing to a priestly or schoolmasterly (that is, an ideal)
interest? Their person seems to them too small, too insignificant—
and is so in fact—to lay claim to everything and be able to put
itself completely in force. There is a sure sign of this in their
dividing themselves into two persons, an eternal and a temporal,
and always caring either only for the one or only for the other,
on Sunday for the eternal, on the work-day for the temporal, in
prayer for the former, in work for the latter. They have the

77. *Die Volksphilosophie unserer Tage* [Neumeister, 1843], p. 22.

priest in themselves, therefore they do not get rid of him, but hear themselves lectured inwardly every Sunday.

How men have struggled and calculated to get at a solution regarding these dualistic essences! Idea followed upon idea, principle upon principle, system upon system, and none knew how to keep down permanently the contradiction of the "worldly" man, the so-called "egoist." Does not this prove that all those ideas were too feeble to take up my whole will into themselves and satisfy it? They were and remained hostile to me, even if the hostility lay concealed for a considerable time. Will it be the same with *self-ownership?* Is it too only an attempt at mediation? Whatever principle I turned to, it might be to that of *reason,* I always had to turn away from it again. Or can I always be rational, arrange my life according to reason in everything? I can, no doubt, *strive* after rationality, I can *love* it, just as I can also love God and every other idea. I can be a philosopher, a lover of wisdom, as I love God. But what I love, what I strive for, is only in my idea, my conception, my thoughts; it is in my heart, my head, it is in me like the heart, but it is not I, I am not it.

To the activity of priestly minds belongs especially what one often hears called *"moral influence."*

Moral influence takes its start where *humiliation* begins; yes, it is nothing else than this humiliation itself, the breaking and bending of the temper[78] down to humility.[79] If I call to some one to run away when a rock is to be blasted, I exert no moral influence by this demand; if I say to a child "You will go hungry if you will not eat what is put on the table," this is not moral influence. But, if I say to it, "You will pray, honor your parents, respect the crucifix, speak the truth, for this belongs to man and is man's calling," or even "this is God's will," then moral influence is complete; then a man is to bend before the *calling* of man, be tractable, become humble, give up his will for an alien one which is set up as rule and law; he is to *abase* himself before something *higher:* self-abasement. "He that abaseth

78. (*Muth*)
79. (*Demuth*)

himself shall be exalted." Yes, yes, children must early be *made* to practice piety, godliness, and propriety; a person of good breeding is one into whom "good maxims" have been *instilled* and *impressed,* poured in through a funnel, thrashed in and preached in.

If one shrugs his shoulders at this, at once the good wring their hands despairingly, and cry: "But, for heaven's sake, if one is to give children no good instruction, why, then they will run straight into the jaws of sin, and become good-for-nothing hoodlums!" Gently, you prophets of evil. Good-for-nothing in your sense they certainly will become; but your sense happens to be a very good-for-nothing sense. The impudent lads will no longer let anything be whined and chattered into them by you, and will have no sympathy for all the follies for which you have been raving and driveling since the memory of man began; they will abolish the law of inheritance; they will not be willing to *inherit* your stupidities as you inherited them from your fathers; they destroy *inherited sin.*[80] If you command them, "Bend before the Most High," they will answer: "If he wants to bend us, let him come himself and do it; we, at least, will not bend of our own accord." And, if you threaten them with his wrath and his punishment, they will take it like being threatened with the bogieman. If you are no more successful in making them afraid of ghosts, then the dominion of ghosts is at an end, and nurses' tales find no —*faith.*

And is it not precisely the liberals again that press for good education and improvement of the educational system? For how could their liberalism, their "liberty within the bounds of law," come about without discipline? Even if they do not exactly educate to the fear of God, yet they demand the *fear of Man* all the more strictly, and awaken "enthusiasm for the truly human calling" by discipline.

———————

A long time passed away, in which people were satisfied with the fancy that they had the *truth,* without thinking seriously whether perhaps they themselves must be true to possess the

80. (Called in English theology "original sin.")

truth. This time was the *Middle Ages*. With the common consciousness—the consciousness which deals with things, that consciousness which has receptivity only for things, or for what is
sensuous and sense-moving—they thought to grasp what did
not deal with things and was not perceptible by the senses. As
one does indeed also exert his eye to see the remote, or laboriously
exercise his hand till its fingers have become dexterous enough
to press the keys correctly, so they chastened themselves in the
most manifold ways, in order to become capable of receiving
the supersensual wholly into themselves. But what they chastened
was, after all, only the sensual man, the common consciousness,
so-called finite or objective thought. Yet as this thought, this
understanding, which Luther decries under the name of reason,
is incapable of comprehending the divine, its chastening contributed just as much to the understanding of the truth as if
one exercised the feet year in and year out in dancing, and hoped
that in this way they would finally learn to play the flute. Luther,
with whom the so-called Middle Ages end, was the first who
understood that the man himself must become other than he
was if he wanted to comprehend truth—must become as true as
truth itself. Only he who already has truth in his belief, only he
who *believes* in it, can become a partaker of it; only the believer
finds it accessible and sounds its depths. Only that organ of
man which is able to blow can attain the further capacity of
flute-playing, and only that man can become a partaker of
truth who has the right organ for it. He who is capable of
thinking only what is sensuous, objective, pertaining to things,
figures to himself in truth only what pertains to things. But
truth is spirit, stuff altogether inappreciable by the senses, and
therefore only for the "higher consciousness," not for that which
is "earthly-minded."

With Luther, accordingly, dawns the perception that truth,
because it is a *thought,* is only for the *thinking* man. And this is
to say that man must henceforth take an utterly different standpoint, to wit, the heavenly, believing, scientific standpoint, or
that of *thought* in relation to its object, the—*thought*—that of

mind in relation to mind. Consequently: only the like apprehend the like. "You are like the spirit that you understand."[81]

Because Protestantism broke the medieval hierarchy, the opinion could take root that hierarchy in general had been shattered by it, and it could be wholly overlooked that it was precisely a "reformation," and so a reinvigoration of the antiquated hierarchy. That medieval hierarchy had been only a weakly one, as it had to let all possible barbarism of unsanctified things run on uncoerced beside it, and it was the Reformation that first steeled the power of hierarchy. If Bruno Bauer thinks:[82] "As the Reformation was mainly the abstract rending of the religious principle from art, State, and science, and so its liberation from those powers with which it had joined itself in the antiquity of the church and in the hierarchy of the Middle Ages, so too the theological and ecclesiastical movements which proceeded from the Reformation are only the consistent carrying out of this abstraction of the religious principle from the other powers of humanity," I regard precisely the opposite as correct, and think that the dominion of spirits, or freedom of mind (which comes to the same thing), was never before so all-embracing and all-powerful, because the present one, instead of rending the religious principle from art, State, and science, lifted the latter altogether out of secularity into the "realm of spirit" and made them religious.

Luther and Descartes have been appropriately put side by side in their "He who believes in God" and "I think, therefore I am" (*cogito, ergo sum*). Man's heaven is thought—mind. Everything can be wrested from him, except thought, except faith. *Particular* faith, like faith of Zeus, Astarte, Jehovah, Allah, may be destroyed, but faith itself is indestructible. In thought is freedom. What I need and what I hunger for is no longer granted to me by any *grace,* by the Virgin Mary, by intercession of the saints, or by the binding and loosing church, but I procure it for myself. In short, my being (the *sum*) is a living in the heaven of thought, of mind, a *cogitare*. But I myself am nothing else than mind, thinking mind (according to Descartes), believing

81. (Goethe, *Faust.*)
82. *Anekdota,* vol. 2, p. 152.

mind (according to Luther). My body I am not; my flesh may *suffer* from appetites or pains. I am not my flesh, but I am *mind,* only mind.

This thought runs through the history of the Reformation till to-day.

Only by the more modern philosophy since Descartes has a serious effort been made to bring Christianity to complete efficacy, by exalting the "scientific consciousness" to be the only true and valid one. Hence it begins with absolute *doubt, dubitare,* with grinding common consciousness to atoms, with turning away from everything that "mind," "thought," does not legitimate. To it *Nature* counts for nothing; the opinion of men, their "human precepts," for nothing: and it does not rest till it has brought reason into everything, and can say "The real is the rational, and only the rational is the real." Thus it has at last brought mind, reason, to victory; and everything is mind, because everything is rational, because all nature, as well as even the perversest opinions of men, contains reason; for "all must serve for the best," that is, lead to the victory of reason.

Descartes's *dubitare* contains the decided statement that only *cogitare,* thought, mind—*is.* A complete break with "common" consciousness, which ascribes reality to *irrational* things! Only the rational is, only mind is! This is the principle of modern philosophy, the genuine Christian principle. Descartes in his own time discriminated the body sharply from the mind, and "the spirit 'tis that builds itself the body," says Goethe.

But this philosophy itself, Christian philosophy, still does not get rid of the rational, and therefore inveighs against the "merely subjective," against "fancies, fortuities, arbitrariness," etc. What it wants is that the *divine* should become visible in everything, and all consciousness become a knowing of the divine, and man behold God everywhere; but God never is, without the *devil.*

For this very reason the name of philosopher is not to be given to him who has indeed open eyes for the things of the world, a clear and undazzled gaze, a correct judgment about the world, but who sees in the world just the world, in objects

only objects, and, in short, everything prosaically as it is; but he
alone is a philosopher who sees, and points out or demonstrates,
heaven in the world, the supernal in the earthly, the—*divine* in the
mundane. The former may be ever so wise, there is no getting
away from this:

> What wise men see not by their wisdom's art
> Is practiced simply by a childlike heart.[83]

It takes this childlike heart, this eye for the divine, to make a
philosopher. The first-named man has only a "common" consciousness, but he who knows the divine, and knows how to tell
it, has a "scientific" one. On this ground Bacon was turned
out of the realm of philosophers. And certainly what is called
English philosophy seems to have got no further than to the
discoveries of so-called "clear heads," such as Bacon and Hume.
The English did not know how to exalt the simplicity of the
childlike heart to philosophic significance, did not know how
to make—philosophers out of childlike hearts. This is as much
as to say, their philosophy was not able to become *theological*
or *theology*, and yet it is only as theology that it can really *live
itself* out, complete itself. The field of its battle to the death
is in theology. Bacon did not trouble himself about theological
questions and cardinal points.

Cognition has its object in life. German thought seeks, more
than that of others, to reach the beginnings and fountain-heads
of life, and sees no life till it sees it in cognition itself. Descartes's
cogito, ergo sum has the meaning "One lives only when one
thinks." Thinking life is called "intellectual life"! Only mind
lives, its life is the true life. Then, just so in nature only the
"eternal laws," the mind or the reason of nature, are its true
life. In man, as in nature, only the thought lives; everything else
is dead! To this abstraction, to the life of generalities or of
that which is *lifeless,* the history of mind had to come. God, who
is spirit, alone lives. Nothing lives but the ghost.

How can one try to assert of modern philosophy or modern
times that they have reached freedom, since they have not freed
us from the power of objectivity? Or am I perhaps free from a

83. (Schiller, *Die Worte des Glaubens.*)

despot when I am not afraid of the personal potentate, to be sure, but of every infraction of the loving reverence which I fancy I owe him? The case is the same with modern times. They only changed the *existing* objects, the real ruler, into *conceived* objects, into *ideas,* before which the old respect not only was not lost, but increased in intensity. Even if people snapped their fingers at God and the devil in their former crass reality, people devoted only the greater attention to their ideas. "They are rid of the Evil One; evil is left."[84] The decision having once been made not to let oneself be imposed on any longer by the extant and palpable, little scruple was felt about revolting against the existing State or overturning the existing laws; but to sin against the *idea* of the State, not to submit to the *idea* of law, who would have dared that? So one remained a "citizen" and a "law-respect-ing," loyal man; yes, one seemed to himself to be only so much more law-respecting, the more rationalistically one abrogated the former defective law in order to do homage to the "spirit of the law." In all this the objects had only suffered a change of form; they had remained in their preponderance and pre-eminence; in short, one was still involved in obedience and possessedness, lived in reflection, and had an object on which one reflected, which one respected, and before which one felt reverence and fear. One had done nothing but transform the *things* into *con-ceptions* of the things, into thoughts and ideas, whereby one's *dependence* became all the more intimate and indissoluble. Thus, it is not hard to emancipate oneself from the commands of parents, or to set aside the admonitions of uncle and aunt, the entreaties of brother and sister; but the renounced obedience easily gets into one's conscience, and the less one does give way to the individual demands, because he rationalistically, by his own reason, recognizes them to be unreasonable, so much the more conscientiously does he hold fast to filial piety and family love, and so much the harder is it for him to forgive himself a trespass against the *conception* which he has formed of family love and of filial duty. Released from dependence as regards the existing

84. (Parodied from the words of Mephistopheles in the witch's kitchen in *Faust.*)

family, one falls into the more binding dependence on the idea of the family; one is ruled by the spirit of the family. The family consisting of John, Maggie, etc., whose dominion has become powerless, is only internalized, being left as "family" in general, to which one just applies the old saying, "We must obey God rather than man," whose significance here is this: "I cannot, to be sure, accommodate myself to your senseless requirements, but, as my 'family,' you still remain the object of my love and care"; for "the family" is a sacred idea, which the individual must never offend against.—And this family internalized and desensualized into a thought, a conception, now ranks as the "sacred," whose despotism is tenfold more grievous because it makes a racket in my conscience. This despotism is broken when the conception, family, also becomes a *nothing* to me. The Christian dicta, "Woman, what have I to do with thee?"[85] "I am come to stir up a man against his father, and a daughter against her mother,"[86] and others, are accompanied by something that refers us to the heavenly or true family, and mean no more than the State's demand, in case of a collision between it and the family, that we obey *its* commands.

The case of morality is like that of the family. Many a man renounces morals, but with great difficulty the conception, "morality." Morality is the "idea" of morals, their intellectual power, their power over the conscience; on the other hand, morals are too material to rule the mind, and do not fetter an "intellectual" man, a so-called independent, a "freethinker."

The Protestant may put it as he will, the "holy[87] Scripture," the "Word of God," still remains sacred[88] for him. He for whom this is no longer "holy" has ceased to—be a Protestant. But herewith what is "ordained" in it, the public authorities appointed by God, etc., also remain sacred for him. For him these things remain indissoluble, unapproachable, "raised above all doubt"; and, as *doubt,* which in practice becomes a *buffeting,* is what

85. John 2. 4.
86. Matt. 10. 35.
87. (*heilig*)
88. (*heilig*)

is most man's own, these things remain "raised" above himself. He who cannot *get away* from them will—*believe;* for to believe in them is to be *bound* to them. Through the fact that in Protestantism the *faith* becomes a more inward faith, the *servitude* has also become a more inward servitude; one has taken those sanctities up into himself, entwined them with all his thoughts and endeavors, made them a *"matter of conscience,"* constructed out of them a *"sacred duty"* for himself. Therefore what the Protestant's conscience cannot get away from is sacred to him, and *conscientiousness* most clearly designates his character.

Protestantism has actually put a man in the position of a country governed by secret police. The spy and eavesdropper, "conscience," watches over every motion of the mind, and all thought and action is for it a "matter of conscience," that is, police business. This tearing apart of man into "natural impulse" and "conscience" (inner populace and inner police) is what constitutes the Protestant. The reason of the Bible (in place of the Catholic "reason of the church") ranks as sacred, and this feeling and consciousness that the word of the Bible is sacred is called —conscience. With this, then, sacredness is "laid upon one's conscience." If one does not free himself from conscience, the consciousness of the sacred, he may act unconscientiously indeed, but never consciencelessly.

The Catholic finds himself satisfied when he fulfils the *command;* the Protestant acts according to his "best judgment and conscience." For the Catholic is only a *layman;* the Protestant is himself a *clergyman.*[89] Just this is the progress of the Reformation period beyond the Middle Ages, and at the same time its curse—that the *spiritual* became complete.

What else was the Jesuit moral philosophy than a continuation of the sale of indulgences? Only that the man who was relieved of his burden of sin now gained also an *insight* into the remission of sins, and convinced himself how really his sin was taken from him, since in this or that particular case (casuists) it was so clearly no sin at all that he committed. The sale of indulgences had made all sins and transgressions permissible,

89. (*Geistlicher,* literally "spiritual man.")

and silenced every movement of conscience. All sensuality might hold sway, if it was only purchased from the church. This favoring of sensuality was continued by the Jesuits, while the strictly moral, dark, fanatical, repentant, contrite, praying Protestants (as the true completers of Christianity, to be sure) acknowledged only the intellectual and spiritual man. Catholicism, especially the Jesuits, gave aid to egoism in this way, found involuntary and unconscious adherents within Protestantism itself, and saved us from the subversion and extinction of *sensuality*. Nevertheless the Protestant spirit spreads its dominion farther and farther; and, as, beside it the "divine," the Jesuit spirit represents only the "diabolic" which is inseparable from everything divine, the latter can never assert itself alone, but must look on and see how in France, for example, the Philistinism of Protestantism[90] wins at last, and mind is on top.

Protestantism is usually complimented on having brought the mundane into repute again, such as marriage, the State, etc. But the mundane itself as mundane, the secular, is even more indifferent to it than to Catholicism, which lets the profane world stand, yes, and relishes its pleasures, while the rational, consistent Protestant sets about annihilating the mundane altogether, and that simply by *hallowing* it. So marriage has been deprived of its naturalness by becoming sacred, not in the sense of the Catholic sacrament, where it only receives its consecration from the church and so is unholy at bottom, but in the sense of being something sacred in itself to begin with, a sacred relation. Just so the State, also. Formerly the pope gave consecration and his blessing to it and its princes; now the State is intrinsically sacred, majesty is sacred without needing the priest's blessing. The order of nature, or natural law, was altogether hallowed as "God's ordinance." Hence it is said in the Augsburg Confession,[91] Art. II: "So now we reasonably abide by the saying, as the

90. [A reference to the success of Calvinism as a more extreme form of Protestantism than Lutheranism.]

91. [A document drafted by Philipp Melanchthon (1497-1560), German theologian and reformer, closely associated with Luther; it was presented to the Diet of German princes meeting in Augsburg in 1530 as a contribution to bringing about unity among Christians once more.]

jurisconsults have wisely and rightly said: that man and woman should be with each other is a natural law. Now, if it is a *natural law, then it is God's ordinance,* therefore implanted in nature, and therefore a *divine* law also." And is it anything more than Protestantism brought up to date, when Feuerbach pronounces moral relations sacred, not as God's ordinance indeed, but, instead, for the sake of the *spirit* that dwells in them? "But marriage—as a free alliance of love, of course—is *sacred of itself,* by the nature of the union that is formed here. *That* marriage alone is a *religious* one that is a *true* one, that corresponds to the *essence* of marriage, love. And so it is with all moral relations. They are *ethical,* are cultivated with a moral mind, only where they rank as *religious of themselves.* True friendship is only where the *limits* of friendship are preserved with religious conscientiousness, with the same conscientiousness with which the believer guards the dignity of his God. Friendship is and must be *sacred* for you, and property, and marriage, and the good of every man, but sacred *in and of itself.*"[92]

That is a very essential consideration. In Catholicism the mundane can indeed be *consecrated* or *hallowed,* but it is not sacred without this priestly blessing; in Protestantism, on the contrary, mundane relations are sacred *of themselves,* sacred by their mere existence. The Jesuit maxim, "the end hallows the means," corresponds precisely to the consecration by which sanctity is bestowed. No means are holy or unholy in themselves, but their relation to the church, their use for the church, hallows the means. Regicide was named as such; if it was committed for the church's behoof, it could be certain of being hallowed by the church, even if the hallowing was not openly pronounced. To the Protestant, majesty ranks as sacred; to the Catholic only that majesty which is consecrated by the pontiff can rank as such; and it does rank as such to him only because the pope, even though it be without a special act, confers this sacredness on it once for all. If he retracted his consecration, the king would be left only a "man of the world or layman," an "unconsecrated" man, to the Catholic.

92. *Essence of Christianity,* p. 403.

If the Protestant seeks to discover a sacredness in the sensual itself, that he may then be linked only to what is holy, the Catholic strives rather to banish the sensual from himself into a separate domain, where it, like the rest of nature, keeps its value for itself. The Catholic church eliminated mundane marriage from its consecrated order, and withdrew those who were its own from the mundane family; the Protestant church declared marriage and family ties to be holy, and therefore not unsuitable for its clergymen.

A Jesuit may, as a good Catholic, hallow everything. He needs only, for example, to say to himself: "I as a priest am necessary to the church, but serve it more zealously when I appease my desires properly; consequently I will seduce this girl, have my enemy there poisoned, etc.; my end is holy because it is a priest's, consequently it hallows the means." For in the end it is still done for the benefit of the church. Why should the Catholic priest shrink from handing Emperor Henry VII[93] the poisoned wafer for the—church's welfare?

The genuinely churchly Protestants inveighed against every "innocent pleasure," because only the sacred, the spiritual, could be innocent. What they could not point out the holy spirit in, the Protestants had to reject—dancing, the theatre, ostentation in the church, and the like.

Compared with this puritanical Calvinism, Lutheranism is again more on the religious, spiritual, track—is more radical. For the former excludes at once a great number of things as sensual and worldly, and *purifies* the church; Lutheranism, on the contrary, tries to bring *spirit* into all things as far as possible, to recognize the holy spirit as an essence in everything, and so to *hallow* everything worldly. ("No one can forbid a kiss in honor." The spirit of honor hallows it.) Hence it was that the Lutheran Hegel (he declares himself such in some passage or

93. [Holy Roman Emperor of the House of Luxemburg (1308-1313), who claimed to be independent of the spiritual power of the pope and encountered a coalition of power against him created in part by Pope Clement V. Stirner's historical reference, regardless of the objections which might be raised by the Jesuits, was incorrect, since the Society of Jesus was not founded until 1534.]

other: he "wants to remain a Lutheran") was completely successful in carrying the idea through everything. In everything there
is reason, holy spirit, or "the real is rational." For the real is
in fact everything; as in each thing, for instance, each lie, the
truth can be detected: there is no absolute lie, no absolute evil,
and the like.

Great "works of mind" were created almost solely by
Protestants, as they alone were the true disciples and consum-
mators of *mind*.

How little man is able to control! He must let the sun
run its course, the sea roll its waves, the mountains rise to heaven.
Thus he stands powerless before the *uncontrollable.* Can he
keep off the impression that he is helpless against this gigantic
world? It is a fixed *law* to which he must submit, it determines
his *fate.* Now, what did pre-Christian humanity work toward?
Toward getting rid of the irruptions of the destinies, not letting
oneself be vexed by them. The Stoics attained this in apathy,
declaring the attacks of nature *indifferent,* and not letting themselves be affected by them. Horace utters the famous *Nil admirari,*
by which he likewise announces the indifference of the *other,*
the world; it is not to influence us, not to rouse our astonishment.
And that *impavidum ferient ruinae* expresses the very same *imperturbability* as Ps. 46.3: "We do not fear, though the earth
should perish." In all this there is room made for the Christian
proposition that the world is empty, for the Christian *contempt
of the world.*

The *imperturbable* spirit of "the wise man," with which the
old world worked to prepare its end, now underwent an *inner
perturbation* against which no ataraxia, no Stoic courage, was
able to protect it. The spirit, secured against all influence of
the world, insensible to its shocks and *exalted* above its attacks,
admiring nothing, not to be disconcerted by any downfall of the
world—foamed over irrepressibly again, because gases (spirits)
were evolved in its own interior, and, after the *mechanical shock*
that comes from without had become ineffective, *chemical ten-
sions,* that agitate within, began their wonderful play.

In fact, ancient history ends with this—that *I* have struggled till I won my ownership of the world. "All things have been delivered to me by my Father" (Matt. 11.27). It has ceased to be overpowering, unapproachable, sacred, divine, for me; it is *undeified,* and now I treat it so entirely as I please that, if I cared, I could exert on it all miracle-working power, that is, power of mind—remove mountains, command mulberry trees to tear themselves up and transplant themselves into the sea (Luke 17.6), and do everything possible, *thinkable:* "All things are possible to him who believes."[94] I am the *lord* of the world, mine is the "glory."[95] The world has become prosaic, for the divine has vanished from it: it is my property, which I dispose of as I (to wit, the mind) choose.

When I had exalted myself to be the *owner of the world,* egoism had won its first complete victory, had vanquished the world, had become *worldless,* and put the acquisitions of a long age under lock and key.

The first property, the first "glory," has been acquired!

But the lord of the world is not yet lord of his thoughts, his feelings, his will: he is not lord and owner of the spirit, for the spirit is still sacred, the "Holy Spirit," and the "worldless" Christian is not able to become "godless." If the ancient struggle was a struggle against the *world,* the medieval (Christian) struggle is a struggle against self, the mind; the former against the outer world, the latter against the inner world. The medieval man is the man "whose gaze is turned inward," the thinking, meditative man.

All wisdom of the ancients is *the science of the world,* all wisdom of the moderns is *the science of God.*

The heathen (Jews included) got through with the *world;* but now the thing was to get through with self, the spirit, too; to become spiritless or godless.

For almost two thousand years we have been working at subjecting the Holy Spirit to ourselves, and little by little we have torn off and trodden under foot many bits of sacredness;

94. Mark 9. 23.

95. (*Herrlichkeit,* which, according to its derivation, means "lord-liness.")

but the gigantic opponent is constantly rising anew under a changed form and name. The spirit has not yet lost its divinity, its holiness, its sacredness. To be sure, it has long ceased to flutter over our heads as a dove; to be sure, it no longer gladdens its saints alone, but lets itself be caught by the laity too; but as spirit of humanity, as spirit of Man, it remains still an *alien* spirit to me or you, still far from becoming our unrestricted *property,* which we dispose of at our pleasure. However, one thing certainly happened, and visibly guided the progress of post-Christian history: this one thing was the endeavor to make the Holy Spirit *more human,* and bring it nearer to men, or men to it. Through this it came about that at last it could be conceived as the "spirit of humanity," and, under different expressions like "idea of humanity, mankind, humaneness, general philanthropy," appeared more attractive, more familiar, and more accessible.

Would not one think that now everybody could possess the Holy Spirit, take up into himself the idea of humanity, bring mankind to form and existence in himself?

No, the spirit is not stripped of its holiness and robbed of its unapproachableness, is not accessible to us, not our property; for the spirit of humanity is not *my* spirit. My *ideal* it may be, and as a thought I call it mine; the *thought* of humanity is my property, and I prove this sufficiently by propounding it quite according to my views, and shaping it to-day so, to-morrow otherwise; we represent it to ourselves in the most manifold ways. But it is at the same time an entail, which I cannot alienate nor get rid of.

Among many transformations, the Holy Spirit became in time the *"absolute idea,"* which again in manifold refractions split into the different ideas of philanthropy, reasonableness, civic virtue, and so on.

But can I call the idea my property if it is the idea of humanity, and can I consider the Spirit as vanquished if I am to serve it, "sacrifice myself" to it? Antiquity, at its close, had gained its ownership of the world only when it had broken the world's overpoweringness and "divinity," recognized the world's power-lessness and "vanity."

The case with regard to the *spirit* corresponds. When I have degraded it to a *spook* and its control over me to a *cranky notion*, then it is to be looked upon as having lost its sacredness, its holiness, its divinity, and then I *use* it, as one uses *nature* at pleasure without scruple.

The "nature of the case," the "concept of the relationship," is to guide me in dealing with the case or in contracting the relation. As if a concept of the case existed on its own account, and was not rather the concept that one forms of the case! As if a relation which we enter into was not, by the uniqueness of those who enter into it, itself unique! As if it depended on how others stamp it! But, as people separated the "essence of Man" from the real man, and judged the latter by the former, so they also separate his action from him, and appraise it by "human value." *Concepts* are to decide everywhere, concepts to regulate life, concepts to *rule*. This is the religious world, to which Hegel gave a systematic expression, bringing method into the nonsense and completing the conceptual precepts into a rounded, firmly-based dogmatic. Everything is sung according to concepts, and the real man, I, am compelled to live according to these conceptual laws. Can there be a more grievous dominion of law, and did not Christianity confess at the very beginning that it meant only to draw Judaism's dominion of law tighter? ("Not a letter of the law shall be lost!")

Liberalism simply brought other concepts on the carpet; human instead of divine, political instead of ecclesiastical, "scientific" instead of doctrinal, or, more generally, real concepts and eternal laws instead of "crude dogmas" and precepts.

Now nothing but *mind* rules in the world. An innumerable multitude of concepts buzz about in people's heads, and what are those doing who endeavor to get further? They are negating these concepts to put new ones in their place! They are saying: "You form a false concept of right, of the State, of man, of liberty, of truth, of marriage; the concept of right, etc., is rather that one which we now set up." Thus the confusion of concepts moves forward.

The history of the world has dealt cruelly with us, and the

spirit has obtained an almighty power. You must have regard for my miserable shoes, which could protect your naked foot, my salt, by which your potatoes would become palatable, and my state-carriage, whose possession would relieve you of all need at once; you must not reach out after them. Man is to recognize the *independence* of all these and innumerable other things: they are to rank in his mind as something that cannot be seized or approached, are to be kept away from him. He must have regard for it, respect it; woe to him if he stretches out his fingers desirously; we call that "being light-fingered!"

How beggarly little is left us, yes, how really nothing! Everything has been removed, we must not venture on anything unless it is given us; we continue to live only by the *grace* of the giver. You must not pick up a pin, unless indeed you have got *leave* to do so. And got it from whom? From *respect!* Only when this lets you have it as property, only when you can *respect* it as property, only then may you take it. And again, you are not to conceive a thought, speak a syllable, commit an action, that should have their warrant in you alone, instead of receiving it from morality or reason or humanity. Happy *unconstraint* of the desirous man, how mercilessly people have tried to slay you on the altar of *constraint!*

But around the altar rise the arches of a church, and its walls keep moving further and further out. What they enclose is *sacred.* You can no longer get to it, no longer touch it. Shrieking with the hunger that devours you, you wander round about these walls in search of the little that is profane, and the circles of your course keep growing more and more extended. Soon that church will embrace the whole world, and you be driven out to the extreme edge; another step, and the *world of the sacred* has conquered: you sink into the abyss. Therefore take courage while it is yet time, wander about no longer in the profane where now it is dry feeding, dare the leap, and rush in through the gates into the sanctuary itself. If you *devour the sacred,* you have made it your *own!* Digest the sacramental wafer, and you are rid of it!

C.—THE FREE

THE ancients and the moderns having been presented above in two divisions, it may seem as if the free were here to be described in a third division as independent and distinct. This is not so. The free are only the more modern and most modern among the "moderns," and are put in a separate division merely because they belong to the present, and what is present, above all, claims our attention here. I give "the free" only as a translation of "the liberals," but must with regard to the concept of freedom (as in general with regard to so many other things whose anticipatory introduction cannot be avoided) refer to what comes later.

1.—POLITICAL LIBERALISM

AFTER the chalice of so-called absolute monarchy had been drained down to the dregs, in the eighteenth century people became aware that their drink did not taste human—too clearly aware not to begin to crave a different cup. Since our fathers were "human beings" after all, they at last desired also to be regarded as such.

Whoever sees in us something else than human beings, in him we likewise will not see a human being, but an inhuman being, and will meet him as an unhuman being; on the other hand, whoever recognizes us as human beings and protects us against the danger of being treated inhumanly, him we will honor as our true protector and guardian.

Let us then hold together and protect the man in each other; then we find the necessary protection in our *holding together,* and in ourselves, *those who hold together,* a fellowship of those who know their human dignity and hold together as "human beings." Our holding together is the *State;* we who hold together are the *nation.*

In our being together as nation or State we are only human beings. How we deport ourselves in other respects as individuals, and what self-seeking impulses we may there succumb to, belongs solely to our *private* life; our public or State life is a *purely human* one. Everything un-human or "egoistic" that clings to us is degraded to a "private matter" and we distinguish the State definitely from "civil society," which is the sphere of "egoism's" activity.

The true man is the nation, but the individual is always an egoist. Therefore strip off your individuality or isolation wherein dwells discord and egoistic inequality, and consecrate yourselves wholly to the true man—the nation or the State. Then you will rank as men, and have all that is man's; the State, the true man, will entitle you to what belongs to it, and give you the "rights of man"; Man gives you his rights!

So runs the speech of the commonalty.

The commonalty[96] is nothing else than the thought that the State is all in all, the true man, and that the individual's human value consists in being a citizen of the State. In being a good citizen he seeks his highest honor; beyond that he knows nothing higher than at most the antiquated—"being a good Christian."

The commonalty developed itself in the struggle against the privileged classes, by whom it was cavalierly treated as "third estate" and confounded with the *canaille*. In other words, up to this time the State had recognized caste.[97] The son of a nobleman was selected for posts to which the most distinguished commoners aspired in vain. The civic feeling revolted against this. No more distinction, no giving preference to persons, no difference of classes! Let all be alike! No *separate interest* is to be pursued longer, but the *general interest of all*. The State is to be a fellowship of free and equal men, and every one is to devote himself to the "welfare of the whole," to be dissolved in the *State*, to make the State his end and ideal. State! State! so ran the general cry, and thenceforth people sought for the "right form of State," the best constitution, and so the State

96. (Or "citizenhood." The word (*das Bürgertum*) means either the condition of being a citizen, or citizen-like principles, of the body of citizens or of the middle or business class, the bourgeoisie.)

97. (*Man hatte im Staate "die ungleiche Person angesehen,"* there had been "respect of unequal persons" in the State.)

in its best conception. The thought of the State passed into all hearts and awakened enthusiasm; to serve it, this mundane god, became the new divine service and worship. The properly *political* epoch had dawned. To serve the State or the nation became the highest ideal, the State's interest the highest interest, State service (for which one does not by any means need to be an official) the highest honor.

So then the separate interests and personalities had been scared away, and sacrifice for the State had become the shibboleth. One must give up *himself,* and live only for the State. One must act "disinterestedly," not want to benefit *himself,* but the State. Hereby the latter has become the true person, before whom the individual personality vanishes; not I live, but it lives in me. Therefore, in comparison with the former self-seeking, this was unselfishness and *impersonality* itself. Before this god—State— all egoism vanished, and before it all were equal; they were without any other distinction—men, nothing but men.

The Revolution took fire from the inflammable material of *property.* The government needed money. Now it must prove the proposition that it is *absolute,* and so master of all property, sole proprietor; it must *take* to itself *its* money, which was only in the possession of the subjects, not their property. Instead of this, it calls States-general, to have this money *granted* to it. The shrinking from strictly logical action destroyed the illusion of an *absolute* government; he who must have something "granted" to him cannot be regarded as absolute. The subjects recognized that they were *real proprietors,* and that it was *their* money that was demanded. Those who had hitherto been subjects attained the consciousness that they were *proprietors.* Bailly[98] depicts this in a few words: "If you cannot dispose of my property without my assent, how much less can you of my person, of all that concerns my mental and social position? All this is my property, like the piece of land that I till; and I have a right, an interest, to make the laws myself." Bailly's words sound, certainly, as

98. [Jean-Sylvain Bailly (1736-1793), famous astronomer and mayor of Paris in first years of the French Revolution, 1789-1793; guillotined during the Reign of Terror in October of the latter year.]

if *every one* was a proprietor now. However, instead of the government, instead of the prince, *the—nation* now became proprietor and master. From this time on the ideal is spoken of as—"popular liberty"—"a free people," etc.

As early as July 8, 1789, the declaration of the bishop of Autun and Barrère[99] took away all semblance of the importance of each and every *individual* in legislation; it showed the complete *powerlessness* of the constituents; the *majority of the representatives* has become *master*. When on July 9 the plan for division of the work on the constitution is proposed, Mirabeau[100] remarks that "the government has only power, no rights; only in the *people* is the source of all *right* to be found." On July 16 this same Mirabeau exclaims: "Is not the people the source of all *power?*" The source, therefore, of all right, and the source of all—power![101] By the way, here the substance of "right" becomes visible; it is —*power*. "He who has power has right."

The commonalty is the heir of the privileged classes. In fact, the rights of the barons, which were taken from them as "usurpations," only passed over to the commonalty. For the commonalty was now called the "nation." "Into the hands of the nation" all *prerogatives* were given back. Thereby they ceased to be "prerogatives":[102] they became "rights."[103] From this time on the nation demands tithes, compulsory services; it has inherited the lord's court, the rights of vert and venison, the —serfs. The night of August 4 was the death-night of privileges or "prerogatives" (cities, communes, boards of magistrates, were also privileged, furnished with prerogatives and seigniorial rights),

99. [Charles Maurice de Talleyrand-Perigord (1754-1838), bishop of Autun and Barrère, 1789-1791. Talleyrand, whose name has become synonymous with craftiness in politics, was one of the prime movers in the concessions made by the French upper classes prior to the bloody phase of the French Revolution.]

100. [Count de Mirabeau (1749-1791) was the principal spokesman for the "third estate" at the National Assembly of 1789-1791 in France, where all the basic steps of the Revolution were taken.]

101. (*Gewalt*, a word which is also commonly used like the English "violence," denoting especially unlawful violence.)

102. (*Vorrechte*)

103. (*Rechte*)

and ended with the new morning of "right," the "rights of the State," the "rights of the nation."

The monarch in the person of the "royal master" had been a paltry monarch compared with this new monarch, the "sovereign nation." This *monarchy* was a thousand times severer, stricter, and more consistent. Against the new monarch there was no longer any right, any privilege at all; how limited the "absolute king" of the *ancien régime* looks in comparison! The Revolution effected the transformation of *limited monarchy* into *absolute monarchy*. From this time on every right that is not conferred by this monarch is an "assumption"; but every prerogative that he besows, a "right." The times demanded *absolute royalty,* absolute monarchy; therefore down fell that so-called absolute royalty which had so little understood how to become absolute that it remained limited by a thousand little lords.

What was longed for and striven for through thousands of years—to wit, to find that absolute lord beside whom no other lords and lordlings any longer exist to clip his power—the *bourgeoisie* has brought to pass. It has revealed the Lord who alone confers "rightful titles," and without whose warrant *nothing is justified.* "So now we know that an idol is nothing in the world, and that there is no other god save the one."[104]

Against *right* one can no longer, as against *a* right, come forward with the assertion that it is "a wrong." One can say now only that it is a piece of nonsense, an illusion. If one called it wrong, one would have to set up *another right* in opposition to it, and measure it by this. If, on the contrary, one rejects right as such, right in and of itself, altogether, then one also rejects the concept of wrong, and dissolves the whole concept of right (to which the concept of wrong belongs).

What is the meaning of the doctrine that we all enjoy "equality of political rights"? Only this—that the State has no regard for my person, that to it I, like every other, am only a man, without having another significance that commands its deference. I do not command its deference as an aristocrat, a nobleman's son, or even as heir of an official whose office belongs

104. 1 Corinthians, 8. 4.

to me by inheritance (as in the Middle Ages countships, etc., and later under absolute royalty, where hereditary offices occur). Now the State has an innumerable multitude of rights to give away; the right to lead a battalion, a company, etc.; the right to lecture at a university, and so forth; it has them to give away because they are its own, namely, State rights or "political" rights. Withal, it makes no difference to it to whom it gives them, if the receiver only fulfills the duties that spring from the delegated rights. To it we are all of us all right, and—*equal*— one worth no more and no less than another. It is indifferent to me who receives the command of the army, says the sovereign State, provided the grantee understands the matter properly. "Equality of political rights" has, consequently, the meaning that every one may acquire every right that the State has to give away, if only he fulfills the conditions annexed thereto—conditions which are to be sought only in the nature of the particular right, not in a predilection for the person (*persona grata*): the nature of the right to become an officer brings with it the necessity that one possess sound limbs and a suitable measure of knowledge, but it does not have noble birth as a condition; if, on the other hand, even the most deserving commoner could not reach that station, then an inequality of political rights would exist. Among the States of to-day one has carried out that maxim of equality more, another less.

The monarchy of estates (so I will call absolute royalty, the time of the kings *before* the revolution) kept the individual in dependence on a lot of little monarchies. These were fellow-ships (societies) like the guilds, the nobility, the priesthood, the burgher class, cities, communes. Everywhere the individual must regard himself *first* as a member of this little society, and yield unconditional obedience to its spirit, the *esprit de corps,* as his monarch. More than the individual nobleman himself must his family, the honor of his race, be to him. Only by means of his *corporation,* his estate, did the individual have relation to the greater corporation, the State—as in Catholicism the individual deals with God only through the priest. To this the third estate now, showing courage to negate *itself as an estate,* made an end. It decided no longer to be and be called an *estate* beside other estates, but to glorify and generalize itself into the "*nation*." Hereby it created a much more complete and absolute monarchy, and the entire previously ruling *principle of estates,* the principle of little monarchies inside the great, went down. Therefore it cannot be said that the Revolution was a revolution against the first two privileged estates. It was against the little monarchies of estates in general. But, if the estates and their despotism were broken (the king too, we know, was only a king of estates, not a citizen-king), the individuals freed from the inequality of estate were left. Were they now really to be without estate and "out of gear," no longer bound by any estate, without a general bond of union? No, for the third estate had declared itself the nation only in order not to remain an estate *beside* other estates, but to become the *sole estate.* This sole *estate* is the nation, the "*State.*" What had the individual now become? A political Protestant, for he had come into immediate connection with his God, the State. He was no longer, as an aristocrat, in the monarchy of the nobility; as a mechanic, in the monarchy of the guild; but he, like all, recognized and acknowledged only —*one lord,* the State, as whose servants they all received the equal title of honor, "citizen."

The *bourgeoisie* is the aristocracy of DESERT; its motto, "Let desert wear its crowns." It fought against the "lazy" aristocracy, for according to it (the industrious aristocracy acquired by industry and desert) it is not the "born" who is free, nor yet I who am free either, but the "deserving" man, the honest *servant* (of his king; of the State; of the people in constitutional States). Through *service* one acquires freedom, that is, acquires "deserts," even if one served—mammon. One must deserve well of the State, of the principle of the State, of its moral spirit. He who *serves* this spirit of the State is a good citizen, let him live to whatever honest branch of industry he will. In its eyes innovators practice a "breadless art." Only the "shopkeeper" is "practical," and the spirit that chases after public offices is as much the shopkeeping spirit as is that which tries in trade to feather its nest or otherwise to become useful to itself and anybody else.

But, if the deserving count as the free (for what does the

comfortable commoner, the faithful office-holder, lack of that freedom that his heart desires?), then the "servants" are the— free. The obedient servant is the free man! What glaring nonsense! Yet this is the sense of the *bourgeoisie,* and its poet, Goethe, as well as its philosopher, Hegel, succeeded in glorifying the dependence of the subject on the object, obedience to the objective world. He who only serves the cause, "devotes himself entirely to it," has the true freedom. And among thinkers the cause was—*reason,* that which, like State and Church, gives— general laws, and puts the individual man in irons by the *thought of humanity.* It determines what is "true," according to which one must then act. No more "rational" people than the honest servants, who primarily are called good citizens as servants of the State.

Be rich as Croesus or poor as Job—the State of the commonalty leaves that to your option; but only have a "good disposition." This it demands of you, and counts it its most urgent task to establish this in all. Therefore it will keep you from "evil promptings," holding the "ill-disposed" in check and silencing their inflammatory discourses under censors' canceling-marks or press-penalties and behind dungeon walls, and will, on the other hand, appoint people of "good disposition" as censors, and in every way have a *moral influence* exerted on you by "well-disposed and well-meaning" people. If it has made you deaf to evil promptings, then it opens your ears again all the more diligently to good *promptings.*

With the time of the *bourgeoisie* begins that of *liberalism.* People want to see what is "rational," "suited to the times," etc., established everywhere. The following definition of liberalism, which is supposed to be pronounced in its honor, characterizes it completely: "Liberalism is nothing else than the knowledge of reason, applied to our existing relations."[105] Its aim is a "rational order," a "moral behavior," a "limited freedom," not anarchy, lawlessness, selfhood. But, if reason rules, then the *person* suc-

105. [Stirner's quotation was from page 12 of Georg Herwegh (ed.), *Ein und zwanzig Bogen aus der Schweiz* (Zurich and Winterthur, 1843). This book, consisting of material by German radicals, was published in Switzerland to escape German press censorship laws.]

cumbs. Art has for a long time not only acknowledged the ugly, but considered the ugly as necessary to its existence, and takes it up into itself; it needs the villain. In the religious domain, too, the extremest liberals go so far that they want to see the most religious man regarded as a citizen—that is, the religious villain; they want to see no more of trials for heresy. But against the "rational law" no one is to rebel, otherwise he is threatened with the severest penalty. What is wanted is not free movement and realization of the person or of me, but of reason—a dominion of reason, a dominion. The liberals are *zealots,* not exactly for the faith, for God, but certainly for *reason,* their master. They brook no lack of breeding, and therefore no self-development and self-determination; they *play the guardian* as effectively as the most absolute rulers.

"Political liberty," what are we to understand by that? Perhaps the individual's independence of the State and its laws? No; on the contrary, the individual's *subjection* in the State and to the State's laws. But why "liberty"? Because one is no longer separated from the State by intermediaries, but stands in direct and immediate relation to it; because one is a—citizen, not the subject of another, not even of the king as a person, but only in his quality as "supreme head of the State." Political liberty, this fundamental doctrine of liberalism, is nothing but a second phase of—Protestantism, and runs quite parallel with "religious liberty."[106]   Or would it perhaps be right to understand by the latter an independence of religion? Anything but that. Independence of intermediaries is all that it is intended to express, independence of mediating priests, the abolition of the "laity," and so, direct and immediate relation to religion or to God. Only on the supposition that one has religion can he enjoy freedom of religion; freedom of religion does not mean being without religion, but inwardness of faith, unmediated intercourse with God. To him who is "religiously free" religion is an affair of

106. Louis Blanc says (*Histoire des dix Ans,* I, 138) of the time of the Restoration: "*Le protestantisme devint le fond des idées et des moeurs.*" [Louis Blanc (1811-1882), probably the most important of the French socialist propagandists; his two-volume *Revolution Française: Histoire de dix Ans, 1830-1840* was published in Paris, 1841-1844.]

the heart, it is to him his *own affair*, it is to him a "sacredly serious matter." So, too, to the "politically free" man the State is a sacredly serious matter; it is his heart's affair, his chief affair, his own affair.

Political liberty means that the *polis,* the State, is free; freedom of religion that religion is free, as freedom of conscience signifies that conscience is free; not, therefore, that I am free from the State, from religion, from conscience, or that I am *rid* of them. It does not mean *my* liberty, but the liberty of a power that rules and subjugates me; it means that one of my *despots,* like State; religion, conscience, is free. State, religion, conscience, these despots, make me a slave, and *their* liberty is my slavery. That in this they necessarily follow the principle, "the end hallows the means," is self-evident. If the welfare of the State is the end, war is a hallowed means; if justice is the State's end, homicide is a hallowed means, and is called by its sacred name, "execution"; the sacred State *hallows* everything that is serviceable to it.

"Individual liberty," over which civic liberalism keeps jealous watch, does not by any means signify a completely free self-determination, by which actions become altogether *mine,* but only independence of *persons.* Individually free is he who is responsible to no *man.* Taken in this sense—and we are not allowed to understand it otherwise—not only the ruler is individually free, *irresponsible toward men* ("before God," we know, he acknowledges himself responsible), but all who are "responsible only to the law." This kind of liberty was won through the revolutionary movement of the century—to wit, independence of arbitrary will, or *tel est notre plaisir.* Hence the constitutional prince must himself be stripped of all personality, deprived of all individual decision, that he may not as a person, as an *individual man,* violate the "individual liberty" of others. The *personal will of the ruler* has disappeared in the constitutional prince; it is with a right feeling, therefore, that absolute princes resist this. Nevertheless these very ones profess to be in the best sense "Christian princes." For this, however, they must bcome a *purely spiritual* power, as the Christian is subject only to *spirit* ("God is spirit"). The purely spiritual power is consistently represented only by

the constitutional prince, he who, without any personal significance, stands there spiritualized to the degree that he can rank
as a sheer, uncanny "spirit," as an *idea*.   The constitutional
king is the truly *Christian* king, the genuine, consistent carrying-
out of the Christian principle.   In the constitutional monarchy
individual dominion—a real ruler that *wills*—has found its end;
here, therefore, *individual liberty* prevails, independence of every
individual dictator, of everyone who could dictate to me with a
tel est notre plaisir.   It is the completed *Christian* State-life, a
spiritualized life.

The behavior of the commonalty is *liberal* through and
through.   Every *personal* invasion of another's sphere revolts
the civic sense; if the citizen sees that one is dependent on the
humor, the pleasure, the will of a man as individual (not as
authorized by a "higher power"), at once he brings his liberalism
to the front and shrieks about "arbitrariness."   In fine, the citizen
asserts his freedom from what is called *orders* (*ordonnance*):
"No one has any business to give me—orders!"   *Orders* carries
the idea that what I am to do is another man's will, while *law*
does not express a personal authority of another.   The liberty
of the commonalty is liberty or independence from the will of
another person, so-called personal or individual liberty; for being
personally free means being only so free that no other person
can dispose of mine, or that what I may or may not do does not
depend on the personal decree of another.   The liberty of the
press, for instance, is such a liberty of liberalism, liberalism
fighting only against the coercion of the censorship as that of
personal wilfulness, but otherwise showing itself extremely inclined
and willing to tyrannize over the press by "press laws"; the civic
liberals want liberty of writing *for themselves;* for, as they are
law-abiding, their writings will not bring them under the law.
Only liberal matter, only lawful matter, is to be allowed to be
printed; otherwise the "press laws" threaten "press-penalties."
If one sees personal liberty assured, one does not notice at all
how, if a new issue happens to arise, the most glaring unfreedom
becomes dominant.   For one is rid of *orders* indeed, and "no
one has any business to give us orders," but one has become

so much the more submissive to the—*law*. One is enthralled now in due legal form.

In the citizen-State there are only "free people," who are *compelled* to thousands of things (to deference, to a confession of faith, and the like). But what does that amount to? Why, it is only the—State, the law, not any man, that compels them!

What does the commonalty mean by inveighing against every personal order, every order not founded on the "cause," on "reason"? It is simply fighting in the interest of the "cause"[107] against the dominion of "persons"! But the mind's cause is the rational, good, lawful, etc.; that is the "good cause." The commonalty wants an *impersonal* ruler.

Furthermore, if the principle is this, that only the cause is to rule man—to wit, the cause of morality, the cause of legality, and so on, then no personal balking of one by the other may be authorized either (as formerly the commoner was balked of the aristocratic offices, the aristocrat of common mechanical trades, etc.); *free competition* must exist. Only through the thing[108] can one balk another (as the rich man balking the impecunious man by money, a thing), not as a person. Henceforth only one lordship, the lordship of the *State,* is admitted; personally no one is any longer lord of another. Even at birth the children belong to the State, and to the parents only in the name of the State, which does not allow infanticide, demands their baptism and so on.

But all the State's children, furthermore, are of quite equal account in its eyes ("civic or political equality"), and they may see to it themselves how they get along with each other; they may *compete*.

Free competition means nothing else than that every one can present himself, assert himself, fight, against another. Of course the feudal party set itself against this, as its existence depended on an absence of competition. The contests in the time of the Restoration in France had no other substance than this—that the *bourgeoisie* was struggling for free competition,

107. (*Sache*, which commonly means thing.)
108. (*Sache*)

and the feudalists were seeking to bring back the guild system.

Now, free competition has won, and against the guild system it had to win. (See below for the further discussion.)

If the Revolution ended in a reaction, this only showed what the Revolution *really was.* For every effort arrives at reaction when it *comes to discreet reflection,* and storms forward in the original action only so long as it is an *intoxication,* an "indiscretion." "Discretion" will always be the cue of the reaction, because discretion sets limits, and liberates what was really wanted, that is, the principle, from the initial "unbridledness" and "unrestrainedness." Wild young fellows, bumptious students, who set aside all considerations, are *really* Philistines, since with them, as with the latter, considerations form the substance of their conduct; only that as swaggerers they are mutinuous against considerations and in negative relations to them, but as Philistines, later, they give themselves up to considerations and have positive relations to them. In both cases all their doing and thinking turns upon "considerations," but the Philistine is *reactionary* in relation to the student; he is the wild fellow come to discreet reflection, as the latter is the unreflecting Philistine. Daily experience confirms the truth of this transformation, and shows how the swaggerers turn to Philistines in turning gray.

So, too, the so-called reaction in Germany gives proof that it was only the *discreet* continuation of the warlike jubilation of liberty.

The Revolution was not directed against *the established,* but against the *establishment in question,* against a *particular* establishment. It did away with *this* ruler, not with *the* ruler— on the contrary, the French were ruled most inexorably; it killed the old vicious rulers, but wanted to confer on the virtuous ones a securely established position, that is, it simply set virtue in the place of vice. (Vice and virtue, again, are on their part distinguished from each other only as a wild young fellow from a Philistine.)

To this day the revolutionary principle has gone no farther than to assail only *one or another* particular establishment, to be *reformatory.* Much as may be *improved,* strongly as "discreet progress" may be adhered to, always there is only a *new master* set in the old one's place, and the overturning is a—building up. We are still at the distinction of the young Philistine from the old one. The Revolution began in *bourgeois* fashion with the uprising of the third estate, the middle class; in *bourgeois* fashion it dries away. It was not the *individual man*—and he alone is *Man*—that became free, but the *citizen*, the *citoyen*, the *political* man, who for that very reason is not *Man* but a specimen of the human species, and more particularly a specimen of the species Citizen, a *free citizen.*

In the Revolution it was not the *individual* who acted so as to affect the world's history, but a *people;* the *nation*, the sovereign nation, wanted to effect everything. A fancied *I*, an idea, such as the nation is, appears acting; the individuals contribute themselves as tools of this idea, and act as "citizens."

The commonalty has its power, and at the same time its limits, in the *fundamental law of the State*, in a charter, in a legitimate[109] or "just"[110] prince who himself is guided, and rules, according to "rational laws," in short, in *legality.* The period of the *bourgeoisie* is ruled by the British spirit of legality. An assembly of provincial estates is ever recalling that its authorization goes only so and so far, and that it is called at all only through favor and can be thrown out again through disfavor. It is always reminding itself of its—*vocation.* It is certainly not to be denied that my father begot me; but, now that I am once begotten, surely his purposes in begetting do not concern me a bit and, whatever he may have *called* me to, I do what I myself will. Therefore even a called assembly of estates, the French assembly in the beginning of the Revolution, recognized quite rightly that it was independent of the caller. It *existed*, and would have been stupid if it did not avail itself of the right of existence, but fancied itself dependent as on a father. The called one no longer has to ask "what did the caller want when he created me?" but "what do I want after I have once followed the call?" Not the caller, not the constituents, not the charter according to which their meeting was called out, nothing will be to him a

109. (Or "righteous." German *rechtlich*.)
110. (*gerecht*)

sacred, inviolable power. He is *authorized* for everything that is in his power; he will know no restrictive "authorization," will not want to be *loyal*. This, if any such thing could be expected from chambers at all, would give a completely *egoistic* chamber, severed from all navel-string and without consideration. But chambers are always devout, and therefore one cannot be surprised if so much half-way or undecided, that is, hypocritical, "egoism" parades in them.

The members of the estates are to remain within the *limits* that are traced for them by the charter, by the king's will, and the like. If they will not or can not do that, then they are to "step out." What dutiful man could act otherwise, could put himself, his conviction, and his will as the *first* thing? Who could be so immoral as to want to assert *himself,* even if the body corporate and everything should go to ruin over it? People keep carefully within the limits of their *authorization;* of course one must remain within the limits of his *power* anyhow, because no one can do more than he can. "My power, or, if it be so, powerlessness, be my sole limit, but authorizations only restraining— precepts? Should I profess this all-subversive view? No, I am a— law-abiding citizen!"

The commonalty professes a morality which is most closely connected with its essence. The first demand of this morality is to the effect that one should carry on a solid business, an honorable trade, lead a moral life. Immoral, to it, is the sharper, the demirep, the thief, robber, and murderer, the gamester, the penniless man without a situation, the frivolous man. The doughty commoner designates the feeling against these "immoral" people as his "deepest indignation."

All these lack settlement, the *solid* quality of business, a solid, seemly life, a fixed income, etc.; in short, they belong, because their existence does not rest on a *secure basis,* to the dangerous "individuals or isolated persons," to the dangerous *proletariat;* they are "individual bawlers" who offer no "guarantee" and have "nothing to lose," and so nothing to risk. The forming of family ties *binds* a man: he who is bound furnishes security, can be taken hold of; not so the street-walker. The gamester stakes everything on the game, ruins himself and

others—no guarantee. All who appear to the commoner suspicious, hostile, and dangerous might be comprised under the
name "vagabonds"; every vagabondish way of living displeases
him. For there are intellectual vagabonds too, to whom the
hereditary dwelling-place of their fathers seems too cramped and
oppressive for them to be willing to satisfy themselves with the
limited space any more: instead of keeping within the limits of a
temperate style of thinking, and taking as inviolable truth what
furnishes comfort and tranquility to thousands, they overlap
all bounds of the traditional and run wild with their impudent
criticism and untamed mania for doubt, these extravagating
vagabonds. They form the class of the unstable, restless, change-
able, of the *proletariat,* and, if they give voice to their unsettled
nature, are called "unruly fellows."

Such a broad sense has the so-called *proletariat,* or pauperism. How much one would err if one believed the commonalty to
be desirous of doing away with poverty (pauperism) to the best
of its ability! On the contrary, the good citizen helps himself
with the incomparably comforting conviction that "the fact is
that the good things of fortune are unequally divided and will
always remain so—according to God's wise decree." The
poverty which surrounds him in every alley does not disturb the
true commoner further than that at most he clears his account
with it by throwing an alms, or finds work and food for an
"honest and serviceable" fellow. But so much the more does
he feel his quiet enjoyment clouded by *innovating* and *discontented* poverty, by those poor who no longer behave quietly
and endure, but begin to *run wild* and become restless. Lock
up the vagabond, thrust the breeder of unrest into the darkest
dungeon! He wants to "arouse dissatisfaction and incite people
against existing institutions" in the State—stone him, stone him!

But from these identical discontented ones comes a reasoning
somewhat as follows: It need not make any difference to the
"good citizens" who protects them and their principles, whether
an absolute king or a constitutional one, a republic, if only they
are protected. And what is their principle, whose protector they
always "love"? Not that of labor; not that of birth either. But
that of *mediocrity,* of the golden mean: a little birth and a little

labor, that is, an *interest-bearing possession.* Possession is here the fixed, the given, inherited (birth); interest-drawing is the exertion about it (labor); *laboring capital,* therefore. Only no immoderation, no ultra, no radicalism! Right of birth certainly, but only hereditary possessions; labor certainly, yet little or none at all of one's own, but labor of capital and of the—subject laborers.

If an age is imbued with an error, some always derive advantage from the error, while the rest have to suffer from it. In the Middle Ages the error was general among Christians that the church must have all power, or the supreme lordship on earth; the hierarchs believed in this "truth" not less than the laymen, and both were spellbound in the like error. But by it the hierarchs had the *advantage* of power, the laymen had to *suffer* subjection. However, as the saying goes, "one learns wisdom by suffering"; and so the laymen at last learned wisdom and no longer believed in the medieval "truth."—A like relation exists between the commalty and the laboring class. Commoner and laborer believe in the "truth" of *money;* they who do not possess it believe in it no less than those who possess it: the laymen, therefore, as well as the priests.

"Money governs the world" is the keynote of the civic epoch. A destitute aristocrat and a destitute laborer, as "starvelings," amount to nothing so far as political consideration is concerned; birth and labor do not do it, but *money* brings *consideration.*[111] The possessors rule, but the State trains up from the destitute its "servants," to whom, in proportion as they are to rule (govern) in its name, it gives money (a salary).

I receive everything from the State. Have I anything without the *State's assent?* What I have without this it *takes* from me as soon as it discovers the lack of a "legal title." Do I not, therefore, have everything through its grace, its assent?

On this alone, on the *legal title,* the commonalty rests. The commoner is what he is through the *protection of the State,* through the State's grace. He would necessarily be afraid of losing everything if the State's power were broken.

111. (*das Geld gibt Geltung.*)

But how is it with him who has nothing to lose, how with the proletarian? As he has nothing to lose, he does not need the protection of the State for his "nothing." He may gain, on the contrary, if that protection of the State is withdrawn from the *protégé*.

Therefore the non-possessor will regard the State as a power protecting the possessor, which privileges the latter, but does nothing for him, the non-possessor, but to—suck his blood. The State is a—*commoners' State,* is the estate of the commonalty. It protects man not according to his labor, but according to his tractableness ("loyalty")—to wit, according to whether the rights entrusted to him by the State are enjoyed and managed in accordance with the will, that is, laws, of the State.

Under the *regime* of the commonalty the laborers always fall into the hands of the possessors, of those who have at their disposal some bit of the State domains (and everything possessible in State domain, belongs to the State, and is only a fief of the individual), especially money and land; of the capitalists, therefore. The laborer cannot *realize* on his labor to the extent of the value that it has for the consumer. "Labor is badly paid!" The capitalist has the greatest profit from it.—Well paid, and more than well paid, are only the labors of those who heighten the splendor and *dominion* of the State, the labors of high State *servants.* The State pays well that its "good citizens," the possessors, may be able to pay badly without danger; it secures to itself by good payment its servants, out of whom it forms a protecting power, a "police" (to the police belong soldiers, officials of all kinds, those of justice, education, etc.—in short, the whole "machinery of the State") for the "good citizens," and the "good citizens" gladly pay high tax-rates to it in order to pay so much lower rates to their laborers.

But the class of laborers, because unprotected in what they essentially are (for they do not enjoy the protection of the State as laborers, but as its subjects they have a share in the enjoyment of the police, a so-called protection of the law), remains a power hostile to this State, this State of possessors, this "citizen kingship." Its principle, labor, is not recognized as to its *value;* it is exploited,[112] a spoil[113] of the possessors, the enemy.

The laborers have the most enormous power in their hands, and, if they once became thoroughly conscious of it and used it, nothing would withstand them; they would only have to stop labor, regard the product of labor as theirs, and enjoy it. This is the sense of the labor disturbances which show themselves here and there.

The State rests on the—*slavery of labor.* If *labor* becomes *free,* the State is lost.

2. — SOCIAL LIBERALISM

We are freeborn men, and wherever we look we see ourselves made servants of egoists! Are we therefore to become egoists too! Heaven forbid! We want rather to make egoists impossible! We want to make them all "ragamuffins"; all of us must have nothing, that "all may have."

So say the Socialists.

Who is this person that you call "All"?—It is "society"!—But is it corporeal, then?—*We* are its body!—You? Why, you are not a body yourselves—you, sir, are corporeal to be sure, you too, and you, but you all together are only bodies, not a body. Accordingly the united society may indeed have bodies at its service, but no one body of its own. Like the "nation" of the politicians, it will turn out to be nothing but a "spirit," its body only semblance.

The freedom of man is, in political liberalism, freedom from *persons,* from personal dominion, from the *master;* the securing of each individual person against other persons, personal freedom.

No one has any orders to give; the law alone gives orders.

But, even if the persons have become *equal,* yet their *possessions* have not. And yet the poor man *needs the rich,* the rich the poor, the former the rich man's money, the latter

112. (*ausgebeutet*)
113. (*Kriegsbeute*)

the poor man's labor. So no one needs another as a *person,* but needs him as a *giver,* and thus as one who has something to give, as holder or possessor. So what he *has* makes the *man.* And in *having,* or in "possessions," people are unequal.

Consequently, social liberalism concludes, *no one must have,* as according to political liberalism *no one was to give orders;* as in that case the *State* alone obtained the command, so now *society* alone obtains the possessions.

For the State, protecting each one's person and property against the other, *separates* them from one another; each one *is* his special part and has his special part. He who is satisfied with what he is and has finds this state of things profitable; but he who would like to be and have more looks around for this "more," and finds it in the power of other *persons.* Here he comes upon a contradiction; as a person no one is inferior to another, and yet one person *has* what another has not but would like to have. So, he concludes, the one person is more than the other, after all, for the former has what he needs, the latter has not; the former is a rich man, the latter a poor man.

He now asks himself further, are we to let what we rightly buried come to life again? Are we to let this circuitously restored inequality of persons pass? No; on the contrary, we must bring quite to an end what was only half accomplished. Our freedom from another's person still lacks the freedom from what the other's person can command, from what he has in his personal power—in short, from "personal property." Let us then do away with *personal property.* Let no one have anything any longer, let every one be a—ragamuffin. Let property be *impersonal,* let it belong to—*society.*

Before the supreme *ruler,* the sole *commander,* we had all become equal, equal persons, that is, nullities.

Before the supreme *proprietor* we all become equal—raga-muffins. For the present, one is still in another's estimation a "ragamuffin," a "have-nothing"; but then this estimation ceases. We are all ragamuffins together, and as the aggregate of Com-munistic society we might call ourselves a "ragamuffin crew."

When the proletarian shall really have founded his purposed

"society" in which the interval between rich and poor is to be removed, then he *will be* a ragamuffin, for then he will feel that it amounts to something to be a ragamuffin, and might lift "Ragamuffin" to be an honorable form of address, just as the Revolution did with the word "Citizen." Ragamuffin is his ideal; we are all to become ragamuffins.

This is the second robbery of the "personal" in the interest of "humanity." Neither command nor property is left to the individual; the State took the former, society the latter.

Because in society the most oppressive evils make themselves felt, therefore the oppressed especially, and consequently the members of the lower regions of society, think they found the fault in society, and make it their task to discover the *right society*. This is only the old phenomenon—that one looks for the fault first in everything but *himself,* and consequently in the State, in the self-seeking of the rich, and so on, which yet have precisely our fault to thank for their existence.

The reflections and conclusions of Communism[114] look very simple. As matters lie at this time—in the present situation with regard to the State, therefore—some, and they the majority, are at a disadvantage compared to others, the minority. In this *state* of things the former are in a *state of prosperity,* the latter in a *state of need.* Hence the present *state* of things, the State itself, must be done away with. And what in its place? Instead of the isolated state of prosperity—a *general state of prosperity,* a *prosperity of all.*

Through the Revolution the *bourgeoisie* became omnipotent, and all inequality was abolished by every one's being raised or degraded to the dignity of a *citizen:* the common man—raised, the aristocrat—degraded; the *third* estate became sole estate, namely, the estate of—*citizens of the State.* Now Communism responds: Our dignity and our essence consist not in our being all—the *equal children* of our mother, the State, all born with

114. [Stirner, as did most of the writers of his time, used the words "Socialism" and "Communism" interchangeably, even as did many of the propagandists of collectivism themselves. It is well after mid-century before the fine qualifications begin and the sectarian conflicts herald the present-day conventional distinctions between the two.]

equal claim to her love and her protection, but in our all existing *for each other*. This is our equality, or herein we are *equal,* in that we, I as well as you and you and all of you, are active or "labor" each one for the rest; in that each of us is a *laborer,* then. The point for us is not what we are *for the State* (citizens), not our *citizenship* therefore, but what we are *for each other,* that each of us exists only through the other, who, caring for my wants, at the same time sees his own satisfied by me. He labors for my clothing (tailor), I for his need of amusement (comedy-writer, rope-dancer), he for my food (farmer), I for his instruction (scientist). It is *labor* that constitutes our dignity and our—equality.

What advantage does citizenship bring us? Burdens! And how high is our labor appraised? As low as possible! But labor is our sole value all the same: that we are *laborers* is the best thing about us, this is our significance in the world, and therefore it must be our consideration too and must come to receive *consideration.* What can you meet us with? Surely nothing but—*labor* too. Only for labor or services do we owe you a recompense, not for your bare existence; not for what you are *for yourselves* either, but only for what you are *for us.* By what have you claims on us? Perhaps by your high birth? No, only by what you do for us that is desirable or useful. Be it thus then: we are willing to be worth to you only so much as we do for you; but you are to be held likewise by us. *Services* determine value, those services that are worth something to us, and consequently *labors for each other, labors for the common good.* Let each one be in the other's eyes a *laborer.* He who accomplishes something useful is inferior to none, or—all laborers (laborers, of course, in the sense of laborers "for the common good," that is, communistic laborers) are equal. But, as the laborer is worth his wages,[115] let the wages too be equal.

As long as faith sufficed for man's honor and dignity, no labor, however harassing, could be objected to if it only did not hinder a man in his faith. Now, on the contrary, when every one is to cultivate himself into man, condemning a man to *machine-*

115. (In German an exact quotation of Luke 10. 7.)

like labor amounts to the same thing as slavery. If a factory worker must tire himself to death twelve hours and more, he is cut off from becoming man. Every labor is to have the intent that the man be satisfied. Therefore he must become a *master* in it too, be able to perform it as a totality. He who in a pin-factory only puts on the heads, only draws the wire, works, as it were, mechanically, like a machine; he remains half-trained, does not become a master: his labor cannot *satisfy* him, it can only *fatigue* him. His labor is nothing by itself, has no object *in itself,* is nothing complete in itself; he labors only into another's hands, and is *used* (exploited) by this other. For this laborer in another's service there is no *enjoyment of a cultivated mind,* at most, crude amusements: *culture,* you see, is barred against him. To be a good Christian one needs only to *believe,* and that can be done under the most oppressive circumstances. Hence the Christian-minded take care only of the oppressed laborers' piety, their patience, submission, etc. Only so long as the downtrodden classes were *Christians* could they bear all their misery: for Christianity does not let their murmurings and exasperation rise. Now the *hushing* of desires is no longer enough, but their *sating* is demanded. The *bourgeoisie* has proclaimed the gospel of the *enjoyment of the world,* of material enjoyment, and now wonders that this doctrine finds adherents among us poor: it has shown that not faith and poverty, but culture and possessions, make a man blessed; we proletarians understand that too.

The commonalty freed us from the orders and arbitrariness of individuals. But that arbitrariness was left which springs from the conjuncture of situations, and may be called the fortuity of circumstances; favoring *fortune,* and those "favored by fortune," still remain.

When, for example, a branch of industry is ruined and thousands of laborers become breadless, people think reasonably enough to acknowledge that it is not the individual who must bear the blame, but that "the evil lies in the situation." Let us change the situation then, but let us change it thoroughly, and so that its fortuity becomes powerless, and a *law!* Let us no longer be slaves of chance! Let us create a new order that makes an end of *fluctuations*. Let this order then be sacred!

Formerly one had to suit the *lords* to come to anything; after the Revolution the word was "Grasp *fortune!*" Luck-hunting or hazard-playing, civil life was absorbed in this. Then, alongside this, the demand that he who has obtained something shall not frivolously stake it again.

Strange and yet supremely natural contradiction. Competition, in which alone civil or political life unrolls itself, is a game of luck through and through, from the speculations of the exchange down to the solicitation of offices, the hunt for customers, looking for work, aspiring to promotion and decorations, the second-hand dealer's petty haggling, etc. If one succeeds in supplanting and outbidding his rivals, then the "lucky throw" is made; for it must be taken as a piece of luck to begin with that the victor sees himself equipped with an ability (even though it has been developed by the most careful industry) against which the others do not know how to rise, consequently that—no abler ones are found. And now those who ply their daily lives in the midst of these changes of fortune without seeing any harm in it are seized with the most virtuous indignation when their own principle appears in naked form and "breeds misfortune" as—*hazard-playing*. Hazard-playing, you see, is too clear, too barefaced a competition, and, like every decided nakedness, offends honorable modesty.

The Socialists want to put a stop to this activity of chance, and to form a society in which men are no longer dependent on *fortune,* but free.

In the most natural way in the world this endeavor first utters itself as hatred of the "unfortunate" against the "fortunate," of those for whom fortune has done little or nothing, against those for whom it has done everything. But properly the ill-feeling is not directed against the fortunate, but against *fortune,* this rotten spot of the commonalty.

As the Communists first declare free activity to be man's essence, they, like all work-day dispositions, need a Sunday; like all material endeavors, they need a God, an uplifting and edification alongside their witless "labor."

That the Communist sees in you the man, the brother, is only the Sunday side of Communism. According to the work-day side he does not by any means take you as man simply, but as human laborer or laboring man. The first view has in it the liberal principle; in the second, illiberality is concealed. If you were a "lazybones," he would not indeed fail to recognize the man in you, but would endeavor to cleanse him as a "lazy man" from laziness and to convert you to the *faith* that labor is man's "destiny and calling."

Therefore he shows a double face: with the one he takes heed that the spiritual man be satisfied, with the other he looks about him for means for the material or corporeal man. He gives man a twofold *post*—an office of material acquisition and one of spiritual.

The commonalty had *thrown open* spiritual and material goods, and left it with each one to reach out for them if he liked.

Communism really procures them for each one, presses them upon him, and compels him to acquire them. It takes seriously the idea that, because only spiritual and material goods make us men, we must unquestionably acquire these goods in order to be man. The commonalty made acquisition free; Communism *compels* to acquisition, and recognizes only the acquirer, him who practices a trade. It is not enough that the trade is free, but you must *take it up*.

So all that is left for criticism to do is to prove that the acquisition of these goods does not yet by any means make us men.

With the liberal commandment that every one is to make a man of himself, or every one to make himself man, there was posited the necessity that every one must gain time for this labor of humanization, that is, that it should become possible for every one to labor on *himself*.

The commonalty thought it had brought this about if it handed over everything human to competition, but gave the individual a right to every human thing. "Each may strive after everything!"

Social liberalism finds that the matter is not settled with the "may," because may means only "it is forbidden to none" but not "it is made possible to every one." Hence it affirms that the commonalty is liberal only with the mouth and in words, supremely illiberal in act. It on its part wants to give all of us the *means* to be able to labor on ourselves.

By the principle of labor that of fortune or competition is certainly outdone. But at the same time the laborer, in his consciousness that the essential thing in him is "the laborer," holds himself aloof from egoism and subjects himself to the supremacy of a society of laborers, as the commoner clung with self-abandonment to the competition-State. The beautiful dream of a "social duty" still continues to be dreamed. People think again that society *gives* what we need, and we are *under obligations* to it on that account, owe it everything.[116] They are still at the point of wanting to *serve* a "supreme giver of all good." That society is no ego at all, which could give, bestow, or grant, but an instrument or means, from which we may derive benefit; that we have no social duties, but solely interests for the pursuance of which society must serve us; that we owe society no sacrifice, but, if we sacrifice anything, sacrifice it to ourselves—of this the Socialists do not think, because they—as liberals—are imprisoned in the religious principle, and zealously aspire after—a sacred society, such as the State was hitherto.

Society, from which we have everything, is a new master, a new spook, a new "supreme being," which "takes us into its service and allegiance!"

The more precise appreciation of political as well as social liberalism must wait to find its place further on. For the present we pass this over, in order first to summon them before the tribunal of humane or critical liberalism.

3. — HUMANE LIBERALISM

As liberalism is completed in self-criticizing, "critical"[117] liberalism—in which the critic remains a liberal and does not

---

116. Proudhon (*Création de l'ordre*) cries out, p. 414, "In industry, as in science, the publication of an invention is the first and most sacred of duties!"

117. (In his strictures on "criticism" Stirner refers to a special move-

go beyond the principle of liberalism, Man—this may distinctively be named after Man and called the "humane."

The laborer is counted as the most material and egoistical man. He does nothing at all *for humanity,* does everything for *himself,* for his welfare.

The commonalty, because it proclaimed the freedom of *Man* only as to his birth, had to leave him in the claws of the un-human man (the egoist) for the rest of life. Hence under the regime of political liberalism egoism has an immense field for free utilization.

The laborer will *utilize* society for his *egoistic* ends as the commoner does the State. You have only an egoistic end after all, your welfare, is the humane liberal's reproach to the Socialist; take up a *purely human interest,* then I will be your companion. "But to this there belongs a consciousness stronger, more comprehensive, than a *laborer-consciousness." "*The laborer makes nothing, therefore he has nothing; but he makes nothing because his labor is always a labor that remains individual, calculated strictly for his own want, a labor day by day."[118] In opposition to this one might, for instance, consider the fact that Gutenberg's[119] labor did not remain individual, but begot innumerable

ment known by that name in the early forties of the last century, of which Bruno Bauer was the principal exponent. After his official separation from the faculty of the university of Bonn on account of his views in regard to the Bible, Bruno Bauer in 1843 settled near Berlin and founded the *Allgemeine Literatur-Zeitung,* in which he and his friends, at war with their surroundings, championed the "absolute emancipation" of the individual within the limits of "pure humanity" and fought as their foe "the mass," comprehending in that term the radical aspirations of political liberalism and the communistic demands of the rising Socialist movement of that time. For a brief account of Bruno Bauer's movement of criticism, see John Henry Mackay, *Max Stirner. Sein Leben und sein Werk.*)

[Twelve issues of this journal, published in Charlottenburg in 1843-1844, were subsequently issued in two bound volumes. It does not appear to have been published after the latter date. An earlier and surviving journal with the identical name was currently being published in Halle.]

118. Br. Bauer, *Lit. Ztg.,* V, 18.

119. [A reference to Johannes Gutenberg (1398-1468), perfector of printing from moveable type.]

children, and still lives to-day; it was calculated for the want of humanity, and was an eternal, imperishable labor.

The humane consciousness despises the commoner-consciousness as well as the laborer-consciousness: for the commoner is "indignant" only at vagabonds (at all who have "no definite occupation") and their "immorality"; the laborer is "disgusted" by the idler ("lazybones") and his "immoral," because parasitic and unsocial, principles. To this the humane liberal retorts: The unsettledness of many is only your product, Philistine! But that you, proletarian, demand the *grind* of all, and want to make *drudgery* general, is a part, still clinging to you, of your pack-mule life up to this time. Certainly you want to lighten drudgery itself by *all* having to drudge equally hard, yet only for this reason, that all may gain *leisure* to an equal extent. But what are they to do with their leisure? What does your "society" do, that this leisure may be passed *humanly?* It must leave the gained leisure to egoistic preference again, and the very *gain* that your society furthers falls to the egoist, as the gain of the commonalty, the *masterlessness of man,* could not be filled with a human element by the State, and therefore was left to arbitrary choice.

It is assuredly necessary that man be masterless: but therefore the egoist is not to become master over man again either, but man over the egoist. Man must assuredly find leisure: but, if the egoist makes use of it, it will be lost for man; therefore you ought to have given leisure a human significance. But you laborers undertake even your labor from an egoistic impulse, because you want to eat, drink, live; how should you be less egoists in leisure? You labor only because having your time to yourselves (idling) goes well after work done, and what you are to while away your leisure time with is left to *chance.*

But, if every door is to be bolted against egoism, it would be necessary to strive after completely "disinterested" action, *total* disinterestedness. This alone is human, because only Man is disinterested, the egoist always interested.

If we let disinterestedness pass unchallenged for a while, then we ask, do you mean not to take an interest in anything, not to be enthusiastic for anything, not for liberty, humanity, etc.? "Oh, yes, but that is not an egoistic interest, not *interested-ness,* but a human, a—*theoretical* interest, to wit, an interest not for an individual or individuals ('all'), but for the *idea, for* Man!"

And you do not notice that you too are enthusiastic only for *your* idea, *your* idea of liberty?

And, further, do you not notice that your disinterestedness is again, like religious disinterestedness, a heavenly interestedness? Certainly benefit to the individual leaves you cold, and abstractly you could cry *fiat libertas, pereat mundus.* You do not take thought for the coming day either, and take no serious care for the individual's wants anyhow, not for your own comfort nor for that of the rest; but you make nothing of all this, because you are a—dreamer.

Do you suppose the humane liberal will be so liberal as to aver that everything possible to man is *human?* On the contrary! He does not, indeed, share the Philistine's moral prejudice about the strumpet, but "that this woman turns her body into a money-getting machine"[120] makes her despicable to him as "human being." His judgment is, the strumpet is not a human being; or, so far as a woman is a strumpet, so far is she unhuman, dehumanized. Further: The Jew, the Christian, the privileged person, the theologian, etc., is not a human being; so far as you are a Jew, etc., you are not a human being. Again the imperious postulate: Cast from you everything peculiar, criticize it away! Be not a Jew, not a Christian, but be a human being, nothing but a human being. Assert your *humanity* against every restrictive specification; make yourself, by means of it, a human being, and free from those limits; make yourself a "free man"—recognize humanity as your all-determining *essence.*

I say: You are indeed more than a Jew, more than a Christian, etc., but you are also more than a human being. Those are all ideas, but you are corporeal. Do you suppose, then, that you can ever become a "human being as such?" Do you suppose our posterity will find no prejudices and limits to clear away, for which our powers were not sufficient? Or do you

120. *Lit. Ztg.,* V, 26.

perhaps think that in your fortieth or fiftieth year you have come
so far that the following days have nothing more to dissipate
in you, and that you are a human being? The men of the future
will yet fight their way to many a liberty that we do not even
miss. What do you need that later liberty for? If you meant to
esteem yourself as nothing before you had become a human
being, you would have to wait till the "last judgment," till the
day when man, or humanity, shall have attained perfection. But,
as you will surely die before that, what becomes of your prize
of victory?

Rather, therefore, invert the case, and say to yourself, *I
am a human being!* I do not need to begin by producing the
human being in myself, for he belongs to me already, like all my
qualities.

But, asks the critic, how can one be a Jew and a man at
once? In the first place, I answer, one cannot be either a Jew
or a man at all, if "one" and Jew or man are to mean the same;
"one" always reaches beyond those specifications, and—let Isaacs
be ever so Jewish—a Jew, nothing but a Jew, he cannot be, just
because he is *this* Jew. In the second place, as a Jew one assuredly
cannot be a man, if being a man means being nothing special. But
in the third place—and this is the point—I can, as a Jew, be
entirely what I—*can* be. From Samuel or Moses, and others,
you hardly expect that they should have raised themselves above
Judaism, although you must say that they were not yet "men."
They simply were what they could be. Is it otherwise with the
Jews of to-day? Because you have discovered the idea of
humanity, does it follow from this that every Jew can become
a convert to it? If he can, he does not fail to, and, if he fails
to, he—cannot. What does your demand concern him? What
the *call* to be a man, which you address to him?

———————

As a universal principle, in the "human society" which the
humane liberal promises, nothing "special" which one or another
has is to find recognition, nothing which bears the character of
"private" is to have value. In this way the circle of liberalism,
which has its good principle in man and human liberty, its bad in
the egoist and everything private, its God in the former, its

devil in the latter, rounds itself off completely; and, if the special or private person lost his value in the State (no personal prerogative), if in the "laborers' or ragamuffins' society" special (private) property is no longer recognized, so in "human society" everything special or private will be left out of account; and, when "pure criticism" shall have accomplished its arduous task, then it will be known just what we must look upon as private, and what, "penetrated with a sense of our nothingness," we must—let stand.

Because State and Society do not suffice for humane liberalism, it negates both, and at the same time retains them. So at one time the cry is that the task of the day is "not a political, but a social, one," and then again the "free State" is promised for the future. In truth, "human society" is both—the most general State and the most general society. Only against the limited State is it asserted that it makes too much stir about spiritual private interests (people's religious belief), and against limited society that it makes too much of material private interests. Both are to leave private interests to private people, and, as human society, concern themselves solely about general human interests.

The politicians, thinking to abolish *personal will,* self-will or arbitrariness, did not observe that through *property*[121] our *self-will*[122] gained a secure place of refuge.

The Socialists, taking away *property* too, do not notice that this secures itself a continued existence in *self-ownership.* Is it only money and goods, then, that are a property, or is every opinion something of mine, something of my own?

So every *opinion* must be abolished or made impersonal. The person is entitled to no opinion, but, as self-will was transferred to the State, property to society, so opinion too must be transferred to something *general,* "Man," and thereby become a general human opinion.

If opinion persists, then I have *my* God (why, God exists only as "my God," he is an opinion or my "faith"), and conse-

121. (*Eigentum,* "owndom.")
122. (*Eigenwille,* "own-will.")

quently *my* faith, my religion, my thoughts, my ideals. Therefore
a general human faith must come into existence, the *"fanaticism
of liberty."* For this would be a faith that agreed with the
"essence of man," and, because only "man" is reasonable (you
and I might be very unreasonable!), a reasonable faith.

As self-will and property become *powerless,* so must self-
ownership or egoism in general.

In this supreme development of "free man" egoism, self-
ownership, is combated on principle, and such subordinate ends
as the social "welfare" of the Socialists, etc., vanish before the
lofty "idea of humanity." Everything that is not a "general human"
entity is something separate, satisfies only some or one; or, if
it satisfies all, it does this to them only as individuals, not as
men, and is therefore called "egoistic."

To the Socialists *welfare* is still the supreme aim, as free
rivalry was the approved thing to the political liberals; now
welfare is free too, and we are free to achieve welfare, just as he
who wanted to enter into rivalry (competition) was free to do so.

But to take part in the rivalry you need only to be *commoners;* to take part in the welfare, only to be *laborers.* Neither
reaches the point of being synonymous with "man." It is "truly
well" with man only when he is also "intellectually free!" For
man is mind: therefore all powers that are alien to him, the
mind—all superhuman, heavenly, unhuman powers—must be
overthrown and the name "man" must be above every name.

So in this end of the modern age (age of the moderns) there
returns again, as the main point, what had been the main point
at its beginning: "intellectual liberty."

To the Communist in particular the humane liberal says:
If society prescribes to you your activity, then this is indeed
free from the influence of the individual, the egoist, but it still
does not on that account need to be a *purely human* activity,
nor you to be a complete organ of humanity. What kind of
activity society demands of you remains *accidental,* you know;
it might give you a place in building a temple or something of
that sort, or, even if not that, you might yet on your own impulse
be active for something foolish, therefore unhuman; yes, more
yet, you really labor only to nourish yourself, in general to

live, for dear life's sake, not for the glorification of humanity. Consequently free activity is not attained till you make yourself free from all stupidities, from everything non-human, namely, egoistic (pertaining only to the individual, not to the Man in the individual), dissipate all untrue thoughts that obscure man or the idea of humanity: in short, when you are not merely un-hampered in your activity, but the substance too of your activity is only what is human, and you live and work only for humanity. But this is not the case so long as the aim of your effort is only your *welfare* and that of all; what you do for the society of ragamuffins is not yet anything done for "human society."

Laboring does not alone make you a man, because it is something formal and its object accidental; the question is who you that labor are. As far as laboring goes, you might do it from an egoistic (material) impulse, merely to procure nourish-ment and the like; it must be a labor furthering humanity, cal-culated for the good of humanity, serving historical (human) evolution—in short, a *human* labor. This implies two things: one, that it be useful to humanity; next, that it be the work of a "man." The first alone may be the case with every labor, as even the labors of nature, as of animals, are utilized by humanity for the furthering of science, etc.; the second requires that he who labors should know the human object of his labor; and, as he can have this consciousness only when he *knows himself as man,* the crucial condition is—*self-consciousness.*

Unquestionably much is already attained when you cease to be a "fragment-laborer,"[123] yet therewith you only get a view of the whole of your labor, and acquire a consciousness about it, which is still far removed from a self-consciousness, a con-sciousness about your true "self" or "essence," Man. The laborer has still remaining the desire for a "higher consciousness," which, because the activity of labor is unable to quiet it, he satisfies in a leisure hour. Hence leisure stands by the side of his labor, and he sees himself compelled to proclaim labor and idling human in one breath, yes, to attribute the true elevation to the

123. (Referring to minute subdivision of labor, whereby the single workman produces, not a whole, but a part.)

idler, the leisure-enjoyer. He labors only to get rid of labor; he wants to make labor free, only that he may be free from labor.

In fine, his work has no satisfying substance, because it is only imposed by society, only a stint, a task, a calling; and, conversely, his society does not satisfy, because it gives only work.

His labor ought to satisfy him as a man; instead of that, it satisfies society; society ought to treat him as a man, and it treats him as—a rag-tag laborer, or a laboring ragamuffin.

Labor and society are of use to him not as he needs them as a man, but only as he needs them as an "egoist."

Such is the attitude of criticism toward labor. It points to "mind," wages the war "of mind with the masses,"[124] and pronounces communistic labor unintellectual mass-labor. Averse to labor as they are, the masses love to make labor easy for themselves. In literature, which is to-day furnished in mass, this aversion to labor begets the universally-known *superficiality,* which puts from it "the toil of research."[125]

Therefore humane liberalism says: You want labor; all right, we want it likewise, but we want it in the fullest measure. We want it, not that we may gain spare time, but that we may find all satisfaction in it itself. We want labor because it is our self-development.

But then the labor too must be adapted to that end! Man is honored only by human, self-conscious labor, only by the labor that has for its end no "egoistic" purpose, but Man, and is Man's self-revelation; so that the saying should be *laboro, ergo sum,* I labor, therefore I am a man. The humane liberal wants that labor of the *mind* which *works up* all material; he wants the mind, that leaves no thing quiet or in its existing condition, that acquiesces in nothing, analyzes everything, criticizes anew every result that has been gained. This restless mind is the true laborer, it obliterates prejudices, shatters limits and narrownesses, and raises man above everything that would like to dominate over him, while the Communist labors only for himself, and not even

124. *Lit. Ztg.,* V, 24.
125. *Lit. Ztg., ibid.*

freely, but from necessity—in short, represents a man condemned to hard labor.

The laborer of such a type is not "egoistic," because he does not labor for individuals, neither for himself nor for other individuals, not for *private* men therefore, but for humanity and its progress: he does not ease individual pains, does not care for individual wants, but removes limits within which humanity is pressed, dispels prejudices which dominate an entire time, vanquishes hindrances that obstruct the path of all, clears away errors in which men entangle themselves, discovers truths which are found through him for all and for all time; in short—he lives and labors for humanity.

Now, in the first place, the discoverer of a great truth doubtless knows that it can be useful to the rest of men, and, as a jealous withholding furnishes him no enjoyment, he communicates it; but, even though he has the consciousness that his communication is highly valuable to the rest, yet he has in no wise sought and found his truth for the sake of the rest, but for his own sake, because he himself desired it, because darkness and fancies left him no rest till he had procured for himself light and enlightenment to the best of his powers.

He labors, therefore, for his own sake and for the satisfaction of *his* want. That along with this he was also useful to others, yes, to posterity, does not take from his labor the *egoistic* character.

In the next place, if he did labor only on his own account, like the rest, why should his act be human, those of the rest unhuman, that is, egoistic? Perhaps because this book, painting, symphony, is the labor of his whole being, because he has done his best in it, has spread himself out wholly and is wholly to be known from it, while the work of a handicraftsman mirrors only the handicraftsman, the skill in handicraft, not "the man?" In his poems we have the whole Schiller; in so many hundred stoves, on the other hand, we have before us only the stove-maker, not "the man."

But does this mean more than "in the one work you see *me* as completely as possible, in the other only my skill?" Is it not me again that the act expresses? And is it not more egoistic to offer *oneself* to the world in a work, to work out and shape *oneself*, than to remain concealed behind one's labor? You say, to be sure, that you are revealing Man. But the Man that you reveal is you; you reveal only yourself, yet with this distinction from the handicraftsman—that he does not understand how to compress himself into one labor, but, in order to be known as himself, must be searched out in his other relations of life, and that your want, through whose satisfaction that work came into being, was a—theoretical want.

But you will reply that you reveal quite another man, a worthier, higher, greater, a man that is more man than that other. I will assume that you accomplish all that is possible to man, that you bring to pass what no other succeeds in. Wherein, then, does your greatness consist? Precisely in this, that you are more than other men (the "masses"), more than *men* ordinarily are, more than "ordinary men"; precisely in your elevation above men. You are distinguished beyond other men not by being man, but because you are a "unique"[126] man. Doubtless you show what a man can do; but because you, a man, do it, this by no means shows that others, also men, are able to do as much; you have executed it only as a *unique* man, and are unique therein.

It is not man that makes up your greatness, but you create it, because you are more than man, and mightier than other—men.

It is believed that one cannot be more than man. Rather, one cannot be less!

It is believed further that whatever one attains is good for Man. In so far as I remain at all times a man—or, like Schiller, a Swabian; like Kant, a Prussian; like Gustavus Adolphus, a near-sighted person—I certainly become by my superior qualities a notable man, Swabian, Prussian, or near-sighted person. But the case is not much better with that than with Frederick the Great's cane, which became famous for Frederick's sake.

To "Give God the glory" corresponds the modern "Give Man the glory." But I mean to keep it for myself.

Criticism, issuing the summons to man to be "human,"

126. (*"einziger"*)

enunciates the necessary condition of sociability; for only as a man among men is one *companionable.* Herewith it makes known its *social* object, the establishment of "human society."

Among social theories criticism is indisputably the most complete, because it removes and deprives of value everything that *separates* man from man: all prerogatives, down to the prerogative of faith. In it the love-principle of Christianity, the true social principle, comes to the purest fulfilment, and the last possible experiment is tried to take away exclusiveness and repulsion from men: a fight against egoism in its simplest and therefore hardest form, in the form of singleness,[127] exclusiveness, itself.

"How can you live a truly social life so long as even one exclusiveness still exists between you?"

I ask conversely, How can you be truly single so long as even one connection still exists between you? If you are connected, you cannot leave each other; if a "tie" clasps you, you are something only *with another,* and twelve of you make a dozen, thousands of you a people, millions of you humanity.

"Only when you are human can you keep company with each other as men, just as you can understand each other as patriots only when you are patriotic!"

All right; then I answer, Only when you are single can you have intercourse with each other as what you are.

It is precisely the keenest critic who is hit hardest by the curse of his principle. Putting from him one exclusive thing after another, shaking off churchliness, patriotism, etc., he undoes one tie after another and separates himself from the churchly man, from the patriot, till at last, when all ties are undone, he stands— alone. He, of all men, must exclude all that have anything exclusive or private; and, when you get to the bottom, what can be more exclusive than the exclusive, single person himself!

Or does he perhaps think that the situation would be better if *all* became "man" and gave up exclusiveness? Why, for the very reason that "all" means "every individual" the most glaring contradiction is still maintained, for the "individual" is exclusive-

127. (*Einzigkeit*)

ness itself. If the humane liberal no longer concedes to the individual anything private or exclusive, any private thought, any private folly; if he criticizes everything away from him before his face, since his hatred of the private is an absolute and fanatical hatred; if he knows no tolerance toward what is private, because everything private is *unhuman*—yet he cannot criticize away the private person himself, since the hardness of the individual person resists his criticism, and he must be satisfied with declaring this person a "private person" and really leaving everything private to him again.

What will the society that no longer cares about anything private do? Make the private impossible? No, but "subordinate it to the interests of society, and, e.g., leave it to private will to institute holidays as many as it chooses, if only it does not come in collision with the general interest."[128] Everything private is *left free;* i.e., it has no interest for society.

"By their raising barriers against science the church and religiousness have declared that they are what they always were, only that this was hidden under another semblance when they were proclaimed to be the basis and necessary foundation of the State—a matter of purely private concern. Even when they were connected with the State and made it Christian, they were only the proof that the State had not yet developed its general political idea, that it was only instituting private rights—they were only the highest expression for the fact that the State was a private affair and had to do only with private affairs. When the State shall at last have the courage and strength to fulfil its general destiny and to be free; when, therefore, it is also able

128. Bruno Bauer, *Judenfrage*, p. 66. [Bruno Bauer's *Die Judenfrage*, published in Brunswick in 1843. It was the object of a vigorous controversy, Bauer arguing in part that the Jews did not deserve civil and political rights by the withdrawal of barriers of exclusion on the grounds that they did not abandon their group exclusiveness. This was partially carried on again in the pages of the *Deutsch-französische Jahrbucher*, by Bauer, and Karl Marx, who, along with Arnold Ruge (1803-1880), edited this journal in Paris in 1844. Ruge and Marx proved to be awkward associates, and soon parted company, and this journal had a short-lived existence. Ruge, an editor and author of some stature then and later, discussed this episode in his *Zwei Jahre in Paris* (2 vols. Leipzig, 1846).]

to give separate interests and private concerns their true position—
then religion and the church will be free as they have never been
hitherto. As a matter of the most purely private concern, and a
satisfaction of purely personal want, they will be left to themselves;
and every individual, every congregation and ecclesiastical communion, will be able to care for the blessedness of their souls
as they choose and as they think necessary. Every one will care
for his soul's blessedness so far as it is to him a personal want,
and will accept and pay as spiritual caretaker the one who seems
to him to offer the best guarantee for the satisfaction of his
want. Science is at last left entirely out of the game."[129]

What is to happen, though? Is social life to have an end,
and all companionableness, all fraternization, everything that is
created by the love or society principle, to disappear?

As if one will not always seek the other because he *needs*
him; as if one must accommodate himself to the other when he
needs him. But the difference is this, that then the individual
really *unites* with the individual, while formerly they were *bound
together* by a tie; son and father are bound together before majority, after it they can come together independently; before it
they *belonged* together as members of the family, after it they unite
as egoists; sonship and fatherhood remain, but son and father
no longer pin themselves down to these.

The last privilege, in truth, is "Man"; with it all are privileged
or invested. For, as Bruno Bauer himself says, "privilege remains
even when it is extended to all."[130]

Thus liberalism runs its course in the following transformations: "First, the individual *is* not man, therefore his individual
personality is of no account: no personal will, no arbitrariness,
no orders or mandates!

"Second, the individual *has* nothing human, therefore no
mine and thine, or property, is valid.

"Third, as the individual neither is man nor has anything

129. Bruno Bauer, *Die gute Sache der Freiheit,* pp. 62-63. [Bauer's
Die gute Sache der Freiheit und meine eigene Angelegenheit was published
in Zurich and Winterthur in 1842, probably as a precaution against running
into Saxon or Prussian press censorship obstacles.]
130. Bruno Bauer, *Judenfrage,* p. 60.

human, he shall not exist at all: he shall, as an egoist with his
egoistic belongings, be annihilated by criticism to make room
for Man, 'Man, just discovered.' "

But, although the individual is not Man, Man is yet present
in the individual, and, like every spook and everything divine,
has its existence in him. Hence political liberalism awards to
the individual everything that pertains to him as "a man by birth,"
as a born man, among which there are counted liberty of conscience, the possession of goods—in short, the "rights of man";
Socialism grants to the individual what pertains to him as an
active man, as a "laboring"man; finally, humane liberalism gives
the individual what he has as "a man," that is, everything that
belongs to humanity. Accordingly the single one[131] has nothing
at all, humanity everything; and the necessity of the "regeneration"
preached in Christianity is demanded unambiguously and in the
completest measure. Become a new creature, become "man!"

One might even think himself reminded of the close of the
Lord's Prayer. To Man belongs the *lordship* (the "power" or
dynamis); therefore no individual may be lord, but Man is the
lord of individuals;—Man's is the *kingdom,* the world, consequently the individual is not to be proprietor, but Man, "all,"
command the world as property—to Man is due renown, *glorification* or "glory" (*doxa*) from all, for Man or humanity is the
individual's end, for which he labors, thinks, lives, and for whose
glorification he must become "man."

Hitherto men have always striven to find out a fellowship
in which their inequalities in other respects should become "non-
essential"; they strove for equalization, consequently for *equality,*
and wanted to come all under one hat, which means nothing less
than that they were seeking for one lord, one tie, one faith (" 'Tis
in one God we all believe"). There cannot be for men anything
more fellowly or more equal than Man himself, and in this
fellowship the love-craving has found its contentment: it did not
rest till it had brought on this last equalization, leveled all inequality, laid man on the breast of man. But under this very
fellowship decay and ruin become most glaring. In a more limited

131. (*Einzige*)

fellowship the Frenchman still stood against the German, the Christian against the Mohammedan, and so on. Now, on the contrary, *man* stands against *men,* or, as men are not man, man stands against the un-man.

The sentence "God has become man" is now followed by the other, "Man has become I." This is *the human I.* But we invert it and say: I was not able to find myself so long as I sought myself as Man. But, now that it appears that Man is aspiring to become I and to gain a corporeity in me, I note that, after all, everything depends on me, and Man is lost without me. But I do not care to give myself up to be the shrine of this most holy thing, and shall not ask henceforward whether I am man or un-man in what I set about; let this *spirit* keep off my neck!

Humane liberalism goes to work radically. If you want to be or have anything especial even in one point, if you want to retain for yourself even one prerogative above others, to claim even one right that is not a "general right of man," you are an egoist.

Very good! I do not want to have or be anything especial above others, I do not want to claim any prerogative against them, but—I do not measure myself by others either, and do not want to have any *right* whatever. I want to be all and have all that I can be and have. Whether others are and have anything *similar,* what do I care? The equal, the same, they can neither be nor have. I cause no *detriment* to them, as I cause no detriment to the rock by being "ahead of it" in having motion. If they could have it, they would have it.

To cause other men no *detriment* is the point of the demand to possess no prerogative; to renounce all "being ahead," the strictest theory of *renunciation.* One is not to count himself as "anything especial," such as for example a Jew or a Christian. Well, I do not count myself as anything especial, but as unique.[132] Doubtless I have *similarity* with others; yet that holds good only for comparison or reflection; in fact I am incomparable, unique. My flesh is not their flesh, my mind is not their mind. If you bring them under the generalities "flesh, mind," those are your

132. (*einzig*)

thoughts, which have nothing to do with *my* flesh, *my* mind, and can least of all issue a "call" to mine.

I do not want to recognize or respect in you any thing, neither the proprietor nor the ragamuffin, nor even the man, but to *use you.* In salt I find that it makes food palatable to me, therefore I dissolve it; in the fish I recognize an aliment, therefore I eat it; in you I discover the gift of making my life agreeable, therefore I choose you as a companion. Or, in salt I study crystallization, in the fish animality, in you men, etc. But to me you are only what you are for me—to wit, my object; and, because *my* object, therefore my property.

In humane liberalism ragamuffinhood is completed. We must first come down to the most ragamuffin-like, most poverty-stricken condition if we want to arrive at *owness,* for we must strip off everything alien. But nothing seems more ragamuffin-like than naked—Man.

It is more than ragamuffinhood, however, when I throw away Man too because I feel that he too is alien to me and that I can make no pretensions on that basis. This is no longer mere ragamuffinhood: because even the last rag has fallen off, here stands real nakedness, denudation of everything alien. The ragamuffin has stripped off ragamuffinhood itself, and therewith has ceased to be what he was, a ragamuffin.

I am no longer a ragamuffin, but have been one.

Up to this time the discord could not come to an outbreak, because properly there is current only a contention of modern liberals with antiquated liberals, a contention of those who understand "freedom" in a small measure and those who want the "full measure" of freedom; of the *moderate* and *measureless,* therefore. Everything turns on the question, *how free* must *man* be? That man must be free, in this all believe; therefore all are liberal too. But the un-man[133] who is somewhere in every indi-

133. (It should be remembered that to be an *Unmensch* (un-man) one must be a man. The word means an inhuman or unhuman man, a man who is not man. A tiger, an avalanche, a drought, a cabbage, is not an un-man.)

vidual, how is he blocked? How can it be arranged not to leave
the un-man free at the same time with man?

Liberalism as a whole has a deadly enemy, an invincible
opposite, as God has the devil: by the side of man stands always
the un-man, the individual, the egoist. State, society, humanity,
do not master this devil.

Humane liberalism has undertaken the task of showing the
other liberals that they still do not want "freedom."

If the other liberals had before their eyes only isolated
egoism and were for the most part blind, radical liberalism has
against it egoism "in mass," throws among the masses all who
do not make the cause of freedom their own as it does, so that
now man and un-man rigorously separated, stand over against
each other as enemies, to wit, the "masses" and "criticism";[134]
namely, "free, human criticism," as it is called (*Judenfrage*, p.
114), in opposition to crude, that is, religious criticism.

Criticism expresses the hope that it will be victorious over
all the masses and "give them a general certificate of insolvency."[135]
So it means finally to make itself out in the right, and to represent all contention of the "faint-hearted and timorous" as an
egoistic *stubbornness*,[136] as pettiness, paltriness. All wrangling
loses significance, and petty dissensions are given up, because
in criticism a common enemy enters the field. "You are egoists
altogether, one no better than another!" Now the egoists stand
together against criticism.

Really the egoists? No, they fight against criticism precisely
because it accuses them of egoism; they do not plead guilty of
egoism. Accordingly criticism and the masses stand on the same
basis: both fight against egoism, both repudiate it for themselves
and charge it to each other.

Criticism and the masses pursue the same goal, freedom from
egoism, and wrangle only over which of them approaches nearest
to the goal or even attains it.

The Jews, the Christians, the absolutists, the men of dark-

134. *Lit. Ztg.*, V, 23; as comment, V, 12 ff.
135. *Lit. Ztg·*, V, 15.
136. (*Rechthaberei*, literally the character of always insisting on
making one's self out to be in the right.)

ness and men of light, politicians, Communists—all, in short—hold
the reproach of egoism far from them; and, as criticism brings
against them this reproach in plain terms and in the most extended sense, all *justify* themselves against the accusation of
egoism, and combat—egoism, the same enemy with whom criticism wages war.

Both, criticism and masses, are enemies of egoists, and
both seek to liberate themselves from egoism, as well by clearing
or whitewashing *themselves* as by ascribing it to the opposite party.

The critic is the true "spokesman of the masses" who gives
them the "simple concept and the phrase" of egoism, while
the spokesmen to whom the triumph is denied were only
bunglers.[137] He is their prince and general in the war against
egoism for freedom; what he fights against they fight against.
But at the same time he is their enemy too, only not the enemy
before them, but the friendly enemy who wields the knout behind
the timorous to force courage into them.

Hereby the opposition of criticism and the masses is reduced to the following contradiction: "You are egoists!" "No,
we are not!" "I will prove it to you!" "You shall have our justification!"

Let us then take both for what they give themselves out for,
non-egoists, and what they take each other for, egoists. They are
egoists and are not.

Properly criticism says: You must liberate your ego from
all limitedness so entirely that it becomes a *human* ego. I say:
Liberate yourself as far as you can, and you have done your part;
for it is not given to every one to break through all limits, or,
more expressively: not to every one is that a limit which is a
limit for the rest. Consequently, do not tire yourself with toiling
at the limits of others; enough if you tear down yours. Who
has ever succeeded in tearing down even one limit *for all men?*
Are not countless persons to-day, as at all times, running about
with all the "limitations of humanity?" He who overturns one
of *his* limits may have shown others the way and the means; the
overturning of *their* limits remains their affair. Nobody does

137. *Lit. Ztg.*, V, 24.

anything else either. To demand of people that they become wholly men is to call on them to cast down all human limits. That is impossible, because *Man* has no limits. I have some indeed, but then it is only *mine* that concern me any, and only they can be overcome by me. A human ego I cannot become, just because I am I and not merely man.

Yet let us still see whether criticism has not taught us something that we can lay to heart! I am not free if I am not without interests, not man if I am not disinterested? Well, even if it makes little difference to me to be free or man, yet I do not want to leave unused any occasion to realize *myself* or make myself count. Criticism offers me this occasion by the teaching that, if anything plants itself firmly in me, and becomes indissoluble, I become its prisoner and servant, a possessed man. An interest, be it for what it may, has kidnapped a slave in me if I cannot get away from it, and is no longer my property, but I am its. Let us therefore accept criticism's lesson to let no part of our property become stable, and to feel comfortable only in— *dissolving* it.

So, if criticism says: You are man only when you are restlessly criticizing and dissolving! then we say: Man I am without that, and I am I likewise; therefore I want only to be careful to secure my property to myself; and, in order to secure it, I continually take it back into myself, annihilate in it every movement toward independence, and swallow it before it can fix itself and become a "fixed idea" or a "mania."

But I do that not for the sake of my "human calling," but because I call myself to it. I do not strut about dissolving everything that it is possible for a man to dissolve, and, for example, while not yet ten years old I do not criticize the nonsense of the Commandments, but I am man all the same, and act humanly in just this—that I still leave them uncriticized. In short, I have no calling, and follow none, not even that to be a man.

Do I now reject what liberalism has won in its various exertions? Far be the day that anything won should be lost! Only, after "Man" has become free through liberalism, I turn my gaze back upon myself and confess to myself openly: What Man seems to have gained, *I* alone have gained.

Man is free when "Man is to man the supreme being." So it belongs to the completion of liberalism that every other supreme being be annulled, theology overturned by anthropology, God and his grace laughed down, "atheism" universal.

The egoism of property has given up the last that it had to give when even the "My God" has become senseless; for God exists only when he has at heart the individual's welfare, as the latter seeks his welfare in him.

Political liberalism abolished the inequality of masters and servants: it made people masterless, anarchic. The master was now removed from the individual, the "egoist," to become a ghost—the law or the State. Social liberalism abolishes the inequality of possession, of the poor and rich, and makes people *possessionless* or propertyless. Property is withdrawn from the individual and surrendered to ghostly society. Humane liberalism makes people *godless,* atheistic. Therefore the individual's God, "My God," must be put an end to. Now masterlessness is indeed at the same time freedom from service, possessionlessness at the same time freedom from care, and godlessness at the same time freedom from prejudice: for with the master the servant falls away; with possession, the care about it; with the firmly-rooted God, prejudice. But, since the master rises again as State, the servant appears again as subject; since possession becomes the property of society, care is begotten anew as labor; and, since God as Man becomes a prejudice, there arises a new faith, faith in humanity or liberty. For the individual's God the God of all, to wit, "Man," is now exalted; "for it is the highest thing in us all to be man." But, as nobody can become entirely what the idea "man" imports, Man remains to the individual a lofty other world, an unattained supreme being, a God. But at the same time this is the "true God," because he is fully adequate to us—to wit, our own *"self";* we ourselves, but separated from us and lifted above us.

———————

POSTSCRIPT

THE foregoing review of "free human criticism" was written by bits immediately after the appearance of the books in question, as was also that which elsewhere refers to writings of this tendency, and I did little more than bring together the fragments. But criticism is restlessly pressing forward, and thereby makes it necessary for me to come back to it once more, now that my book is finished, and insert this concluding note.

I have before me the latest (eighth) number of the *Allgemeine Literatur-Zeitung* of Bruno Bauer.

There again "the general interests of society" stand at the top. But criticism has reflected, and given this "society" a specification by which it is discriminated from a form which previously had still been confused with it: the "State," in former passages still celebrated as "free State," is quite given up because it can in no wise fulfill the task of "human society." Criticism only "saw itself compelled to identify for a moment human and political affairs" in 1842; but now it has found that the State, even as "free State," is not human society, or, as it could likewise say, that the people is not "man." We saw how it got through with theology and showed clearly that God sinks into dust before Man; we see it now come to a clearance with politics in the same way, and show that before Man peoples and nationalities fall: so we see how it has its explanation with Church and State, declaring them both unhuman, and we shall see—for it betrays this to us already—how it can also give proof that before Man the "masses," which it even calls a "spiritual being," appear worthless. And how should the lesser "spiritual beings" be able to maintain themselves before the supreme spirit? "Man" casts down the false idols.

So what the critic has in view for the present is the scrutiny of the "masses," which he will place before "Man" in order to combat them from the standpoint of Man. "What is now the object of criticism?" "The masses, a spiritual being!" These the critic will "learn to know," and will find that they are in contradiction with Man; he will demonstrate that they are unhuman, and will succeed just as well in this demonstration as in the former ones, that the divine and the national, or the concerns of Church and of State, were the unhuman.

The masses are defined as "the most significant product of the Revolution, as the deceived multitude which the illusions of political Illumination, and in general the entire Illumination movement of the eighteenth century, have given over to boundless disgruntlement." The Revolution satisfied some by its result, and left others unsatisfied; the satisfied part is the commonalty (*bourgeoisie*, etc.), the unsatisfied is the—masses. Does not the critic, so placed, himself belong to the "masses"?

But the unsatisfied are still in great mistiness, and their discontent utters itself only in a "boundless disgruntlement." This the likewise unsatisfied critic now wants to master: he cannot want and attain more than to bring that "spiritual being," the masses, out of its disgruntlement, and to "uplift" those who were only disgruntled, to give them the right attitude toward those results of the Revolution which are to be overcome;—he can become the head of the masses, their decided spokesman. Therefore he wants also to "abolish the deep chasm which parts him from the multitude." From those who want to "uplift the lower classes of the people" he is distinguished by wanting to deliver from "disgruntlement," not merely these, but himself too.

But assuredly his consciousness does not deceive him either, when he takes the masses to be the "natural opponents of theory," and forsees that, "the more this theory shall develop itself, so much the more will it make the masses compact." For the critic cannot enlighten or satisfy the masses with his *presupposition,* Man. If over against the commonalty they are only the "lower classes of the people," politically insignificant masses, over against "Man" they must still more be mere "masses," humanly insignificant—yes, unhuman—masses, or a multitude of un-men.

The critic clears away everything human; and, starting from the presupposition that the human is the true, he works against himself, denying it wherever it had been hitherto found. He proves only that the human is to be found nowhere except in his head, but the unhuman everywhere. The unhuman is the real, the extant on all hands, and by the proof that it is "not human" the critic only enunciates plainly the tautological sentence that it is the unhuman.

But what if the unhuman, turning its back on itself with resolute heart, should at the same time turn away from the disturbing critic and leave him standing, untouched and unstung by his remonstrance? "You call me the unhuman," it might say to him, "and so I really am—for you; but I am so only because you bring me into opposition to the human, and I could despise myself only so long as I let myself be hypnotized into this opposition. I was contemptible because I sought my 'better self' outside me; I was the unhuman because I dreamed of the 'human'; I resembled the pious who hunger for their 'true self' and always remain 'poor sinners'; I thought of myself only in comparison to another; enough, I was not all in all, was not—*unique*.[138] But now I cease to appear to myself as the unhuman, cease to measure myself and let myself be measured by man, cease to recognize anything above me: consequently—adieu, humane critic! I only have been the unhuman, am it now no longer, but am the unique, yes, to your loathing, the egoistic; yet not the egoistic as it lets itself be measured by the human, humane, and unselfish, but the egoistic as the—unique."

We have to pay attention to still another sentence of the same number. "Criticism sets up no dogmas, and wants to learn to know nothing but *things*."

The critic is afraid of becoming "dogmatic" or setting up dogmas. Of course: why, thereby he would become the opposite of the critic—the dogmatist; he would now become bad, as he is good as critic, or would become from an unselfish man an egoist. "Of all things, no dogma!" This is his—dogma. For the critic remains on one and the same ground with the dogmatist —that of *thoughts*. Like the latter he always starts from a thought, but varies in this, that he never ceases to keep the principle-thought in the *process of thinking*, and so does not let it become stable. He only asserts the thought-process against the thought-faith, the progress of thinking against stationariness in it.

138. (*einzig*)

From criticism no thought is safe, since criticism is thought or the thinking mind itself.

Therefore I repeat that the religious world—and this is the world of thought—reaches its completion in criticism, where thinking extends its encroachments over every thought, no one of which may "egoistically" establish itself. Where would the "purity of criticism," the purity of thinking, be left if even one thought escaped the process of thinking? This explains the fact that the critic has even begun already to gibe gently here and there at the thought of Man, of humanity and humaneness, because he suspects that here a thought is approaching dogmatic fixity. But yet he cannot decompose this thought till he has found a— "higher" in which it dissolves; for he moves only—in thoughts. This higher thought might be enunciated as that of the movement or process of thinking itself. as the thought of thinking or of criticism, for example.

Freedom of thinking has in fact become complete hereby, freedom of mind celebrates its triumph: for the individual, "egoistic" thoughts have lost their dogmatic truculence. There is nothing left but the—dogma of free thinking or of criticism.

Against everything that belongs to the world of thought, criticism is in the right, that is, in might: it is the victor. Criticism, and criticism alone, is "up to date." From the standpoint of thought there is no power capable of being an overmatch for criticism's, and it is a pleasure to see how easily and sportively this dragon swallows all other serpents of thought. Each serpent twists, to be sure, but criticism crushes it in all its "turns."

I am no opponent of criticism. I am no dogmatist, and do not feel myself touched by the critic's tooth with which he tears the dogmatist to pieces. If I were a "dogmatist," I should place at the head a dogma, a thought, an idea, a principle, and should complete this as a "systematist," spinning it out to a system, a structure of thought. Conversely, if I were a critic, an opponent of the dogmatist, I should carry on the fight of free thinking against the enthralling thought, I should defend thinking against what was thought. But I am neither the champion of a thought nor the champion of thinking; for "I," from whom I start, am not a thought, nor do I consist in thinking. Against

me, the unnameable, the realm of thoughts, thinking, and mind
is shattered.

Criticism is the possessed man's fight against possession as
such, against all possession: a fight which is founded in the
consciousness that everywhere possession, or, as the critic calls
it, a religious and theological attitude, is extant. He knows that
people stand in a religious or believing attitude not only toward
God, but toward other ideas as well, like right, the State, law;
he recognizes possession in all places. So he wants to break up
thoughts by thinking; but I say, only thoughtlessness really saves
me from thoughts. It is not thinking, but my thoughtlessness,
or I the unthinkable, incomprehensible, that frees me from
possession.

A jerk does me the service of the most anxious thinking,
a stretching of the limbs shakes off the torment of thoughts, a
leap upward hurls from my breast the nightmare of the religious
world, a jubilant Hoopla throws off year-long burdens. But the
monstrous significance of unthinking jubilation could not be
recognized in the long night of thinking and believing.

"What clumsiness and frivolity, to want to solve the most
difficult problems, acquit yourself of the most comprehensive
tasks, by a *breaking off*!"

But have you tasks if you do not set them to yourself? So
long as you set them, you will not give them up, and I certainly
do not care if you think, and, thinking, create a thousand thoughts.
But you who have set the tasks, are you not to be able to upset
them again? Must you be bound to these tasks, and must they
become absolute tasks?

To cite only one thing, the government has been disparaged
on account of its resorting to forcible means against thoughts,
interfering against the press by means of the police power of the
censorship, and making a personal fight out of a literary one.
As if it were solely a matter of thoughts, and as if one's attitude
toward thoughts must be unselfish, self-denying, and self-sacrificing! Do not those thoughts attack the governing parties themselves, and so call out egoism? And do the thinkers not set
before the attacked ones the *religious* demand to reverence the
power of thought, of ideas? They are to succumb voluntarily

and resignedly, because the divine power of thought, Minerva, fights on their enemies' side. Why, that would be an act of possession, a religious sacrifice. To be sure, the governing parties are themselves held fast in a religious bias, and follow the leading power of an idea or a faith; but they are at the same time unconfessed egoists, and right here, against the enemy, their pent-up egoism breaks loose: possessed in their faith, they are at the same time unpossessed by their opponents' faith; they are egoists toward this. If one wants to make them a reproach, it could only be the converse—to wit, that they are possessed by their ideas.

Against thoughts no egoistic power is to appear, no police power and the like. So the believers in thinking believe. But thinking and its thoughts are not sacred to *me, an*d I defend *my skin* against them as against other things. That may be an unreasonable defense; but, if I am in duty bound to reason, then I, like Abraham, must sacrifice my dearest to it!

In the kingdom of thought, which, like that of faith, is the kingdom of heaven, every one is assuredly wrong who uses *unthinking* force, just as every one is wrong who in the kingdom of love behaves unlovingly, or, although he is a Christian and therefore lives in the kingdom of love, yet acts un-Christianly; in these kingdoms, to which he supposes himself to belong though he nevertheless throws off their laws, he is a "sinner" or "egoist." But it is only when he he becomes a *criminal* against these kingdoms that he can throw off their dominion.

Here too the result is this, that the fight of the thinkers against the government is indeed in the right, namely, in might— so far as it is carried on against the government's thoughts (the government is dumb, and does not succeed in making any literary rejoinder to speak of), but is, on the other hand, in the wrong, to wit, in impotence, so far as it does not succeed in bringing into the field anything but thoughts against a personal power (the egoistic power stops the mouths of the thinkers). The theoretical fight cannot complete the victory, and the sacred power of thought succumbs to the might of egoism. Only the egoistic fight, the fight of egoists on both sides, clears up everything.

This last now, to make thinking an affair of egoistic option, an affair of the single person,[139] a mere pastime or hobby as it were, and to take from it the importance of "being the last decisive power"; this degradation and desecration of thinking; this equalization of the unthinking and thoughtful ego; this clumsy but real "equality"—criticism is not able to produce, because it itself is only the priest of thinking, and sees nothing beyond thinking but —the deluge.

Criticism does indeed affirm, that free criticism may overcome the State, but at the same time it defends itself against the reproach which is laid upon it by the State government, that it is "self-will and impudence"; it thinks, then, that "self-will and impudence" may not overcome, it alone may. The truth is rather the reverse: the State can be really overcome only by impudent self-will.

It may now, to conclude with this, be clear that in the critic's new change of front he has not transformed himself, but only "made good an oversight," "disentangled a subject," and is saying too much when he speaks of "criticism criticizing itself"; it, or rather he, has only criticized its "oversight" and cleared it of its "inconsistencies." If he wanted to criticize criticism, he would have to look and see if there was anything in its presupposition.

I on my part start from a presupposition in presupposing *myself*; but my presupposition does not struggle for its perfection like "Man struggling for his perfection," but only serves me to enjoy it and consume it. I consume my presupposition, and nothing else, and exist only in consuming it. But that presupposition is therefore not a presupposition at all: for, as I am the Unique, I know nothing of the duality of a presupposing and a presupposed ego (an "incomplete" and a "complete" ego or man); but this, that I consume myself, means only that I am. I do not presuppose myself, because I am every moment just positing or creating myself, and am I only by being not presupposed but posited, and, again, posited only in the moment when I posit myself; that is, I am creator and creature in one.

If the presuppositions that have hitherto been current are to melt away in a full dissolution, they must not be dissolved

139. (*des Einzigen*)

into a higher presupposition again—a thought, or thinking itself, criticism. For that dissolution is to be for *my* good; otherwise it would belong only in the series of the innumerable dissolutions which, in favor of others (as this very Man, God, the State, pure morality, etc.), declared old truths to be untruths and did away with long-fostered presuppositions.

PART SECOND

I

At the entrance of the modern time stands the "God-man." At its exit will only the God in the God-man evaporate? And can the God-man really die if only the God in him dies? They did not think of this question, and thought they were through when in our days they brought to a victorious end the work of the Illumination, the vanquishing of God: they did not notice that Man has killed God in order to become now—"*sole God on high.*" The *other world outside us* is indeed brushed away, and the great undertaking of the Illuminators completed; but the *other world in us* has become a new heaven and calls us forth to renewed heaven-storming: God has had to give place, yet not to us, but to—Man. How can you believe that the God-man is dead before the Man in him, besides the God, is dead?

III

Ownness[1]

"DOES not the spirit thirst for freedom?"—Alas, not my spirit alone, my body too thirsts for it hourly! When before the odorous castle-kitchen my nose tells my palate of the savory dishes that are being prepared therein, it feels a fearful pining at its dry bread; when my eyes tell the hardened back about soft down on which one may lie more delightfully than on its compressed straw, a suppressed rage seizes it; when—but let us not follow the pains further.—And you call that a longing for freedom? What do you want to become free from, then? From your hardtack and your straw bed? Then throw them away!—But that seems not to serve you: you want rather to have the freedom to enjoy delicious foods and downy beds. Are men to give you this "freedom"—are they to permit it to you? You do not hope that from their philanthropy, because you know they all think like—you: each is the nearest to himself! How, therefore, do you mean to come to the enjoyment of those foods and beds? Evidently not otherwise than in making them your property!

If you think it over rightly, you do not want the freedom to have all these fine things, for with this freedom you still do not have them; you want really to have them, to call them *yours* and possess them as *your property*. Of what use is a freedom

1. (This is a literal translation of the German word *Eigenheit*, which, with its primitive *eigen*, "own," is used in this chapter in a way that the German dictionaries do not quite recognize. The author's conception being new, he had to make an innovation in the German language to express it. The translator is under the like necessity. In most passages "self-ownership," or else "personality," would translate the word, but there are some where the thought is so *eigen*, that is, so peculiar or so thoroughly the author's *own*, that no English word I can think of would express it. It will explain itself to one who has read Party First intelligently.)

to you, indeed, if it brings in nothing? And, if you became free from everything, you would no longer have anything; for freedom is empty of substance. Whoso knows not how to make use of it, for him it has no value, this useless permission; but how I make use of it depends on my personality.[2]

I have no objection to freedom, but I wish more than freedom for you: you should not merely *be rid* of what you do not want; you should not only be a "freeman," you should be an "owner" too.

Free—from what? Oh! what is there that cannot be shaken off? The yoke of serfdom, of sovereignty, of aristocracy and princes, the dominion of the desires and passions; yes, even the dominion of one's own will, of self-will, for the completest self-denial is nothing but freedom—freedom, to wit, from self-determination, from one's own self. And the craving for freedom as for something absolute, worthy of every praise, deprived us of ownness: it created self-denial. However, the freer I become, the more compulsion piles up before my eyes; and the more impotent I feel myself. The unfree son of the wilderness does not yet feel anything of all the limits that crowd a civilized man: he seems to himself freer than this latter. In the measure that I conquer freedom for myself I create for myself new bounds and new tasks: if I have invented railroads, I feel myself weak again because I cannot yet sail through the skies like the bird;[3] and, if I have solved a problem whose obscurity disturbed my mind, at once there await me innumerable others, whose perplexities impede my progress, dim my free gaze, make the limits of my *freedom* painfully sensible to me. "Now that you have become free from sin, you have become servants of righteousness."[4] Republicans in their broad freedom, do they not become servants of the law? How true Christian hearts at all times longed to "become free," how they pined to see themselves delivered from

2. (*Eigenheit*)
3. [Even the achievement of flight through space has not dimmed Stirner's point; contemporary physicists and astronomers describe with anguish the staggering difficulties in the way of reaching even the nearest star.]
4. Rom. 6. 18.

the "bonds of this earth-life"! They looked out toward the land of freedom. ("The Jerusalem that is above is the freewoman; she is the mother of us all." Gal. 4. 26.)

Being free from anything—means only being clear or rid. "He is free from headache" is equal to "he is rid of it." "He is free from this prejudice" is equal to "he has never conceived it" or "he has got rid of it." In "less" we complete the freedom recommended by Christianity, in sinless, godless, moralityless, etc.

Freedom is the doctrine of Christianity. "Ye, dear brethren, are called to freedom."[5] "So speak and so do, as those who are to be judged by the law of freedom."[6]

Must we then, because freedom betrays itself as a Christian ideal, give it up? No, nothing is to be lost, freedom no more than the rest; but it is to become our own, and in the form of freedom it cannot.

What a difference between freedom and ownness! One can get *rid* of a great many things, one yet does not get rid of all; one becomes free from much, not from everything. Inwardly one may be free in spite of the condition of slavery, although, too, it is again only from all sorts of things, not from everything; but from the whip, the domineering temper, of the master, one does not as slave become *free*. "Freedom lives only in the realm of dreams!" Ownness, on the contrary, is my whole being and existence, it is I myself. I am free from what I am *rid* of, owner of what I have in my *power* or what I *control*. *My own* I am at all times and under all circumstances, if I know how to have myself and do not throw myself away on others. To be free is something that I cannot truly *will*, because I cannot make it, cannot create it: I can only wish it and—aspire toward it, for it remains an ideal, a spook. The fetters of reality cut the sharpest welts in my flesh every moment. But *my own* I remain. Given up as serf to a master, I think only of myself and my advantage; his blows strike me indeed, I am not *free* from them; but I endure them only for *my benefit*, perhaps in order to deceive him and make him secure by the semblance of patience, or,

5. 1 Pet. 2. 16.
6. James 2. 12.

again, not to draw worse upon myself by contumacy. But, as I keep my eye on myself and my selfishness, I take by the forelock the first good opportunity to trample the slaveholder into the dust. That I then become *free* from him and his whip is only the consequence of my antecedent egoism. Here one perhaps says I was "free" even in the condition of slavery—to wit, "intrinsically" or "inwardly." But "intrinsically free" is not "really free," and "inwardly" is not "outwardly." I was own, on the other hand, my own, altogether, inwardly and outwardly. Under the dominion of a cruel master my body is not "free" from torments and lashes; but it is *my* bones that moan under the torture, *my* fibres that quiver under the blows, and *I* moan because *my* body moans. That *I* sigh and shiver proves that I have not yet lost *myself*, that I am still my own. My leg is not "free" from the master's stick, but it is *my* leg and is inseparable. Let him tear it off me and look and see if he still has my leg! He retains in his hand nothing but the—corpse of my leg, which is as little my leg as a dead dog is still a dog: a dog has a pulsating heart, a so-called dead dog has none and is therefore no longer a dog.

If one opines that a slave may yet be inwardly free, he says in fact only the most indisputable and trivial thing. For who is going to assert that any man is *wholly* without freedom? If I am an eye-servant, can I therefore not be free from innumerable things, from faith in Zeus, from the desire for fame, and the like? Why then should not a whipped slave also be able to be inwardly free from un-Christian sentiments, from hatred of his enemy, etc.? He then has "Christian freedom," is rid of the un-Christian; but has he absolute freedom, freedom from everything, as from the Christian delusion, or from bodily pain?

In the meantime, all this seems to be said more against names than against the thing. But is the name indifferent, and has not a word, a shibboleth, always inspired and—fooled men? Yet between freedom and ownness there lies still a deeper chasm than the mere difference of the words.

All the world desires freedom, all long for its reign to come. Oh, enchantingly beautiful dream of a blooming "reign of freedom," a "free human race"!—who has not dreamed it? So men shall become free, entirely free, free from all constraint! From all contraint, really from all? Are they never to put constraint on themselves any more? "Oh yes, that, of course; don't you see, that is no constraint at all?" Well, then at any rate they are to become free from religious faith, from the strict duties of morality, from the inexorability of the law, from—"What a fearful misunderstanding!" Well, *what* are they to be free from then, and what not?

The lovely dream is dissipated; awakened, one rubs his half-opened eyes and stares at the prosaic questioner. "What men are to be free from?"—From blind credulity, cries one. What's that? exclaims another, all faith is blind credulity; they must become free from all faith. No, no, for God's sake—inveighs the first again—do not cast all faith from you, else the power of brutality breaks in. We must have the republic—a third makes himself heard—and become—free from all commanding lords. There is no help in that, says a fourth: we only get a new lord then, a "dominant majority"; let us rather free ourselves from this dreadful inequality.—O, hapless equality, already I hear your plebeian roar again! How I had dreamed so beautifully just now of a paradise of *freedom,* and what—impudence and licentiousness now raises its wild clamor! Thus the first laments, and gets on his feet to grasp the sword against "unmeasured freedom." Soon we no longer hear anything but the clashing of the swords of the disagreeing dreamers of freedom.

What the craving for freedom has always come to has been the desire for a *particular* freedom, such as freedom of faith; the believing man wanted to be free and independent; of what? of faith perhaps? no! but of the inquisitors of faith. So now "political or civil" freedom. The citizen wants to become free not from citizenhood, but from bureaucracy, the arbitrariness of princes, and the like. Prince Metternich[7] once said he had "found

7. [Metternich (1773-1859), a minister in various capacities under Austrian emperors between the time of Napoleon and the Revolutions of 1848, was the very symbol of reaction to Stirner's Liberal contemporaries, mainly as a consequence of his grim resistance to the extension of political democracy within the Austrian Empire.]

a way that was adapted to guide men in the path of *genuine* freedom for all the future." The Count of Provence[8] ran away from France precisely at the time when she was preparing the "reign of freedom," and said: "My imprisonment had become intolerable to me; I had only one passion, the desire for *freedom;* I thought only of it."

The craving for a *particular* freedom always includes the purpose of a new *dominion,* as it was with the Revolution, which indeed "could give its defenders the uplifting feeling that they were fighting for freedom," but in truth only because they were after a particular freedom, therefore a new *dominion,* the "dominion of the law."

Freedom you all want, you want *freedom.* Why then do you higgle over a more or less? *Freedom* can only be the whole of freedom; a piece of freedom is not *freedom.* You despair of the possibility of obtaining the whole of freedom, freedom from everything—yes, you consider it insanity even to wish this?—Well, then leave off chasing after the phantom, and spend your pains on something better than the—*unattainable.*

"Ah, but there is nothing better than freedom!"

What have you then when you have freedom—for I will not speak here of your piecemeal bits of freedom—complete freedom? Then you are rid of everything that embarrasses you, everything, and there is probably nothing that does not once in your life embarrass you and cause you inconvenience. And for whose sake, then, did you want to be rid of it? Doubtless *for your* sake, because it is in *your* way! But, if something were not inconvenient to you; if, on the contrary, it were quite to your mind (such as the gently but *irresistibly commanding* look of your loved one)—then you would not want to be rid of it and free from it. Why not? For *your sake* again! So you take *yourselves* as measure and judge over all. You gladly let freedom go when unfreedom, the "sweet service of love," suits *you;* and you take up your freedom again on occasion when it begins to

8. [Brother of Louis XVI of France, who fled the country in the days after the uprising of the Paris mob which stormed the Bastille in July, 1789]

suit *you* better—that is, supposing, which is not the point here, that you are not afraid of such a Repeal of the Union for other (perhaps religious) reasons.

Why will you not take courage now to really make *yourselves* the central point and the main thing altogether? Why grasp in the air at freedom, your dream? Are you your dream? Do not begin by inquiring of your dreams, your notions, your thoughts, for that is all "hollow theory." Ask yourselves and ask after yourselves—that is *practical,* and you know you want very much to be "practical." But there the one hearkens what his God (of course what he thinks of at the name God is his God) may be going to say to it, and another what his moral feelings, his conscience, his feeling of duty, may determine about it, and a third calculates what folks will think of it—and, when each has thus asked his Lord God (folks are a Lord God just as good as, nay, even more compact than, the other-worldly and imaginary one: *vox populi, vox dei*), then he accommodates himself to his Lord's will and listens no more at all for what *he himself* would like to say and decide.

Therefore turn to yourselves rather than to your gods or idols. Bring out from yourselves what is in you, bring it to the light, bring yourselves to revelation.

How one acts only from himself, and asks after nothing further, the Christians have realized in the notion "God." He acts "as it pleases him." And foolish man, who could do just so, is to act as it "pleases God" instead.—If it is said that even God proceeds according to eternal laws, that too fits me, since I too cannot get out of my skin, but have my law in my whole nature, in myself.

But one needs only admonish you of yourselves to bring you to despair at once. "What am I?" each of you asks himself. An abyss of lawless and unregulated impulses, desires, wishes, passions, a chaos without light or guiding star! How am I to obtain a correct answer, if, without regard to God's commandments or to the duties which morality prescribes, without regard to the voice of reason, which in the course of history, after bitter experiences, has exalted the best and most reasonable thing into law, I simply appeal to myself? My passion would advise me to do the most senseless thing possible.—Thus each deems himself the—devil; for, if, so far as he is unconcerned about religion, he only deemed himself a beast, he would easily find that the beast, which does follow only *its* impulse (as it were, its advice), does not advise and impel itself to do the "most senseless" things, but takes very correct steps. But the habit of the religious way of thinking has biased our mind so grievously that we are— terrified at *ourselves* in our nakedness and naturalness; it has degraded us so that we deem ourselves depraved by nature, born devils. Of course it comes into your head at once that your calling requires you to do the "good," the moral, the right. Now, if you ask *yourselves* what is to be done, how can the right voice sound forth from you, the voice which points the way of the good, the right, the true? What concord have God and Belial?

But what would you think if one answered you by saying: "That one is to listen to God, conscience, duties, laws, and so forth, is flim-flam with which people have stuffed your head and heart and made you crazy"? And if he asked you how it is that you know so surely that the voice of nature is a seducer? And if he even demanded of you to turn the thing about and actually to deem the voice of God and conscience to be the devil's work? There are such graceless men; how will you settle them? You cannot appeal to your parsons, parents, and good men, for precisely these are designated by them as your *seducers,* as the true seducers and corrupters of youth, who busily sow broadcast the tares of self-contempt and reverence to God, who fill young hearts with mud and young heads with stupidity.

But now those people go on and ask: For whose sake do you care about God's and the other commandments? You surely do not suppose that this is done merely out of complaisance toward God? No, you are doing it—*for your sake* again.—Here too, therefore, *you* are the main thing, and each must say to himself, *I* am everything to myself and I do everything *on my account.* If it ever became clear to you that God, the command-ments, and so on, only harm you, that they reduce and ruin *you,* to a certainty you would throw them from you just as the Christians once condemned Apollo or Minerva or heathen mo-rality. They did indeed put in the place of these Christ and afterward Mary, as well as a Christian morality; but they did this for the sake of *their* souls' welfare too, therefore out of egoism or ownness.

And it was by this egoism, this ownness, that they got *rid* of the old world of gods and became *free* from it. Ownness *created* a new *freedom;* for ownness is the creator of everything, as genius (a definite ownness), which is always originality, has for a long time already been looked upon as the creator of new productions that have a place in the history of the world.

If your efforts are ever to make "freedom" the issue, then exhaust freedom's demands. Who is it that is to become free? You, I, we. Free from what? From everything that is not you, not I, not we. I, therefore, am the kernel that is to be delivered from all wrappings and—freed from all cramping shells. What is left when I have been freed from everything that is not I? Only I; nothing but I. But freedom has nothing to offer to this I himself. As to what is now to happen further after I have become free, freedom is silent—as our governments, when the prisoner's time is up, merely let him go, thrusting him out into abandonment.

Now why, if freedom is striven after for love of the I after all—why not choose the I himself as beginning, middle, and end? Am I not worth more than freedom? Is it not I that make myself free, am not I the first? Even unfree, even laid in a thousand fetters, I yet am; and I am not, like freedom, extant only in the future and in hopes, but even as the most abject of slaves I am—present.

Think that over well, and decide whether you will place on your banner the dream of "freedom" or the resolution of "egoism," of "ownness." "Freedom" awakens your *rage* against everything that is not you; "egoism" calls you to *joy* over yourselves, to self-enjoyment; "freedom" is and remains a *longing,* a romantic plaint, a Christian hope for unearthliness and futurity; "ownness" is a reality, which *of itself* removes just so much unfreedom as by barring your own way hinders you. What does not disturb you, you will not want to renounce; and, if it begins to disturb you, why, you know that "you must obey *yourselves* rather than men!"

Freedom teaches only: Get yourselves rid, relieve yourselves, of everything burdensome; it does not teach you who you yourselves are. Rid, rid! so call, get rid even of yourselves, "deny yourselves." But ownness calls you back to yourselves, it says "Come to yourself!" Under the aegis of freedom you get rid of many kinds of things, but something new pinches you again: "you are rid of the Evil One; evil is left."[9] As *own* you are *really rid of everything,* and what clings to you *you have accepted;* it is your choice and your pleasure. The *own* man is the *free-born,* the man free to begin with; the free man, on the contrary, is only the *eleutheromaniac,* the dreamer and enthusiast.

The former is *originally free,* because he recognizes nothing but himself; he does not need to free himself first, because at the start he rejects everything outside himself, because he prizes nothing more than himself, rates nothing higher, because, in short, he starts from himself and "comes to himself." Constrained by childish respect, he is nevertheless already working at "freeing" himself from this constraint. Ownness works in the little egoist, and procures him the desired—freedom.

Thousands of years of civilization have obscured to you what you are, have made you believe you are not egoists but are *called* to be idealists ("good men"). Shake that off! Do not seek for freedom, which does precisely deprive you of yourselves, in "self-denial"; but seek for *yourselves,* become egoists, become each of you an *almighty ego.* Or, more clearly: Just recognize yourselves again, just recognize what you really are, and let go your hypocritical endeavors, your foolish mania to be something else than you are. Hypocritical I call them because you have yet remained egoists all these thousands of years, but sleeping, self-deceiving, crazy egoists, you Heautontimorumenoses, you self-tormentors. Never yet has a religion been able to dispense with "promises," whether they referred us to the other world or to this ("long life," etc.); for man is *mercenary* and does nothing "gratis." But how about that "doing the good for the good's sake" without prospect of reward? As if here too the pay was not contained in the satisfaction that it is to afford.

9. (See note 84, previous chapter.)

Even religion, therefore, is founded on our egoism and—exploits it; calculated for our *desires,* it stifles many others for the sake of one. This then gives the phenomenon of *cheated* egoism, where I satisfy, not myself, but one of my desires, such as the impulse toward blessedness. Religion promises me the—"supreme good"; to gain this I no longer regard any other of my desires, and do not slake them.—All your doings are *unconfessed,* secret, covert, and concealed egoism. But because they are egoism that you are unwilling to confess to yourselves, that you keep secret from yourselves, hence not manifest and public egoism, consequently unconscious egoism—therefore they are *not egoism,* but thraldom, service, self-renunciation; you are egoists, and you are not, since you renounce egoism. Where you seem most to be such, you have drawn upon the word "egoist"—loathing and contempt.

I secure my freedom with regard to the world in the degree that I make the world my own, "gain it and take possession of it" for myself, by whatever might, by that of persuasion, of petition, of categorical demand, yes, even by hypocrisy, cheating, etc.; for the means that I use for it are determined by what I am. If I am weak, I have only weak means, like the aforesaid, which yet are good enough for a considerable part of the world. Besides, cheating, hypocrisy, lying, look worse than they are. Who has not cheated the police, the law? Who has not quickly taken on an air of honorable loyalty before the sheriff's officer who meets him, in order to conceal an illegality that may have been committed? He who has not done it has simply let violence be done to him; he was a *weakling* from—conscience. I know that my freedom is diminished even by my not being able to carry out my will on another object, be this other something without will, like a rock, or something with will, like a government, an individual; I deny my ownness when—in presence of another— I give myself up, give way, desist, submit; therefore by *loyalty, submission.* For it is one thing when I give up my previous course because it does not lead to the goal, and therefore turn out of a wrong road; it is another when I yield myself a prisoner. I get around a rock that stands in my way, till I have powder enough to blast it; I get around the laws of a people, till I have gathered strength to overthrow them. Because I cannot grasp the moon, is it therefore to be "sacred" to me, an Astarte? If I only could grasp you, I surely would, and, if I only find a means to get up to you, you shall not frighten me! You inapprehensible one, you shall remain inapprehensible to me only till I have acquired the might for apprehension and call you my *own;* I do not give myself up before you, but only bide my time. Even if for the present I put up with my inability to touch you, I yet remember it against you.

Vigorous men have always done so. When the "loyal" had exalted an unsubdued power to be their master and had adored it, when they had demanded adoration from all, then there came some such son of nature who would not loyally submit, and drove the adored power from its inaccessible Olympus. He cried his "Stand still" to the rolling sun, and made the earth go round; the loyal had to make the best of it; he laid his axe to the sacred oaks, and the "loyal" were astonished that no heavenly fire consumed him; he threw the pope off Peter's chair, and the "loyal" had no way to hinder it; he is tearing down the divine-right business, and the "loyal" croak in vain, and at last are silent.

My freedom becomes complete only when it is my—*might;* but by this I cease to be a merely free man, and become an own man. Why is the freedom of the peoples a "hollow word"? Because the peoples have no might! With a breath of the living ego I blow peoples over, be it the breath of a Nero, a Chinese emperor, or a poor writer. Why is it that the G. . . . .[10] legislatures pine in vain for freedom, and are lectured for it by the cabinet ministers? Because they are not of the "mighty"! Might is a fine

10. (Meaning "German." Written in this form because of the censorship.) [The legislatures of the various German states in the 1840s were relatively powerless, and their demands for a larger voice in the conduct of public policy usually brought serious reproaches from the administrative ministers of state appointed by the princes who controlled executive power. The issue was so touchy in 1843-1844 that even Stirner tip-toed around it, for fear his work might be confiscated upon publication, for even mentioning the subject. According to Mackay, *Der Einzige* actually was impounded by the Saxon Ministry of the Interior for a short time following its publication, but was soon released; perhaps no censor in the Ministry was capable of understanding it.]

thing, and useful for many purposes; for "one goes further with a handful of might than with a bagful of right." You long for freedom? You fools! If you took might, freedom would come of itself. See, he who has might "stands above the law." How does this prospect taste to you, you "law-abiding" people? But you have no taste!

The cry for "freedom" rings loudly all around. But is it felt and known what a donated or chartered freedom must mean? It is not recognized in the full amplitude of the word that all freedom is essentially—self-liberation—that I can have only so much freedom as I procure for myself by my ownness. Of what use is it to sheep that no one abridges their freedom of speech? They stick to bleating. Give one who is inwardly a Mohammedan, a Jew, or a Christian, permission to speak what he likes: he will yet utter only narrow-minded stuff. If, on the contrary, certain others rob you of the freedom of speaking and hearing, they know quite rightly wherein lies their temporary advantage, as you would perhaps be able to say and hear something whereby those "certain" persons would lose their credit.

If they nevertheless give you freedom, they are simply knaves who give more than they have. For then they give you nothing of their own, but stolen wares: they give you your own freedom, the freedom that you must take for yourselves; and they *give* it to you only that you may not take it and call the thieves and cheats to an account to boot. In their slyness they know well that given (chartered) freedom is no freedom, since only the freedom one *takes* for himself, therefore the egoist's freedom, rides with full sails. Donated freedom strikes its sails as soon as there comes a storm—or calm; it requires always a—gentle and moderate breeze.

Here lies the difference between self-liberation and emancipation (manumission, setting free). Those who to-day "stand in the opposition" are thirsting and screaming to be "set free." The princes are to "declare their peoples of age," that is, emancipate them! Behave as if you were of age, and you are so without any declaration of majority; if you do not behave accordingly, you are not worthy of it, and would never be of age even by a declaration of majority. When the Greeks were of age, they drove out their tyrants, and, when the son is of age, he makes himself independent of his father. If the Greeks had waited till their tyrants graciously allowed them their majority, they might have waited long. A sensible father throws out a son who will not come of age, and keeps the house to himself; it serves the noodle right.

The man who is set free is nothing but a freed man, a *libertinus,* a dog dragging a piece of chain with him: he is an unfree man in the garment of freedom, like the ass in the lion's skin. Emancipated Jews are nothing bettered in themselves, but only relieved as Jews, although he who relieves their condition is certainly more than a churchly Christian, as the latter cannot do this without inconsistency. But, emancipated or not emancipated, Jew remains Jew; he who is not self-freed is merely an—emancipated man. The Protestant State can certainly set free (emancipate) the Catholics; but, because they do not make themselves free, they remain simply—Catholics.

Selfishness and unselfishness have already been spoken of. The friends of freedom are exasperated against selfishness because in their religious striving after freedom they cannot—free themselves from that sublime thing, "self-renunciation." The liberal's anger is directed against egoism, for the egoist, you know, never takes trouble about a thing for the sake of the thing, but for his sake: the thing must serve him. It is egoistic to ascribe to no thing a value of its own, an "absolute" value, but to seek its value in me. One often hears that pot-boiling study which is so common counted among the most repulsive traits of egoistic behavior, because it manifests the most shameful desecration of science; but what is science for but to be consumed? If one does not know how to use it for anything better than to keep the pot boiling, then his egoism is a petty one indeed, because this egoist's power is a limited power; but the egoistic element in it, and the desecration of science, only a possessed man can blame.

Because Christianity, incapable of letting the individual count as an ego,[11] thought of him only as a dependent, and was properly nothing but a *social theory*—a doctrine of living to-

11. (*Einzige*)

gether, and that of man with God as well as of man with man—
therefore in it everything "own" must fall into most woeful
disrepute: selfishness, self-will, ownness, self-love, and the like.
The Christian way of looking at things has on all sides gradually
re-stamped honorable words into dishonorable; why should they
not be brought into honor again? So *Schimpf* (contumely) is
in its old sense equivalent to jest, but for Christian seriousness
pastime became a dishonor,[12] for that seriousness cannot take a
joke; *frech* (impudent) formerly meant only bold, brave; *Frevel*
(wanton outrage) was only daring. It is well known how askance
the word "reason" was looked at for a long time.

Our language has settled itself pretty well to the Christian
standpoint, and the general consciousness is still too Christian
not to shrink in terror from everything un-Christian as from something incomplete or evil. Therefore "selfishness" is in a bad
way too.

Selfishness,[13] in the Christian sense, means something like
this: I look only to see whether anything is of use to me as a
sensual man. But is sensuality then the whole of my ownness?
Am I in my own senses when I am given up to sensuality? Do
I follow myself, my *own* determination, when I follow that? I
am my *own* only when I am master of myself, instead of being
mastered either by sensuality or by anything else (God, man,
authority, law, State, Church); what is of use to me, this self-
owned or self-appertaining one, my selfishness pursues.

Besides, one sees himself every moment compelled to believe
in that constantly-blasphemed selfishness as an all-controlling
power. In the session of February 10, 1844, Welcker[14] argues

12. (I take *Entbehrung*, "destitution," to be a misprint for *Enteh-rung*.) [The 1892 (Reclam) edition reprinted this error.]

13. (*Eigennutz*, literally "own-use.")

14. [Karl Theodor Welcker (1790-1869), a prominent German liberal,
teacher and student of law, a member of the Baden legislature for a time
beginning in 1831. He was a widely-known and controversial fighter for
freedom of the press. See his *Die volkommene und ganze Pressfreiheit*
(Freiburg, 1830), and, jointly, with Wilhelm Schulz, *Die geheime Inquisition; die Censur und Kabinetsjustiz im verderblichen Bunde* (Karls-
ruhe, 1845).]

a motion on the dependence of the judges, and sets forth in a detailed speech that removable, dismissable, transferable, and pensionable judges—in short, such members of a court of justice as can by mere administrative process be damaged and endangered —are wholly without reliability, yes, lose all respect and all confidence among the people. The whole bench, Welcker cries, is demoralized by this dependence! In blunt words this means nothing else than that the judges find it more to their advantage to give judgment as the ministers would have them than to give it as the law would have them. How is that to be helped? Perhaps by bringing home to the judges' hearts the ignominiousness of their venality, and then cherishing the confidence that they will repent and henceforth prize justice more highly than their selfishness? No, the people does not soar to this romantic confidence, for it feels that selfishness is mightier than any other motive. Therefore the same persons who have been judges hitherto may remain so, however thoroughly one has convinced himself that they behaved as egoists; only they must not any longer find their selfishness favored by the venality of justice, but must stand so independent of the government that by a judgment in conformity with the facts they do not throw into the shade their own cause, their "well-understood interest," but rather secure a comfortable combination of a good salary with respect among the citizens.

So Welcker and the commoners of Baden consider themselves secured only when they can count on selfishness. What is one to think, then, of the countless phrases of unselfishness with which their mouths overflow at other times?

To a cause which I am pushing selfishly I have another relation than to one which I am serving unselfishly. The following criterion might be cited for it; against the one I can *sin* or commit a *sin*, the other I can only *trifle away*, push from me, deprive myself of—commit an imprudence. Free trade is looked at in both ways, being regarded partly as a freedom which may *under certain circumstances* be granted or withdrawn, partly as one which is to be held *sacred under all circumstances*.

If I am not concerned about a thing in and for itself, and do not desire it for its own sake, then I desire it solely as a *means to an end,* for its usefulness; for the sake of another end, as in oysters for a pleasant flavor. Now will not every thing whose final end he himself is, serve the egoist as means? And is he to protect a thing that serves him for nothing—for example, the proletarian to protect the State?

Ownness includes in itself everything own, and brings to honor again what Christian language dishonored. But ownness has not any alien standard either, as it is not in any sense an *idea* like freedom, morality, humanity, and the like: it is only a description of the—*owner*.

IV

The Owner

I—DO I come to myself and mine through liberalism?

Whom does the liberal look upon as his equal? Man! Be only man—and that you are anyway—and the liberal calls you his brother. He asks very little about your private opinions and private follies, if only he can espy "Man" in you.

But, as he takes little heed of what you are *privatim*—nay, in a strict following out of his principle sets no value at all on it—he sees in you only what you are *generatim*. In other words, he sees in you, not *you*, but the *species;* not Tom or Jim, but Man; not the real or unique one,[1] but your essence or your concept; not the bodily man, but the *spirit*.

As Tom you would not be his equal, because he is Jim, therefore not Tom; as man you are the same that he is. And, since as Tom you virtually do not exist at all for him (so far, to wit, as he is a liberal and not unconsciously an egoist), he has really made "brother-love" very easy for himself: he loves in you not Tom, of whom he knows nothing and wants to know nothing, but Man.

To see in you and me nothing further than "men," that is running the Christian way of looking at things, according to which one is for the other nothing but a *concept* (a man called to salvation, for instance), into the ground.

Christianity properly so called gathers us under a less utterly general concept: there we are "sons of God" and "led by the Spirit of God."[2] Yet not all can boast of being God's sons, but "the same Spirit which witnesses to our spirit that we are sons of God reveals also who are the sons of the devil."[3] Consequently,

1. (*Einzigen*)
2. Rom. 8. 14.
3. Cf. 1 John 3. 10 with Rom. 8. 16.

to be a son of God one must not be a son of the devil; the sonship of God excluded certain men. To be *sons of men*— that is, men—on the contrary, we need nothing but to belong to the human *species,* need only to be specimens of the same species. What I am as this I is no concern of yours as a good liberal, but is my *private affair* alone; enough that we are both sons of one and the same mother, to wit, the human species: as "a son of man" I am your equal.

What am I now to you? Perhaps this *bodily* I as I walk and stand? Anything but that. This bodily I, with its thoughts, decisions, and passions, is in your eyes a "private affair" which is no concern of yours: it is an "affair by itself." As an "affair for you" there exists only my concept, my generic concept, only *the Man,* who, as he is called Tom, could just as well be Joe or Dick. You see in me not me, the bodily man, but an unreal thing, the spook, a *Man.*

In the course of the Christian centuries we declared the most various persons to be "our equals," but each time in the measure of that *spirit* which we expected from them—each one in whom the spirit of the need of redemption may be assumed, then later each one who has the spirit of integrity, finally each one who shows a human spirit and a human face. Thus the fundamental principle of "equality" varied.

Equality being now conceived as equality of the *human spirit,* there has certainly been discovered an equality that includes *all* men; for who could deny that we men have a human spirit, that is, no other than a human!

But are we on that account further on now than in the beginning of Christianity? Then we were to have a *divine spirit,* now a *human;* but, if the divine did not exhaust us, how should the human wholly express what *we* are? Feuerbach thinks, that if he humanizes the divine, he has found the truth. No, if God has given us pain, "Man" is capable of pinching us still more torturingly. The long and the short of it is this: that we are men is the slightest thing about us, and has significance only in so far as it is one of our *qualities,*[4] our property.[5] I am indeed

4. (*Eigenschaften*)   5. (*Eigentum*)

among other things a man, as I am a living being, therefore an animal, or a European, a Berliner, and the like; but he who chose to have regard for me only as a man, or as a Berliner, would pay me a regard that would be very unimportant to me. And wherefore? Because he would have regard only for one of my *qualities,* not for *me.*

It is just so with the *spirit too.* A Christian spirit, an upright spirit, and the like may well be my acquired quality, my property, but I am not this spirit: it is mine, not I its.

Hence we have in liberalism only the continuation of the old Christian depreciation of the I, the bodily Tom. Instead of taking me as I am, one looks solely at my property, my qualities, and enters into marriage bonds with me only for the sake of my —possessions; one marries, as it were, what I have, not what I am. The Christian takes hold of my spirit, the liberal of my humanity.

But, if the spirit, which is not regarded as the *property* of the bodily ego but as the proper ego itself, is a ghost, then the Man too, who is not recognized as my quality but as the proper I, is nothing but a spook, a thought, a concept.

Therefore the liberal too revolves in the same circle as the Christian. Because the spirit of mankind, Man, dwells in you, you are a man, as when the spirit of Christ dwells in you you are a Christian; but, because it dwells in you only as a second ego, even though it be as your proper or "better" ego, it remains otherworldly to you, and you have to strive to become wholly man. A striving just as fruitless as the Christian's to become wholly a blessed spirit!

One can now, after liberalism has proclaimed Man, declare openly that herewith was only completed the consistent carrying out of Christianity, and that in truth Christianity set itself no other task from the start than to realize "man," the "true man." Hence, then, the illusion that Christianity ascribes an infinite value to the ego (as in the doctrine of immortality, in the cure of souls, etc.) comes to light. No, it assigns this value to *Man* alone. Only *Man* is immortal, and only because I am Man am I too immortal. In fact, Christianity had to teach that no one is lost, just as liberalism too puts all on an equality as men;

but that eternity, like this equality, applied only to the *Man* in me, not to me. Only as the bearer and harborer of Man do I not die, as notoriously "the king never dies." Louis dies, but the king remains; I die, but my spirit, Man, remains. To identify me now entirely with Man the demand has been invented, and stated, that I must become a "real generic being."[6]

The HUMAN *religion* is only the last metamorphosis of the Christian religion. For liberalism is a religion because it separates my essence from me and sets it above me, because it exalts "Man" to the same extent as any other religion does its God or idol, because it makes what is mine into something otherworldly, because in general it makes out of what is mine, out of my qualities and my property, something alien—to wit, an "essence"; in short, because it sets me beneath Man, and thereby creates for me a "vocation." But liberalism declares itself a religion in form too when it demands for this supreme being, Man, a zeal of faith, "a faith that some day will at last prove its fiery zeal too, a zeal that will be invincible."[7] But, as liberalism is a human religion, its professor takes a *tolerant* attitude toward the professor of any other (Catholic, Jewish, etc.), as Frederick the Great[8] did toward every one who performed his duties as a subject, whatever fashion of becoming blest he might be inclined toward. This religion is now to be raised to the rank of the generally customary one, and separated from the others as mere "private follies," toward which, besides, one takes a highly *liberal* attitude on account of their unessentialness.

One may call it the *State-religion,* the religion of the "free State," not in the sense hitherto current that it is the one favored or privileged by the State, but as that religion which the "free State" not only has the right, but is compelled, to demand from each of those who belong to it, let him be *privatim* a Jew, a Christian, or anything else. For it does the same service to the State as filial piety to the family. If the family is to be recognized

6. Karl Marx, in the *Deutsch-französische Jahrbücher,* p. 197.
7. Bruno Bauer, *Judenfrage,* p. 61.
8. [Frederick II (1712-1786), King of Prussia from 1740 to 1786, widely known for his indifference to the religious professions and preferences of his subjects.]

and maintained, in its existing condition, by each one of those who belong to it, then to him the tie of blood must be sacred, and his feeling for it must be that of piety, of respect for the ties of blood, by which every blood-relation becomes to him a consecrated person. So also to every member of the State-community this community must be sacred, and the concept which is the highest to the State must likewise be the highest to him.

But what concept is the highest to the State? Doubtless that of being a really human society, a society in which every one who is really a man, that is, *not an un-man,* can obtain admission as a member. Let a State's tolerance go ever so far, toward an un-man and toward what is inhuman it ceases. And yet this "un-man" is a man, yet the "inhuman" itself is something human, yes, possible only to a man, not to any beast; it is, in fact, something "possible to man." But, although every un-man is a man, yet the State excludes him; it locks him up, or transforms him from a fellow of the State into a fellow of the prison (fellow of the lunatic asylum or hospital, according to Communism).

To say in blunt words what an un-man is is not particularly hard: it is a man who does not correspond to the *concept* man, as the inhuman is something human which is not conformed to the concept of the human. Logic calls this a "self-contradictory judgment." Would it be permissible for one to pronounce this judgment, that one can be a man without being a man, if he did not admit the hypothesis that the concept of man can be separated from the existence, the essence from the appearance? They say, he *appears* indeed as a man, but *is* not a man.

Men have passed this "self-contradictory judgment" through a long line of centuries! Nay, what is still more, in this long time there were only—*un-men.* What individual can have corresponded to his concept? Christianity knows only one Man, and this one—Christ—is at once an un-man again in the reverse sense, to wit, a superhuman man, a "God." Only the—un-man is a *real* man.

Men that are not men, what should they be but *ghosts?* Every real man, because he does not correspond to the concept "man," or because he is not a "generic man," is a spook. But do I still remain an un-man even if I bring Man (who towered above me and remained otherworldly to me only as my ideal, my task, my essence or concept) down to be my *quality,* my own and inherent in me; so that Man is nothing else than my humanity, my human existence, and everything that I do is human precisely because *I* do it, but not because it corresponds to the *concept* "man"? *I* am really Man and the un-man in one; for I am a man and at the same time more than a man; I am the ego of this my mere quality.

It had to come to this at last, that it was no longer merely demanded of us to be Christians, but to become men; for, though we could never really become even Christians, but always remained "poor sinners" (for the Christian was an unattainable ideal too), yet in this the contradictoriness did not come before our consciousness so, and the illusion was easier than now when of us, who are men act humanly (yes, cannot do otherwise than be such and act so), the demand is made that we are to be men, "real men."

Our States of to-day, because they still have all sorts of things sticking to them, left from their churchly mother, do indeed load those who belong to them with various obligations (such as churchly religiousness) which properly do not a bit concern them, the States; yet on the whole they do not deny their significance, since they want to be looked upon as *human societies,* in which man as man can be a member, even if he is less privileged than other members; most of them admit adherence of every religious sect, and receive people without distinction of race or nation: Jews, Turks, Moors, etc., can become French citizens. In the act of reception, therefore, the State looks only to see whether one is a *man.* The Church, as a society of believers, could not receive every man into her bosom; the State, as a society of men, can. But, when the State has carried its principle clear through, of presupposing in its constituents nothing but that they are men (even the North Americans still presuppose in theirs that they have religion, at least the religion of integrity, of responsibility), then it has dug its grave. While it will fancy that those whom it possesses are without exception men, these have meanwhile become without exception *egoists,* each of whom utilizes it according to his egoistic powers and ends. Against the egoists "human society" is wrecked; for they no longer have to do with each other as *men,* but appear egoistically as an *I against* a You altogether different from me and in opposition to me.

If the State must count on our humanity, it is the same if one says it must count on our *morality.* Seeing Man in each other, and acting as men toward each other, is called moral behavior. This is every whit the "spiritual love" of Christianity. For, if I see Man in you, as in myself I see Man and nothing but Man, then I care for you as I would care for myself; for we represent, you see, nothing but the mathematical proposition: $A = C$ and $B = C$, consequently $A = B$—I nothing but man and you nothing but man, consequently I and you the same. Morality is incompatible with egoism, because the former does not allow validity to *me,* but only to the Man in me. But, if the State is a *society of men,* not a union of egos each of whom has only himself before his eyes, then it cannot last without morality, and must insist on morality.

Therefore we two, the State and I, are enemies. I, the egoist, have not at heart the welfare of this "human society," I sacrifice nothing to it, I only utilize it; but to be able to utilize it completely I transform it rather into my property and my creature; that is, I annihilate it, and form in its place the *Union of Egoists.*[9]

So the State betrays its enmity to me by demanding that I be a man, which presupposes that I may also not be a man, but rank for it as an "un-man"; it imposes being a man upon me as a *duty.* Further, it desires me to do nothing along with which *it* cannot last; so *its permanence* is to be sacred for me. Then I am not to be an egoist, but a "respectable, upright," thus moral,

9. [Stirner's *Verein von Egoisten* has drawn the attention of a number of students, critics and commentators over the years. It is the closest he came to suggesting an alternative socio-political system to that he abominated, and does not go beyond the very outline of a "new order." At the minimum it suggests a loose association of conscious "egoists" drawn together voluntarily by the attraction of their mutual interests, and contracting out the recourse to force as their starting point.]

man. Enough: before it and its permanence I am to be impotent
and respectful.

This State, not a present one indeed, but still in need of
being first created, is the ideal of advancing liberalism. There
is to come into existence a true "society of men," in which every
"man" finds room. Liberalism means to realize "Man," create
a world for him; and this should be the *human* world or the
general (Communistic) society of men. It was said, "The Church
could regard only the spirit, the State is to regard the whole
man."[10] But is not "Man" "spirit"? The kernel of the State
is simply "Man," this unreality, and it itself is only a "society
of men." The world which the believer (believing spirit) creates
is called Church, the world which the man (human or humane
spirit) creates is called State. But that is not *my* world. I
never execute anything *human* in the abstract, but always my *own*
things; *my* human act is diverse from every other human act, and
only by this diversity is it a real act belonging to me. The human
in it is an abstraction, and, as such, spirit, abstracted essence.

Bruno Bauer states (*Judenfrage,* p. 84) that the truth of
criticism is the final truth, and in fact the truth sought for by
Christianity itself—to wit, "Man." He says, "The history of the
Christian world is the history of the supreme fight for truth, for
in it—and in it only!—the thing at issue is the discovery of the
final or the primal truth—man and freedom."

All right, let us accept this gain, and let us take *man* as the
ultimately found result of Christian history and of the religious
or ideal efforts of man in general. Now, who is Man? *I* am!
Man, the end and outcome of Christianity, is, as *I,* the beginning
and raw material of the new history, a history of enjoyment after
the history of sacrifices, a history not of man or humanity, but of
—*me. Man* ranks as the general. Now then, I and the egoistic
are the really general, since every one is an egoist and of para-
mount importance to himself. The Jewish is not the purely

10. Hess, *Triarchie,* p. 76. [Moses Hess (1812-1875), a contemporary
of Marx in the propagation of Socialist views; his *Die Europäische
Triarchie* was published in Leipzig in 1841 by the same house which
brought out Stirner, Otto Wigand.]

egoistic, because the Jew still devotes *himself* to Jehovah; the Christian is not, because the Christian lives on the grace of God and subjects *himself* to him. As Jew and as Christian alike a man satisfies only certain of his wants, only a certain need, not *himself*: a *half*-egoism, because the egoism of a half-man, who is half he, half Jew, or half his own proprietor, half a slave. Therefore, too, Jew and Christian always half-way exclude each other; as men they recognize each other, as slaves they exclude each other, because they are servants of two different masters. If they could be complete egoists, they would exclude each other *wholly* and hold together so much the more firmly. Their ignominy is not that they exclude each other, but that this is done only *half-way*. Bruno Bauer, on the contrary, thinks Jews and Christians cannot regard and treat each other as "men" till they give up the separate essence which parts them and obligates them to eternal separation, recognize the general essence of "Man," and regard this as their "true essence."

According to his representation the defect of the Jews and the Christians alike lies in their wanting to be and have something "particular" instead of only being men and endeavoring after what is human—to wit, the "general rights of man." He thinks their fundamental error consists in the belief that they are "privileged," possess "prerogatives"; in general, in the belief in *prerogative*.[11] In opposition to this he holds up to them the general rights of man. The rights of man!—

Man is *man in general,* and in so far every one who is a man. Now every one is to have the eternal rights of man, and, according to the opinion of Communism, enjoy them in the complete "democracy," or, as it ought more correctly to be called—anthropocracy. But it is I alone who have everything that I—procure for myself; as man I have nothing. People would like to give every man an affluence of all good, merely because he has the title "man." But I put the accent on *me,* not on my being *man.*

Man is something only as *my quality*[12] (property),[13] like

11. (*Vorrecht,* literally "precedent right.")
12. (*Eigenschaft*)   13. (*Eigentum*)

masculinity or femininity. The ancients found the ideal in one's being *male* in the full sense; their virtue is *virtus* and *arete*—manliness. What is one to think of a woman who should want only to be perfectly "woman?" That is not given to all, and many a one would therein be fixing for herself an unattainable goal. *Feminine,* on the other hand, she is anyhow, by nature; femininity is her quality, and she does not need "true femininity." I am a man just as the earth is a star. As ridiculous as it would be to set the earth the task of being a "thorough star," so ridiculous it is to burden me with the call to be a "thorough man."

When Fichte says, "The ego is all," this seems to harmonize perfectly with my thesis. But it is not that the ego *is* all, but the ego *destroys* all, and only the self-dissolving ego, the never-being ego, the—*finite* ego is really I. Fichte speaks of the "absolute" ego, but I speak of me, the transitory ego.

How natural is the supposition that *man* and *ego* mean the same! And yet one sees, as by Feuerbach, that the expression "man" is to designate the absolute ego, the *species,* not the transitory, individual ego. Egoism and humanity (humaneness) ought to mean the same, but according to Feuerbach the individual can "only lift himself above the limits of his individuality, but not above the laws, the positive ordinances, of his species."[14] But the species is nothing, and, if the individual lifts himself above the limits of his individuality, this is rather his very self as an individual; he exists only in raising himself, he exists only in not remaining what he is; otherwise he would be done, dead. Man with the great M is only an ideal, the species only something thought of. To be a man is not to realize the ideal of *Man,* but to present *oneself,* the individual. It is not how I realize the *generally human* that needs to be my task, but how I satisfy myself. *I* am my species, am without norm, without law, without model, and the like. It is possible that I can make very little out of myself; but this little is everything, and is better than what I allow to be made out of me by the might of others, by the training of custom, religion, the laws, the State. Better—if the talk is to be of better at all—better an unmannerly child than

14. *Essence of Christianity,* 2nd ed., p. 401.

an old head on young shoulders, better a mulish man than a man compliant in everything. The unmannerly and mulish fellow is still on the way to form himself according to his own will; the prematurely knowing and compliant one is determined by the "species," the general demands—the species is law to him. He is *determined*[15] by it; for what else is the species to him but his "destiny,"[16] his "calling?" Whether I look to "humanity," the species, in order to strive toward this ideal, or to God and Christ with like endeavor, where is the essential dissimilarity? At most the former is more washed-out than the latter. As the individual is the whole of nature, so he is the whole of the species too.

Everything that I do, think—in short, my expression or manifestation—is indeed *conditioned* by what I am. The Jew can will only thus or thus, can "present himself" only thus; the Christian can present and manifest himself only Christianly, etc. If it were possible that you could be a Jew or Christian, you would indeed bring out only what was Jewish or Christian; but it is not possible; in the most rigorous conduct you yet remain an *egoist,* a sinner against that concept— *you* are not the precise equivalent of Jew. Now, because the egoistic always keeps peeping through, people have inquired for a more perfect concept which should really wholly express what you are, and which, because it is your true nature, should contain all the laws of your activity. The most perfect thing of the kind has been attained in "Man." As a Jew you are too little, and the Jewish is not your task; to be a Greek, a German, does not suffice. But be a—man, then you have everything; look upon the human as your calling.

Now I know what is expected of me, and the new catechism can be written. The subject is again subjected to the predicate, the individual to something general; the dominion is again secured to an *idea,* and the foundation laid for a new *religion.* This is a step *forward* in the domain of religion, and in particular of Christianity; not a step out beyond it.

To step out beyond it leads into the *unspeakable.* For me

15. (*bestimmt*)
16. (*Bestimmung*)

paltry language has no word, and "the Word," the Logos, is to me a "mere word."

My *essence* is sought for. If not the Jew, the German, then at any rate it is—the man. "Man is my essence."

I am repulsive or repugnant to myself; I have a horror and loathing of myself, I am a horror to myself, or, I am never enough for myself and never do enough to satisfy myself. From such feelings springs self-dissolution or self-criticism. Religious-ness begins with self-renunciation, ends with completed criticism.

I am possessed, and want to get rid of the "evil spirit." How do I set about it? I fearlessly commit the sin that seems to the Christian the direst, the sin and blasphemy against the Holy Spirit. "He who blasphemes the Holy Spirit has no forgiveness forever, but is liable to the eternal judgment!"[17] I want no forgiveness, and am not afraid of the judgment.

Man is the last evil *spirit* or spook, the most deceptive or most intimate, the craftiest liar with honest mien, the father of lies.

The egoist, turning against the demands and concepts of the present, executes pitilessly the most measureless—*desecration.* Nothing is holy to him!

It would be foolish to assert that there is no power above mine. Only the attitude that I take toward it will be quite another than that of the religious age: I shall be the *enemy* of every higher power, while religion teaches us to make it our friend and be humble toward it.

The *desecrator* puts forth his strength against every *fear of God,* for fear of God would determine him in everything that he left standing as sacred. Whether it is the God or the Man that exercises the hallowing power in the God-man—whether, therefore, anything is held sacred for God's sake or for Man's (Humanity's)—this does not change the fear of God, since Man is revered as "supreme essence," as much as on the specifically religious standpoint God as "supreme essence" calls for our fear and reverence; both overawe us.

17. Mark 3.29.

The fear of God in the proper sense was shaken long ago, and a more or less conscious "atheism," externally recognizable by a wide-spread "unchurchliness," has involuntarily become the mode. But what was taken from God has been superadded to Man, and the power of humanity grew greater in just the degree that that of piety lost weight: "Man" is the God of to-day, and fear of Man has taken the place of the old fear of God.

But, because Man represents only another Supreme Being, nothing in fact has taken place but a metamorphosis in the Supreme Being, and the fear of Man is merely an altered form of the fear of God.

Our atheists are pious people.

If in the so-called feudal times we held everything as a fief from God, in the liberal period the same feudal relation exists with Man. God was the Lord, now Man is the Lord; God was the Mediator, now Man is; God was the Spirit, now Man is. In this three fold regard the feudal relation has experienced a transformation. For now, firstly, we hold as a fief from all-powerful Man our *power,* which, because it comes from a higher, is not called power or might, but "right"—the "rights of man"; we further hold as a fief from him our position in the world, for he, the mediator, mediates our *intercourse* with others, which therefore may not be otherwise than "human"; finally, we hold as a fief from him ourselves—to wit, our own value, or all that we are worth—inasmuch as we are worth nothing when *he* does not dwell in us, and when or where we are not "human." The power is Man's, the world is Man's, I am Man's.

But am I not still unrestrained from declaring *myself* the entitler, the mediator, and the own self? Then it runs thus:

My power is *my* property.

My power *gives* me property.

My power *am* I myself, and through it am I my property.

A. — MY POWER

RIGHT[18] is the *spirit of society*. If society has a *will*, this will
is simply right: society exists only through right. But, as
it endures only exercising a *sovereignty* over individuals, right is
its SOVEREIGN WILL. Aristotle says justice is the advantage
of *society*.

All existing right is—*foreign law;* some one makes me out
to be in the right, "does right by me." But should I therefore
be in the right if all the world made me out so? And yet what else
is the right that I obtain in the State, in society, but a right of
those *foreign* to me? When a blockhead makes me out in the
right, I grow distrustful of my rightness; I don't like to receive
it from him. But, even when a wise man makes me out in the
right, I nevertheless am not in the right on that account. Whether
I am in the right is completely independent of the fool's making
out and of the wise man's.

All the same, we have coveted this right till now. We seek
for right, and turn to the court for that purpose. To what? To
a royal, a papal, a popular court, etc. Can a sultanic court
declare another right than that which the sultan has ordained
to be right? Can it make me out in the right if I seek for a right
that does not agree with the sultan's law? Can it, for instance,
concede to me high treason as a right, since it is assuredly not a
right according to the sultan's mind? Can it as a court of censorship allow me the free utterance of opinion as a right, since the
sultan will hear nothing of this *my* right? What am I seeking
for in this court, then? I am seeking for sultanic right, not
my right; I am seeking for—*foreign* right. As long as this
foreign right harmonizes with mine, to be sure, I shall find in it
the latter too.

The State does not permit pitching into each other man to
man; it opposes the *duel*. Even every ordinary appeal to blows,
notwithstanding that neither of the fighters calls the police to it,
is punished; except when it is not an I whacking away at a you,

18. (This word has also, in German, the meaning of "common law,"
and will sometimes be translated "law" in the following paragraphs.)

but, say, the *head of a family* at the child. The *family* is entitled to this, and in its name the father; I as Ego am not.

The *Vossische Zeitung*[19] presents to us the "commonwealth of right." There everything is to be decided by the judge and a *court*. It ranks the supreme court of censorship as a "court" where "right is declared." What sort of a right? The right of the censorship. To recognize the sentences of that court as right one must regard the censorship as right. But it is thought nevertheless that this court offers a protection. Yes, protection against an individual censor's error: it protects only the censorship-legislator against false interpretation of his will, at the same time making his statute, by the "sacred power of right," all the firmer against writers.

Whether I am in the right or not there is no judge but myself. Others can judge only whether they endorse my right, and whether it exists as right for them too.

In the meantime let us take the matter yet another way. I am to reverence sultanic law in the sultanate, popular law in republics, canon law in Catholic communities. To these laws I am to subordinate myself; I am to regard them as sacred. A "sense of right" and "law-abiding mind" of such a sort is so firmly planted in people's heads that the most revolutionary persons of our days want to subject us to a new "sacred law," the "law of society," the law of mankind, the "right of all," and the like. The right of "all" is to go before *my* right. As a right of all it would indeed be my right among the rest, since I, with the rest, am included in all; but that it is at the same time a right of others, or even of all others, does not move me to its upholding. Not as a *right of all* will I defend it, but as *my* right; and then every other may see to it how he shall likewise maintain it for himself. The right of all (for example, to eat) is a right of every individual. Let each keep this right unabridged for *himself,* then all exercise it spontaneously; let him not take care for all though— let him not grow zealous for it as for a right of all.

19. [The oldest and most respected newspaper in Berlin, founded in the 18th century. For a time it was published under the title *Königlich privilegirte Berliner Zeitung.*]

But the social reformers preach to us a *"law of society."*
There the individual becomes society's slave, and is in the right
only when society *makes him out* in the right, when he lives
according to society's *statutes* and so is—*loyal.* Whether I am
loyal under a despotism or in a "society" *a la* Weitling,[20] it is the
same absence of right in so far as in both cases I have not *my*
right but *foreign* right.

In consideration of right the question is always asked, "What
or who gives me the right to it?" Answer: God, love, reason,
nature, humanity, etc. No, only *your might, your* power gives
you the right (your reason, therefore, may give it to you).

Communism, which assumes that men "have equal rights
by nature," contradicts its own proposition till it comes to this,
that men have no right at all by nature. For it is not willing to
recognize, for instance, that parents have "by nature" rights
as against their children, or the children as against the parents:
it abolishes the family. Nature gives parents, brothers, and so on,
no right at all. Altogether, this entire revolutionary or Babouvist
principle[21] rests on a religious, that is, false, view of things. Who
can ask after "right" if he does not occupy the religious standpoint
himself? Is not "right" a religious concept, something sacred?
Why, *"equality of rights,"* as the Revolution propounded it, is
only another name for "Christian equality," the "equality of
the brethren," "of God's children," "of Christians"; in short,
fraternité. Each and every inquiry after right deserves to be
lashed with Schiller's words:

20. [Wilhelm Christian Weitling (1809-1871), born in Magdeburg,
a very active participant in communist propaganda in Germany between
1842 and 1848. He was one of the radicals who came to America after the
latter date, and all his activities were confined to the United States
thereafter. Weitling was a favorite target of Stirner's.]

21. Cf. *Die Kommunisten in der Schweiz,* committee report, p. 3.
[The reference is to François-Noël Babeuf (1764-1797), one of the
earliest theorists of equalitarian communism during the French Revolution;
Babouvism became the term which described the substance of his overall
views. The source cited by Stirner is *Die Kommunisten in der Schweiz
nach den bei Weitling vorgefundenen Papieren; Wörtlicher Abdruck des
Kommissionalberichtes an die Regierung des Standes* (Zurich, 1843). It

> Many a year I've used my nose
> To smell the onion and the rose;
> Is there any proof which shows
> That I've a right to that same nose?

When the Revolution stamped equality as a "right," it took flight into the religious domain, into the region of the sacred, of the ideal. Hence, since then, the fight for the "sacred, inalienable rights of man." Against the "eternal rights of man" the "well-earned rights of the established order" are quite naturally, and with equal right, brought to bear: right against right, where of course one is decried by the other as "wrong." This has been the *contest of rights*[22] since the Revolution.

You want to be "in the right" as against the rest. That you cannot; as against them you remain forever "in the wrong"; for they surely would not be your opponents if they were not in "their right" too; they will always make you out "in the wrong." But, as against the right of the rest, yours is a higher, greater, *more powerful* right, is it not? No such thing! Your right is not more powerful if you are not more powerful. Have Chinese subjects a right to freedom? Just bestow it on them, and then look how far you have gone wrong in your attempt: because they do not know how to use freedom they have no right to it, or, in clearer terms, because they have not freedom they have not the right to it. Children have no right to the condition of majority because they are not of age, because they are children. Peoples that let themselves be kept in nonage have no rights to the condition of majority; if they ceased to be in nonage, then only would they have the right to be of age. This means nothing else than "What you have the *power* to be you have the *right* to." I derive all right and all warrant from *me;* I am *entitled* to everything that I have in my power. I am entitled to overthrow Zeus, Jehovah, God, if I *can;* if I cannot, then these gods will always remain in the right and in power as against me, and what I do will be to fear their right and their power in impotent "god-

---

was reprinted in another form by inclusion within another publication, presumably to outwit the press censors, in Schaffhausen in the same year.]

22. (*Rechtsstreit,* a word which usually means "lawsuit.")

fearingness," to keep their commandments and believe that I do right in everything that I do according to *their* right, about as the Russian boundary-sentinels think themselves rightfully entitled to shoot dead the suspicious persons who are escaping, since they murder "by superior authority," "with right."[23] But I am entitled by myself to murder if I myself do not forbid it to myself, if I myself do not fear murder as a "wrong." This view of things lies at the foundation of Chamisso's poem, "The Valley of Murder," where the gray-haired Indian murderer compels reverence from the white man whose brethren he has murdered. The only thing I am not entitled to is what I do not do with a free cheer, that is, what I do not entitle myself to.

I decide whether it is the *right thing* in me; there is no right *outside* me. If it is right for me,[24] it is right. Possibly this may not suffice to make it right for the rest; that is their care, not mine: let them defend themselves. And if for the whole world something were not right, but it were right for me, that is, I wanted it, then I would ask nothing about the whole world. So every one does who knows how to value *himself*, every one in the degree that he is an egoist; for might goes before right, and that—with perfect right.

Because I am "by nature" a man I have an equal right to the enjoyment of all goods, says Babeuf. Must he not also say: because I am "by nature" a first-born prince I have a right to the throne? The rights of man and the "well-earned rights" come to the same thing in the end, to wit, to *nature,* which *gives* me a right, that is, to *birth* (and, further, inheritance). "I am born as a man" is equal to "I am born as a king's son." The natural man has only a natural right (because he has only a natural power) and natural claims: he has right of birth and claims of birth. But *nature* cannot entitle me, give me capacity or might, to that to which only my act entitles me. That the king's child sets himself above other children, even this is his act, which

23. [There is an electrifying contemporary ring to this example of Stirner's, though it is probably superfluous to mention that he is speaking of circumstances nearly a century and a quarter ago.]

24. (A common German phrase for "it suits me.")

secures to him the precedence; and that the other children approve and recognize this act is their act, which makes them worthy to be —subjects.

Whether nature gives me a right, or whether God, the people's choice, etc., does so, all of that is the same *foreign* right, a right that I do not give or take to myself.

Thus the Communists say, equal labor entitles man to equal enjoyment. Formerly the question was raised whether the "virtuous" man must not be "happy" on earth. The Jews actually drew this inference: "That it may go well with thee on earth." No, equal labor does not entitle you to it, but equal enjoyment alone entitles you to equal enjoyment. Enjoy, then you are entitled to enjoyment. But, if you have labored and let the enjoyment be taken from you, then—"it serves you right."

If you *take* the enjoyment, it is your right; if, on the contrary, you only pine for it without laying hands on it, it remains as before, a "well-earned right" of those who are privileged for enjoyment. It is *their* right, as by laying hands on it would become *your* right.

The conflict over the "right of property" wavers in vehement commotion. The Communists affirm[25] that "the earth belongs rightfully to him who tills it, and its products to those who bring them out." I think it belongs to him who knows how to take it, or who does not let it be taken from him, does not let himself be deprived of it. If he appropriates it, then not only the earth, but the right to it too, belongs to him. This is *egoistic right:* it is right for me, therefore it is right.

Aside from this, right does have "a wax nose." The tiger that assails me is in the right, and I who strike him down am also in the right. I defend against him not my *right,* but *myself.*

As human right is always something given, it always in reality reduces to the right which men give, "concede," to each other. If the right to existence is conceded to new-born children, then they have the right; if it is not conceded to them, as was the case among the Spartans and ancient Romans, then they do not have it. For only society can give or concede it to them; they

25. A. Becker, *Volksphilosophie,* p. 22 f.

themselves cannot take it, or give it to themselves. It will be objected, the children had nevertheless "by nature" the right to exist; only the Spartans refused *recognition* to this right. But then they simply had no right to this recognition—no more than they had to recognition of their life by the wild beasts to which they were thrown.

People talk so much about *birthright,* and complain:
> There is—alas!—no mention of the rights
> That were born with us.[26]

What sort of right, then, is there that was born with me? The right to receive an entailed estate, to inherit a throne, to enjoy a princely or noble education; or, again, because poor parents begot me, to—get free schooling, be clothed out of contributions of alms, and at last earn my bread and my herring in the coal-mines or at the loom? Are these not birthrights, rights that have come down to me from my parents through *birth?* You think—no; you think these are only rights improperly so called, it is just these rights that you aim to abolish through the *real birthright.* To give a basis for this you go back to the simplest thing and affirm that every one is by birth *equal* to another—to wit, a *man.* I will grant you that every one is born as man, hence the new-born are therein *equal* to each other. Why are they? Only because they do not yet show and exert themselves as anything but bare—*children of men,* naked little human beings. But thereby they are at once different from those who have already made something out of themselves, who thus are no longer bare "children of man," but—children of their own creation. The latter possesses more than bare birthrights: they have *earned* rights. What an antithesis, what a field of combat! The old combat of the birthrights of man and well-earned rights. Go right on appealing to your birthrights; people will not fail to oppose to you the well-earned. Both stand on the "ground of right"; for each of the two has a "right" against the other, the one the birthright of natural right, the other the earned or "well-earned" right.

If you remain on the ground of right, you remain in—

26. (Mephistopheles in *Faust.*)

Rechthaberei.[27] The other cannot give you your right; he cannot "mete out right" to you. He who has might has—right; if you have not the former, neither have you the latter. Is this wisdom so hard to attain? Just look at the mighty and their doings! We are talking here only of China and Japan, of course. Just try it once, you Chinese and Japanese, to make them out in the wrong, and learn by experience how they throw you into jail. (Only do not confuse with this the "well-meaning counsels" which —in China and Japan—are permitted, because they do not hinder the mighty one, but possibly *help him on.*) For him who should want to make them out in the wrong there would stand open only one way thereto, that of might. If he deprives them of their *might,* then he has *really* made them out in the wrong, deprived them of their right; in any other case he can do nothing but clench his little fist in his pocket, or fall a victim as an obtrusive fool.

In short, if you Chinese or Japanese did not ask after right, and in particular if you did not ask after the rights "that were born with you," then you would not need to ask at all after the well-earned rights either.

You start back in fright before others, because you think you see beside them the *ghost of right,* which, as in the Homeric combats, seems to fight as a goddess at their side, helping them. What do you do? Do you throw the spear? No, you creep around to gain the spook over to yourselves, that it may fight on your side: you woo for the ghost's favor. Another would simply ask thus: Do I will what my opponent wills? "No!" Now then, there may fight for him a thousand devils or gods, I go at him all the same!

The "commonwealth of right," as the *Vossische Zeitung* among others stands for it, asks that office-holders be removable only by the *judge,* not by the *administration.* Vain illusion! If it were settled by law that an office-holder who is once seen

27. "I beg you, spare my lungs! He who insists on proving himself right, if he but has one of these things called tongues, can hold his own in all the world's despite!" (Faust's words to Mephistopheles, slightly mis-quoted.—For *Rechthaberei* see note 136 in second chapter.)

drunken shall lose his office, then the judges would have to condemn him on the word of the witnesses. In short, the lawgiver would only have to state precisely all the possible grounds which entail the loss of office, however laughable they might be (that is, he who laughs in his superiors' faces, who does not go to church every Sunday, who does not take the communion every four weeks, who runs in debt, who has disreputable associates, who shows no determination, etc., shall be removed. These things the lawgiver might take it into his head to prescribe for a court of honor); then the judge would solely have to investigate whether the accused had "become guilty" of those "offenses," and, on presentation of the proof, pronounce sentence of removal against him "in the name of the law."

The judge is lost when he ceases to be *mechanical,* when he "is forsaken by the rules of evidence." Then he no longer has anything but an opinion like everybody else; and, if he decides according to this *opinion,* his action is *no longer an official action.* As judge he must decide only according to the law. Commend me rather to the old French parliaments, which wanted to examine for themselves what was to be matters of right, and to register it only after their own approval. They at least judged according to a right of their own, and were not willing to give themselves up to be machines of the lawgiver, although as judges they must, to be sure, become their own machines.

It is said that punishment is the criminal's right. But impunity is just as much his right. If his undertaking succeeds, it serves him right, and, if it does not succeed, it likewise serves him right. You make your bed and lie in it. If some one goes foolhardily into dangers and perishes in them, we are apt to say, "It serves him right; he would have it so." But, if he conquered the dangers, if his *might* was victorious, then he would be in the *right* too. If a child plays with the knife and gets cut, it is served right; but, if it doesn't get cut, it is served right too. Hence right befalls the criminal, doubtless, when he suffers what he risked; why, what did he risk it for, since he knew the possible consequences? But the punishment that we decree against him is only our right, not his. Our right reacts against his, and he is—"in the wrong at last" because—we get the upper hand.

———————

But what is right, what is matter of right in a society, is voiced too—in the *law*.[28]

Whatever the law may be, it must be respected by the— loyal citizen. Thus the law-abiding mind of Old England is eulogized. To this that Euripidean sentiment (Orestes, 418) entirely corresponds: "We serve the gods, whatever the gods are." *Law as such, God as such,* thus far we are to-day.

People are at pains to distinguish *law* from arbitrary *orders,* from an ordinance: the former comes from a duly entitled authority . But a law over human action (ethical law, State law, etc.) is always a *declaration of will,* and so an order. Yes, even if I myself gave myself the law, it would yet be only my order, to which in the next moment I can refuse obedience. One may well enough declare what he will put up with, and so deprecate the opposite of the law, making known that in the contrary case he will treat the transgressor as his enemy; but no one has any business to command *my* actions, to say what course I shall pursue and set up a code to govern it. I must put up with it that he treats me as his *enemy,* but never that he makes free with me as his *creature,* and that he makes *his* reason, or even unreason, my plumb-line.

States last only so long as there is a *ruling will* and this ruling will is looked upon as tantamount to the own will. The lord's will is—law. What do your laws amount to if no one obeys them? What your orders, if nobody lets himself be ordered? The State cannot forbear the claim to determine the individual's will, to speculate and count on this. For the State it is indispensable that nobody have an *own will;* if one had, the State would have to exclude (lock up, banish, etc.) this one; if all had, they would do away with the State. The State is not thinkable without lordship and servitude (subjection); for the State must will to be the lord of all that it embraces, and this will is called the "will of the State."

28. (*Gesetz,* statute; no longer the same German word as "right.")

He who, to hold his own, must count on the absence of
will in others is a thing made by these others, as the master
is a thing made by the servant. If submissiveness ceased, it would
be all over with lordship.

The *own will* of Me is the State's destroyer; it is therefore
branded by the State as "self-will." Own will and the State
are powers in deadly hostility, between which no "eternal peace"
is possible. As long as the State asserts itself, it represents own
will, its ever-hostile opponent, as unreasonable, evil; and the
latter lets itself be talked into believing this—nay, it really is
such, for no more reason than this, that it still lets itself be
talked into such belief: it has not yet come to itself and to the
consciousness of its dignity; hence it is still incomplete, still
amenable to fine words.

Every State is a *despotism*, be the despot one or many,
or (as one is likely to imagine about a republic) if all be lords,
that is, despotize one over another. For this is the case when
the law given at any time, the expressed volition of (it may be)
a popular assembly, is thenceforth to be *law* for the individual,
to which *obedience is due* from him or toward which he has the
duty of obedience. If one were even to conceive the case that
every individual in the people had expressed the same will, and
hereby a complete "collective will" had come into being, the
matter would still remain the same. Would I not be bound to-day
and henceforth to my will of yesterday? My will would in
this case be *frozen*. Wretched *stability!* My creature— to wit, a
particular expression of will—would have become my commander. But I in my will, I the creator, should be hindered
in my flow and my dissolution. Because I was a fool yesterday
I must remain such my life long. So in the State-life I am at
best—I might just as well say, at worst—a bondman of myself.
Because I was a willer yesterday, I am to-day without will:
yesterday voluntary, to-day involuntary.

How change it? Only be recognizing no *duty*, not *binding*
myself nor letting myself be bound. If I have no duty, then I
know no law either.

"But they will bind me!" My will nobody can bind, and my
disinclination remains free.

"Why, everything must go topsy-turvy if every one could do what he would!" Well, who says that every one can do everything? What are you there for, pray, you who do not need to put up with everything? Defend yourself, and no one will do anything to you! He who would break your will has to do with you, and is your *enemy*. Deal with him as such. If there stand behind you for your protection some millions more, then you are an imposing power and will have an easy victory. But, even if as a power you overawe your opponent, still you are not on that account a hallowed authority to him, unless he be a simpleton. He does not owe you respect and regard, even though he will have to consider your might.

We are accustomed to classify States according to the different ways in which "the supreme might" is distributed. If an individual has it—monarchy; if all have it—democracy; etc. Supreme might then! Might against whom? Against the individual and his "self-will." The State practices "violence," the individual must not do so. The State's behavior is violence, and it calls its violence "law"; that of the individual, "crime." Crime,[29] then—so the individual's violence is called; and only by crime does he overcome[30] the State's violence when he thinks that the State is not above him, but he is above the State.

Now, if I wanted to act ridiculously, I might, as a well-meaning person, admonish you not to make laws which impair my self-development, self-activity, self-creation. I do not give this advice. For, if you should follow it, you would be unwise, and I should have been cheated of my entire profit. I request nothing at all from you; for, whatever I might demand, you would still be dictatorial lawgivers, and must be so, because a raven cannot sing, nor a robber live without robbery. Rather do I ask those who would be egoists what they think the more egoistic—to let laws be given them by you, and to respect those that are given, or to practice *refractoriness,* yes, complete disobedience. Good-hearted people think the laws ought to prescribe only what is accepted in the people's feeling as right and proper.

29. (*Verbrechen*)
30. (*brechen*)

But what concern is it of mine what is accepted in the nation and by the nation? The nation will perhaps be against the blasphemer; therefore a law against blasphemy. Am I not to blaspheme on that account? Is this law to be more than an "order" to me? I put the question.

Solely from the principle that all *right* and all *authority* belong to the *collectivity of the people* do all forms of government arise. For none of them lacks this appeal to the collectivity, and the despot, as well as the president or any aristocracy, acts and commands "in the name of the State." They are in possession of the "authority of the State," and it is perfectly indifferent whether, were this possible, the people as a *collectivity* (all individuals) exercise this State-*authority,* or whether it is only the representatives of this collectivity, be there many of them as in aristocracies or one as in monarchies. Always the collectivity is above the individual, and has a power which is called *legitimate,* which is law.

Over against the sacredness of the State, the individual is only a vessel of dishonor, in which "exuberance, malevolence, mania for ridicule and slander, frivolity," are left as soon as he does not deem that object of veneration, the State, to be worthy of recognition. The spiritual *haughtiness* of the servants and subjects of the State has fine penalties against unspiritual 'exuberance."

When the government designates as punishable all play of mind *against* the State, the moderate liberals come and opine that fun, satire, wit, humor, must have free play anyhow, and *genius* must enjoy freedom. So not the *individual man* indeed, but still *genius,* is to be free. Here the State, or in its name the government, says with perfect right: He who is not for me is against me. Fun, wit, etc.—in short, the turning of State affairs into a comedy—have undermined States from of old: they are not "innocent." And, further, what boundaries are to be drawn between guilty and innocent wit? At this question the moderates fall into great perplexity, and everything reduces itself to the prayer that the State (government) would please not be so *sensitive,* so *ticklish;* that it would not immediately scent malevolence in "harmless' things, and would in general be a little "more tolerant." Exaggerated sensitiveness is certainly a weakness, its avoidance may be praiseworthy virtue; but in time of war one cannot be sparing, and what may be allowed under peaceable circumstances ceases to be permitted as soon as a state of siege is declared. Because the well-meaning liberals feel this plainly, they hasten to declare that, considering "the devotion of the people," there is assuredly no danger to be feared. But the government will be wiser, and not let itself be talked into believing anything of that sort. It knows too well how people stuff one with fine words, and will not let itself be satisfied with the Barmecide dish.[31]

But they are bound to have their play-ground, for they are children, you know, and cannot be so staid as old folks; boys will be boys. Only for this play-ground, only for a few hours of jolly running about, they bargain. They ask only that the State should not, like a splenetic papa, be too cross. It should permit some Processions of the Ass and plays of fools, as the church allowed them in the Middle Ages. But the times when it could grant this without danger are past. Children that now once come *into the open,* and live through an hour without the rod of discipline, are no longer willing to go into the *cell.* For the open is now no longer a *supplement* to the cell, no longer a refreshing *recreation,* but its *opposite,* an *aut—aut.* In short, the State must either no longer put up with anything, or put up with everything and perish; it must be either sensitive through and through, or, like a dead man, insensitive. Tolerance is done with. If the State but gives a finger, they take the whole hand at once. There can be no more "jesting," and all jest, such as fun, wit, humor, becomes bitter earnest.

The clamor of the Liberals for freedom of the press runs counter to their own principle, their proper *will.* They will what they *do not will;* they wish, they would like. Hence it is too that they fall away so easily when once so-called freedom of the press

31. [A figure of speech for a particularly disappointing illusion, referring to the story in *The Arabian Nights,* wherein a member of the Barmecide family pretended to serve a feast to a beggar but set before him only a succession of empty dishes.]

appears; then they would like censorship. Quite naturally. The
State is sacred even to them; likewise morals. They behave
toward it only as ill-bred brats, as tricky children who seek to
utilize the weaknesses of their parents. Papa State is to permit
them to say many things that do not please him, but papa has the
right, by a stern look, to blue-pencil their impertinent gabble.
If they recognize in him their papa, they must in his presence
put up with the censorship of speech, like every child.

If you let yourself be made out in the right by another, you
must no less let yourself be made out in the wrong by him; if
justification and reward come to you from him, expect also his
arraignment and punishment. Alongside right goes wrong, alongside legality *crime*. What are *you?—You* are a—*criminal!*

"The criminal is in the utmost degree the State's own crime!"
says Bettina.[32] One may let this sentiment pass, even if Bettina
herself does not understand it exactly so. For in the State the
unbridled I—I, as I belong to myself alone—cannot come to
my fulfilment and realization. Every ego is from birth a criminal
to begin with against the people, the State. Hence it is that it
does really keep watch over all; it sees in each one an—egoist,
and it is afraid of the egoist. It presumes the worst about each
one, and takes care, police-care, that "no harm happens to the
State," *ne quid respublica detrimenti capiat.* The unbridled ego—
and this we originally are, and in our secret inward parts we
remain so always—is the never-ceasing criminal in the State.
The man whom his boldness, his will, his inconsiderateness and
fearlessness lead is surrounded with spies by the State, by the
people. I say, by the people! The people (think it something
wonderful, you good-hearted folks, what you have in the people)—
the people is full of police sentiments through and through.—
Only he who renounces his ego, who practices "self-renunciation,"
is acceptable to the people.

32. *This Book Belongs to the King,* p. 376. [The pseudonym of
Elizabeth Brentano, Countess von Arnim (1785-1859), a writer and belated
socialist propagandist, best remembered for her correspondence with
Goethe, published in 1835. *Dies Buch gehört dem König,* cited by Stirner,
was published in Berlin in 1843.]

In the book cited Bettina is throughout good-natured enough
to regard the State as only sick, and to hope for its recovery,
a recovery which she would bring about through the "demagogues";[33] but it is not sick; rather is it in its full strength, when
it puts from it the demagogues who want to acquire something
for the individuals, for "all." In its believers it is provided with
the best demagogues (leaders of the people). According to Bettina,
the State is to[34] "develop mankind's germ of freedom; otherwise
it is a raven-mother[35] and caring for raven-fodder!" It cannot
do otherwise, for in its very caring for "mankind" (which, besides,
would have to be the "humane" or "free" State to begin with)
the "individual" is raven-fodder for it. How rightly speaks the
burgomaster, on the other hand:[36] "What? the State has no other
duty than to be merely the attendant of incurable invalids?—
That isn't to the point. From of old the healthy State has relieved
itself of the diseased matter, and not mixed itself with it. It does
not need to be so economical with its juices. Cut off the robber-
branches without hesitation, that the others may bloom.—Do
not shiver at the State's harshness; its morality, its policy and
religion, point it to that. Accuse it of no want of feeling; its
sympathy revolts against this, but its experience finds safety only
in this severity! There are diseases in which only drastic remedies
will help. The physician who recognizes the disease as such,
but timidly turns to palliatives, will never remove the disease,
but may well cause the patient to succumb after a shorter or
longer sickness." Frau Rat's question, "If you apply death as a
drastic remedy, how is the cure to be wrought then?" isn't to
the point. Why, the State does not apply death against itself,
but against an offensive member; it tears out an eye that offends
it, etc.

"For the invalid State the only way of salvation is to make
man flourish in it."[37] If one here, like Bettina, understand by
man the concept "Man," she is right; the "invalid" State will

33. [Bettina, *This Book*,] p. 376.
34. [Bettina, *This Book*,] p. 374.
35. (An unnatural mother.)
36. [Bettina, *This Book*,] p. 381.
37. [Bettina, *This Book*,] p. 385.

recover by the flourishing of "Man," for, the more infatuated the individuals are with "Man," the better it serves the State's turn. But, if one referred it to the individuals, to "all" (and the authoress half-does this too, because about "Man" she is still involved in vagueness), then it would sound somewhat like the following: For an invalid band of robbers the only way of salvation is to make the loyal citizen flourish in it! Why, thereby the band of robbers would simply go to ruin as a band of robbers; and, because it perceives this, it prefers to shoot every one who has a leaning toward becoming a "steady man."

In this book Bettina is a patriot, or, what is little more, a philanthropist, a worker for human happiness. She is discontented with the existing order in quite the same way as is the title-ghost of her book, along with all who would like to bring back the good old faith and what goes with it. Only she thinks, contrariwise, that the politicians, place-holders, and diplomats ruined the State, while those lay it at the door of the malevolent, the "seducers of the people."

What is the ordinary criminal but one who has committed the fatal mistake of endeavoring after what is the people's instead of seeking for what is his? He has sought despicable *alien* goods, has done what believers do who seek after what is God's. What does the priest who admonishes the criminal do? He sets before him the great wrong of having desecrated by his act what was hallowed by the State, its property (in which, of course, must be included even the life of those who belong to the State); instead of this, he might rather hold up to him the fact that he has befouled *himself* in not despising the alien thing, but thinking it worth stealing; he could, if he were not a parson. Talk with the so-called criminal as with an egoist, and he will be ashamed, not that he transgressed against your laws and goods, but that he considered your laws worth evading, your goods worth desiring; he will be ashamed that he did not—despise you and yours together, that he was too little an egoist. But you cannot talk egoistically with him, for you are not so great as a criminal, you—commit no crime! You do not know that an ego who is his own cannot desist from being a criminal, that crime is his life. And yet you should know it, since you believe that "we are all miserable sinners"; but you think surreptitiously to get beyond sin, you do not comprehend—for you are devil-fearing—that guilt is the value of a man. Oh, if you were guilty! But now you are "righteous."[38] Well—just put every thing nicely to rights[39] for your master!

When the Christian consciousness, or the Christian man, draws up a criminal code, what can the concept of *crime* be there but simply—*heartlessness?* Each severing and wounding of a *heart relation,* each *heartless behavior* toward a sacred being, is crime. The more heartfelt the relation is supposed to be, the more scandalous is the deriding of it, and the more worthy of punishment the crime. Everyone who is subject to the lord should love him; to deny this love is a high treason worthy of death. Adultery is a heartlessness worthy of punishment; one has no heart, no enthusiasm, no pathetic feeling for the sacredness of marriage. So long as the heart or soul dictates laws, only the heartful or soulful man enjoys the protection of the laws. That the man of soul makes laws means properly that the *moral* man makes them: what contradicts these men's "moral feeling," this they penalize. How should disloyalty, secession, breach of oaths— in short, all *radical breaking off,* all tearing asunder of venerable *ties*—not be flagitious and criminal in their eyes? He who breaks with these demands of the soul has for enemies all the moral, all the men of soul. Only Krummacher and his mates are the right people to set up consistently a penal code of the heart, as a certain bill sufficiently proves. The consistent legislation of the Christian State must be placed wholly in the hands of the— *parsons,* and will not become pure and coherent so long as it is worked out only by—the *parson-ridden,* who are always only *half-parsons.* Only then will every lack of soulfulness, every heartlessness, be certified as an unpardonable crime, only then will every agitation of the soul become condemnable, every objection of criticism and doubt be anathematized; only then is the own man, before the Christian consciousness, a convicted— *criminal* to begin with.

38. (*Gerechte*)
39. (*macht Alles huebsch gerecht*)

The men of the Revolution often talked of the people's "just revenge" as its "right." Revenge and right coincide here. Is this an attitude of an ego to an ego? The people cries that the opposite party has committed "crimes" against it. Can I assume that one commits a crime against me, without assuming that he has to act as I see fit? And this action I call the right, the good, etc.; the divergent action, a crime. So I think that the others must aim at the *same* goal with me; I do not treat them as unique beings[40] who bear their law in themselves and live according to it, but as beings who are to obey some "rational" law. I set up what "Man" is and what acting in a "truly human" way is, and I demand of every one that this law become norm and ideal to him; otherwise he will expose himself as a "sinner and criminal." But upon the "guilty" falls the "penalty of the law"!

One sees here how it is "Man" again who sets on foot even the concept of crime, of sin, and therewith that of right. A man in whom I do not recognize "man" is "sinner, a guilty one."

Only against a sacred thing are there criminals; you against me can never be a criminal, but only an opponent. But not to hate him who injures a sacred thing is in itself a crime, as St. Just cries out against Danton:[41] "Are you not a criminal and responsible for not having hated the enemies of the fatherland?" —

If, as in the Revolution, what "Man" is is apprehended as "good citizen," then from this concept of "Man" we have the well-known "political offenses and crimes."

In all this the individual, the individual man, is regarded as refuse, and on the other hand the general man, "Man," is honored. Now, according to how this ghost is named—as Christian, Jew, Mussulman, good citizen, loyal subject, freeman, patriot, etc.—just so do those who would like to carry through a divergent concept of man, as well as those who want to put *themselves* through, fall before victorious "Man."

---

40. (*Einzige*)

41. [Georges Jacques Danton (1759-1794), along with Robespierre, Marat and St. Just, leaders of the French Revolution. Danton fell afoul of an intra-revolutionary coup, charged with insufficient zeal in his opposition to the country's foreign enemies, and was guillotined in April, 1794.]

And with what unction the butchery goes on here in the name of the law, of the sovereign people, of God, etc.!

Now, if the persecuted trickily conceal and protect themselves from the stern parsonical judges, people stigmatize them as St. Just does those whom he accuses in the speech against Danton. One is to be a fool, and deliver himself up to their Moloch.

Crimes spring from *fixed ideas*. The sacredness of marriage is a fixed idea. From the sacredness it follows that infidelity is a *crime,* and therefore a certain marriage law imposes upon it a shorter or longer *penalty*. But by those who proclaim "freedom as sacred" this penalty must be regarded as a crime against freedom, and only in this sense has public opinion in fact branded the marriage law.

Society would have *every one* come to his right indeed, but yet only to that which is sanctioned by society, to the society-right, not really to *his* right. But I give or take to myself the right out of my own plenitude of power, and against every superior power I am the most impenitent criminal. Owner and creator of my right, I recognize no other source of right than— me, neither God nor the State nor nature nor even man himself with his "eternal rights of man," neither divine nor human right.

Right "in and for itself." Without relation to me, therefore! "Absolute right." Separated from me, therefore! A thing that exists in and for itself! An absolute! An eternal right, like an eternal truth!

According to the liberal way of thinking, right is to be obligatory for me because it is thus established by *human reason,* against which *my reason* is "unreason." Formerly people inveighed in the name of divine reason against weak human reason; now, in the name of strong human reason, against egoistic reason, which is rejected as "unreason." And yet none is real but this very "unreason." Neither divine nor human reason, but only your and my reason existing at any given time, is real, as and because you and I are real.

The thought of right is originally my thought; or, it has its origin in me. But, when it has sprung from me, when the "Word" is out, then it has "become flesh," it is a *fixed idea.* Now I no longer get rid of the thought; however I turn, it stands before me. Thus men have not become masters again of the thought "right," which they themselves created; their creature is running away with them. This is absolute right, that which is absolved or unfastened from me. We, revering it as absolute, cannot devour it again, and it takes from us the creative power: the creature is more than the creator, it is "in and for itself."

Once you no longer let right run around free, once you draw it back into its origin, into you, it is *your* right; and that is right which suits you.

Right has had to suffer an attack within itself, from the standpoint of right; war being declared on the part of liberalism against "privilege."[42]

Privileged and *endowed with equal rights*—on these two concepts turns a stubborn fight. Excluded or admitted—would mean the same. But where should there be a power—be it an imaginary one like God, law, or a real one like I, you—of which it should not be true that before it all are "endowed with equal rights," that is, no respect of persons holds? Every one is equally dear to God if he adores him, equally agreeable to the law if only he is a law-abiding person; whether the lover of God and the law is humpbacked and lame, whether poor or rich, and the like, that amounts to nothing for God and the law; just so, when you are at the point of drowning, you like a Negro as rescuer as well as the most excellent Caucasian—yes, in this situation you esteem a dog not less than a man. But to whom will not every one be also, contrariwise, a preferred or disregarded person? God punishes the wicked with his wrath, the law chastises the lawless, you let one visit you every moment and show the other the door.

The "equality of right" is a phantom just because right is nothing more and nothing less than admission, *a matter of grace,* which, be it said, one may also acquire by his desert; for desert and grace are not contradictory, since even grace wishes to be "deserved" and our gracious smile falls only to him who knows how to force it from us.

So people dream of "all citizens of the State having to stand

42. (Literally, "precedent right.")

side by side, with equal rights." As citizens of the State they are
certainly all equal for the State. But it will divide them, and
advance them or put them in the rear, according to its special
ends, if on no other account; and still more must it distinguish
them from one another as good and bad citizens.

Bruno Bauer disposes of the Jew question from the standpoint that "privilege" is not justified. Because Jew and Christian
have each some point of advantage over the other, and in having
this point of advantage are exclusive, therefore before the critic's
gaze they crumble into nothingness. With them the State lies
under the like blame, since it justifies their having advantages
and stamps it as a "privilege" or prerogative, but thereby derogates
from its calling to become a "free State."

But now every one has something of advantage over another—to wit, himself or his individuality; in this everybody
remains exclusive.

And, again, before a third party every one makes his peculiarity count for as much as possible, and (if he wants to win him
at all) tries to make it appear attractive before him.

Now, is the third party to be insensible to the difference of
the one from the other? Do they ask that of the free State or
of humanity? Then these would have to be absolutely without
self-interest, and incapable of taking an interest in any one
whatever. Neither God (who divides his own from the wicked)
nor the State (which knows how to separate good citizens from
bad) was thought of as so indifferent.

But they are looking for this very third party that bestows
no more "privilege." Then it is called perhaps the free State,
or humanity, or whatever else it may be.

As Christian and Jew are ranked low by Bruno Bauer on
account of their asserting privileges, it must be that they could
and should free themselves from their narrow standpoint by
self-renunciation or unselfishness. If they threw off their "egoism,"
the mutual wrong would cease, and with it Christian and Jewish
religiousness in general; it would be necessary only that neither
of them should any longer want to be anything peculiar.

But, if they gave up this exclusiveness, with that the ground
on which their hostilities were waged would in truth not yet

be forsaken. In case of need they would indeed find a third thing on which they could unite, a "general religion," a "religion of humanity," and the like; in short, an equalization, which need not be better than that which would result if all Jews became Christians, by this likewise the "privilege" of one over the other would have an end. The *tension*[43] would indeed be done away, but in this consisted not the essence of the two, but only their neighborhood. As being distinguished from each other they must necessarily be mutually resistant,[44] and the disparity will always remain. Truly it is not a failing in you that you stiffen[45] yourself against me and assert your distinctness or peculiarity: you need not give way or renounce yourself.

People conceive the significance of the opposition too *formally* and weakly when they want only to "dissolve" it in order to make room for a third thing that shall "unite." The opposition deserves rather to be *sharpened*. As Jew and Christian you are in too slight an opposition, and are contending only about religion, as it were about the emperor's beard, about a fiddlestick's end. Enemies in religion indeed, *in the rest* you still remain good friends, and equal to each other, as men. Nevertheless the rest too is unlike in each; and the time when you no longer merely *dissemble* your opposition will be only when you entirely recognize it, and everybody asserts himself from top to toe as *unique*.[46] Then the former opposition will assuredly be dissolved, but only because a stronger has taken it up into itself.

Our weakness consists not in this, that we are in opposition to others, but in this, that we are not completely so; that we are not entirely *severed* from them, or that we seek a "communion," a "bond," that in communion we have an ideal. One faith, one God, one idea, one hat, for all! If all were brought under one hat, certainly no one would any longer need to take off his hat before another.

The last and most decided opposition, that of unique against

43. (*Spannung*)
44. (*gespannt*)
45. (*spannen*)
46. (*einzig*)

unique, is at bottom beyond what is called opposition, but without having sunk back into "unity" and unison. As unique you have nothing in common with the other any longer, and therefore nothing divisive or hostile either; you are not seeking to be in the right against him before a *third* party, and are standing with him neither "on the ground of right" nor on any other common ground. The opposition vanishes in complete—*severance* or singleness.[47] This might indeed be regarded as the new point in common or a new parity, but here the parity consists precisely in the disparity, and is itself nothing but disparity, a par of disparity, and that only for him who institutes a "comparison."

The polemic against privilege forms a characteristic feature of liberalism, which fumes against "privilege" because it itself appeals to "right." Further than to fuming it cannot carry this; for privileges do not fall before right falls, as they are only forms of right. But right falls apart into its nothingness when it is swallowed up by might, when one understands what is meant by "Might goes before right." All right explains itself then as privilege, and privilege itself as power, as—*superior power*.

But must not the mighty combat against superior power show quite another face than the modest combat against privilege, which is to be fought out before a first judge, "Right," according to the judge's mind?

Now, in conclusion, I have still to take back the half-way form of expression of which I was willing to make use only so long as I was still rooting among the entrails of right, and letting the word at least stand. But, in fact, with the concept the word too loses its meaning. What I called "my right" is no longer "right" at all, because right can be bestowed only by a spirit, be it the spirit of nature or that of the species, of mankind, the Spirit of God or that of His Holiness or His Highness, etc. What I have without an entitling spirit I have without right; I have it solely and alone through my power.

47. (*Einzigkeit*)

I do not demand any right, therefore I need not recognize any either. What I can get by force I get by force, and what I do not get by force I have no right to, nor do I give myself airs, or consolation, with my imprescriptible right.

With absolute right, right itself passes away; the dominion of the "concept of right" is canceled at the same time. For it is not to be forgotten that hitherto concepts, ideas, or principles ruled us, and that among these rulers the concept of right, or of justice, played one of the most important parts.

Entitled or unentitled—that does not concern me, if I am only *powerful,* I am of myself *empowered,* and need no other empowering or entitling.

Right—is a wheel in the head, put there by a spook; power— that am I myself, I am the powerful one and owner of power. Right is above me, is absolute, and exists in one higher, as whose grace it flows to me: right is a gift of grace from the judge; power and might exist only in me the powerful and mighty.

B. — MY INTERCOURSE

IN society the human demand at most can be satisfied, while the egoistic must always come short.

Because it can hardly escape anybody that the present shows no such living interest in any question as in the "social," one has to direct his gaze especially to society. Nay, if the interest felt in it were less passionate and dazzled, people would not so much, in looking at society, lose sight of the individuals in it, and would recognize that a society cannot become new so long as those who form and constitute it remain the old ones. If, for example, there was to arise in the Jewish people a society which should spread a new faith over the earth, these apostles could in no case remain Pharisees.

As you are, so you present yourself, so you behave toward men: a hypocrite as a hypocrite, a Christian as a Christian. There-fore the character of a society is determined by the character of its members: they are its creators. So much at least one must perceive even if one were not willing to put to the test the concept "society" itself.

Ever far from letting *themselves* come to their full development and consequence, men have hitherto not been able to found their societies on *themselves;* or rather, they have been able only to found "societies" and to live in societies. The societies were always persons, powerful persons, so-called "moral persons," ghosts, before which the individual had the appropriate wheel in his head, the fear of ghosts. As such ghosts they may most suitably be designated by the respective names "people" and "peoplet": the people of the patriarchs, the people of the Hellenes, etc., at last the—people of men, Mankind (Anacharsis Cloots[48] was enthusiastic for the "nation" of mankind); then every subdivision of this "people," which could and must have its special societies, the Spanish, French people, etc.; within it again classes, cities, in short all kinds of corporations; lastly, tapering to the finest point, the little peoplet of the—*family.* Hence, instead of saying that the person that walked as ghost in all societies hitherto has been the people, there might also have been named the two extremes— to wit, either "mankind" or the "family," both the most "natural-born units." We choose the word "people"[49] because its derivation has been brought into connection with the Greek *polloi,* the "many" or "the masses," but still more because "national efforts" are at present the order of the day, and because even the newest mutineers have not yet shaken off this deceptive person, although on the other hand the latter consideration must give the preference to the expression "mankind," since on all sides they are going in for enthusiasm over "mankind."

The people, then—mankind or the family—have hitherto, as it seems, played history: no *egoistic* interest was to come up in these societies, but solely general ones, national or popular interests, class interests, family interests, and "general human

48. [Jean Baptiste, Baron de Cloots (1755-1794), of Dutch origin, a writer and rationalist, instrumental in the famous action in the French Revolution, known as the "Abolition of the worship of God," in November, 1793. Cloots was one of the followers of Hébert who was guillotined by Robespierre in March, 1794.]

49. (*Volk;* but the etymological remark following applies equally to the English word "people." See Liddell & Scott's Greek lexicon, under *pimplemi.*)

interests." But who has brought to their fall the peoples whose decline history relates? Who but the egoist, who was seeking *his* satisfaction! If once an egoistic interest crept in, the society was "corrupted" and moved toward its dissolution, as Rome proves with its highly developed system of private rights, or Christianity with the incessantly-breaking-in "rational self-determination," "self-consciousness," the "autonomy of the spirit," and so on.

The Christian people has produced two societies whose duration will keep equal measure with the permanence of that people: these are the societies *State* and *Church*. Can they be called a union of egoists? Do we in them pursue an egoistic, personal, own interest, or do we pursue a popular, an interest of the Christian *people,* to wit, a State, and Church interest? Can I and may I be myself in them? May I think and act as I will, may I reveal myself, live myself out, busy myself? Must I not leave untouched the majesty of the State, the sanctity of the Church?

Well, I may not do so as I will. But shall I find in any society such an unmeasured freedom of maying? Certainly no! Accordingly we might be content? Not a bit! It is a different thing whether I rebound from an ego or from a people, a generalization. There I am my opponent's opponent, born his equal; here I am a despised opponent, bound and under a guardian: there I stand man to man; here I am a schoolboy who can accomplish nothing against his comrade because the latter has called father and mother to aid and has crept under the apron, while I am well scolded as an ill-bred brat, and I must not "argue": there I fight against a bodily enemy; here against mankind, against a generalization, against a "majesty," against a spook. But to me no majesty, nothing sacred, is a limit; nothing that I know how to overpower. Only that which I cannot overpower still limits my might; and I of limited might am temporarily a limited I, not limited by the might *outside* me, but limited by my *own* still deficient might, by my *own impotence.* However, "the Guard dies, but does not surrender!" Above all, only a bodily opponent!

I dare meet every foeman
Whom I can see and measure with my eye,
Whose mettle fires my mettle for the fight—etc.

Many privileges have indeed been cancelled with time, but
solely for the sake of the common weal, of the State and the
State's weal, by no means for the strengthening of me. Vassalage
was abrogated only that a single liege lord, the lord of the people,
the monarchical power, might be strengthened: vassalage under
the one became yet more rigorous thereby. Only in favor of
the monarch, be he called "prince" or "law," have privileges
fallen. In France the citizens are not, indeed, vassals of the
king, but are instead vassals of the "law" (the Charter). *Subordination* was retained, only the Christian State recognized that
man cannot serve two masters (the lord of the manor and the
prince); therefore one obtained all the prerogatives; now he
can again *place* one above another, he can make "men in high
place."

But of what concern to me is the common weal? The
common weal as such is not *my weal,* but only the furthest
extremity of *self-renunciation.* The common weal may cheer
aloud while I must "down";[50] the State may shine while I starve.
In what lies the folly of the political liberals but in their opposing
the people to the government and talking of people's rights?
So there is the people going to be of age, etc. As if one who
has no mouth could be *mündig!*[51] Only the individual is able
to be *mündig.* Thus the whole question of the liberty of the
press is turned upside down when it is laid claim to as a "right
of the people." It is only a right, or better the might, of the
individual. If a people has liberty of the press, then I, although
in the midst of this people, have it not; a liberty of the people
is not *my* liberty, and the liberty of the press as a liberty of
the people must have at its side a press law directed against *me.*

50. (*Kuschen,* a word whose only use is in ordering dogs to keep
quiet.)

51. (This is the word for "of age"; but it is derived from *Mund,*
"mouth," and refers properly to the right of speaking through one's own
mouth, not by a guardian.)

This must be insisted on all around against the present-day efforts for liberty:

Liberty of the *people* is not *my* liberty!

Let us admit these categories, liberty of the people and right of the people: for example, the right of the people that everybody may bear arms. Does one not forfeit such a right? One cannot forfeit his own right, but may well forfeit a right that belongs not to me but to the people. I may be locked up for the sake of the liberty of the people; I may, under sentence, incur the loss of the right to bear arms.

Liberalism appears as the last attempt at a creation of the liberty of the people, a liberty of the commune, of "society," of the general, of mankind; the dream of a humanity, a people, a commune, a "society," that shall be of age.

A people cannot be free otherwise than at the individual's expense; for it is not the individual that is the main point in this liberty, but the people. The freer the people, the more bound the individual; the Athenian people, precisely at its freest time, created ostracism, banished the atheists, poisoned the most honest thinker.

How they do praise Socrates for his conscientiousness, which makes him resist the advice to get away from the dungeon! He is a fool that he concedes to the Athenians a right to condemn him. Therefore it certainly serves him right; why then does he remain standing on an equal footing with the Athenians? Why does he not break with them? Had he known, and been able to know, what he was, he would have conceded to such judges no claim, no right. That *he did not escape* was just his weakness, his delusion of still having something in common with the Athenians, or the opinion that he was a member, a mere member of this people. But he was rather this people itself in person, and could only be his own judge. There was no *judge over him,* as he himself had really pronounced a public sentence on himself and rated himself worthy of the Prytaneum. He should have stuck to that, and, as he had uttered no sentence of death against himself, should have despised that of the Athenians too and escaped. But he subordinated himself and recognized in the *people* his *judge;* he seemed little to himself before the majesty of the people. That he subjected himself to *might* (to which alone he could succumb) as to a "right" was treason against himself: it was *virtue*. To Christ, who, it is alleged, refrained from using the power over his heavenly legions, the same scrupulousness is thereby ascribed by the narrators. Luther did very well and wisely to have the safety of his journey to Worms[52] warranted to him in black and white, and Socrates should have known that the Athenians were his *enemies*, he alone his judge. The self-deception of a "reign of law," etc., should have given way to the perception that the relation was a relation of *might*.

It was with pettifoggery and intrigues that Greek liberty ended. Why? Because the ordinary Greeks could still less attain that logical conclusion which not even their hero of thought, Socrates, was able to draw. What then is pettifoggery but a way of utilizing something established without doing away with it? I might add "for one's own advantage," but, you see, that lies in "utilizing." Such pettifoggers are the theologians who "wrest" and "force" God's word; what would they have to wrest if it were not for the "established" Word of God? So those liberals who only shake and wrest the "established order." They are all perverters, like those perverters of the law. Socrates recognized law, right; the Greeks constantly retained the authority of right and law. If with this recognition they wanted nevertheless to assert their advantage, every one his own, then they had to seek it in perversion of the law, or intrigue. Alcibiades, an intriguer of genius, introduces the period of Athenian "decay"; the Spartan Lysander and others show that intrigue had become universally Greek. Greek *law,* on which the Greek *States* rested, had to be perverted and undermined by the egoists within these States, and the *States* went down that the *individuals* might become free, the Greek people fell because the individuals cared less for this people than for themselves. In general, all States, constitutions, churches, have sunk by the *secession* of individuals;

52. [A reference to Martin Luther's safe-conduct pass under which he journeyed to the grand Diet of the German princes at Worms in 1521 to defend himself of charges of heresy.]

for the individual is the irreconcilable enemy of every *generality*, every *tie,* every fetter. Yet people fancy to this day that man needs "sacred ties": he, the deadly enemy of every "tie." The history of the world shows that no tie has yet remained unrent, shows that man tirelessly defends himself against ties of every sort; and yet, blinded, people think up new ties again and again, and think that they have arrived at the right one if one puts upon them the tie of a so-called free constitution, a beautiful, constitutional tie; decoration ribbons, the ties of confidence between "— — —," do seem gradually to have become somewhat infirm, but people have made no further progress than from apron-strings to garters and collars.

Everything sacred is a tie, a fetter.

Everything sacred is and must be perverted by perverters of the law; therefore our present time has multitudes of such perverters in all spheres. They are preparing the way for the break-up of law, for lawlessness.

Poor Athenians who are accused of pettifoggery and sophistry! poor Alcibiades, of intrigue! Why, that was just your best point, your first step in freedom. Your Aeschylus, Herodotus, etc., only wanted to have a free Greek *people;* you were the first to surmise something of *your* freedom.

A people represses those who tower above *its majesty,* by ostracism against too-powerful citizens, by the Inquisition against the heretics of the Church, by the—Inquisition against traitors in the State.

For the people is concerned only with its self-assertion; it demands "patriotic self-sacrifice" from everybody. To it, accordingly, every one *in himself* is indifferent, a nothing, and it cannot do, not even suffer, what the individual and he alone must do—to wit, *turn him to account.* Every people, every State, is unjust toward the *egoist.*

As long as there still exists even one institution which the individual may not dissolve, the ownness and self-appurtenance of Me is still very remote. How can I be free when I must bind myself by oath to a constitution, a charter, a law, "vow body and soul" to my people? How can I be my own when my faculties may develop only so far as they "do not disturb the harmony of society" (Weitling)?

The fall of peoples and mankind will invite *me* to my rise.

Listen, even as I am writing this, the bells begin to sound, that they may jingle in for to-morrow the festival of the thousand years' existence of our dear Germany.[53] Sound, sound its knell! You do sound solemn enough, as if your tongue was moved by the presentiment that it is giving convoy to a corpse. The German people and German peoples have behind them a history of a thousand years: what a long life! O, go to rest, never to rise again—that all may become free whom you so long have held in fetters.—The *people* is dead.—Up with *me*!

O thou my much-tormented German people—what was thy torment? It was the torment of a thought that cannot create itself a body, the torment of a walking spirit that dissolves into nothing at every cock-crow and yet pines for deliverance and fulfillment. In me too thou hast lived long, thou dear—thought, thou dear—spook. Already I almost fancied I had found the word of thy deliverance, discovered flesh and bones for the wandering spirit; then I hear them sound, the bells that usher thee into eternal rest; then the last hope fades out, then the notes of the last love die away, then I depart from the desolate house of those who now are dead and enter at the door of the—living one:

For only he who is alive is in the right.

Farewell, thou dream of so many millions; farewell, thou who hast tyrannized over thy children for a thousand years!

To-morrow they carry thee to the grave; soon thy sisters, the peoples, will follow thee. But, when they have all followed, then — — mankind is buried, and I am my own, I am the laughing heir!

The word *Gesellschaft* (society) has its origin in the word *Sal* (hall). If one hall encloses many persons, then the hall

53. [Written in 1843, the thousandth anniversary of the Treaty of Verdun, when the empire of Charlemagne was divided into three parts, the part from the Rhine to the easterly marches of the empire becoming what was essentially Germany upon unification in 1870, though it was a confederation of several separate political units in Stirner's time.]

causes these persons to be in society. They *are* in society, and at most constitute a parlor-society by talking in the traditional forms of parlor speech. When it comes to real *intercourse,* this is to be regarded as independent of society: it may occur or be lacking, without altering the nature of what is named society. Those who are in the hall are a society even as mute persons, or when they put each other off solely with empty phrases of courtesy. Intercourse is mutuality, it is the action, the *commercium,* of individuals; society is only community of the hall, and even the statues of a museum-hall are in society, they are "grouped." People are accustomed to say "they *haben inne*[54] this hall in common," but the case is rather that the hall has us *inne* or in it. So far the natural signification of the word society. In this it comes out that society is not generated by me and you, but by a third factor which makes associates out of us two, and that it is just this third factor that is the creative one, that which creates society.

Just so a prison society or prison companionship (those who enjoy[55] the same prison). Here we already hit upon a third factor fuller of significance than was that merely local one, the hall. Prison no longer means a space only, but a space with express reference to its inhabitants: for it is a prison only through being destined for prisoners, without whom it would be a mere building. What gives a common stamp to those who are gathered in it? Evidently the prison, since it is only by means of the prison that they are prisoners. What, then, determines the *manner of life* of the prison society? The prison! What determines their intercourse? The prison too, perhaps? Certainly they can enter upon intercourse only as prisoners, only so far as the prison laws allow it; but that *they themselves* hold intercourse, I with you, this the prison cannot bring to pass; on the contrary, it must have an eye to guarding against such egoistic, purely personal intercourse (and only as such is it really intercourse between me and you). That we *jointly* execute a job,

54. ("Occupy"; literally, "have within").
55. (The word *Genosse,* "companion," signifies originally a companion in *enjoyment.*)

run a machine, effectuate anything in general—for this a prison will indeed provide; but that I forget that I am a prisoner, and engage in intercourse with you who likewise disregard it, brings danger to the prison, and not only cannot be caused by it, but must not even be permitted. For this reason the saintly and moral-minded French chamber decides to introduce solitary confinement, and other saints will do the like in order to cut off "demoralizing intercourse." Imprisonment is the established and —sacred condition, to injure which no attempt must be made. The slightest push of that kind is punishable, as is every uprising against a sacred thing by which man is to be charmed and chained.

Like the hall, the prison does form a society, a companionship, a communion (as in a communion of labor), but no *intercourse,* no reciprocity, no *union.* On the contrary, every union in the prison bears within it the dangerous seed of a "plot," which under favorable circumstances might spring up and bear fruit.

Yet one does not usually enter the prison voluntarily, and seldom remains in it voluntarily either, but cherishes the egoistic desire for liberty. Here, therefore, it sooner becomes manifest that personal intercourse is in hostile relations to the prison society and tends to the dissolution of this very society, this joint incarceration.

Let us therefore look about for such communions as, it seems, we remain in gladly and voluntarily, without wanting to endanger them by our egoistic impulses.

As a communion of the required sort the *family* offers itself in the first place. Parents, husbands and wife, children, brothers and sisters, represent a whole or form a family, for the further widening of which the collateral relatives also may be made to serve if taken into account. The family is a true communion only when the law of the family, piety[56] or family love, is observed by its members. A son to whom parents, brothers,

56. (This word in German does not mean religion, but, as in Latin, faithfulness to family ties—as we speak of "filial piety." But the word elsewhere translated "pious" (*fromm*) means "religious," as usually in English.)

and sisters have become indifferent *has been* a son; for, as the sonship no longer shows itself efficacious, it has no greater significance than the long-past connection of mother and child by the navel-string.   That one has once lived in this bodily juncture cannot as a fact be undone; and so far one remains irrevocably this mother's son and the brother of the rest of her children; but it would come to a lasting connection only by lasting piety, this spirit of the family.   Individuals are members of a family in the full sense only when they make the *persistence* of the family their task; only as *conservative* do they keep aloof from doubting their basis, the family.   To every member of the family one thing must be fixed and sacred—to wit, the family itself, or, more expressively, piety.   That the family is to *persist* remains to its member, so long as he keeps himself free from that egoism which is hostile to the family, an unassailable truth.   In a word:—If the family is sacred, then nobody who belongs to it may secede from it; else he becomes a "criminal" against the family: he may never pursue an interest hostile to the family, form a misalliance.   He who does this has "dishonored the family," "put it to shame," etc.

Now, if in an individual the egoistic impulse has not force enough, he complies and makes a marriage which suits the claims of the family, takes a rank which harmonizes with its position, and the like; in short, he "does honor to the family."

If, on the contrary, the egoistic blood flows fierily enough in his veins, he prefers to become a "criminal" against the family and to throw off its laws.

Which of the two lies nearer my heart, the good of the family or my good?   In innumerable cases both go peacefully together; the advantage of the family is at the same time mine, and *vice versa*.   Then it is hard to decide whether I am thinking *selfishly* or *for the common benefit,* and perhaps I complacently flatter myself with my unselfishness.   But there comes the day when a necessity of choice makes me tremble, when I have it in mind to dishonor my family tree, to affront parents, brothers, and kindred.   What then?   Now it will appear how I am disposed at the bottom of my heart; now it will be revealed whether piety ever stood above egoism for me, now the selfish one can no longer skulk behind the semblance of unselfishness. A wish rises in my soul, and, growing from hour to hour, becomes a passion. To whom does it occur at first blush that the slightest thought which may result adversely to the spirit of the family (piety) bears within it a transgression against this? Nay, who at once, in the first moment, becomes completely conscious of the matter? It happens so with Juliet in "Romeo and Juliet." The unruly passion can at last no longer be tamed, and undermines the building of piety. You will say, indeed, it is from self-will that the family casts out of its bosom those wilful ones that grant more of a hearing to their passion than to piety; the good Protestants used the same excuse with much success against the Catholics, and believed in it themselves. But it is just a subterfuge to roll the fault off oneself, nothing more. The Catholics had regard for the common bond of the church, and thrust those heretics from them only because these did not have so much regard for the bond of the church as to sacrifice their convictions to it; the former, therefore, held the bond fast, because the bond, the Catholic (common and united) church, was sacred to them; the latter, on the contrary, disregarded the bond. Just so those who lack piety. They are not thrust out, but thrust themselves out, prizing their passion, their wilfulness, higher than the bond of the family.

But now sometimes a wish glimmers in a less passionate and wilful heart than Juliet's. The pliable girl brings herself as a *sacrifice* to the peace of the family. One might say that here too selfishness prevailed, for the decision came from the feeling that the pliable girl felt herself more satisfied by the unity of the family than by the fulfillment of her wish. That might be; but what if there remained a sure sign that egoism had been sacrificed to piety? What if, even after the wish that had been directed against the peace of the family was sacrificed, it remained at least as a recollection of a "sacrifice" brought to a sacred tie? What if the pliable girl were conscious of having left her self-will unsatisfied and humbly subjected herself to a higher power? Subjected and sacrificed, because the superstition of piety exercised its dominion over her!

There egoism won, here piety wins and the egoistic heart

bleeds; there egoism was strong, here it was—weak. But the weak, as we have long known, are the—unselfish. For them, for these its weak members, the family cares, because they *belong* to the family, do not belong to themselves and care for themselves. This weakness Hegel praises when he wants to have match-making left to the choice of the parents.

As a sacred communion to which, among the rest, the individual owes obedience, the family has the judicial function too vested in it; such a "family court" is described in the *Cabanis* of Wilibald Alexis.[57] There the father, in the name of the "family council," puts the intractable son among the soldiers and thrusts him out of the family, in order to cleanse the smirched family again by means of this act of punishment.—The most consistent development of family responsibility is contained in Chinese law, according to which the whole family has to expiate the individual's fault.

To-day, however, the arm of family power seldom reaches far enough to take seriously in hand the punishment of apostates (in most cases the State protects even against disinheritance). The criminal against the family (family-criminal) flees into the domain of the State and is free, as the State-criminal who gets away to America is no longer reached by the punishments of his State. He who has shamed his family, the graceless son, is protected against the family's punishment because the State, this protecting lord, takes away from family punishment its "sacredness" and profanes it, decreeing that it is only—"revenge": it restrains punishment, this sacred family right, because before its, the State's, "sacredness" the subordinate sacredness of the family always pales and loses its sanctity as soon as it comes in conflict with this higher sacredness. Without the conflict, the State lets pass the lesser sacredness of the family; but in the opposite case it even commands crime against the family, charging, for example, the son to refuse obedience to his parents

57. [The pseudonym of Georg Wilhelm Häring (1798-1871), a novelist, resident of Breslau, descended from a refugee family from Brittany. *Cabanis* was published in Berlin in 1832, and was one of his most famous stories; seven editions appeared in the following sixty years.]

as soon as they want to beguile him to a crime against the State.

Well, the egoist has broken the ties of the family and found in the State a lord to shelter him against the grievously affronted spirit of the family. But where has he run now? Straight into a new *society,* in which his egoism is awaited by the same snares and nets that it has just escaped. For the State is likewise a society, not a union; it is the broadened *family* ("Father of the Country—Mother of the Country—children of the country").

What is called a State is a tissue and plexus of dependence and adherence; it is a *belonging together,* a holding together, in which those who are placed together fit themselves to each other, or, in short, mutually depend on each other: it is the *order* of this *dependence.* Suppose the king, whose authority lends authority to all down to the beadle, should vanish: still all in whom the will for order was awake would keep order erect against the disorders of bestiality. If disorder were victorious, the State would be at an end.

But is this thought of love, to fit ourselves to each other, to adhere to each other and depend on each other, really capable of winning us? According to this the State should be *love* realized, the being for each other and living for each other of all. Is not self-will being lost while we attend to the will for order? Will people not be satisfied when order is cared for by authority, when authority sees to it that no one "gets in the way of" another; when, then, the *herd* is judiciously distributed or ordered? Why, then everything is in "the best order," and it is this best order that is called—State!

Our societies and States *are* without our *making* them, are united without our uniting, are predestined and established, or have an independent standing[58] of their own, are the indissolubly established against us egoists. The fight of the world to-day is, as it is said, directed against the "established." Yet people are wont to misunderstand this as if it were only that what is now established was to be exchanged for another, a better, established

58. (It should be remembered that the words "establish" and "State" are both derived from the root "stand.")

system. But war might rather be declared against establishment itself, the *State,* not a particular State, not any such thing as the mere condition of the State at the time; it is not another State (such as a "people's State") that men aim at, but their *union,* uniting, this ever-fluid uniting of everything standing.—A State exists even without my co-operation: I am born in it, brought up in it, under obligations to it, and must "do it homage."[59] It takes me up into its "favor,"[60] and I live by its "grace." Thus the independent establishment of the State founds my lack of independence; its condition as a "natural growth," its organism, demands that my nature do not grow freely, but be cut to fit it. That *it* may be able to unfold in natural growth, it applies to me the shears of "civilization"; it gives me an education and culture adapted to it, not to me, and teaches me to respect the laws, to refrain from injury to State property (that is, private property), to reverence divine and earthly highness, etc.; in short, it teaches me to be—*unpunishable,* "sacrificing" my ownness to "sacredness" (everything possible is sacred; property, others' life, etc.). In this consists the sort of civilization and culture that the State is able to give me: it brings me up to be a "serviceable instrument," a "serviceable member of society."

This every State must do, the people's State as well as the absolute or constitutional one. It must do so as long as we rest in the error that it is an *I,* as which it then applies to itself the name of a "moral, mystical, or political person." I, who really am I, must pull off this lion-skin of the I from the stalking thistle-eater. What manifold robbery have I not put up with in the history of the world! There I let sun, moon, and stars, cats and crocodiles, receive the honor of ranking as I; there Jehovah, Allah, and Our Father came and were invested with the I; there families, tribes, peoples, and at last actually mankind, came and were honored as I's; there the Church, the State, came with the pretension to be I—and I gazed calmly on all. What wonder if then there was always a real I too that joined the company and affirmed in my face that it was not my *you* but my real *I.* Why,

59. (*huldigen*)
60. (*Huld*)

the Son of Man *par excellence* had done the like; why should not *a* son of man do it too? So I saw my I always above me and outside me, and could never really come to myself.

I never believed in myself; I never believed in my present, I saw myself only in the future. The boy believes he will be a proper I, a proper fellow, only when he has become a man; the man thinks, only in the other world will he be something proper. And, to enter more closely upon reality at once, even the best are to-day still persuading each other that one must have received into himself the State, his people, mankind, and what not, in order to be a real I, a "free burgher," a "citizen," a "free or true man"; they too see the truth and reality of me in the reception of an alien I and devotion to it. And what sort of an I? An I that is neither an I nor a you, a *fancied* I, a spook.

While in the Middle Ages the church could well brook many States living united in it, the States learned after the Reformation, especially after the Thirty Years' War, to tolerate many churches (confessions) gathering under one crown. But all States are religious and, as the case may be, "Christian States," and make it their task to force the intractable, the "egoists," under the bond of the unnatural, that is, Christianize them. All arrangements of the Christian State have the object of *Christianizing the people*. Thus the court has the object of forcing people to justice, the school that of forcing them to mental culture—in short, the object of protecting those who act Christianly against those who act un-Christianly, of bringing Christian action to *dominion,* of making it *powerful.* Among these means of force the State counted the *Church* too, it demanded a—particular religion from everybody. Dupin[61] said lately against the clergy, "Instruction and education belong to the State."

Certainly everything that regards the principle of morality is a State affair. Hence it is that the Chinese State meddles so much in family concerns, and one is nothing there if one is not first of all a good child to his parents. Family concerns are

61. [Andre Marie J. — J. Dupin (1783-1865), formidable and versatile French politician, a judge and one time president of the Chamber of Deputies, and active under several quite different regimes; Stirner's quote presumably came from a newspaper comment on a current speech.]

altogether State concerns with us too, only that our State—puts confidence in the families without painful oversight; it holds the family bound by the marriage tie, and this tie cannot be broken without it.

But that the State makes me responsible for my principles, and demands certain ones from me, might make me ask, what concern has it with the "wheel in my head" (principle)? Very much, for the State is the—*ruling principle*. It is supposed that in divorce matters, in marriage law in general, the question is of the proportion of rights between Church and States. Rather, the question is of whether anything sacred is to rule over man, be it called faith or ethical law (morality). The State behaves as the same ruler that the Church was. The latter rests on godliness, the former on morality.

People talk of the tolerance, the leaving opposite tendencies free, and the like, by which civilized States are distinguished. Certainly some are strong enough to look with complacency on even the most unrestrained meetings, while others charge their catchpole to go hunting for tobacco-pipes. Yet for one State as for another the play of individuals among themselves, their buzzing to and fro, their daily life, is an *incident* which it must be content to leave to themselves because it can do nothing with this. Many, indeed, still strain out gnats and swallow camels, while others are shrewder. Individuals are "freer" in the latter, because less pestered. But *I* am free in *no* State. The lauded tolerance of States is simply a tolerating of the "harmless," the "not dangerous"; it is only elevation above pettymindedness, only a more estimable, grander, prouder—despotism. A certain State seemed for a while to mean to be pretty well elevated above *literary* combats, which might be carried on with all heat; England is elevated above *popular turmoil* and—tobacco-smoking. But woe to the literature that deals blows at the State itself, woe to the mobs that "endanger" the State. In that certain State they dream of a "free science," in England of a "free popular life."

The State does let individuals *play* as freely as possible, only they must not be in *earnest,* must not forget *it.* Man must not carry on intercourse with man *unconcernedly,* not without "superior oversight and mediation." I must not execute all that I am able to, but only so much as the State allows; I must not turn to account *my* thoughts, nor *my* work, nor, in general, anything of mine.

The State always has the sole purpose to limit, tame, subordinate, the individual—to make him subject to some *generality* or other; it lasts only so long as the individual is not all in all, and it is only the clearly-marked *restriction of me,* my limitation, my slavery. Never does a State aim to bring in the free activity of individuals, but always that which is bound to the *purpose of the State.* Through the State nothing *in common* comes to pass either, as little as one can call a piece of cloth the common work of all the individual parts of a machine; it is rather the work of the whole machine as a unit, *machine work.* In the same style everything is done by the *State machine* too; for it moves the clockwork of the individual minds, none of which follow their own impulse. The State seeks to hinder every free activity by its censorship, its supervision, its police, and holds this hindering to be its duty, because it is in truth a duty of self-preservation. The State wants to make something out of man, therefore there live in it only *made* men; every one who wants to be his own self is its opponent and is nothing. "He is nothing" means as much as, the State does not make use of him, grants him no position, no office, no trade, and the like.

Edgar Bauer,[62] in the *Liberalen Bestrebungen* (vol. II, p. 50), is still dreaming of a "government which, proceeding out of the people, can never stand in opposition to it." He does indeed (p. 69) himself take back the word "government": "In the republic no government at all obtains, but only an executive authority. An authority which proceeds purely and alone out of the people; which has not an independent power, independent

62. What was said in the concluding remarks after Humane Liberalism holds good of the following—to wit, that it was likewise written immediately after the appearance of the book cited. [Edgar Bauer (1820-1886), younger brother of Bruno and a collaborator on a number of literary projects, as well as being ideologically allied to him. A third Bauer brother, Egbert, did not figure in Stirner's polemical discussions. *Die Liberalen Bestrebungen in Deutschland* was published in Zurich and Winterthur in 1843.]

principles, independent officers, over against the people; but which has its foundation, the fountain of its power and of its principles, in the sole, supreme authority of the State, in the people. The concept government, therefore, is not at all suitable in the people's State." But the thing remains the same. That which has "proceeded, been founded, sprung from the fountain" becomes something "independent" and, like a child delivered from the womb, enters upon opposition at once. The government, if it were nothing independent and opposing, would be nothing at all.

"In the free State there is no government," etc. (p. 94). This surely means that the people, when it is the *sovereign,* does not let itself be conducted by a superior authority. Is it perchance different in absolute monarchy? Is there *there* for the *sovereign,* perchance, a government standing over him? *Over* the sovereign, be he called prince or people, there never stands a government: that is understood of itself. But over *me* there will stand a government in every "State," in the absolute as well as in the republican or "free." *I* am as badly off in one as in the other.

The republic is nothing whatever but—absolute monarchy; for it makes no difference whether the monarch is called prince or people, both being a "majesty." Constitutionalism itself proves that nobody is able and willing to be only an instrument. The ministers domineer over their master the prince, the deputies over their master the people. Here, then, the *parties* at least are already free—*videlicet,* the office-holders' party (so-called people's party). The prince must conform to the will of the ministers, the people dance to the pipe of the chambers. Constitutionalism is further than the republic, because it is the *State* in incipient *dissolution.*

Edgar Bauer denies (p. 56) that the people is a "personality" in the constitutional State; *per contra,* then, in the republic? Well, in the constitutional State the people is—a *party,* and a party is surely a "personality" if one is once resolved to talk of a "political" (p. 76) moral person anyhow. The fact is that a moral person, be it called people's party or people or even "the Lord," is in no wise a person, but a spook.

Further, Edgar Bauer goes on (p. 69): "guardianship is the characteristic of a government." Truly, still more that of a people and "people's State"; it is the characteristic of all *dominion.*

A people's State, which "unites in itself all completeness of power," the "absolute master," cannot let me become powerful. And what a chimera, to be no longer willing to call the "people's officials" "servants, instruments," because they "execute the free, rational law-will of the people!" (p. 73). He thinks (p. 74): "Only by all official circles subordinating themselves to the government's views can unity be brought into the State"; but his "people's State" is to have "unity" too; how will a lack of subordination be allowed there? subordination to the —people's will.

"In the constitutional State it is the regent and his *disposition* that the whole structure of government rests on in the end." (p. 130.) How would that be otherwise in the "people's State"? Shall *I* not there be governed by the people's *disposition* too, and does it make a difference *for me* whether I see myself kept in dependence by the prince's disposition or by the people's disposition, so-called "public opinion"? If dependence means as much as "religious relation," as Edgar Bauer rightly alleges, then in the people's State the people remains *for me* the superior power, the "majesty" (for God and prince have their proper essence in "majesty") to which I stand in religious relations.— Like the sovereign regent, the sovereign people too would be reached by no *law.* Edgar Bauer's whole attempt comes to a *change of masters.* Instead of wanting to make the *people* free, he should have had his mind on the sole realizable freedom, his own.

In the constitutional State *absolutism* itself has at last come in conflict with itself, as it has been shattered into a duality; the government wants to be absolute, and the people wants to be absolute. These two absolutes will wear out against each other.

Edgar Bauer inveighs against the determination of the regent by *birth,* by *chance.* But, when "the people" have become "the sole power in the State" (p. 132), have *we* not then in it a master from *chance*? Why, what is the people? The people has always been only the *body* of the government: it is many under one hat (a prince's hat) or many under one constitution. And the constitution is the—prince. Princes and peoples will persist so long as both do not *collapse,* that is, fall *together.* If under one constitution there are many "peoples"—as in the ancient

Persian monarchy and to-day—then these "peoples" rank only as "provinces." For me the people is in any case an—accidental power, a force of nature, an enemy that I must overcome.

What is one to think of under the name of an "organized" people (p. 132)? A people "that no longer has a government," that governs itself. In which, therefore, no ego stands out prominently; a people organized by ostracism. The banishment of egos, ostracism, makes the people autocrat.

If you speak of the people, you must speak of the prince; for the people, if it is to be a subject[63] and make history, must, like everything that acts, have a *head,* its "supreme head." Weitling sets this forth in [*Die Europäische*] *Triarchie,* and Proudhon declares, "*une société, pour ainsi dire acéphale, ne peut vivre.*"[64]

The *vox populi* is now always held up to us, and "public opinion" is to rule our princes. Certainly the *vox populi* is at the same time *vox dei;* but is either of any use, and is not the *vox principis* also *vox dei*?

At this point the "Nationals" may be brought to mind. To demand of the thirty-eight States of Germany that they shall act as *one nation* can only be put alongside the senseless desire that thirty-eight swarms of bees, led by thirty-eight queen-bees, shall unite themselves into one swarm. *Bees* they all remain; but it is not the bees as bees that belong together and can join themselves together, it is only that the *subject* bees are connected with the *ruling* queens. Bees and peoples are destitute of will, and the *instinct* of their queens leads them.

If one were to point the bees to their beehood, in which at any rate they are all equal to each other, one would be doing the same thing that they are now doing so stormily in pointing the Germans to their Germanhood. Why, Germanhood is just like beehood in this very thing, that it bears in itself the necessity of cleavages and separations, yet without pushing on to the last separation, where, with the complete carrying through of the process of separating, its end appears: I mean, to the separation

63. (In the philosophical sense (a thinking and acting being), not in the political sense.)

64. *Création de l'ordre,* p. 485.

of man from man. Germanhood does indeed divide itself into different peoples and tribes, beehives; but the individual who has the quality of being a German is still as powerless as the isolated bee. And yet only individuals can enter into union with each other, and all alliances and leagues of peoples are and remain mechanical compoundings, because those who come together, at least so far as the "peoples" are regarded as the ones that have come together, are *destitute of will.* Only with the last separation does separation itself end and change to unification.

Now the Nationals are exerting themselves to set up the abstract, lifeless unity of beehood; but the self-owned are going to fight for the unity willed by their own will, for union. This is the token of all reactionary wishes, that they want to set up something *general,* abstract, an empty, lifeless *concept,* in distinction from which the self-owned aspire to relieve the robust, lively *particular* from the trashy burden of generalities. The reactionaries would be glad to smite a *people,* a *nation,* forth from the earth; the self-owned have before their eyes only themselves. In essentials the two efforts that are just now the order of the day —to wit, the restoration of provincial rights and of the old tribal divisions (Franks, Bavarians, Lusatia,[65] etc.), and the restoration of the entire nationality—coincide in one. But the Germans will come into unison, unite *themselves,* only when they knock over their beehood as well as all the beehives; in other words, when they are more than—Germans: only then can they form a "German Union." They must not want to turn back into their nationality, into the womb, in order to be born again, but let every one turn in *to himself.* How ridiculously sentimental when one German grasps another's hand and presses it with sacred awe because "he too is a German!" With that he is something great! But this will certainly still be thought touching as long as people are enthusiastic for "brotherliness," as long as they have a *"family disposition."* From the superstition of "piety," from "brotherliness" or "childlikeness" or however else the soft-hearted

65. [A 10th century district or march created between the Elbe and Oder Rivers to serve as a buffer and advance frontier against the Eastern enemies of the Saxon and Salian emperors.]

piety-phrases run—from the *family spirit*—the Nationals, who
want to have a great *family of Germans,* cannot liberate themselves.

Aside from this, the so-called Nationals would only have to
understand themselves rightly in order to lift themselves out of
their juncture with the good-natured Teutomaniacs. For the uniting for material ends and interests, which they demand of the
Germans, comes to nothing else than a voluntary union. Carrière,
inspired, cries out,[66] "Railroads are to the more penetrating eye
the way to a *life of the people* such as has not yet anywhere
appeared in such significance." Quite right, it will be a life of
the people that has nowhere appeared, because it is not a—life
of the people.—So Carrière then combats himself (p. 10): "Pure
humanity or manhood cannot be better represented than by a
people fulfilling its mission." Why, by this nationality only is
represented. "Washed-out generality is lower than the form
complete in itself, which is itself a whole, and lives as a living
member of the truly general, the organized." Why, the people
is this very "washed-out generality," and it is only a man that
is the "form complete in itself."

The impersonality of what they call "people, nation," is
clear also from this: that a people which wants to bring its
I into view to the best of its power puts at its head the ruler
without will. It finds itself in the alternative either to be subjected
to a prince who realizes only *himself, his individual pleasure*—
then it does not recognize in the "absolute master" its own will,
the so-called will of the people—or to seat on the throne a prince
who gives effect to *no* will of his *own*—then it has a prince *without
will,* whose place some ingenious clockwork would perhaps fill
just as well.—Therefore insight need go only a step farther;
then it becomes clear of itself that the I of the people is an impersonal, "spiritual" power, the—law. The people's I, therefore,
is a—spook, not an I. I am I only by this, that I make myself;
that it is not another who makes me, but I must be my own

66. [Moriz Carrière (1817-1895), a German writer, and professor of
philosophy at Giessen and later Munich. Stirner quoted from page four of
Carrière's *Der Kölner Dom als freie deutsche Kirche: Gedanken über
Nationalität, Kunst und Religion beim Wiederbeginn des Baues,* published
in Stuttgart in 1843.]

work. But how is it with this I of the people? *Chance* plays it into the people's hand, chance gives it this or that born lord, accidents procure it the chosen one; he is not its (the *"sovereign"* people's) product, as I am *my* product. Conceive of one wanting to talk you into believing that you were not your I, but Tom or Jack was your I! But so it is with the people, and rightly. For the people has an I as little as the eleven planets counted together have an I, though they revolve around a common *centre.*

Bailly's utterance is representative of the slave-disposition that folks manifest before the sovereign people, as before the prince. "I have," says he, "no longer any extra reason when the general reason has pronounced itself. My first law was the nation's will; as soon as it had assembled I knew nothing beyond its sovereign will." He would have no "extra reason," and yet this extra reason alone accomplishes everything. Just so Mirabeau inveighs in the words, "No power on earth has the *right* to say to the nation's representatives, It is my will!"

As with the Greeks, there is now a wish to make man a *zoon politicon,* a citizen of the State or political man. So he ranked for a long time as a "citizen of heaven." But the Greek fell into ignominy along with his *State,* the citizen of heaven likewise falls with heaven; we, on the other hand, are not willing to go down along with the *people,* the nation and nationality, not willing to be merely *political* men or politicians. Since the Revolution they have striven to "make the people happy," and in making the people happy, great, and the like, they make us unhappy: the people's good hap is—my mishap.

What empty talk the political liberals utter with emphatic decorum is well seen again in Nauwerck's *On Taking Part in the State.*[67]. There complaint is made of those who are indifferent and do not take part, who are not in the full sense citizens, and the author speaks as if one could not be man at all if one were not a politician. In this he is right; for, if the State ranks as the warder of everything "human," we can have nothing human without taking part in it. But what does this make out against the

67. [Karl Nauwerck, *Uber die Teilnahme am Staate,* published by **Wigand** in Leipzig, 1844.]

egoist? Nothing at all, because the egoist is to himself the warder of the human, and has nothing to say to the State except "Get out of my sunshine." Only when the State comes in contact with his ownness does the egoist take an active interest in it. If the condition of the State does not bear hard on the closet-philosopher, is he to occupy himself with it because it is his "most sacred duty?" So long as the State does according to his wish, what need has he to look up from his studies? Let those who from an interest of their own want to have conditions otherwise busy themselves with them. Not now, nor evermore, will "sacred duty" bring folks to reflect about the State—as little as they become disciples of science, artists, etc., from "sacred duty." Egoism alone can impel them to it, and will as soon as things have become much worse. If you showed folks that their egoism demanded that they busy themselves with State affairs, you would not have to call on them long; if, on the other hand, you appeal to their love of fatherland and the like, you will long preach to deaf hearts in behalf of this "service of love." Certainly, in your sense the egoists wil not participate in State affairs at all.

Nauwerck utters a genuine liberal phrase on p. 16: "Man completely fulfils his calling only in feeling and knowing himself as a member of humanity, and being active as such. The individual cannot realize the idea of *manhood* if he does not stay himself upon all humanity, if he does not draw his powers from it like Antaeus."

In the same place it is said: "Man's relation to the *res publica* is degraded to a purely private matter by the theological view; is, accordingly, made away with by denial." As if the political view did otherwise with religion! There religion is a "private matter."

If, instead of "sacred duty," "man's destiny," the "calling to full manhood," and similar commandments, it were held up to people that their *self-interest* was infringed on when they let everything in the State go as it goes, then, without declamations, they would be addressed as one will have to address them at the decisive moment if he wants to attain his end. Instead of this, the theology-hating author says, "If there has ever been a time when the *State* laid claim to all that are *hers,* such a time is ours. —The thinking man sees in participation in the theory and practice of the State a *duty,* one of the most sacred duties that rest upon him"—and then takes under closer consideration the "unconditional necessity that everybody participate in the State."

He in whose head or heart or both the *State* is seated, he who is possessed by the State, or the *believer in the State,* is a politician, and remains such to all eternity.

"The State is the most necessary means for the complete development of mankind." It assuredly has been so as long as we wanted to develop mankind; but, if we want to develop ourselves, it can be to us only a means of hindrance.

Can State and people still be reformed and bettered now? As little as the nobility, the clergy, the church, etc.: they can be abrogated, annihilated, done away with, not reformed. Can I change a piece of nonsense into sense by reforming it, or must I drop it outright?

Henceforth what is to be done is no longer about the *State* (the form of the State, etc.), but about me. With this all questions about the prince's power, the constitution, and so on, sink into their true abyss and their true nothingness. I, this nothing, shall put forth my *creations* from myself.

To the chapter of society belongs also "the party," whose praise has of late been sung.

In the State the *party* is current. "Party, party, who should not join one!" But the individual is *unique,*[68] not a member of the party. He unites freely, and separates freely again. The party is nothing but a State in the State, and in this smaller bee-State "peace" is also to rule just as in the greater. The very people who cry loudest that there must be an *opposition* in the State inveigh against every discord in the party. A proof that they too want only a—State. All parties are shattered not against the State, but against the ego.[69]

One hears nothing oftener now than the admonition to remain true to his party; party men despise nothing so much as a mugwump. One must run with his party through thick and thin, and

68. (*einzig*)
69. (*am Einzigen*)

unconditionally approve and represent its chief principles. It does not indeed go quite so badly here as with closed societies, because these bind their members to fixed laws or statutes (such as the orders, the Society of Jesus, etc.). But yet the party ceases to be a union at the same moment at which it makes certain principles *binding* and wants to have them assured against attacks; but this moment is the very birth-act of the party. As party it is already a *born society,* a dead union, an idea that has become fixed. As party of absolutism it cannot will that its members should doubt the irrefragable truth of this principle; they could cherish this doubt only if they were egoistic enough to want still to be something outside their party, non-partisans. Non-partisans they cannot be as party-men, but only as egoists. If you are a Protestant and belong to that party, you must only justify Protestantism, at most "purge" it, not reject it; if you are a Christian and belong among men to the Christian party, you cannot be beyond this as a member of this party, but only when your egoism, non-partisanship, impels you to it. What exertions the Christians, down to Hegel and the Communists, have put forth to make their party strong! They stuck to it that Christianity must contain the eternal truth, and that one needs only to get at it, make sure of it, and justify it.

In short, the party cannot bear non-partisanship, and it is in this that egoism appears. What matters the party to me? I shall find enough anyhow who *unite* with me without swearing allegiance to my flag.

He who passes over from one party to another is at once abused as a "turncoat." Certainly *morality* demands that one stand by his party, and to become apostate from it is to spot oneself with the stain of "faithlessness"; but ownness knows no commandment of "faithlessness"; adhesion, and the like, ownness permits everything, even apostasy, defection. Unconsciously even the moral themselves let themselves be led by this principle when they have to judge one who passes over to *their* party—nay, they are likely to be making proselytes; they should only at the same time acquire a consciousness of the fact that one must commit *immoral* actions in order to commit his own—here, that one must break faith, yes, even his oath, in order to determine

himself instead of being determined by moral considerations. In
the eyes of people of strict moral judgment an apostate always
shimmers in equivocal colors, and will not easily obtain their
confidence; for there sticks to him the taint of "faithlessness,"
of an immorality. In the lower man this view is found almost
generally; advanced thinkers fall here too, as always, into an
uncertainty and bewilderment, and the contradiction necessarily
founded in the principle of morality does not, on account of the
confusion of their concepts, come clearly to their consciousness.
They do not venture to call the apostate immoral downright, because they themselves entice to apostasy, to defection from one
religion to another; still, they cannot give up the standpoint of
morality either. And yet here the occasion was to be seized
to step outside of morality.

Are the Own or Unique[70] perchance a party? How could
they be *own* if they were such as *belonged* to a party?

Or is one to hold with no party? In the very act of joining
them and entering their circle one forms a *union* with them that
lasts as long as party and I pursue one and the same goal. But
to-day I still share the party's tendency, as by to-morrow I can
do so no longer and I become "untrue" to it. The party has
nothing *binding* (obligatory) for me, and I do not have respect
for it; if it no longer pleases me, I become its foe.

In every party that cares for itself and its persistence, the
members are unfree (or better, unown) in that degree, they lack
egoism in that degree, in which they serve this desire of the party.
The independence of the party conditions the lack of independence
in the party-members.

A party, of whatever kind it may be, can never do without
a *confession of faith*. For those who belong to the party must
believe in its principle, it must not be brought in doubt or put in
question by them, it must be the certain, indubitable thing for
the party-member. That is: One must belong to a party body
and soul, else one is not truly a party-man, but more or less—
an egoist. Harbor a doubt of Christianity, and you are already
no longer a true Christian, you have lifted yourself to the

70. (*Einzigen*)

"effrontery" of putting a question beyond it and haling Christianity before your egoistic judgment-seat. You have—*sinned* against Christianity, this party cause (for it is surely not for example a cause for the Jews, another party.) But well for you if you do not let yourself be affrighted: your effrontery helps you to ownness.

So then an egoist could never embrace a party or take up with a party? Oh, yes, only he cannot let himself be embraced and taken up by the party. For him the party remains all the time nothing but a gathering: he is one of the party, he takes part.

The best State will clearly be that which has the most loyal citizens, and the more the devoted mind for *legality* is lost, so much the more will the State, this system of morality, this moral life itself, be diminished in force and quality. With the "good citizens" the good State too perishes and dissolves into anarchy and lawlessness. "Respect for the law!" By this cement the total of the State is held together. "The law is *sacred,* and he who affronts it a *criminal."* Without crime no State: the moral world—and this the State is—is crammed full of scamps, cheats, liars, thieves. Since the State is the "lordship of law," its hierarchy, it follows that the egoist, in all cases where *his* advantage runs against the State's, can satisfy himself only by crime.

The State cannot give up the claim that its *laws* and ordinances are *sacred.*[71] At this the individual ranks as the *unholy*[72] (barbarian, natural man, "egoist") over against the State, exactly as he was once regarded by the Church; before the individual the State takes on the nimbus of a saint.[73] Thus it issues a law against dueling. Two men who are both at one in this, that they are willing to stake their life for a cause (no matter what), are not to be allowed this, because the State wil not have it: it imposes a penalty on it. Where is the liberty of self-determination then? It is at once quite another situation if, as in North America, society determines to let the duelists bear certain evil *consequences*

71. (*heilig*)
72. (*unheilig*)
73. (*Heiliger*)

of their act, such as withdrawal of the credit hitherto enjoyed. To refuse credit is everybody's affair, and, if a society wants to withdraw it for this or that reason, the man who is hit cannot therefore complain of encroachment on his liberty: the society is simply availing itself of its own liberty. That is no penalty for sin, no penalty for a *crime*. The duel is no crime there, but only an act against which the society adopts counter-measures, resolves on a *defense*. The State, on the contrary, stamps the duel as a crime, as an injury to its sacred law: it makes it a *criminal case*. The society leaves it to the individual's decision whether he will draw upon himself evil consequences and inconveniences by his mode of action, and hereby recognizes his free decision; the State behaves in exactly the reverse way, denying all right to the individual's decision and, instead, ascribing the sole right to its own decision, the law of the State, so that he who transgresses the State's commandment is looked upon as if he were acting against God's commandment—a view which likewise was once maintained by the Church. Here God is the Holy in and of himself, and the commandments of the Church, as of the State, are the commandments of this Holy One, which he transmits to the world through his anointed and Lords-by-the-Grace-of-God. If the Church had *deadly sins,* the State has *capital crimes;* if the one had *heretics,* the other has *traitors;* the one *ecclesiastical penalties,* the other *criminal penalties;* the one *inquisitorial* processes, the other *fiscal*; in short, there sins, here crimes, there inquisition and here—inquisition. Will the sanctity of the State not fall like the Church's? The awe of its laws, the reverence for its highness, the humility of its "subjects," will this remain? Will the "saint's" face not be stripped of its adornment?

What a folly, to ask of the State's authority that it should enter into an honorable fight with the individual, and, as they express themselves in the matter of freedom of the press, share sun and wind equally! If the State, this thought, is to be a *de facto* power, it simply must be a superior power against the individual. The State is "sacred" and must not expose itself to the "impudent attacks" of individuals. If the State is *sacred,* there must be censorship. The political liberals admit the former and dispute the inference. But in any case they concede repressive measures to it, for—they stick to this, that State is *more* than the individual and exercises a justified revenge, called punishment.

Punishment has a meaning only when it is to afford expiation for the injuring of a *sacred* thing. If something is sacred to any one, he certainly deserves punishment when he acts as its enemy. A man who lets a man's life continue in existence *because* to him it is sacred and he has a *dread* of touching it is simply a—*religious* man.

Weitling lays crime at the door of "social disorder," and lives in the expectation that under Communistic arrangements crimes will become impossible, because the temptations to them, such as money, fall away. As, however, his organized society is also exalted into a sacred and inviolable one, he miscalculates in that good-hearted opinion. Such as with their mouth professed allegiance to the Communistic society, but worked underhand for its ruin, would not be lacking. Besides, Weitling has to keep on with "curative means against the natural remainder of human diseases and weaknesses," and "curative means" always announce to begin with that individuals will be looked upon as "called" to a particular "salvation" and hence treated according to the requirements of this "human calling." *Curative means* or *healing* is only the reverse side of *punishment,* the *theory of cure* runs parallel with the *theory of punishment;* if the latter sees in an action a sin against right, the former takes it for a sin of the man *against himself,* as a decadence from his health. But the correct thing is that I regard it either as an action that *suits me* or as one that *does not suit me,* as hostile or friendly to *me,* that I treat it as my *property,* which I cherish or demolish. "Crime" or "disease" are not either of them an *egoistic* view of the matter, a judgment *starting from me,* but starting from *another*—to wit, whether it injures *right,* general right, or the *health* partly of the individual (the sick one), partly of the generality (*society*). "Crime" is treated inexorably, "disease" with "loving gentleness, compassion," and the like.

Punishment follows crime. If crime falls because the sacred vanishes, punishment must not less be drawn into its fall; for it too has significance only over against something sacred. Ecclesiastical punishments have been abolished. Why? Because how one behaves toward the "holy God" is his own affair. But, as this one punishment, *ecclesiastical punishment,* has fallen, so all *punishments* must fall. As sin against the so-called God is a man's own affair, so is that against every kind of the so-called sacred. According to our theories of penal law, with whose "improvement in conformity to the times" people are tormenting themselves in vain, they want to *punish* men for this or that "inhumanity"; and therein they make the silliness of these theories especially plain by their consistency, hanging the little thieves and letting the big ones run. For injury to property they have the house of correction, and for "violence to thought," suppression of "natural rights of man," only—representations and petitions.

The criminal code has continued existence only through the sacred, and perishes of itself if punishment is given up. Now they want to create everywhere a new penal law, without indulging in a misgiving about punishment itself. But it is exactly punishment that must make room for satisfaction, which, again, cannot aim at satisfying right or justice, but at procuring *us* a satisfactory outcome. If one does to us what we *will not put up with,* we break his power and bring our own to bear: we satisfy *ourselves* on him, and do not fall into the folly of wanting to satisfy right (the spook). It is not the *sacred* that is to defend itself against man, but man against man; as *God* too, you know, no longer defends himself against man, God to whom formerly (and in part, indeed, even now) all the "servants of God" offered their hands to punish the blasphemer, as they still at this very day lend their hands to the sacred. This devotion to the sacred brings it to pass also that, without lively participation of one's own, one only delivers misdoers into the hands of the police and courts: a non-participating making over to the authorities, "who, of course, will best administer sacred matters." The people is quite crazy for hounding the police on against everything that seems to it to be immoral, often only unseemly, and this popular rage for the moral protects the police institution more than the government could in any way protect it.

In crime the egoist has hitherto asserted himself and mocked at the sacred; the break with the sacred, or rather of the sacred, may become general. A revolution never returns, but a mighty, reckless, shameless, conscienceless, proud—*crime,* does it not rumble in distant thunders, and do you not see how the sky grows presciently silent and gloomy?

He who refuses to spend his powers for such limited societies as family, party, nation, is still always longing for a worthier society, and thinks he has found the true object of love, perhaps, in "human society" or "mankind," to sacrifice himself to which constitutes his honor; from now on he "lives for and serves *mankind.*"

People is the name of the body, *State* of the spirit, of that *ruling person* that has hitherto suppressed me. Some have wanted to trasfigure peoples and States by broadening them out to "mankind" and "general reason"; but servitude would only become still more intense with this widening, and philanthropists and humanitarians are as absolute masters as politicians and diplomats.

Modern critics inveigh against religion because it sets God, the divine, moral, etc., *outside* of man, or makes them something objective, in opposition to which the critics rather transfer these very subjects *into* man. But those critics none the less fall into the proper error of religion, to give man a "destiny," in that they too want to have him divine, human, and the like: morality, freedom and humanity, etc., are his essence. And, like religion politics too wanted to *"educate"* man, to bring him to the realization of his "essence," his "destiny," to *make* something out of him—to wit, a "true man," the one in the form of the "true believer," the other in that of the "true citizen or subject." In fact, it comes to the same whether one calls the destiny the divine or human.

Under religion and politics man finds himself at the standpoint of *should*: he *should* become this and that, should be so and so. With this postulate, this commandment, every one steps not only in front of another but also in front of himself. Those critics say: You should be a whole, free man. Thus they too stand in the temptation to proclaim a new *religion,* to set up a new absolute, an ideal—to wit, freedom. Men *should* be free.

Then there might even arise *missionaries* of freedom, as Christianity, in the conviction that all were properly destined to become Christians, sent out missionaries of the faith. Freedom would then (as have hitherto faith as Church, morality as State) constitute itself as a new *community* and carry on a like "propaganda" therefrom. Certainly no objection can be raised against a getting together; but so much the more must one oppose every renewal of the old *care* for us, of culture directed toward an end—in short, the principle of *making something* out of us, no matter whether Christians, subjects, or freemen and men.

One may well say with Feuerbach and others that religion has displaced the human from man, and has transferred it so into another world that, unattainable, it went on with its own existence there as something personal in itself, as a "God": but the error of religion is by no means exhausted with this. One might very well let fall the personality of the displaced human, might transform God into the divine, and still remain religious. For the religious consists in discontent with the *present* men, in the setting up of a "perfection" to be striven for, in "man wrestling for his completion."[74] ("Ye therefore *should* be perfect as your father in heaven is perfect." Matt. 5, 48): it consists in the fixation of an ideal, an absolute. Perfection is the "supreme good," the *finis bonorum;* every one's ideal is the perfect man, the true, the free man, etc.

The efforts of modern times aim to set up the ideal of the "free man." If one could find it, there would be a new—religion, because a new ideal; there would be a new longing, a new torment, a new devotion, a new deity, a new contrition.

With the ideal of "absolute liberty," the same turmoil is made as with everything absolute, and according to Hess, it is said to "be realizable in absolute human society."[75] Nay, this realization is immediately afterward styled a "vocation"; just so he then defines liberty as "morality": the kingdom of "justice" (equality) and "morality" (liberty) is to begin, etc.

74. B. Bauer, *Lit. Ztg.,* No. VIII, p. 22.
75. [This is cited from Hess's "Philosophie der Tat," in Herweg (ed.), *Ein und zwanzig Bogen,* pp. 89 ff.]

Ridiculous is he who, while fellows of his tribe, family, nation, rank high, is—nothing but "puffed up" over the merit of his fellows; but blinded too is he who wants only to be "man." Neither of them puts his worth in *exclusiveness,* but in *connectedness,* or in the "tie" that conjoins him with others, in the ties of blood, of nationality, of humanity.

Through the "Nationals" of to-day the conflict has again been stirred up between those who think themselves to have merely human blood and human ties of blood, and the others who brag of their special blood and the special ties of blood.

If we disregard the fact that pride may mean conceit, and take it for consciousness alone, there is found to be a vast difference between pride in "belonging to" a nation and therefore being its property, and that in calling a nationality one's property. Nationality is my quality, but the nation my owner and mistress. If you have bodily strength, you can apply it at a suitable place and have a self- consciousness or pride of it; if, on the contrary, your strong body has you, then it pricks you everywhere, and at the most unsuitable place, to show its strength: you can give nobody your hand without squeezing his.

The perception that one is more than a member of the family, more than a fellow of the tribe, more than an individual of the people, has finally led to saying, one is more than all this because one is man, or, the man is more than the Jew, German, etc. "Therefore be every one wholly and solely—man." Could one not rather say: Because we are more than what has been stated, therefore we will be this, as well as that "more" also? Man and Germans, then, man and Guelph?[76] The Nationals are in the right; one cannot deny his nationality: and the humanitarians are in the right; one must not remain in the narrowness of the national. In *uniqueness*[77] the contradiction is solved; the national is my quality. But I am not swallowed up in my quality—as the human

76. [It is not clear from the context whether Stirner meant the partisans of the pope against the Ghibelline aristocratic faction in medieval Italy or the secret society of the same name in then-contemporary Italy with political ambitions not very different from nationalistic liberals in Germany.]

77. (*Einzigkeit*)

too is my quality, but I give to man his existence first through my uniqueness.

History seeks for Man: but he is I, you, we. Sought as a mysterious *essence,* as the divine, first as *God,* then as Man (humanity, humaneness, and mankind), he is found as the individual, the finite, the unique one.

I am owner of humanity, am humanity, and do nothing for the good of another humanity. Fool, you who are a unique humanity, that you make a merit of wanting to live for another than you are.

The hitherto-considered relation of me to the *world of men* offers such a wealth of phenomena that it will have to be taken up again and again on other occasions, but here, where it was only to have its chief outlines made clear to the eye, it must be broken off to make place for an apprehension of two other sides toward which it radiates. For, as I find myself in relation not merely to men so far as they present in themselves the concept "man" or are children of men (children of *Man,* as children of God are spoken of), but also to that which they have of man and call their own, and as therefore I relate myself not only to that which they *are* through man, but also to their human *possessions*: so, besides the world of men, the world of the senses and of ideas will have to be included in our survey, and somewhat said of what men call their own of sensuous goods, and of spiritual as well.

According as one had developed and clearly grasped the concept of man, he gave it to us to respect as this or that *person of respect,* and from the broadest understanding of this concept there proceeded at last the command "to respect Man in every one." But if I respect Man, my respect must likewise extend to the human, or what is Man's.

Men have somewhat of their *own,* and *I* am to recognize this own and hold it sacred. Their own consists partly in outward, partly in inward *possessions.* The former are things, the latter spiritualities, thoughts, convictions, noble feelings. But I am always to respect only *rightful* or *human* possessions: the wrongful and unhuman I need not spare, for only *Man's* own is men's real own. An inward possession of this sort is, for example, religion; because *religion* is free, that is, is Man's, *I* must not strike at it. Just so *honor* is an inward possession; it is free and must not be struck at my me. (Action for insult, caricatures, etc.) Religion and honor are "spiritual property." In tangible property the person stands foremost: my person is my first property. Hence freedom of the person; but only the *rightful* or human person is free, the other is locked up. Your life is your property; but it is sacred for men only if it is not that of an inhuman monster.

What a man as such cannot defend of bodily goods, we may take from him: this is the meaning of competition, of freedom of occupation. What he cannot defend of spiritual goods falls a prey to us likewise: so far goes the liberty of discussion, of science, of criticism.

But *consecrated* goods are inviolable. Consecrated and guaranteed by whom? Proximately by the State, society, but properly by man or the "concept," the "concept of the thing"; for the concept of consecrated goods is this, that they are truly human, or rather that the holder possesses them as man and not as un-man.[78]

On the spiritual side man's faith is such goods, his honor, his moral feeling—yes, his feeling of decency, modesty, etc. Actions (speeches, writings) that touch honor are punishable; attacks on "the foundations of all religion"; attacks on political faith; in short, attacks on everything that a man "rightly" has.

How far critical liberalism would extend the sanctity of goods—on this point it has not yet made any pronouncement, and doubtless fancies itself to be ill-disposed toward all sanctity; but, as it combats egoism, it must set limits to it, and must not let the un-man pounce on the human. To its theoretical contempt for the "masses" there must correspond a practical snub if it should get into power.

What extension the concept "man" receives, and what comes to the individual man through it—what, therefore, man and the human are—on this point the various grades of liberalism differ, and the political, the social, the humane man are each always

78. (See note 133 in second chapter.)

claiming more than the other for "man." He who has best grasped this concept knows best what is "man's." The State still grasps this concept in political restriction, society in social; mankind, so it is said, is the first to comprehend it entirely, or "the history of mankind develops it." But, if "man is discovered," then we know also what pertains to man as his own, man's property, the human.

But let the individual man lay claim to ever so many rights because Man or the concept man "entitles" him to them, because his being man does it: what do *I* care for his right and his claim? If he has his right only from Man and does not have it from *me,* then for *me* he has no right. His life, for example, counts to *me* only for what it is *worth* to *me.* I respect neither a so-called right of property (or his claim to tangible goods) nor yet his right to the "sanctuary of his inner nature" (or his right to have the spiritual goods and divinities, his gods, remain unaggrieved). His goods, the sensuous as well as the spiritual, are *mine,* and I dispose of them as proprietor, in the measure of my—might.

In the *property question* lies a broader meaning than the limited statement of the question allows to be brought out. Referred solely to what men call our possessions, it is capable of no solution; the decision is to be found in him "from whom we have everything." Property depends on the *owner.*

The Revolution directed its weapons against everything which came "from the grace of God," against divine right, in whose place the human was confirmed. To that which is granted by the grace of God, there is opposed that which is derived "from the essence of man."

Now, as men's relation to each other, in opposition to the religious dogma which commands a "Love one another for God's sake," had to receive its human position by a "Love each other for man's sake," so the revolutionary teaching could not do otherwise than, first, as to what concerns the relation of men to the things of this world, settle it that the world, which hitherto was arranged according to God's ordinance, henceforth belongs to "Man."

The world belongs to "Man," and is to be respected by me as his property.

Property is what is mine!

Property in the civic sense means *sacred* property, such that I must *respect* your property. "Respect for property!" Hence the politicians would like to have every one possess his little bit of property, and they have in part brought about an incredible parcellation by this effort. Each must have his bone on which he may find something to bite.

The position of affairs is different in the egoistic sense. I do not step shyly back from your property, but look upon it always as *my* property, in which I need to "respect" nothing. Pray do the like with what you call my property!

With this view we shall most easily come to an understanding with each other.

The political liberals are anxious that, if possible, all servitudes be dissolved, and every one be free lord on his ground, even if this ground has only so much area as can have its requirements adequately filled by the manure of one person. (The farmer in the story married even in his old age "that he might profit by his wife's dung.") Be it ever so little, if one only has somewhat of his own—to wit, a *respected* property! The more such owners, such cotters,[79] the more "free people and good patriots" has the State.

Political liberalism, like everything religious, counts on *respect*, humaneness, the virtues of love. Therefore does it live in incessant vexation. For in practice people respect nothing, and every day the small possessions are bought up again by greater proprietors, and the "free people" change into day-laborers.

If, on the contrary, the "small proprietors" had reflected that the great property was also theirs, they would not have respectfully shut themselves out from it, and would not have been shut out.

Property as the civic liberals understand it deserves the attacks of the Communists and Proudhon: it is untenable, because

79. (The words "cot" and "dung" are alike in German.)

the civic proprietor is in truth nothing but a propertyless man, one who is everywhere *shut out*. Instead of owning the world, as he might, he does not own even the paltry point on which he turns around.

Proudhon wants not the *propriétaire* but the *possesseur* or *usufruitier*.[80] What does that mean? He wants no one to own the land; but the benefit of it—even though one were allowed only the hundredth part of this benefit, this fruit—is at any rate one's property, which he can dispose of at will. He who has only the benefit of a field is assuredly not the proprietor of it; still less he who, as Proudhon would have it, must give up so much of this benefit as is not required for his wants; but he is the proprietor of the share that is left him. Proudhon, therefore, denies only such and such property, not *property* itself. If we want no longer to leave the land to the landed proprietors, but to appropriate it to ourselves, we unite ourselves to this end, form a union, a *société*, that makes *itself* proprietor; if we have good luck in this, then those persons cease to be landed proprietors. And, as from the land, so we can drive them out of many another property yet, in order to make it *our* property, the property of the —conquerors. The conquerors form a society which one may imagine so great that it by degrees embraces all humanity; but so-called humanity too is as such only a thought (spook); the individuals are its reality. And these individuals as a collective mass will treat land and earth not less arbitrarily than an isolated individual or so-called *propriétaire*. Even so, therefore, *property* remains standing, and that as exclusive" too, in that *humanity,* this great society, excludes the *individual* from its property (perhaps only leases to him, gives his as a fief, a piece of it) as it besides excludes everything that is not humanity, does not allow animals to have property.—So too it will remain, and will grow to be. That in which *all* want to have a *share* will be withdrawn from that individual who wants to have it for himself alone: it is made a *common estate*. As a *common estate* every one has his *share* in it, and this share

80. *Qu'est-ce que la Propriété*, p. 83. [This was published in Paris in 1840.]

is his *property*. Why, so in our old relations a house which belongs to five heirs is their common estate; but the fifth part of
the revenue is each one's property. Proudhon might spare his
prolix pathos if he said: "There are some things that belong
only to a few, and to which we others will from now on lay
claim or—siege. Let us take them, because one comes to property
by taking, and the property of which for the present we are
still deprived came to the proprietors likewise only by taking.
It can be utilized better if it is in the hands of *us all* than if the
few control it. Let us therefore associate ourselves for the
purpose of this robbery (*vol*)."—Instead of this, he tries to get
us to believe that society is the original possessor and the sole
proprietor, of imprescriptible right; against it the so-called proprietors have become thieves (*La propriété c'est le vol*); if it
now deprives of his property the present proprietor, it robs him
of nothing, as it is only availing itself of its imprescriptible right.
—So far one comes with the spook of society as a *moral person*.
On the contrary, what man can obtain belongs to him: the world
belongs to *me*. Do you say anything else by your opposite
proposition? "The world belongs to *all*"? All are I and again
I, etc. But you make out of the "all" a spook, and make it
sacred, so that then the "all" become the individual's fearful
master. Then the ghost of "right" places itself on their side.

Proudhon, like the Communists, fights against *egoism*. Therefore they are continuations and consistent carryings-out of the
Christian principle, the principle of love, of sacrifice for something
general, something alien. They complete in property, only what
has long been extant as a matter of fact—to wit, the propertylessness of the individual. When the laws says, *Ad reges potestas
omnium pertinet, ad singulos proprietas; omnia rex imperio
possidet, singuli dominio,* this means: The king is proprietor,
for he alone can control and dispose of "everything," he has
potesta and *imperium* over it. The Communists make this
clearer, transferring that *imperium* to the "society of all." Therefore: Because enemies of egoism, they are on that account—
Christians, or, more generally speaking, religious men, believers
in ghosts, dependents, servants of some generality (God, society,
etc.). In this too Proudhon is like the Christians, that he

ascribes to God that which he denies to men. He names him
(on page 90) the Propriétaire of the earth. Herewith he proves
that he cannot think away the *proprietor as such;* he comes to a
proprietor at last, but removes him to the other world.

Neither God nor Man ("human society") is proprietor, but
the individual.

———————

Proudhon (Weitling too) thinks he is telling the worst about
property when he calls it theft (*vol*). Passing quite over the
embarrassing question, what well-founded objection could be
made against theft, we only ask: Is the concept "theft" at all
possible unless one allows validity to the concept "property"?
How can one steal if property is not already extant? What
belongs to no one cannot be *stolen;* the water that one draws
out of the sea he does *not steal.* Accordingly property is not
theft, but a theft becomes possible only through property.
Weitling has to come to this too, as he does regard everything
as the *property of all*: if something is "the property of all,"
then indeed the individual who appropriates it to himself steals.

Private property lives by grace of the *law.* Only in the
law has it its warrant—for possession is not yet property, it
becomes "mine" only by assent of the law; it is not a fact, not
un fait as Proudhon thinks, but a fiction, a thought. This is
legal property, legitimate property, guaranteed property. It is
mine not through *me* but through the—*law.*

Nevertheless, property is the expression for *unlimited
dominion* over somewhat (thing, beast, man) which "I can
judge and dispose of as seems good to me." According to Roman
law, indeed, *jus utendi et abutendi re sua, quatenus juris ratio
patitur,* an *exclusive* and *unlimited right;* but property is conditioned by might. What I have in my power, that is my own.
So long as I assert myself as holder, I am the proprietor of the
thing; if it gets away from me again, no matter by what power,
as through my recognition of a title of others to the thing—
then the property is extinct. Thus property and possession
coincide. It is not a right lying outside my might that legitimizes
me, but solely my might: if I no longer have this, the thing
vanishes away from me. When the Romans no longer had any

might against the Germans, the world-empire of Rome *belonged* to the latter, and it would sound ridiculous to insist that the Romans had nevertheless remained properly the proprietors. Whoever knows how to take and to defend the thing, to him it belongs till it is again taken from him, as liberty belongs to him who *takes* it.

Only might decides about property, and, as the State (no matter whether State or well-to-do citizens or of ragamuffins or of men in the absolute) is the sole mighty one, it alone is proprietor; I, the unique,[81] have nothing, and am only enfeoffed, am vassal and as such, servitor. Under the dominion of the State there is no property of *mine*.

I want to raise the value of myself, the value of ownness, and should I cheapen property? No, as I was not respected hitherto because people, mankind, and a thousand other generalities were put higher, so property too has to this day not yet been recognized in its full value. Property too was only the property of a ghost, the people's property; my whole existence "belonged to the fatherland"; *I* belonged to the fatherland, the people, the State, and therefore also everything that I called *my own*. It is demanded of States that they make away with pauperism. It seems to me this is asking that the State should cut off its own head and lay it at its feet; for so long as the State is the ego the individual ego must remain a poor devil, a non-ego. The State has an interest only in being itself rich; whether Michael is rich and Peter poor is alike to it; Peter might also be rich and Michael poor. It looks on indifferently as one grows poor and the other rich, unruffled by this alternation. As *individuals* they are really equal before its face; in this it is just: before it both of them are—nothing, as we "are altogether sinners before God"; on the other hand, it has a very great interest in this, that those individuals who make it their ego should have a part in *its* wealth; it makes them partakers in *its property*. Through property, with which it rewards the individuals, it tames them; but this remains *its* property, and every one has the usufruct of it only so long as he bears in himself the ego of the

81. (*Einzige*)

State, or is a "loyal member of society"; in the opposite case the property is confiscated, or made to melt away by vexatious lawsuits. The property, then, is and remains *State property,* not property of the ego. That the State does not arbitrarily deprive the individual of what he has from the State means simply that the State does not rob itself. He who is State-ego, a good citizen or subject, holds his fief undisturbed as *such an ego,* not as being an ego of his own. According to the code, property is what I call mine "by virtue of God and law." But it is mine by virtue of God and law only so long as—the State has nothing against it.

In expropriations, disarmaments, and the like (as, when the exchequer confiscates inheritances if the heirs do not put in an appearance early enough) how plainly the else-veiled principle that only the *people,* "the State," is proprietor, while the individual is feoffee, strikes the eye!

The State, I mean to say, cannot intend that anybody should *for his own sake* have property or actually be rich, nay, even well-to-do; it can acknowledge nothing, yield nothing, grant nothing to me as me. The State cannot check pauperism, because the poverty of possession is a poverty of me. He who *is* nothing but what chance or another—to wit, the State— makes out of him also *has* quite rightly nothing but what another gives him. And this other will *give* him only what he *deserves,* what he is worth by *service.* It is not he that realizes a value from himself; the State realizes a value from him.

National economy busies itself much with this subject. It lies far out beyond the "national," however, and goes beyond the concepts and horizon of the State, which knows only State property and can distribute nothing else. For this reason it binds the possessions of property to *conditions*—as it binds everything to them, as in marriage, allowing validity only to the marriage sanctioned by it, and wresting this out of my power. But property is *my* property only when I hold it *unconditionally:* only I, an *unconditional* ego, have property, enter a relation of love, carry on free trade.

The State has no anxiety about me and mine, but about itself and its: I count for something to it only as *its child,* as "a son of the country"; as *ego* I am nothing at all for it. For the State's understanding, what befalls me as ego is something accidental, my wealth as well as my impoverishment. But, if I with all that is mine am an accident in the State's eyes, this proves that it cannot comprehend *me: I* go beyond its concepts, or, its understanding is too limited to comprehend me. Therefore it cannot do anything for me either.

Pauperism is the *valuelessness of me,* the phenomenon that I cannot realize value from myself. For this reason State and pauperism are one and the same. The State does not let me come to my value, and continues in existence only through my valuelessness: it is forever intent on *getting benefit* from me, exploiting me, turning me to account, using me up, even if the use it gets from me consists only in my supplying a *proles* (*proletariat*); it wants me to be "its creature."

Pauperism can be removed only when I as ego *realize value* from myself, when I give my own self value, and make my price myself. I must rise in revolt to rise in the world.

What I produce, flour, linen, or iron and coal, which I toilsomely win from the earth, is my work that I want to realize value from. But then I may long complain that I am not paid for my work according to its value: the payer will not listen to me, and the State likewise will maintain an apathetic attitude so long as it does not think it must "appease" me that *I* may not break out with my dreaded might. But this "appeasing" will be all, and, if it comes into my head to ask for more, the State turns against me with all the force of its lion-paws and eagle-claws: for it is the king of beasts, it is lion and eagle. If I refuse to be content with the price that it fixes for my ware and labor, if I rather aspire to determine the price of my ware myself, that is, "to pay myself," in the first place I come into a conflict with the buyers of the ware. If this were stilled by a mutual understanding, the State would not readily make objections; for how individuals get along with each other troubles it little, so long as therein they do not get in its way. Its damage and its danger begin only when they do not agree, but, in the absence of a settlement, take each other by the hair. The State cannot endure that man stand in a direct relation to man; it must step between as—*mediator,* must—*intervene.* What Christ was, what the saints, the Church were, the State has become— to wit, "mediator." It tears man from man to put itself between them as "spirit." The laborers who ask for higher pay are treated as criminals as soon as they want to *compel* it. What are they to do? Without compulsion they don't get it, and in compulsion the State sees a self-help, a determination of price by the ego, a genuine, free realization of value from his property, which it cannot admit of. What then are the laborers to do? Look to themselves and ask nothing about the State? — —

But, as is the situation with regard to my material work, so it is with my intellectual too. The State allows me to realize value from all my thoughts and to find customers for them (I do realize value from them, in the very fact that they bring me honor from the listeners, and the like); but only so long as *my* thoughts are—*its* thoughts. If, on the other hand, I harbor thoughts that it cannot approve (make its own), then it does not allow me at all to realize value from them, to bring them into *exchange* into *commerce.* *My* thoughts are free only if they are granted to me by the State's *grace,* if they are the State's thoughts. It lets me philosophize freely only so far as I approve myself a "philosopher of State"; *against* the State I must not philosophize, gladly as it tolerates my helping it out of its "deficiencies," "furthering" it.—Therefore, as I may behave only as an ego most graciously permitted by the State, provided with its testimonial of legitimacy and police pass, so too it is not granted me to realize value from what is mine, unless this proves to be its, which I hold as fief from it. My ways must be its ways, else it distrains me; my thoughts its thoughts, else it stops my mouth.

The State has nothing to be more afraid of than the value of me, and nothing must it more carefully guard against than every occasion that offers itself to me for *realizing value* from myself. *I* am the deadly enemy of the State, which always hovers between the alternatives, it or I. Therefore it strictly insists not only on not letting *me* have a standing, but also on keeping down what is *mine.* In the State there is no property, no property of the individual, but only State property. Only

through the State have I what I have, as I am only through it
what I am.   My private property is only that which the State
leaves to me of *its, cutting off* others from it (depriving them,
making it private); it is State property.

But, in opposition to the State, I feel more and more clearly
that there is still left me a great might, the might over myself,
over everything that pertains only to me and that *exists* only in
being my own.

What do I do if my ways are no longer its ways, my thoughts
no longer its thoughts?   I look to myself, and ask nothing about
it!   In *my* thoughts, which I get sanctioned by no assent, grant,
or grace, I have my real property, a property with which I can
trade.   For as mine they are my *creatures,* and I am in a position
to give them away in return for *other* thoughts: I give them up
and take in exchange for them others, which then are my new
purchased property.

What then is *my* property?   Nothing but what is in my
power!   To what property am I entitled?   To every property
to which I—*empower* myself.[82]   I give myself the right of
property in taking property to myself, or giving myself the proprietor's *power,* full power, empowerment.

Everything over which I have might that cannot be torn
from me remains my property; well, then let might decide about
property, and I will expect everything from my might!   Alien
might, might that I leave to another, makes me an owned slave:
then let my own might make me an owner.   Let me then withdraw the might that I have conceded to others out of ignorance
regarding the strength of my *own* might!   Let me say to myself,
what my might reaches to is my property; and let me claim as
property everything that I feel myself strong enough to attain,
and let me extend my actual property as far as *I* entitle, that is,
empower, myself to take.

Here egoism, selfishness, must decide; not the principle of
love, not love-motives like mercy, gentleness, good-nature, or
even justice and equity (for *justitia* too is a phenomenon of—

82. (A German idiom for "take upon myself," "assume.")

love, a product of love): love knows only *sacrifices* and demands "self-sacrifice."

Egoism does not think of sacrificing anything, giving away anything that it wants; it simply decides, what I want I must have and will procure.

All attempts to enact rational laws about property have put out from the bay of *love* into a desolate sea of regulations. Even Socialism and Communism cannot be excepted from this. Every one is to be provided with adequate means, for which it is little to the point whether one socialistically finds them still in a personal property, or communistically draws them from the community of goods. The individual's mind in this remains the same; it remains a mind of dependence. The distributing *board of equity* lets me have only what the sense of equity, its *loving* care for all, prescribes. For me, the individual, there lies no less of a check in *collective wealth* than in that of *individual others;* neither that is mine, nor this: whether the wealth belongs to the collectivity, which confers part of it on me, or to individual possessors, is for me the same constraint, as I cannot decide about either of the two. On the contrary, Communism, by the abolition of all personal property, only presses me back still more into dependence on another, to wit, on the generality or collectivity; and, loudly as it always attacks the "State," what it intends is itself again a State, a *status,* a condition hindering my free movement, a sovereign power over me. Communism rightly revolts against the pressure that I experience from individual proprietors; but still more horrible is the might that it puts in the hands of the collectivity.

Egoism takes another way to root out the non-possessing rabble. It does not say: Wait for what the board of equity will— bestow on you in the name of the collectivity (for such bestowal took place in "States" from the most ancient times, each receiving "according to his desert," and therefore according to the measure in which each was able to *deserve* it, to acquire it by *service*), but: Take hold, and take what you require! With this the war of all against all is declared. I alone decide what I will have.

"Now, that is truly no new wisdom, for self-seekers have acted so at all times!" Not at all necessary either that the thing be new, if only *consciousness* of it is present. But this latter will not be able to claim great age, unless perhaps one counts in the Egyptian and Spartan law; for how little current it is appears even from the stricture above, which speaks with contempt of "self-seekers." One is to know just this, that the procedure of taking hold is not contemptible, but manifests the pure deed of the egoist at one with himself.

Only when I expect neither from individuals nor from a collectivity what I can give to myself, only then do I slip out of the snares of—love; the rabble ceases to be rabble only when it *takes hold.* Only the dread of taking hold, and the corresponding punishment thereof, makes it a rabble. Only that taking hold is *sin,* crime—only this dogma creates a rabble. For the fact that the rabble remains what it is, it (because it allows validity to that dogma) is to blame as well as, more especially, those who "self-seekingly" (to give them back their favorite word) demand that the dogma be respected. In short, the lack of *consciousness* of that "new wisdom," the old consciousness of sin, alone bears the blame.

If men reach the point of losing respect for property, every one will have property, as all slaves become free men as soon as they no longer respect the master as master. *Unions* will then, in this matter too, multiply the individual's means and secure his assailed property.

According to the Communists' opinion the commune should be proprietor. On the contrary, *I* am proprietor, and I only come to an understanding with others about my property. If the commune does not do what suits me, I rise against it and defend my property. I am proprietor, but property is *not sacred.* I should be merely possessor? No, hitherto one was only possessor, secured in the possession of a parcel by leaving others also in possession of a parcel; but now *everything* belongs to me, I am proprietor of *everything that I require* and can get possession of. If it is said socialistically, society gives me what I require—then the egoist says, I take what I require. If the Communists conduct themselves as ragamuffins, the egoist behaves as proprietor.

All swan-fraternities,[83] and attempts at making the rabble happy, that spring from the principle of love, must miscarry. Only from egoism can the rabble get help, and this help it must give to itself and—will give to itself. If it does not let itself be coerced into fear, it is a power. "People would lose all respect if one did not coerce them into fear," says bugbear Law in *Der gestiefelte Kater*.[84]

Property, therefore, should not and cannot be abolished; it must rather be torn from ghostly hands and become *my* property; then the erroneous consciousness, that I cannot entitle myself to as much as I require, will vanish. —

"But what cannot man require!" Well, whoever requires much, and understands how to get it, has at all times helped himself to it, as Napoleon did with the Continent and France with Algiers.[85] Hence the exact point is that the respectful "rabble" should learn at last to help itself to what it requires. If it reaches out too far for you, why, then defend yourselves. You have no need at all to good-heartedly—bestow anything on it; and, when it learns to know itself, it—or rather: whoever of the rabble learns to know himself, he—casts off the rabble-quality in refusing your alms with thanks. But it remains ridiculous that you declare the rabble "sinful and criminal" if it is not pleased to live from your favors because it can do something in its own favor. Your bestowals cheat it and put it off. Defend your property, then you will be strong; if, on the other hand, you want to retain your ability to bestow, and perhaps actually have the more political rights the more alms (poor-rates) you

83. [This word mystified Byington; the reference was to the famous Renaissance *Schwanenorden*, the oldest order of the Hohenzollern house, established September 29, 1440, open to both men and women, with its principal object being the founding and conducting of charitable enterprises and societies. It had been reorganized and renewed, after a long period of neglect, by the romanticist Kaiser Frederick Wilhelm IV in 1843, the year Stirner was at work on his book.]

84. [*Puss in Boots,* one of the stories of Johann Ludwig Tieck (1773-1853), a Romantic period writer of prodigious output; twenty volumes of his novels were published in Berlin between 1828 and 1846.]

85. [A French army captured Algiers on July 5, 1830 and proceeded to make Algeria a French colony.]

can give, this will work just as long as the recipients let you work it.[86]

In short, the property question cannot be solved so amicably as the Socialists, yes, even the Communists, dream. It is solved only by the war of all against all. The poor become free and proprietors only when they—*rise*. Bestow ever so much on them, they will still always want more; for they want nothing less than that at last—nothing more be bestowed.

It will be asked, but how then will it be when the have-nots take heart? Of what sort is the settlement to be? One might as well ask that I cast a child's nativity. What a slave will do as soon as he has broken his fetters, one must—await.

In Kaiser's pamphlet,[87] worthless for lack of form as well as substance, he hopes from the *State* that it will bring about a leveling of property. Always the State! Herr Papa! As the Church was proclaimed and looked upon as the "mother" of believers, so the State has altogether the face of the provident father.

Competition shows itself most strictly connected with the principle of civism. Is it anything else than *equality* (*égalité*)? And is not equality a product of that same Revolution which was brought on by the commonalty, the middle classes? As no one is barred from competing with all in the State (except the prince, because he represents the State itself) and working himself up to their height, yes, overthrowing or exploiting them for his own advantage, soaring above them and by stronger exertion depriving them of their favorable circumstances—this serves as a clear proof that before the State's judgment-seat every one has only the value of a "simple individual" and may not count on any

86. In a registration bill for Ireland the government made the proposal to let those be electors who pay £5 sterling of poor-rates. He who gives alms, therefore, acquires political rights, or elsewhere becomes a swanknight. [The *Schwanenritter* (*Chevalier au Cygne* in French), legendary figures of the 12th and 13th centuries, rescuers of those in need or distress, as Godfrey of Bouillon, and later, Lohengrin.]

87. [*Die Personlichkeit des Eigentums in Bezug auf den Sozialismus und Communismus im heutigen Frankreich,* by Heinrich Wilhelm Kaiser, published in Bremen in 1843.]

favoritism. Outrun and outbid each other as much as you like and can; that shall not trouble me, the State! Among yourselves you are free in competing, you are competitors; that is your *social* position. But before me, the State, you are nothing but "simple individuals"![88]

What in the form of principle or theory was propounded as the equality of all has found here in competition its realization and practical carrying out; for *égalité* is—free competition. All are, before the State—simple individuals; in society, or in relation to each other—competitors.

I need be nothing further than a simple individual to be able to compete with all others aside from the prince and his family: a freedom which formerly was made impossible by the fact that only by means of one's corporation, and within it, did one enjoy any freedom of effort.

In the guild and feudality the State is in an intolerant and fastidious attitude, granting *privileges;* in competition and liberalism it is in a tolerant and indulgent attitude, granting only *patents* (letters assuring the applicant that the business stands open (patent) to him) or "concessions." Now, as the State has thus left everything to the *applicants,* it must come in conflict with all, because each and all are entitled to make application. It will be "stormed," and will go down in this storm.

Is "free competition" then really "free?" nay, is it really a

---

88. Minister Stein used this expression about Count von Reisach, when he cold-bloodedly left the latter at the mercy of the Bavarian government because to him, as he said, "a government like Bavaria must be worth more than a simple individual." Reisach had written against Montgelas at Stein's bidding, and Stein later agreed to the giving up of Reisach, which was demanded by Montgelas on account of this very book. See Hinrichs, *Politische Vorlesungen,* I, 280. [*Politische Vorlesungen* by Hermann F.W. Hinrichs (1794-1861) was published in two volumes in Halle in 1843; the principals in the statecraft described by Stirner, Baron vom Stein (1757-1831), Baron von Montgelas (1757-1838), Minister to Maximilian Joseph of Bavaria, and Karl August, Count von Reisach, were all well-known figures in then-recent German affairs. The work which led to Reisach's prosecution was his *Beitrage zur kenntniss der neuen Einrichtungen in Baiern, der Ursachen des Widerstandes, welche man finden wird* (Nürnberg, 1802.]

"competition"—to wit, one of *persons*—as it gives itself out to be because on this title it bases its right? It originated, you know, in persons becoming free of all personal rule. Is a competition "free" which the State, this ruler in the civic principle, hems in by a thousand barriers? There is a rich manufacturer doing a brilliant business, and I should like to compete with him. "Go ahead," says the State, "I have no objection to make to your *person* as competitor." Yes, I reply, but for that I need a space for buildings, I need money! "That's bad; but, if you have no money, you cannot compete. You must not take anything from anybody, for I protect property and grant it privileges." Free competition is not "free," because I lack the THINGS for competition. Against my *person* no objection can be made, but because I have not the things my person too must step to the rear. And who has the necessary things? Perhaps that manufacturer? Why, from him I could take them away! No, the State has them as property, the manufacturer only as fief, as possession.

But, since it is no use trying it with the manufacturer, I will compete with that professor of jurisprudence; the man is a booby, and I, who know a hundred times more than he, shall make his class-room empty. "Have you studied and graduated, friend?" No, but what of that? I understand abundantly what is necessary for instruction in that department. "Sorry, but competition is not 'free' here. Against your person there is nothing to be said, but the *thing,* the doctor's diploma, is lacking. And this diploma I, the State, demand. Ask me for it respectfully first; then we will see what is to be done."

This, therefore, is the "freedom" of competition. The State, *my lord,* first qualifies me to compete.

But do *persons* really compete? No, again *things* only! Moneys in the first place, etc.

In the rivalry one will always be left behind another (as, a poetaster behind a poet). But it makes a difference whether the means that the unlucky competitor lacks are personal or material, and likewise whether the material means can be won by *personal energy* or are to be obtained only by *grace,* only as a present; as when the poorer man must leave, that is, present, to the rich man his riches. But, if I must all along wait for the State's *approval*

to obtain or to use (as in the case of graduation) the means, I
have the means by the *grace of the State*.[89]

Free competition, therefore, has only the following meaning:
To the State all rank as its equal children, and every one can
scud and run to earn the *State's goods and largess*. Therefore all
do chase after havings, holdings, possessions (be it of money or
offices, titles of honor, etc.), after the *things*.

In the mind of the commonalty every one is possessor or
"owner." Now, whence comes it that the most have in fact next
to nothing? From this, that the most are already joyful over
being possessors at all, even though it be of some rags, as
children are joyful in their first trousers or even the first penny
that is presented to them. More precisely, however, the matter is
to be taken as follows. Liberalism came forward at once with the
declaration that it belonged to man's essence not to be property,
but proprietor. As the consideration here was about "man," not
about the individual, the how-much (which formed exactly the
point of the individual's special interest) was left to him. Hence
the individual's egoism retained room for the freest play in this
how-much, and carried on an indefatigable competition.

However, the lucky egoism had to become a snag in the
way of the less fortunate, and the latter, still keeping its feet
planted on the principle of humanity, put forward the question
as to how-much of possession, and answered it to the effect that
"man must have as much as he requires."

Will it be possible for *my* egoism to let itself be satisfied
with that? What "man" requires furnishes by no means a scale
for measuring me and my needs; for I may have use for less or
more. I must rather have so much as I am competent to appropriate.

Competition suffers from the unfavorable circumstance that

89. In colleges and universities poor men compete with rich. But
they are able to do so in most cases only through scholarships, which—
a significant point—almost all come down to us from a time when free
competition was still far from being a controlling principle. The principle
of competition founds no scholarship, but says, Help yourself; provide
yourself the means. What the State gives for such purposes it pays out
from interested motives, to educate "servants" for itself.

the *means* for competing are not at every one's command, because they are not taken from personality, but from accident. Most are *without means,* and for this reason *without goods.*

Hence the Socialists demand the *means* for all, and aim at a society that shall offer means. Your money value, say they, we no longer recognize as your "competence"; you must show another competence—to wit, your *working force.* In the possession of a property, or as "possessor," man does certainly show himself as man; it was for this reason that we let the possessor, whom we called "proprietor," keep his standing so long. Yet you possess the things only so long as you are not "put out of this property."

The possessor is competent, but only so far as the others are incompetent. Since your ware forms your competence only so long as you are competent to defend it (as *we* are not competent to do anything with it), look about you for another competence; for we now, by our might, surpass your alleged competence.

It was an extraordinarily large gain made, when the point of being regarded as possessors was put through. Therein bondservice was abolished, and every one who till then had been bound to the lord's service, and more or less had been his property, now became a "lord." But henceforth your having, and what you have, are no longer adequate and no longer recognized; *per contra,* your working and your work rise in value. We now respect your *subduing* things, as we formerly did your possessing them. Your work is your competence! You are lord or possessor only of what comes by *work,* not by *inheritance.* But as at the time everything has come by inheritance, and every copper that you possess bears not a labor-stamp but an inheritance-stamp, everything must be melted over.

But is my work then really, as the Communists suppose, my sole competence? or does not this consist rather in everything that I am competent for? And does not the workers' society itself have to concede this, in supporting also the sick, children, old men—in short, those who are incapable of work? These are still competent for a good deal, for instance, to preserve their life instead of taking it. If they are competent to cause you to desire their continued existence, they have a power over you.

To him who exercised utterly no power over you, you would vouchsafe nothing; he might perish.

Therefore, what you are *competent* for is your *competence!* If you are competent to furnish pleasure to thousands, then thousands will pay you an honorarium for it; for it would stand in your power to forbear doing it, hence they must purchase your deed. If you are not competent to *captivate* any one, you may simply starve.

Now am I, who am competent for much, perchance to have no advantage over the less competent?

We are all in the midst of abundance; now shall I not help myself as well as I can, but only wait and see how much is left me in an equal division?

Against competition there rises up the principle of ragamuffin society—*partition.*

To be looked upon as a mere *part,* part of society, the individual cannot bear—because he is *more;* his uniqueness puts from it this limited conception.

Hence he does not await his competence from the sharing of others, and even in the workers' society there arises the misgiving that in an equal partition the strong will be exploited by the weak; he awaits his competence rather from himself, and says now, what I am competent to have, that is my competence.

What competence does not the child possess in its smiling, its playing, its screaming! in short, in its mere existence! Are you capable of resisting its desire? Or do you not hold out to it, as mother, your breast; as father, as much of your possessions as it needs? It compels you, therefore it possesses what you call yours.

If your person is of consequence to me, you pay me with your very existence; if I am concerned only with one of your qualities, then your compliance, perhaps, or your aid, has a value (a money value) for me, and I *purchase* it.

If you do not know how to give yourself any other than a money value in my estimation, there may arise the case of which history tells us, that Germans, sons of the fatherland, were sold to America. Should those who let themselves to be traded in be worth more to the seller? He preferred the cash to this living ware that did not understand how to make itself precious to him. That he discovered nothing more valuable in it was assuredly a defect of his competence; but it takes a rogue to give more than he has. How should he show respect when he did not have it, nay, hardly could have it for such a pack!

You behave egoistically when you respect each other neither as possessors nor as ragamuffins or workers, but as a part of your competence, as *"useful bodies."* Then you will neither give anything to the possessor ("proprietor") for his possessions, nor to him who works, but only to him whom *you require.* The North Americans ask themselves, Do we require a king? and answer, Not a farthing are he and his work worth to us.

If it is said that competition throws every thing open to all, the expression is not accurate, and it is better put thus: competition makes everything purchasable. In *abandoning*[90] it to them, competition leaves it to their appraisal[91] or their estimation, and demands a price[92] for it.

But the would-be buyers mostly lack the means to make themselves buyers: they have no money. For money, then, the purchasable things are indeed to be had ("For money everything is to be had!"), but it is exactly money that is lacking. Where is one to get money, this current or circulating property? Know then, you have as much money[93] as you have—might; for you count[94] for as much as you make yourself count for.

One pays not with money, of which there may come a lack, but with his competence, by which alone we are "competent";[95] for one is proprietor only so far as the arm of our power reaches.

Weitling has thought out a new means of payment—work. But the true means of payment remains, as always, *competence.* With what you have "within your competence" you pay. Therefore think on the enlargement of your competence.

90. (*preisgeben*)
91. (*Preis*)
92. (*Preis*)
93. (*Geld*)
94. (*gelten*)
95. (Equivalent in ordinary German use to our "possessed of a competence.")

This being admitted, they are nevertheless right on hand again with the motto, "To each according to his competence!" Who is to *give* to me according to my competence? Society? Then I should have to put up with its estimation. Rather, I shall *take* according to my competence.

"All belongs to all!" This proposition springs from the same unsubstantial theory. To each belongs only what he is competent for. If I say, The world belongs to me, properly that too is empty talk, which has a meaning only in so far as I respect no alien property. But to me belongs only as much as I am competent for, or have within my competence.

One is not worthy to have what one, through weakness, lets be taken from him; one is not worthy of it because one is not capable of it.

They raise a mighty uproar over the "wrong of a thousand years" which is being committed by the rich against the poor. As if the rich were to blame for poverty, and the poor were not in like manner responsible for riches! Is there another difference between the two than that of competence and incompetence, of the competent and incompetent? Wherein, pray, does the crime of the rich consist? "In their hardheartedness." But who then have maintained the poor? Who have cared for their nourishment? Who have given alms, those alms that have even their name from mercy (*eleemosyne*)? Have not the rich been "merciful" at all times? Are they not to this day "tender-hearted," as poor-taxes, hospitals, foundations of all sorts, etc., prove?

But all this does not satisfy you! Doubtless, then, they are to *share* with the poor? Now you are demanding that they shall abolish poverty. Aside from the point that there might be hardly one among you who would act so, and that this one would be a fool for it, do ask yourselves: why should the rich let go their fleeces and give up *themselves,* thereby pursuing the advantage of the poor rather than their own? You, who have your thaler daily, are rich above thousands who live on four groschen. Is it for your interest to share with the thousands, or is it not rather for theirs?— —

With competition is connected less the intention to do the thing *best* than the intention to make it as *profitable,* as productive, as possible. Hence people study to get into the civil service (pot-boiling study), study cringing and flattery, routine and "acquaintance with business," work "for appearance." Hence, while it is apparently a matter of doing "good service," in truth only a "good business" and earning of money are looked out for. The job is done only ostensibly for the job's sake, but in fact on account of the gain that it yields. One would indeed prefer not to be censor, but one wants to be—advanced; one would like to judge, administer, etc., according to his best convictions, but one is afraid of transference or even dismissal; one must, above all things—live.

Thus these goings-on are a fight for *dear life,* and, in gradation upward, for more or less of a "good living."

And yet, withal, their whole round of toil and care brings in for most only "bitter life" and "bitter poverty." All the bitter painstaking for this!

Restless acquisition does not let us take breath, take a calm *enjoyment*: we do not get the comfort of our possessions.

But the organization of labor touches only such labors as others can do for us, slaughtering, tillage, and the like; the rest remain egoistic, because no one can in your stead elaborate your musical compositions, carry out your projects of painting, etc.; nobody can replace Raphael's labors. The latter are labors of a unique person,[96] which only he is competent to achieve, while the former deserved to be called "human," since what is anybody's *own* in them is of slight account, and almost "any man" can be trained to it.

Now, as society can regard only labors for the common benefit, *human* labors, he who does anything *unique* remains without its care; nay, he may find himself disturbed by its intervention. The unique person will work himself forth out of society all right, but society brings forth no unique person.

Hence it is at any rate helpful that we come to an agreement about *human* labors, that they may not, as under competition, claim all our time and toil. So far Communism will bear its fruits. For before the dominion of the commonalty even that

96. (*Einzige*)

for which all men are qualified, or can be qualified, was tied up to a few and withheld from the rest: it was a privilege. To the commonalty it looked equitable to leave free all that seemed to exist for every "man." But, because left[97] free, it was yet given to no one, but rather left to each to be got hold of by his *human* power. By this the mind was turned to the acquisition of the human, which henceforth beckoned to every one; and there arose a movement which one hears so loudly bemoaned under the name of "materialism."

Communism seeks to check its course, spreading the belief that the human is not worth so much discomfort, and, with sensible arrangements, could be gained without the great expense of time and powers which has hitherto seemed requisite.

But for whom is time to be gained? For what does man require more time than is necessary to refresh his wearied powers of labor? Here Communism is silent.

For what? To take comfort in himself as the unique, after he has done his part as man!

In the first joy over being allowed to stretch out their hands toward everything human, people forgot to want anything else; and they competed away vigorously, as if the possession of the human were the goal of all our wishes.

But they have run themselves tired, and are gradually noticing that "possession does not give happiness." Therefore they are thinking of obtaining the necessary by an easier bargain, and spending on it only so much time and toil as its indispensableness exacts. Riches fall in price, and contented poverty, the care-free ragamuffin, becomes the seductive ideal.

Should such human activities, that every one is confident of his capacity for, be highly salaried, and sought for with toil and expenditure of all life-forces? Even in the every-day form of speech, "If I were minister, or even the . . ., then it should go quite otherwise," that confidence expresses itself—that one holds himself capable of playing the part of such a dignitary; one does get a perception that to things of this sort there belongs not uniqueness, but only a culture which is attainable, even if not

97. (Literally, "given.")

exactly by all, at any rate by many; that for such a thing one need only be an ordinary man.

If we assume that, as *order* belongs to the essence of the State, so *subordination* too is founded in its nature, then we see that the subordinates, or those who have received preferment, disproportionately *overcharge* and *overreach* those who are put in the lower ranks. But the latter take heart (first from the Socialist standpoint, but certainly with egoistic consciousness later, of which we will therefore at once give their speech some coloring) for the question, By what then is your property secure, you creatures of preferment?—and give themselves the answer, By our refraining from interference! And so by *our* protection! And what do you give us for it? Kicks and disdain you give to the "common people"; police supervision, and a catechism with the chief sentence "Respect what is *not yours,* what belongs to *others!* respect others, and especially your superiors!" But we reply, "If you want our respect, *buy* it for a price agreeable to us. We will leave you your property, if you give a due equivalent for this leaving." Really, what equivalent does the general in time of peace give for the many thousands of his yearly income?—another for the sheer hundred-thousands and millions yearly? What equivalent do you give for our chewing potatoes and looking calmly on while you swallow oysters? Only buy the oysters of us as dear as we have to buy the potatoes of you, then you may go on eating them. Or do you suppose the oysters do not belong to us as much as to you? You will make an outcry over *violence* if we reach out our hands and help consume them, and you are right. Without violence we do not get them, as you no less have them by doing violence to us.

But take the oysters and have done with it, and let us consider our nearer property, labor; for the other is only posses-sion. We distress ourselves twelve hours in the sweat of our face, and you offer us a few groschen for it. Then take the like for your labor too. Are you not willing? You fancy that our labor is richly repaid with that wage, while yours on the other hands is worth a wage of many thousands. But, if you did not rate yours so high, and gave us a better chance to realize value from ours, then we might well, if the case demanded it, bring to pass still more important things than you do for the many thousand thalers; and, if you got only such wages as we, you would soon grow more industrious in order to receive more. But, if you render any service that seems to us worth ten and a hundred times more than our own labor, why, then you shall get a hundred times more for it too; we, on the other hand, think also to produce for you things for which you will requite us more highly than with the ordinary day's wages. We shall be willing to get along with each other all right, if only we have first agreed on this—that neither any longer needs to—*present* anything to the other. Then we may perhaps actually go so far as to pay even the cripples and sick and old an appropriate price for not parting from us by hunger and want; for, if we want them to live, it is fitting also that we—purchase the fulfillment of our will. I say "purchase," and therefore do not mean a wretched "alms." For their life is the property even of those who cannot work; if we (no matter for what reason) want them not to withdraw this life from us, we can mean to bring this to pass only by purchase; nay, we shall perhaps (maybe because we like to have friendly faces about us) even want a life of comfort for them. In short, we want nothing presented by you, but neither will we present you with anything. For centuries we have handed alms to you from good-hearted—stupidity, have doled out the mite of the poor and given to the masters the things that are—not the masters'; now just open your wallet, for henceforth our ware rises in price quite enormously. We do not want to take from you anything, anything at all, only you are to pay better for what you want to have. What then have you? "I have an estate of a thousand acres." And I am your plowman, and will henceforth attend to your fields only for one thaler a day wages. "Then I'll take another." You won't find any, for we plowmen are no longer doing otherwise, and, if one puts in an appearance who takes less, then let him beware of us. There is the housemaid, she too is now demanding as much, and you will no longer find one below this price. "Why, then it is all over with me." Not so fast! You will doubtless take in as much as we; and, if it should not be so, we will take off so much that you shall have wherewith to live like us. "But I am accustomed to live better." We have nothing against that, but it is not our lookout; if you can clear more, go ahead. Are we to hire out under rates, that you may have a good living? The rich man always puts off the poor with the words, "What does your want concern me? See to it how you make your way through the world; that is *your affair,* not mine." Well, let us let it be our affair, then, and let us not let the means that we have to realize value from ourselves be pilfered from us by the rich. "But you uncultured people really do not need so much." Well, we are taking somewhat more in order that for it we may procure the culture that we perhaps need. "But, if you thus bring down the rich, who is then to support the arts and sciences hereafter?" Oh, well, we must make it up by num- bers; we club together, that gives a nice little sum—besides, you rich men now buy only the most tasteless books and the most lamentable Madonnas or a pair of lively dancer's legs. "O ill-starred equality!" No, my good old sir, nothing of equality. We only want to count for what we are worth, and, if you are worth more, you shall count for more right along. We only want to be *worth our price,* and think to show ourselves worth the price that you will pay.

Is the State likely to be able to awaken so secure a temper and so forceful a self-consciousness in the menial? Can it make man feel himself? Nay, may it even do so much as set this goal for itself? Can it want the individual to recognize his value and realize this value from himself? Let us keep the parts of the double question separate, and see first whether the State can bring about such a thing. As the unanimity of the plowmen is required, only this unanimity can bring it to pass, and a State law would be evaded in a thousand ways by competition and in secret. But can the State bear with it? The State cannot possibly bear with people's suffering coercion from another than it; it could not, therefore, admit the self-help of the unanimous plowmen against those who want to engage for lower wages. Suppose, however, that the State made the law, and all the plow- men were in accord with it: could the State bear with it then?

In the isolated case—yes; but the isolated case is more than that, it is a case of *principle.* The question therein is of the whole range of *the ego's self-realization of value from himself,* and therefore also of his self-consciousness *against* the State. So far the Communists keep company; but, as self-realization of value from self necessarily directs itself against the State, so it does against *society* too, and therewith reaches out beyond the commune and the communistic—out of egoism.

Communism makes the maxim of the commonalty, that every one is a possessor ("proprietor"), into an irrefragable truth, into a reality, since the anxiety about *obtaining* now ceases and every one *has* from the start what he requires. In his labor-force he *has* his competence, and, if he makes no use of it, that is his fault. The grasping and hounding is at an end, and no competition is left (as so often now) without fruit, because with every stroke of labor an adequate supply of the needful is brought into the house. Now for the first time one is a *real possessor,* because what one has in his labor-force can no longer escape from him as it was continually threatening to do under the system of competition. One is a *care-free* and assured possessor. And one is this precisely by seeking his competence no longer in a ware, but in his own labor, his competence for labor; and therefore by being a *ragamuffin,* a man of only ideal wealth. *I,* however, cannot content myself with the little that I scrape up by my competence for labor, because my competence does not consist merely in my labor.

By labor I can perform the official functions of a president, a minister, etc.; these offices demand only a general culture— to wit, such a culture as is generally attainable (for general culture is not merely that which every one has attained, but broadly that which every one can attain, and therefore every special culture, medical, military, philological, of which no "cultivated man" believes that they surpass his powers), or, broadly, only a skill possible to all.

But, even if these offices may vest in every one, yet it is only the individual's unique force, peculiar to him alone, that gives them, so to speak, life and significance. That he does not manage his office like an "ordinary man," but puts in the competence of his uniqueness, this he is not yet paid for when he is paid only in general as an official or a minister. If he has done it so as to earn your thanks, and you wish to retain this thankworthy force of the unique one, you must not pay him like a mere man who performed only what was human, but as one who accomplishes what is unique. Do the like with your labor, do!

There cannot be a general schedule-price fixed for my uniqueness as there can for what I do as man. Only for the latter can a schedule-price be set.

Go right on, then, setting up a general appraisal for human labors, but do not deprive your uniqueness of its desert.

Human or *general* needs can be satisfied through society; for satisfaction of *unique* needs you must do some seeking. A friend and a friendly service, or even an individual's service, society cannot procure you. And yet you will every moment be in need of such a service, and on the slightest occasions require somebody who is helpful to you. Therefore do not rely on society, but see to it that you have the wherewithal to—purchase the fulfilment of your wishes.

Whether money is to be retained among egoists? To the old stamp an inherited possession adheres. If you no longer let yourselves be paid with it, it is ruined: if you do nothing for this money, it loses all power. Cancel the *inheritance,* and you have broken off the executor's court-seal. For now everything is an inheritance, whether it be already inherited or await its heir. If it is yours, wherefore do you let it be sealed up from you? Why do you respect the seal?

But why should you not create a new money? Do you then annihilate the ware in taking from it the hereditary stamp? Now, money is a ware, and an essential *means* or competence. For it protects against the ossification of resources, keeps them in flux and brings to pass their exchange. If you know a better medium of exchange, go ahead; yet it will be a "money" again. It is not the money that does you damage, but your incompetence to take it. Let your competence take effect, collect yourselves, and there will be no lack of money—of your money, the money of *your* stamp. But working I do not call "letting your competence take effect." Those who are only "looking for work" and "willing to work hard" are preparing for their own selves the infallible upshot—to be out of work.

Good and bad luck depend on money. It is a power in the

bourgeois period for this reason, that it is only wooed on all hands like a girl, indissolubly wedded by nobody. All the romance and chivalry of *wooing* for a dear object come to life again in competition. Money, an object of longing, is carried off by the bold "knights of industry."⁵⁸

He who has luck takes home the bride. The ragamuffin has luck; he takes her into his household, "society," and destroys the virgin. In his house she is no longer bride, but wife; and with her virginity her family name is also lost. As housewife the maiden Money is called "Labor," for "Labor" is her husband's name. She is a possession of her husband's.

To bring this figure to an end, the child of Labor and Money is again a girl, an unwedded one and therefore Money but with the certain descent from Labor, her father. The form of the face, the "effigy," bears another stamp.

Finally, as regards competition once more, it has a continued existence by this very means, that all do not attend to *their affair* and come to an *understanding* with each other about it. Bread is a need of all the inhabitants of a city; therefore they might easily agree on setting up a public bakery. Instead of this, they leave the furnishing of the needful to the competing bakers. Just so meat to the butchers, wine to wine-dealers, etc.

Abolishing competition is not equivalent to favoring the guild. The difference is this: In the *guild* baking, etc., is the affair of the guild-brothers; in *competition,* the affair of chance competitors; in the *union,* of those who require baked goods, and therefore my affair, yours, the affair of neither the guildic nor the concessionary baker, but the affair of the *united.*

If *I* do not trouble myself about *my* affair, I must be *content* with what it pleases others to vouchsafe me. To have bread is my affair, my wish and desire, and yet people leave that to the bakers and hope at most to obtain through their wrangling, their getting ahead of each other, their rivalry—in short, their competition—an advantage which one could not count on in the case of the guild-brothers who were lodged *entirely* and *alone* in the proprietorship of the baking franchise.—What every one requires,

98. (A German phrase for sharpers.)

every one should also take a hand in procuring and producing; it is *his* affair, his property, not the property of the guildic or concessionary master.

Let us look back once more. The world belongs to the children of this world, the children of men; it is no longer God's world, but man's. As much as every man can procure of it, let him call his; only the true man, the State, human society or mankind, will look to it that each shall make nothing else his own than what he appropriates as man, in human fashion. Unhuman appropriation is that which is not consented to by man, that is, it is a "criminal" appropriation, as the human, *vice versa,* is a "rightful" one, one acquired in the "way of law."

So they talk since the Revolution.

But my property is not a thing, since this has an existence independent of me; only my might is my own. Not this tree, but my might or control over it, is what is mine.

Now, how is this might perversely expressed? They say I have a *right* to this tree, or it is my *rightful* property. So I have *earned* it by might. That the might must last in order that the tree may also be *held*—or better, that the might is not a thing existing of itself, but has existence solely in the *mighty ego,* in me the mighty—is forgotten. Might, like other of my *qualities* (humanity, majesty, etc.), is exalted to something existing of itself, so that it still exists long after it has ceased to be *my* might. Thus transformed into a ghost, might is—*right*. This *eternalized* might is not extinguished even with my death, but is transferred to "bequeathed."

Things now really belong not to me, but to right.

On the other side, this is nothing but a hallucination of vision. For the individual's might becomes permanent and a right only by others joining their might with his. The delusion consists in their believing that they cannot withdraw their might. The same phenomenon over again; might is separated from me. I cannot take back the might that I gave to the possessor. One has "granted power of attorney," has given away his power, has renounced coming to a better mind.

The proprietor can give up his might and his right to a thing by giving the thing away, squandering it, and the like. And *we*

should not be able likewise to let go the might that we lend
to him?

The rightful man, the *just,* desires to call nothing his own
that he does not have "rightly" or have the right to, and therefore
only *legitimate property.*

Now, who is to be judge, and adjudge his right to him? At
last, surely, Man, who imparts to him the rights of man: then
he can say, in an infinitely broader sense than Terence, *humani
nihil a me alienum puto,* that is, *the human is my property.* However he may go about it, so long as he occupies this standpoint
he cannot get clear of a judge; and in our time the multifarious
judges that had been selected have set themselves against each
other in two persons at deadly enmity—to wit, in God and Man.
The one party appeal to divine right, the other to human right
or the rights of man.

So much is clear, that in neither case does the individual
do the entitling himself.

Just pick me out an action to-day that would not be a
violation of right! Every moment the rights of man are trampled
under foot by one side, while their opponents cannot open their
mouth without uttering a blasphemy against divine right. Give
an alms, you mock at a right of man, because the relation of
beggar and benefactor is an inhuman relation; utter a doubt, you
sin against a divine right. Eat dry bread with contentment, you
violate the right of man by your equanimity; eat it with discontent,
you revile divine right by your repining. There is not one among
you who does not commit a crime at every moment; your speeches
are crimes, and every hindrance to your freedom of speech is no
less a crime. Ye are criminals altogether!

Yet you are so only in that you all stand on the *ground of
right,* in that you do not even know, and understand how to value,
the fact that you are criminals.

Inviolable or *sacred* property has grown on this very ground:
it is a *juridical concept.*

A dog sees the bone in another's power, and stands off
only if it feels itself too weak. But man respects the other's *right*
to his bone. The latter action, therefore, ranks as *human,* the
former as *brutal* or "egoistic."

And as here, so in general, it is called *"human"* when one sees in everything something *spiritual* (here right), makes everything a ghost and takes his attitude toward it as toward a ghost, which one can indeed scare away at its appearance, but cannot kill. It is human to look at what is individual not as individual, but as a generality.

In nature as such I no longer respect anything, but know myself to be entitled to everything against it; in the tree in that garden, on the other hand, I must respect *alienness* (they say in one-sided fashion "property"), I must keep my hand off it. This comes to an end only when I can indeed leave that tree to another as I leave my stick, etc., to another, but do not in advance regard it as alien to me, sacred. Rather, I make to myself no *crime* of felling it if I will, and it remains my property, however long as I resign it to others: it is and remains *mine*. In the banker's fortune I as little see anything alien as Napoleon did in the territories of kings: we have no *dread* of *"conquering"* it, and we look about us also for the means thereto. We strip off from it, therefore, the *spirit* of *alienness,* of which we had been afraid.

Therefore it is necessary that I do not lay claim to anything more *as man,* but to everything as I, this I; and accordingly to nothing human, but to mine; that is, nothing that pertains to me as man, but—what I will and because I will it.

Rightful, or legitimate, property of another will be only that which *you* are content to recognize as such. If your content ceases, then this property has lost legitimacy for you, and you will laugh at absolute right to it.

Besides the hitherto discussed property in the limited sense, there is held up to our reverent heart another property against which we are far less "to sin." This property consists in spiritual goods, in the "sanctuary of the inner nature." What a man holds sacred, no other is to gibe at; because, untrue as it may be, and zealously as one may "in loving and modest wise" seek to convince of a true sanctity the man who adheres to it and believes in it, yet *the sacred* itself is always to be honored in it: the mistaken man does believe in the sacred, even though in an incorrect essence of it, and so his belief in the sacred must at least be respected.

In ruder times than ours it was customary to demand a particular faith, and devotion to a particular sacred essence, and they did not take the gentlest way with those who believed otherwise; since, however, "freedom of belief" spread itself more and more abroad, the "jealous God and sole Lord" gradually melted into a pretty general "supreme being," and it satisfied humane tolerance if only every one revered "something sacred."

Reduced to the most human expression, this sacred essence is "man himself" and "the human." With the deceptive semblance as if the human were altogether our own, and free from all the otherworldliness with which the divine is tainted—yes, as if Man were as much as I or you—there may arise even the proud fancy that the talk is no longer of a "sacred essence" and that we now feel ourselves everywhere at home and no longer in the uncanny,[99] in the sacred and in sacred awe: in the ecstasy over "Man discovered at last" the egoistic cry of pain passes unheard, and the spook that has become so intimate is taken for our true ego.

But "Humanus is the saint's name" (see Goethe), and the humane is only the most clarified sanctity.

The egoist makes the reverse declaration. For this precise reason, because you hold something sacred, I gibe at you; and, even if I respected everything in you, your sanctuary is precisely what I should not respect.

With these opposed views there must also be assumed a contradictory relation to spiritual goods: the egoist insults them, the religious man (every one who puts his "essence" above himself) must consistently—protect them. But what kind of spiritual goods are to be protected, and what left unprotected, depends entirely on the concept that one forms of the "supreme being"; and he who fears God, for example, has more to shelter than he (the liberal) who fears Man.

In spiritual goods we are (in distinction from the sensuous) injured in a spiritual way, and the sin against them consists in a direct *desecration,* while against the sensuous a purloining or

99. (Literally, "unhomely.")

alienation takes place; the goods themselves are robbed of value and of consecration, not merely taken away; the sacred is immediately compromised. With the word "irreverence" or "flippancy" is designated everything that can be committed as *crime* against spiritual goods, against everything that is sacred for us; and scoffing, reviling, contempt, doubt, and the like, are only different shades of *criminal flippancy.*

That desecration can be practiced in the most manifold way is here to be passed over, and only that desecration is to be preferentially mentioned which threatens the sacred with danger through an *unrestricted press.*

As long as respect is demanded even for one spiritual essence, speech and the press must be enthralled in the name of this essence; for just so long the egoist might "trespass" against it by his *utterances,* from which thing he must be hindered by "due punishment" at least, if one does not prefer to take up the more correct means against it, the preventive use of police authority, such as censorship.

What a sighing for liberty of the press! What then is the press to be liberated from? Surely from a dependence, a belonging, and a liability to service! But to liberate himself from that is every one's affair, and it may with safety be assumed that, when you have delivered yourself from liability to service, that which you compose and write will also belong to you as your *own* instead of having been thought and indicted *in the service* of some power. What can a believer in Christ say and have printed, that should be freer from that belief in Christ than he himself is? If I cannot or may not write something, perhaps the primary fault lies with *me.* Little as this seems to hit the point, so near is the application nevertheless to be found. By a press-law I draw a boundary for my publications, or let one be drawn, beyond which wrong and its *punishment* follows. I myself *limit* myself.

If the press was to be free, nothing would be so important as precisely its liberation from every coercion that could be put on it in the *name of a law.* And, that it might come to that, I my own self should have to have absolved myself from obedience to the law.

Certainly, the absolute liberty of the press is like every absolute liberty, a nonentity. The press can become free from full many a thing, but always only from what I too am free from. If we make ourselves free from the sacred, if we have become *graceless* and *lawless,* our words too will become so.

As little as *we* can be declared clear of every coercion in the world, so little can our writing be withdrawn from it. But as free as we are, so free we can make it too.

It must therefore become our *own,* instead of, as hitherto, serving a spook.

People do not yet know what they mean by their cry for liberty of the press. What they ostensibly ask is that the State shall set the press free; but what they are really after, without knowing it themselves, is that the press become free from the the State, or clear of the State. The former is a *petition to* the State, the latter an *insurrection against* the State. As a "petition for right," even as a serious demanding of the right of liberty of the press, it presupposes the State as the giver, and can hope only for a *present,* a permission, a chartering. Possible, no doubt, that a State acts so senselessly as to grant the demanded present; but you may bet everything that those who receive the present will not know how to use it so long as they regard the State as a truth: they will not trespass against this "sacred thing," and will call for a penal press-law against every one who would be willing to dare this.

In a word, the press does not become free from what I am not free from.

Do I perhaps hereby show myself an opponent of the liberty of the press? On the contrary, I only assert that one will never get it if one wants only it, the liberty of the press, if one sets out only for an unrestricted permission. Only beg right along for this permission: you may wait forever for it, for there is no one in the world who could give it to you. As long as you want to have yourselves "entitled" to the use of the press by a permission, you live in vain hope and complaint.

"Nonsense! Why, you yourself, who harbor such thoughts as stand in your book, can unfortunately bring them to publicity only through a lucky chance or by stealth; nevertheless you will inveigh against one's pressing and importuning his own State till it gives the refused permission to print?" But an author thus addressed would perhaps—for the impudence of such people goes far—give the following reply: "Consider well what you say! What then do I do to procure myself liberty of the press for my book? Do I ask for permission, or do I not rather, without any question of legality, seek a favorable occasion and grasp it in complete recklessness of the State and its wishes? I—the terrifying word must be uttered—I cheat the State. You unconsciously do the same. From your tribunes you talk it into the idea that it must give up its sanctity and inviolability, it must lay itself bare to the attacks of writers, without needing on that account to fear danger. But you are imposing on it; for its existence is done for as soon as it loses its unapproachableness. To *you* indeed it might well accord liberty of writing, as England has done; you are *believers in the State* and incapable of writing against the State, however much you would like to reform it and 'remedy its defects.' But what if opponents of the State availed themselves of free utterance, and stormed out against Church, State, morals, and everything 'sacred' with inexorable reasons? You would then be the first, in terrible agonies, to call into life the *September laws.*[100] Too late would you then rue the stupidity that earlier made you so ready to fool and palaver into compliance the State, or the government of the State.—But, I prove by my act only two things. This for one, that the liberty of the press is always bound to 'favorable opportunities,' and accordingly will never be an absolute liberty; but secondly this, that he who would enjoy it must seek out and, if possible, create the favorable opportunity, availing himself of his *own advantage* against the State; and counting himself and his will more than the State and every 'superior' power. Not in the State, but only against it, can the liberty of the press be carried through; if it is to be established, it is to be obtained not as the consequence of a *petition* but as the work of an *insurrection.* Every petition and

100. [A series of very repressive measures enacted in France in September, 1835 in the reign of Louis Philippe; one of them was a severe press restriction, aimed at curtailing the expression of radical views and opinions.]

every motion for liberty of the press is already an insurrection, be it conscious or unconscious: a thing which Philistine halfness alone will not and cannot confess to itself until, with a shrinking shudder, it shall see it clearly and irrefutably by the outcome. For the requested liberty of the press has indeed a friendly and well-meaning face at the beginning, as it is not in the least minded ever to let the 'insolence of the press' come into vogue; but little by little its heart grows more hardened, and the inference flatters its way in that really a liberty is not a liberty if it stands in the *service* of the State, of morals, or of the law. A liberty indeed from the coercion of censorship, it is yet not a liberty from the coercion of law. The press, once seized by the lust for liberty, always wants to grow freer, till at last the writer says to himself, really I am not wholly free till I ask about nothing; and writing is free only when it is my *own,* dictated to me by no power or authority, by no faith, no dread; the press must not be free—that is too little—it must be *mine:—ownness of the press* or *property in the press,* that is what I will take.

"Why, liberty of the press is only *permission of the press,* and the State never will or can voluntarily permit me to grind it to nothingness by the press."

Let us now, in conclusion, bettering the above language, which is still vague, owing to the phrase 'liberty of the press,' rather put it thus: "*liberty of the press,* the liberals' loud demand, is assuredly possible in the State; yes, it is possible only *in* the State, because it is a *permission,* and consequently the permitter (the State) must not be lacking. But as permission it has its limit in this very State, which surely should not in reason permit more than is compatible with itself and its welfare: the State fixes for it this limit as the *law* of its existence and of its extension. That one State brooks more than another is only a quantitative distinction, which alone, nevertheless, lies at the heart of the political liberals: they want in Germany, for example, only a '*more extended, broader* accordance of free utterance.' The liberty of the press which is sought for is an affair of the *people's,* and before the people (the State) possesses it I may make no use of it. From the standpoint of property in the press, the situation is different. Let my people, if they will, go without liberty of free press, I will manage to print by force or ruse; I get my permission to print only from—*myself* and my strength.

If the press is *my own,* I as little need a permission of the State for employing it as I seek that permission in order to blow my nose. The press is my *property* from the moment when nothing is more to me than myself; for from this moment State, Church, people, society, and the like, cease, because they have to thank for their existence only the disrespect that I have for myself, and with the vanishing of this undervaluation they themselves are extinguished: they exist only when they exist *above me,* exist only as *powers* and *power-holders.* Or can you imagine a State whose citizens one and all think nothing of it? It would be as certainly a dream, an existence in seeming, as 'united Germany.'

The press is my own as soon as I myself am my own, a self-owned man: to the egoist belongs the world, because he belongs to no power of the world.

With this my press might still be very *unfree,* as at this moment. But the world is large, and one helps himself as well as he can. If I were willing to abate from the *property* of my press, I could easily attain the point where I might everywhere have as much printed as my fingers produced. But, as I want to assert my property, I must necessarily swindle my enemies. 'Would you not accept their permission if it were given you?' Certainly, with joy; for their permission would be to me a proof that I had fooled them and started them on the road to ruin. I am not concerned for their permission, but so much the more for their folly and their overthrow. I do not sue for their permission as if I flattered myself (like the political liberals) that we both, they and I, could make out peaceably alongside and with each other, yes, probably raise and prop each other; but I sue for it in order to make them bleed to death by it, that the permitters themselves may cease at last. I act as a conscious enemy, overreaching them and *utilizing* their heedlessness.

The press is *mine* when I recognize outside myself no *judge* whatever over its utilization, when my writing is no longer determined by morality or religion or respect for the State laws or the like, but by me and my egoism!"

Now, what have you to reply to him who gives you so impudent an answer?—We shall perhaps put the question most strikingly by phrasing it as follows: Whose is the press, the people's (State's) or mine? The politicals on their side intend nothing further than to liberate the press from personal and arbitrary interferences of the possessors of power, without thinking of the point that to be really open for everybody it would also have to be free from the laws, from the people's (State's) will. They want to make a "people's affair" of it.

But, having become the people's property, it is still far from being mine; rather, it retains for me the subordinate significance of a *permission*. The people plays judge over my thoughts; it has the right of calling me to account for them, or, I am responsible to it for them. Jurors, when their fixed ideas are attacked, have just as hard heads as the stiffest despots and their servile officials.

In the *Liberalen Bestrebungen*[101] Edgar Bauer asserts that liberty of the press is impossible in the absolutist and the constitutional State, whereas in the "free State" it finds its place. "Here," the statement is, "it is recognized that the individual, because he is no longer an individual but a member of a true and rational generality, has the right to utter his mind." So not the individual, but the "member," has liberty of the press. But, if for the purpose of liberty of the press the individual must first give proof of himself regarding his belief in the generality, the people; if he does not have this liberty *through might of his own*—then it is a *people's liberty,* a liberty that he is invested with for the sake of his faith, his "membership." The reverse is the case: it is precisely as an individual that every one has open to him the liberty to utter his mind. But he has not the "right": that liberty is assuredly not his "sacred right." He has only the *might;* but the might alone makes him owner. I need no concession for the liberty of the press, do not need the people's consent to it, do not need the "right" to it, nor any "justification." The liberty of the press too, like every liberty, I must "take"; the people, "as being the sole judge," cannot *give* it to me. It

101. Vol. II, p. 91 ff. See my note above.

can put up with me the liberty that I take, or defend itself against it; give, bestow, grant it it cannot. I exercise it *despite* the people, purely as an individual; I get it by fighting the people, my—enemy, and obtain it only when I really get it by such fighting, *take* it. But I take it because it is my property.

Sander, against whom E. Bauer writes, lays claim (page 99) to the liberty of the press "as the right and the liberty of the *citizens in the State.*" What else does Edgar Bauer do? To him also it is only a right of the free *citizen*.

The liberty of the press is also demanded under the name of a "general human right." Against this the objection was well-founded that not every man knew how to use it rightly, for not every individual was truly man. Never did a government refuse it to *Man* as such; but *Man* writes nothing, for the reason that he is a ghost. It always refused it to *individuals* only, and gave it to others, its organs. If then one would have it for all, one must assert outright that it is due to the individual, me, not to man or to the individual so far as he is man. Besides, another than a man (a beast) can make no use of it. The French government, for example, does not dispute the liberty of the press as a right of man, but demands from the individual a security for his really being man; for it assigns liberty of the press not to the individual, but to man.

Under the exact pretense that it was *not human,* what was mine was taken from me! What was human was left to me undiminished.

Liberty of the press can bring about only a *responsible* press; the *irresponsible* proceeds solely from property in the press.

For intercourse with men an express law (conformity to which one may venture at times sinfully to forget, but the absolute value of which one at no time ventures to deny) is placed foremost among all who live religiously: this is the law— of *love,* to which not even those who seem to fight against its principle, and who hate its name, have as yet become untrue; for they also still have love, yes, they love with a deeper and more sublimated love, they love "man and mankind."

If we formulate the sense of this law, it will be about as

follows: Every man must have a something that is more to him than himself. You are to put your "private interest" in the background when it is a question of the welfare of others, the weal of the fatherland, of society, the common weal, the weal of mankind, the good cause, and the like! Fatherland, society, mankind, must be more to you than yourself, and as against their interest your "private interest" must stand back; for you must not be an—egoist.

Love is a far-reaching religious demand, which is not, as might be supposed, limited to love to God and man, but stands foremost in every regard. Whatever we do, think, will, the ground of it is always to be love. Thus we may indeed judge, but only "with love." The Bible may assuredly be criticized, and that very thoroughly, but the critic must before all things *love* it and see in it the sacred book. Is this anything else than to say he must not criticize it to death, he must leave it standing, and that as a sacred thing that cannot be upset?—In our criticism on men too, love must remain the unchanged key-note. Certainly judgments that hatred inspires are not at all our *own* judgments, but judgments of the hatred that rules us, "rancorous judgments." But are judgments that love inspires in us any more our *own*? They are judgments of the love that rules us, they are "loving, lenient" judgments, they are not our *own,* and accordingly not real judgments at all. He who burns with love for justice cries out, *fiat justitia, pereat mundus!* He can doubtless ask and investigate what justice properly is or demands, and *in what* it consists, but not *whether* it is anything.

It is very true, "He who abides in love abides in God, and God in him." (I John 4. 16.) God abides in him, he does not get rid of God, does not become godless; and he abides in God, does not come to himself and into his own home, abides in love to God and does not become loveless.

"God is love! All times and all races recognize in this word the central point of Christianity." God, who is love, is an officious God: he cannot leave the world in peace, but wants to make it *blest.* "God became man to make men divine."[102] He

102. Athanasius. [A Greek Father of the Church, Bishop of Alex-

has his hand in the game everywhere, and nothing happens without it; everywhere he has his "best purposes," his "incomprehensible plans and decrees." Reason, which he himself is, is to be forwarded and realized in the whole world. His fatherly care deprives us of all independence. We can do nothing sensible without its being said, God did that, and can bring upon ourselves no misfortune without hearing, God ordained that; we have nothing that we have not from him, he "gave" everything. But, as God does, so does Man. God wants perforce to make the world *blest,* and Man wants to make it *happy,* to make all men happy. Hence every "man" wants to awaken in all men the reason which he supposes his own self to have: everything is to be rational throughout. God torments himself with the devil, and the philosopher does it with unreason and the accidental. God lets no being go *its own* gait, and Man likewise wants to make us walk only in human wise.

But whoso is full of sacred (religious, moral, humane) love loves only the spook, the "true man," and persecutes with dull mercilessness the individual, the real man, under the phlegmatic legal title of measures against the "un-man." He finds it praiseworthy and indispensable to exercise pitilessness in the harshest measure; for love to the spook or generality commands him to hate him who is not ghostly, the egoist or individual; such is the meaning of the renowned love-phenomenon that is called "justice."

The criminally arraigned man can expect no forbearance, and no one spreads a friendly veil over his unhappy nakedness. Without emotion the stern judge tears the last rags of excuse from the body of the poor accused; without compassion the jailer drags him into his damp abode; without placability, when the time of punishment has expired, he thrusts the branded man again among men, his good, Christian, loyal brethren, who contemptuously spit on him. Yes, without grace a criminal "deserving of death" is led to the scaffold, and before the eyes of a jubilating crowd the appeased moral law celebrates its sublime—revenge. For only one can live, the moral law or the criminal. Where criminals

andria, born late in the 3rd century, died 373 A.D., and subsequently canonized a saint.]

live unpunished, the moral law has fallen; and, where this prevails, those must go down. Their enmity is indestructible.

The Christian age is precisely that of *mercy, love,* solicitude to have men receive what is due them, yes, to bring them to fulfill their human (divine) calling. Therefore the principle has been put foremost for intercourse, that this and that is man's essence and consequently his calling, to which either God has called him or (according to the concepts of to-day) his being man (the species) calls him. Hence the zeal for conversion. That the Communists and the humane expect from man more than the Christians do does not change the standpoint in the least. Man shall get what is human! If it was enough for the pious that what was divine became his part, the humane demand that he be not curtailed of what is human. Both set themselves against what is egoistic. Of course; for what is egoistic cannot be accorded to him or vested in him (a fief); he must procure it for himself. Love imparts the former, the latter can be given to me by myself alone.

Intercourse hitherto has rested on love, *regardful* behavior, doing for each other. As one owed it to himself to make himself blessed, or owed himself the bliss of taking up into himself the supreme essence and bringing it to a *vérité* (a truth and reality), so one owed it to *others* to help them realize their essence and their calling: in both cases one owed it to the essence of man to contribute to its realization.

But one owes it neither to himself to make anything out of himself, nor to others to make anything out of them; for one owes nothing to his essence and that of others. Intercourse resting on essence is an intercourse with the spook, not with anything real. If I hold intercourse with the supreme essence, I am not holding intercourse with myself, and, if I hold intercourse with the essence of man, I am not holding intercourse with men.

The natural man's love becomes through culture a *commandment.* But as commandment it belongs to *Man* as such, not to me; it is my *essence,*[103] about which much ado[104] is made, not

103. (*Wesen*)
104. (*Wesen*)

my property. *Man,* humanity, presents that demand to me; love
is *demanded,* it is my *duty.* Instead, therefore, of being really
won for *me,* it has been won for the generality, *Man,* as his
property or peculiarity: "it becomes man, every man, to love;
love is the duty and calling of man," etc.

Consequently I must again vindicate love for *myself,* and
deliver it out of the power of Man with the great M.

What was originally *mine,* but *accidentally* mine, instinctively
mine, I was invested with as the property of Man; I became
feoffee in loving, I became the retainer of mankind, only a
specimen of this species, and acted, loving, not as *I,* but as *man,*
as a specimen of man, the humanly. The whole condition of
civilization is the *feudal system,* the property being Man's or
mankind's, not *mine.* A monstrous feudal State was founded, the
individual robbed of everything, everything left to "man." The
individual had to appear at last as a "sinner through and through."

Am I perchance to have no lively interest in the person of
another, are *his* joy and *his* weal not to lie at my heart, is the
enjoyment that I furnish him not to be more to me than other
enjoyments of my own? On the contrary, I can with joy sacrifice
to him numberless enjoyments, I can deny myself numberless
things for the enhancement of *his* pleasure, and I can hazard for
him what without him was the dearest to me, my life, my welfare,
my freedom. Why, it constitutes my pleasure and my happiness
to refresh myself with his happiness and his pleasure. But *myself,*
my own self, I do not sacrifice to him, but remain an egoist and
—enjoy him. If I sacrifice to him everything that but for my
love to him I should keep, that is very simple, and even more
usual in life than it seems to be; but it proves nothing further
than that this one passion is more powerful in me than all the
rest. Christianity too teaches us to sacrifice all other passions
to this. But, if to one passion I sacrifice others, I do not on
that account go so far as to sacrifice *myself,* nor sacrifice anything
of that whereby I truly am myself; I do not sacrifice my peculiar
value, my *ownness.* Where this bad case occurs, love cuts no
better figure than any other passion that I obey blindly. The
ambitious man, who is carried away by ambition and remains
deaf to every warning that a calm moment begets in him, has

let this passion grow up into a despot against whom he abandons all power of dissolution: he has given up himself, because he cannot *dissolve* himself, and consequently cannot absolve himself from the passion: he is possessed.

I love men too—not merely individuals, but every one. But I love them with the consciousness of egoism; I love them because love makes *me* happy, I love because loving is natural to me, because it pleases me. I know no "commandment of love." I have a *fellow-feeling* with every feeling being, and their torment torments, their refreshment refreshes me too; I can kill them, not torture them. *Per contra,* the high-souled, virtuous Philistine prince Rudolph in *The Mysteries of Paris,*[105] because the wicked provoke his "indignation," plans their torture. That fellow-feeling proves only that the feeling of those who feel is mine too, my property; in opposition to which the pitiless dealing of the "righteous" man (as against notary Ferrand) is like the unfeelingness of that robber [Procrustes] who cut *off* or stretched his prisoners' legs to the measure of his bedstead: Rudolph's bedstead, which he cuts men to fit, is the concept of the "good." The feeling for right, virtue, etc., makes people hard-hearted and intolerant. Rudolph does not feel like the notary, but the reverse; he feels that "it serves the rascal right"; that is no fellow-feeling.

You love man, therefore you torture the individual man, the egoist; your philanthropy (love of men) is the tormenting of men.

If I see the loved one suffer, I suffer with him, and I know no rest till I have tried everything to comfort and cheer him; if I see him glad, I too become glad over his joy. From this it does not follow that suffering or joy is caused in me by the same thing that brings out this effect in him, as is sufficiently proved by every bodily pain which I do not feel as he does; his tooth pains him, but his pain pains me.

But, because I cannot bear the troubled crease on the beloved forehead, for that reason, and therefore for my sake, I kiss it away. If I did not love this person, he might go right

---

105. [*Mystères de Paris,* the major work of Marie-Joseph Sue (1804-1857), celebrated French novelist, published in Paris, 1842-1843; the author was known as Eugène Sue.]

on making creases, they would not trouble me; I am only driving away *my* trouble.

How now, has anybody or anything, whom and which I do not love, a *right* to be loved by me? Is my love first, or is his right first? Parents, kinsfolk, fatherland, nation, native town, etc., finally fellowmen in general ("brothers, fraternity"), assert that they have a right to my love, and lay claim to it without further ceremony. They look upon it as *their property,* and upon me, if I do not respect this, as a robber who takes from them what pertains to them and is theirs. I *should* love. If love is a commandment and law, then I must be educated into it, cultivated up to it, and, if I trespass against it, punished. Hence people will exercise as strong a "moral influence" as possible on me to bring me to love. And there is no doubt that one can work up and seduce men to love as one can to other passions—if you like, to hate. Hate runs through whole races merely because the ancestors of the one belonged to the Guelphs, those of the other to the Ghibellines.

But love is not a commandment, but, like each of my feelings, *my property.* *Acquire,* purchase, my property, and then I will make it over to you. A church, a nation, a fatherland, a family, etc., that does not know how to acquire my love, I need not love; and I fix the purchase price of my love quite at my pleasure.

Selfish love is far distant from unselfish, mystical, or romantic love. One can love everything possible, not merely men, but an "object" in general (wine, one's fatherland, etc.). Love becomes blind and crazy by a *must* taking it out of my power (infatuation), romantic by a *should* entering into it, by the "objects" becoming sacred for me, or my becoming bound to it by duty, conscience, oath. Now the object no longer exists for me, but I for it.

Love is a possessedness, not as my feeling—as such I rather keep it in my possession as property—but through the alienness of the object. For religious love consists in the commandment to love in the beloved a "holy one," or to adhere to a holy one; for unselfish love there are objects *absolutely lovable* for which my heart is to beat, such as fellow-men, or my wedded mate, kinsfolk, etc. Holy Love loves the holy in the beloved, and therefore exerts itself also to make of the beloved more and more a holy one (a "man").

The beloved is an object that *should* be loved by me. He is not an object of my love on account of, because of, or by, my loving him, but is an object of love in and of himself. Not I make him an object of love, but he is such to begin with; for it is here irrelevant that he has become so by my choice, if so it be (as with a *fiancée,* a spouse, and the like), since even so he has in any case, as the person once chosen, obtained a "right of his own to my love," and I, because I have loved him, am under obligation to love him forever. He is therefore not an object of *my* love, but of love in general: an object that *should* be loved. Love appertains to him, is due to him, or is his *right,* while I am under *obligation* to love him. My love, the toll of love that I pay him, is in truth *his* love, which he only collects from me as toll.

Every love to which there clings but the smallest speck of obligation is an unselfish love, and, so far as this speck reaches, a possessedness. He who believes that he *owes* the object of his love anything loves romantically or religiously.

Family love, as it is usually understood as "piety," is a religious love; love of fatherland, preached as "patriotism," likewise. All our romantic loves move in the same pattern: everywhere the hypocrisy, or rather self-deception, of an "unselfish love," an interest in the object for the object's sake, not for my sake and mine alone.

Religious or romantic love is distinguished from sensual love by the difference of the object indeed, but not by the dependence of the relation to it. In the latter regard both are possessedness; but in the former the one object is profane, the other sacred. The dominion of the object over me is the same in both cases, only that it is one time a sensuous one, the other time a spiritual (ghostly) one. My love is my own only when it consists altogether in a selfish and egoistic interest, and when consequently the object of my love is really *my* object or my property. I owe my property nothing, and have no duty to it, as little as I might have a duty to my eye; if nevertheless I guard it with the greatest care, I do so on my account.

Antiquity lacked love as little as do Christian times; the god of love is older than the God of Love. But the mystical possessedness belongs to the moderns.

The possessedness of love lies in the alienation of the object, or in my powerlessness as against its alienness and superior power. To the egoist nothing is high enough for him to humble himself before it, nothing so independent that he would live for love of it, nothing so sacred that he would sacrifice himself to it. The egoist's love rises in selfishness, flows in the bed of selfishness, and empties into selfishness again.

Whether this can still be called love? If you know another word for it, go ahead and choose it; then the sweet word love may wither with the departed world; for the present I at least find none in our *Christian* language, and hence stick to the old sound and "love" *my* object, my—property.

Only as one of my feelings do I harbor love; but as a power above me, as a divine power, as Feuerbach says, as a passion that I am not to cast off, as a religious and moral duty, I—scorn it. As my feeling it is *mine;* as a principle to which I consecrate and "vow" my soul it is a dominator and *divine,* just as hatred as a principle is *diabolical;* one not better than the other. In short, egoistic love, my love, is neither holy nor unholy, neither divine nor diabolical.

"A love that is limited by faith is an untrue love. The sole limitation that does not contradict the essence of love is the self-limitation of love by reason, intelligence. Love that scorns the rigor, the law, of intelligence, is theoretically a false love, practically a ruinous one."[106] So love is in its essence *rational!* So thinks Feuerbach; the believer, on the contrary, thinks, Love is in its essence *believing.* The one inveighs against *irrational,* the other against *unbelieving,* love. To both it can at most rank as a *splendidum vitium.* Do not both leave love standing, even in the form of unreason and unbelief? They do not dare to say, irrational or unbelieving love is nonsense, is not love; as little

106. Feuerbach, *Essence of Christianity,* p. 394.

as they are willing to say, irrational or unbelieving tears are not tears. But, if even irrational love, etc., must count as love, and if they are nevertheless to be unworthy of man, there follows simply this: love is not the highest thing, but reason or faith; even the unreasonable and the unbelieving can love; but love has value only when it is that of a rational or believing person. It is an illusion when Feuerbach calls the rationality of love its "self-limitation"; the believer might with the same right call belief its "self-limitation." Irrational love is neither "false" nor "ruinous"; its does its service as love.

Toward the world, especially toward men, I am to *assume a particular feeling,* and "meet them with love," with the feeling of love, from the beginning. Certainly, in this there is revealed far more free-will and self-determination than when I let myself be stormed, by way of the world, by all possible feelings, and remain exposed to the most checkered, most accidental impressions. I go to the world rather with a preconceived feeling, as if it were a prejudice and a preconceived opinion; I have prescribed to myself in advance my behavior toward it, and, despite all its temptations, feel and think about it only as I have once determined to. Against the dominion of the world I secure myself by the principle of love; for, whatever may come, I—love. The ugly, for example, makes a repulsive impression on me; but, determined to love, I master this impression as I do every antipathy.

But the feeling to which I have determined and—condemned myself from the start is a *narrow* feeling, because it is a pre-destined one, of which I myself am not able to get clear or to declare myself clear. Because preconceived, it is a *prejudice. I* no longer show myself in face of the world, but my love shows itself. The *world* indeed does not rule me, but so much the more inevitably does the spirit of *love* rule this spirit.

If I first said, I love the world, I now add likewise: I do not love it, for I *annihilate* it as I annihilate myself; I *dissolve it.* I do not limit myself to one feeling for men, but give free play to all that I am capable of. Why should I not dare speak it out in all its glaringness? Yes, I *utilize* the world and men! With this I can keep myself open to every impression without being torn away from myself by one of them. I can love, love with a full heart, and let the most consuming glow of passion burn in my heart, without taking the beloved one for anything else than the *nourishment* of my passion, on which it ever refreshes itself anew. All my care for him applies only to the *object of my love,* only to him whom my love *requires,* only to him, the "warmly loved." How indifferent would he be to me without this—my love! I feed only my love with him, I *utilize* him for this only: I *enjoy* him.

Let us choose another convenient example. I see how men are fretted in dark superstition by a swarm of ghosts. If to the extent of my powers I let a bit of daylight fall in on the nocturnal spookery, is it perchance because love to you inspires this in me? Do I write out of love to men? No, I write because I want to procure for *my* thoughts an existence in the world; and, even if I foresaw that these thoughts would deprive you of your rest and your peace, even if I saw the bloodiest wars and the fall of many generations springing up from this seed of thought—I would nevertheless scatter it. Do with it what you will and can, that is your affair and does not trouble me. You will perhaps have only trouble, combat, and death from it, very few will draw joy from it. If your weal lay at my heart, I should act as the church did in withholding the Bible from the laity, or Christian governments, which make it a sacred duty for themselves to "protect the common people from bad books."

But not only not for your sake, not even for truth's sake either do I speak out what I think. No—

> I sing as the bird sings
>   That on the bough alights;
> The song that from me springs
>   Is pay that well requites.

I sing because—I am a singer. But I *use*[107] you for it because I—need ears.[108]

Where the world comes in my way—and it comes in my way everywhere—I consume it to quiet the hunger of my egoism. For me you are nothing but—my food, even as I too am fed upon

107. (*gebrauche*)
108. (*brauche*)

and turned to use by you. We have only one relation to each other, that of *usableness,* of utility, of use. We owe *each other* nothing, for what I seem to owe you I owe at most to myself. If I show you a cheery air in order to cheer you likewise, then your cheeriness is of consequence to *me,* and my air serves *my* wish; to a thousand others, whom I do not aim to cheer, I do not show it.

One has to be educated up to that love which founds itself on the "essence of man" or, in the ecclesiastical and moral period, lies upon us as a "commandment." In what fashion moral influence, the chief ingredient of our education, seeks to regulate the intercourse of men shall here be looked at with egoistic eyes in one example at least.

Those who educate us make it their concern early to break us of lying and to inculcate the principle that one must always tell the truth. If selfishness were made the basis for this rule, every one would easily understand how by lying he fools away that confidence in him which he hopes to awaken in others, and how correct the maxim proves, Nobody believes a liar even when he tells the truth. Yet, at the same time, he would also feel that he had to meet with truth only him whom *he* authorized to hear the truth. If a spy walks in disguise through the hostile camp, and is asked who he is, the askers are assuredly entitled to inquire after his name, but the disguised man does not give them the right to learn the truth from him; he tells them what he likes, only not the fact. And yet morality demands, "Thou shalt not lie!" By morality those persons are vested with the right to expect the truth; but by me they are not vested with that right, and I recognize only the right that *I* impart. In a gathering of revolutionists the police force their way in and ask the orator for his name; everybody knows that the police have the right to do so, but they do not have it from the *revolutionist,* since he is their enemy; he tells them a false name and—cheats them with a lie. The police do not act so foolishly either as to count on their enemies' love of truth; on the contrary, they do not believe without further ceremony, but have the questioned individual "identified" if they can. Nay, the State everywhere proceeds incredulously with individuals, because in their egoism it recognizes its natural enemy; it invariably demands a "voucher," and he who cannot show vouchers falls a prey to its investigating inquisition. The State does not believe nor trust the individual, and so of itself places itself with him in the *convention of lying;* it trusts me only when it has *convinced* itself of the truth of my statement, for which there often remains to it no other means than the oath. How clearly, too, this (the oath) proves that the State does not count on our credibility and love of truth, but on our *interest,* our selfishness: it relies on our not wanting to fall foul of God by a perjury.

Now, let one imagine a French revolutionist in the year 1788, who among friends let fall the now well-known phrase, "the world will have no rest till the last king is hanged with the guts of the last priest." The king then still had all power, and, when the utterance is betrayed by an accident, yet without its being possible to produce witnesses, confession is demanded from the accused. Is he to confess or not? If he denies, he lies and— remains unpunished; if he confesses, he is candid and—is beheaded. If truth is more than everything else to him, all right, let him die. Only a paltry poet could try to make a tragedy out of the end of his life; for what interest is there in seeing how a man succumbs from cowardice? But, if he had the courage not to be a slave of truth and sincerity, he would ask somewhat thus: Why need the judges know what I have spoken among friends? If I had *wished* them to know, I should have said it to them as I said it to my friends. I will not have them know it. They force themselves into my confidence without my having called them to it and made them my confidants; they *will* learn what I *will* keep secret. Come on then, you who wish to break my will by your will, and try your arts. You can torture me by the rack, you can threaten me with hell and eternal damnation, you can make me so nerveless that I swear a false oath, but the truth you shall not press out of me, for I *will* lie to you because I have given you no claim and no right to my sincerity. Let God, "who is truth," look down ever so threateningly on me, let lying come ever so hard to me, I have nevertheless the courage of a lie; and, even if I were weary of my life, even if nothing appeared to me more welcome than your executioner's sword, you nevertheless should not have the joy of finding in me a slave of truth, whom by your priestly arts you make a traitor to his *will*. When I spoke those treasonable words, I would not have had you know anything of them; I now retain the same will, and do not let myself be frightened by the curse of the lie.

Sigismund is not a miserable caitiff because he broke his princely word,[109] but he broke the word because he was a caitiff; he might have kept his word and would still have been a caitiff, a priest-ridden man. Luther, driven by a higher power, became unfaithful to his monastic vow: he became so for God's sake. Both broke their oath as possessed persons: Sigismund, because he wanted to appear as a *sincere* professor of the divine *truth,* that is, of the true, genuinely Catholic faith; Luther, in order to give testimony for the gospel *sincerely* and with entire truth. with body and soul; both became perjured in order to be sincere toward the "higher truth." Only, the priests absolved the one, the other abolved himself. What else did both observe than what is contained in those apostolic words, "Thou hast not lied to men, but to God?" They lied to men, broke their oath before the world's eyes, in order not to lie to God, but to serve him. Thus they show us a way to deal with truth before men. For God's glory, and for God's sake, a—breach of oath, a lie, a prince's word broken!

How would it be, now, if we changed the thing a little and wrote, A perjury and lie for—*my sake?* Would not that be pleading for every baseness? It seems so, assuredly, only in this it is altogether like the "for God's sake." For was not every baseness committed for God's sake, were not all the scaffolds filled for his sake and all the *autos-da-fé* held for his sake, was not all stupefaction introduced for his sake? And do they not to-day still for God's sake fetter the mind in tender children by religious education? Were not sacred vows broken for his sake,

109. [A reference to the safe-conduct pass given by Sigismund, the King of Bohemia (from 1410 to 1437) to John Hus, accused of preaching heresy, that the latter might attend the Council of Constance, in 1415, and defend himself of the charges. But the king then allowed him to be arrested, and he was subsequently tried and burned at the stake.]

and do not missionaries and priests still go around every day to bring Jews, heathen, Protestants or Catholics, to treason against the faith of their fathers—for his sake? And that should be worse with the *for my sake?* What then does *on my account* mean? There people immediately think of *"filthy lucre."* But he who acts from love of filthy lucre does it on his own account indeed, as there is nothing anyhow that one does not do for his own sake—among other things, everything that is done for God's glory; yet he, for whom he seeks the lucre, is a slave of lucre, not raised above lucre; he is one who belongs to lucre, the money-bag, not to himself; he is not his own. Must not a man whom the passion of avarice rules follow the commands of this *master?* And, if a weak goodnaturedness once beguiles him, does this not appear as simply an exceptional case of precisely the same sort as when pious believers are sometimes forsaken by their Lord's guidance and ensnared by the arts of the "devil?" So an avaricious man is not a self-owned man, but a servant; and he can do nothing for his own sake without at the same time doing it for his lord's sake—precisely like the godly man.

Famous is the breach of oath which Francis I committed against Emperor Charles V.[110] Not later, when he ripely weighed his promise, but at once, when he swore the oath, King Francis took it back in thought as well as by a secret protestation documentarily subscribed before his councillors; he uttered a perjury aforethought. Francis did not show himself disinclined to buy his release, but the price that Charles put on it seemed to him too high and unreasonable. Even though Charles behaved himself in a sordid fashion when he sought to extort as much as possible, it was yet shabby of Francis to want to purchase his freedom for a lower ransom; and his later dealings, among which there occurs yet a second breach of his word, prove sufficiently how the

110. [In the first war (1521-1526) of the Holy Roman Emperor Charles V against Francis I, King of France, Francis was routed and personally captured in 1525. At the treaty of peace signed at Madrid the following year, Francis agreed to a number of humiliating provisions in order to obtain his release, but in 1527 denounced the terms on the grounds that they had been wrung from him by extortion, and were therefore not binding.]

huckster spirit held him enthralled and made him a shabby
swindler. However, what shall we say to the reproach of perjury
against him? In the first place, surely, this again: that not the
perjury, but his sordidness, shamed him; that he did not deserve
contempt for his perjury, but made himself guilty of perjury
because he was a contemptible man. But Francis's perjury, regarded in itself, demands another judgment. One might say
Francis did not respond to the confidence that Charles put in
him in setting him free. But, if Charles had really favored him
with confidence, he would have named to him the price that
he considered the release worth, and would then have set him
at liberty and expected Francis to pay the redemption-sum. Charles
harbored no such trust, but only believed in Francis's impotence
and credulity, which would not allow him to act against his oath;
but Francis deceived only this—credulous calculation. When
Charles believed he was assuring himself of his enemy by an
oath, right there he was freeing him from every obligation. Charles
had given the king credit for a piece of stupidity, a narrow
conscience, and, without confidence in Francis, counted only on
Francis's stupidity, that is, conscientiousness: he let him go from
the Madrid prison only to hold him the more securely in the
prison of conscientiousness, the great jail built about the mind
of man by religion: he sent him back to France locked fast in
invisible chains, what wonder if Francis sought to escape and
sawed the chains apart? No man would have taken it amiss of
him if he had secretly fled from Madrid, for he was in an enemy's
power; but every good Christian cries out upon him, that he
wanted to loose himself from God's bonds too. (It was only
later that the pope absolved him from his oath.)

It is despicable to deceive a confidence that we voluntarily
call forth; but it is no shame to egoism to let every one who
wants to get us into his power by an oath bleed to death by
the unsuccessfulness of his untrustful craft. If you have wanted
to bind me, then learn that I know how to burst your bonds.

The point is whether I give the confider the right to confidence. If the pursuer of my friend asks me where he has fled
to, I shall surely put him on a false trail. Why does he ask
precisely me, the pursued man's friend? In order not to be a

false, traitorous friend, I prefer to be false to the enemy. I might certainly in courageous conscientiousness, answer, "I will not tell" (so Fichte decides the case); by that I should salve my love of truth and do for my friend as much as—nothing, for, if I do not mislead the enemy, he may accidentally take the right street, and my love of truth would have given up my friend as a prey, because it hindered me from the—courage for a lie. He who has in the truth an idol, a sacred thing, must *humble* himself before it, must not defy its demands, not resist courageously; in short, he must renounce the *heroism of the lie*. For to the lie belongs not less courage than to the truth: a courage that young men are most apt to be defective in, who would rather confess the truth and mount the scaffold for it than confound the enemy's power by the impudence of a lie. To them the truth is "sacred," and the sacred at all times demands blind reverence, submission, and self-sacrifice. If you are not impudent, not mockers of the sacred, you are tame and its servants. Let one but lay a grain of truth in the trap for you, you peck at it to a certainty, and the fool is caught. You will not lie? Well, then, fall as sacrifices to the truth and become—martyrs! Martyrs!—for what? For yourselves, for self-ownership? No, for your goddess—the truth. You know only two *services,* only two kinds of servants: servants of the truth and servants of the lie. Then in God's name serve the truth!

Others, again, serve the truth also; but they serve it "in moderation," and make a great distinction between a simple lie and a lie sworn to. And yet the whole chapter of the oath coincides with that of the lie, since an oath, everybody knows, is only a strongly assured statement. You consider yourselves entitled to lie, if only you do not swear to it besides? One who is particular about it must judge and condemn a lie as sharply as a false oath. But now there has been kept up in morality an ancient point of controversy, which is customarily treated of under the name of the "lie of necessity." No one who dares plead for this can consistently put from him an "oath of necessity." If I justify my lie as a lie of necessity, I should not be so pusillanimous as to rob the justified lie of the strongest corroboration. Whatever I do, why should I not do it entirely and without reservations (*reservatio mentalis*)? If I once lie, why then not lie completely, with entire consciousness and all my might? As a spy I should have to swear to each of my false statements at the enemy's demand; determined to lie to him, should I suddenly become cowardly and undecided in face of an oath? Then I should have been ruined in advance for a liar and spy; for, you see, I should be voluntarily putting into the enemy's hands a means to catch me.—The State too fears the oath of necessity, and for this reason does not give the accused a chance to swear. But you do not justify the State's fear; you lie, but do not swear falsely. If you show some one a kindness, and he is not to know it, but he guesses it and tells you so to your face, you deny; if he insists, you say, "honestly, no!" If it came to swearing, then you would refuse; for, from fear of the sacred, you always stop half way. *Against* the sacred you have no *will of your own.* You lie in—moderation, as you are free "in moderation," religious "in moderation" (the clergy are not to "encroach"; over this point the most rapid of controversies is now being carried on, on the part of the university against the church), monarchically disposed "in moderation" (you want a monarch limited by the constitution, by a fundamental law of the State), everything nicely *tempered*, lukewarm, half God's, half the devil's.

There was a university where the usage was that every word of honor that must be given to the university judge was looked upon by the students as null and void. For the students saw in the demanding of it nothing but a snare, which they could not escape otherwise than by taking away all its significance. He who at that same university broke his word of honor to one of the fellows was infamous; he who gave it to the university judge derided, in union with these very fellows, the dupe who fancied that a word had the same value among friends and among foes. It was less a correct theory than the constraint of practice that had there taught the students to act so, as, without that means of getting out, they would have been pitilessly driven to treachery against their comrades. But, as the means approved itself in practice, so it has its theoretical probation too. A word of honor, an oath, is one only for him whom I entitle to receive it; he who forces me to it obtains only a forced, a *hostile* word, the word of a foe, whom one has no right to trust; for the foe does not give us the right.

Aside from this, the courts of the State do not even recognize the inviolability of an oath. For, if I had sworn to one who comes under examination that I would not declare anything against him, the court would demand my declaration in spite of the fact that an oath binds me, and, in case of refusal, would lock me up till I decided to become—an oath-breaker. The court "absolves me from my oath";—how magnanimous! If any power can absolve me from the oath, I myself am surely the very first power that has a claim to.

As a curiosity, and to remind us of customary oaths of all sorts, let place be given here to that which Emperor Paul[111] commanded the captured Poles (Kosciuszko, Potocki, Niemcewicz, and others) to take when he released them: "We not merely swear fidelity and obedience to the emperor, but also further promise to pour out our blood for his glory; we obligate ourselves to discover everything threatening to his person or his empire that we ever learn; we declare finally that, in whatever part of the earth we may be, a single word of the emperor shall suffice to make us leave everything and repair to him at once."

In one domain the principle of love seems to have been long outsoared by egoism, and to be still in need only of sure consciousness, as it were of victory with a good conscience. This domain is speculation, in its double manifestation as thinking and as trade. One thinks with a will, whatever may come of it; one speculates, however many may suffer under our speculative undertakings. But, when it finally becomes serious, when even the last remnant of religiousness, romance, or "humanity" is to be done away, then the pulse of religious conscience beats, and one at least *professes* humanity. The avaricious speculator throws some coppers into the poor-box and "does good," the bold thinker

111. [Czar Paul I of Russia (1796-1801), who forced this upon the Polish patriots following their unsuccessful insurrection and the subsequent third partition of Poland in 1795; the revolt had begun in 1794 led by Thaddeus Kosciuszko (1746-1817), famous for his earlier part in the American Revolution.]

consoles himself with the fact that he is working for the advance-
ment of the human race and that his devastation "turns to the
good" of mankind, or, in another case, that he is "serving the
idea"; mankind, the idea, is to him that something of which he
must say, It is more to me than myself.

To this day thinking and trading have been done for—God's
sake. Those who for six days were trampling down everything
by their selfish aims sacrificed on the seventh to the Lord; and
those who destroyed a hundred "good causes" by their reckless
thinking still did this in the service of another "good cause,"
and had yet to think of another—besides themselves—to whose
good their self-indulgence should turn; of the people, mankind,
and the like. But this other thing is a being above them, a
higher or supreme being; and therefore I say, they are toiling
for God's sake.

Hence I can also say that the ultimate basis of their actions
is—love. Not a voluntary love however, not their own, but a
tributary love, or the higher being's own (God's, who himself is
love); in short, not the egoistic, but the religious; a love that
springs from their fancy that they *must* discharge a tribute of
love, that they must not be "egoists."

If *we* want to deliver the world from many kinds of unfreedom, we want this not on its account but on ours; for, as we
are not world-liberators by profession and out of "love," we
only want to win it away from others. We want to make it
our own; it is not to be any longer *owned as serf* by God (the
church) nor by the law (State), but to be *our own*; therefore
we seek to "win" it, to "captivate" it, and, by meeting it half-
way and "devoting" ourselves to it as to ourselves as soon as
it belongs to us, to complete and make superfluous the force
that it turns against us. If the world is ours, it no longer attempts
any force *against* us, but only *with us*. My selfishness has an
interest in the liberation of the world, that it may become—my
property.

Not isolation or being alone, but society, is man's original
state. Our existence begins with the most intimate conjunction,
as we are already living with our mother before we breathe;
when we see the light of the world, we at once lie on a human

being's breast again, her love cradles us in the lap, leads us in the go-cart, and chains us to her person with a thousand ties. Society is our *state of nature*. And this is why, the more we learn to feel ourselves, the connection that was formerly most intimate becomes ever looser and the dissolution of the original society more unmistakable. To have once again for herself the child that once lay under her heart, the mother must fetch it from the street and from the midst of its playmates. The child prefers the *intercourse* that it enters into with *its fellows* to the *society* that it has not entered into, but only been born in.

But the dissolution of *society* is *intercourse* or *union*. A society does assuredly arise by union too, but only as a fixed idea arises by a thought—to wit, by the vanishing of the energy of the thought (the thinking itself, this restless taking back all thoughts that make themselves fast) from the thought. If a union[112] has crystallized into a society, it has ceased to be a coalition;[113] for coalition is an incessant self-uniting; it has become a unitedness, come to a standstill, degenerated into a fixity; it is—*dead* as a union, it is the corpse of the union or the coalition, it is—society, community. A striking example of this kind is furnished by the *party*.

That a society (such as the society of the State) diminishes my *liberty* offends me little. Why, I have to let my liberty be limited by all sorts of powers and by every one who is stronger; nay, by every fellow-man; and, were I the autocrat of all the R . . . . . ,* I yet should not enjoy absolute liberty. But *ownness* I will not have taken from me. And ownness is precisely what every society has designs on, precisely what is to succumb to its power.

A society which I join does indeed take from me many liberties, but in return it affords me other liberties; neither does it matter if I myself deprive myself of this and that liberty (such

112. (*Verein*)
113. (*Vereinigung*)
* [Stirner is undoubtedly referring here to the Czar "of all the Russians," but for reasons again of probable censorship on the grounds of invidious reference to a contemporary and not unfriendly monarch, has chosen to disguise it in this manner.]

as by any contract). On the other hand, I want to hold jealously to my ownness. Every community has the propensity, stronger or weaker according to the fullness of its power, to become an *authority* to its members and to set *limits* for them: it asks, and must ask, for a "subject's limited understanding"; it asks that those who belong to it be subjected to it, be its "subjects"; it exists only by *subjection*. In this a certain tolerance need by no means be excluded; on the contrary, the society will welcome improvements, corrections, and blame, so far as such are calculated for its gain: but the blame must be "well-meaning," it may not be "insolent and disrespectful"—in other words, one must leave uninjured, and hold sacred, the substance of the society. The society demands that those who belong to it shall not *go beyond it* and exalt themselves, but remain "within the bounds of legality," that is, allow themselves only so much as the society and its law allow them.

There is a difference whether my liberty or my ownness is limited by a society. If the former only is the case, it is a coalition, an agreement, a union; but, if ruin is threatened to ownness, it is a *power of itself,* a power *above me,* a thing unattainable by me, which I can indeed admire, adore, reverence, respect, but cannot subdue and consume, and that for the reason that I *am resigned.* It exists by my *resignation,* my *self- renunciation,* my spiritlessness,[114] called — HUMILITY.[115] My humility makes its courage,[116] my submissiveness gives it its dominion.

But in reference to *liberty,* State and union are subject to no essential difference. The latter can just as little come into existence, or continue in existence, without liberty's being limited in all sorts of ways, as the State is compatible with unmeasured liberty. Limitation of liberty is inevitable everywhere, for one cannot get *rid* of everything; one cannot fly like a bird merely because one would like to fly so, for one does not get free from his own weight; one cannot live under water as long as he likes,

114. (*Muthlosigkeit*)
115. (*Demuth*)
116. (*Muth*)

like a fish, because one cannot do without air and cannot get free from this indispensable necessity; and the like. As religion, and most decidedly Christianity, tormented man with the demand to realize the unnatural and self-contradictory, so it is to be looked upon only as the true logical outcome of that religious overstraining and overwroughtness that finally *liberty itself, absolute liberty,* was exalted into an ideal, and thus the nonsense of the impossible to come glaringly to the light.—The union will assuredly offer a greater measure of liberty, as well as (and especially because by it one escapes all the coercion peculiar to State and society life) admit of being considered as "a new liberty"; but nevertheless it will still contain enough of unfreedom and involuntariness. For its object is not this—liberty (which on the contrary it sacrifices to ownness), but only *ownness.* Referred to this, the difference between State and union is great enough. The former is an enemy and murderer of *ownness,* the latter a son and co-worker of it; the former a spirit that would be adored in spirit and in truth, the latter my work, my *product;* the State is the lord of my spirit, who demands faith and prescribes to me articles of faith, the creed of legality; it exerts moral influence, dominates my spirit, drives away my ego to put itself in its place as "my true ego"—in short, the State is *sacred,* and as against me, the individual man, it is the true man, the spirit, the ghost; but the union is my own creation, my creature, not sacred, not a spiritual power above my spirit, as little as any association of whatever sort. As I am not willing to be a slave of my maxims, but lay them bare to my continual criticism without *any warrant,* and admit no bail at all for their persistence, so still less do I obligate myself to the union for my future and pledge my soul to it, as is said to be done with the devil, and is really the case with the State and all spiritual authority; but I am and remain *more* to myself than State, Church, God, and the like; consequently infinitely more than the union too.

That society which Communism wants to found seems to stand nearest to *coalition.* For it is to aim at the "welfare of all," oh, yes, of all, cries Weitling innumerable times, of all! That does really look as if in it no one needed to take a back seat. But what then will this welfare be? Have all one and the same welfare, are all equally well off with one and the same thing? If that be so, the question is of the "true welfare." Do we not with this come right to the point where religion begins its dominion of violence? Christianity says, Look not on earthly toys, but seek your true welfare, become—pious Christians; being Christians is the true welfare. It is the true welfare of "all," because it is the welfare of Man as such (this spook). Now, the welfare of all is surely to be *your* and *my* welfare too? But, if you and I do not look upon that welfare as *our* welfare, will care then be taken for that in which *we* feel well? On the contrary, society has decreed a welfare as the "true welfare," if this welfare were called "enjoyment honestly worked for"; but if you preferred enjoyable laziness, enjoyment without work, then society, which cares for the "welfare of all," would wisely avoid caring for that in which you are well off. Communism, in proclaiming the welfare of all, annuls outright the well-being of those who hitherto lived on their income from investments and apparently felt better in that than in the prospect of Weitling's strict hours of labor. Hence the latter asserts that with the welfare of thousands the welfare of millions cannot exist, and the former must give up *their* special welfare "for the sake of the general welfare." No, let people not be summond to sacrifice their special welfare for the general, for this Christian admonition will not carry you through; they will better understand the opposite admonition, not to let their *own* welfare be snatched from them by anybody, but to put it on a permanent foundation. Then they are of themselves led to the point that they care best for their welfare if they *unite* with others for this purpose, that is, "sacrifice a part of their liberty," yet not to the welfare of others, but to their own. An appeal to men's self-sacrificing disposition and self-renouncing love ought at least to have lost its seductive plausibility when, after an activity of thousands of years, it has left nothing behind but the—*misère* of to-day. Why then still fruitlessly expect self-sacrifice to bring us better times? Why not rather hope for them from *usurpation*? Salvation comes no longer from the giver, the bestower, the loving one, but from the *taker*, the

appropriator (usurper), the owner. Communism, and, consciously, egoism-reviling humanism, still count on *love*.

If community is once a need of man, and he finds himself
furthered by it in his aims, then very soon, because it has become
his principle, it prescribes to him its laws too, the laws of—
society. The principle of men exalts itself into a sovereign power
over them, becomes their supreme essence, their God, and, as
such—lawgiver. Communism gives this principle the strictest
effect, and Christianity is the religion of society, for, as Feuerbach
rightly says, although he does not mean it rightly, love is the
essence of man; that is, the essence of society or of societary
(Communistic) man. All religion is a cult of society, this principle by which societary (cultivated) man is dominated; neither
is any god an ego's exclusive god, but always a society's or
community's, be it of the society, "family" (Lar, Penates[117]) or
of a "people" ("national god") or of "all men" ("he is a Father
of all men").

Consequently one has a prospect of extirpating religion down
to the ground only when one antiquates *society* and everything
that flows from this principle. But it is precisely in Communism
that this principle seeks to culminate, as in it everything is to
become *common* for the establishment of—"equality." If this
"equality" is won, "liberty" too is not lacking. But whose liberty?
Society's! Society is then all in all, and men are only "for each
other." It would be the glory of the—love-State.

But I would rather be referred to men's selfishness than to
their "kindnesses,"[118] their mercy, pity, etc. The former demands
reciprocity (as thou to me, so I to thee), does nothing "gratis,"
and may be won and—*bought*. But with what shall I obtain
the kindness? It is a matter of chance whether I am at the time
having to do with a "loving" person. The affectionate one's
service can be had only by—*begging*, be it by my lamentable
appearance, by my need of help, my misery, my—*suffering*. What
can I offer him for his assistance? Nothing! I must accept it

117. [In Roman mythology, the traditional household or family
deities.]
118. (Literally, "love-services.")

as a—present. Love is *unpayable,* or rather, love can assuredly be paid for, but only by counter-love ("One good turn deserves another"). What paltriness and beggarliness does it not take to accept gifts year in and year out without service in return, as they are regularly collected, for instance, from the poor day-laborer? What can the receiver do for him and his donated pennies, in which his wealth consists? The day-laborer would really have more enjoyment if the receiver with his laws, his institutions, etc., all of which the day-laborer has to pay for though, did not exist at all. And yet, with it all, the poor wight *loves* his master.

No, community, as the "goal" of history hitherto, is impossible. Let us rather renounce every hypocrisy of community, and recognize that, if we are equal as men, we are not equal for the very reason that we are not men. We are equal *only in thoughts,* only when "we" are *thought,* not as we really and bodily are. I am ego, and you are ego: but I am not this thought-of ego; this ego in which we are all equal is only *my thought.* I am man, and you are man: but "man" is only a thought, a generality; neither you and I are speakable, we are *unutterable,* because only *thoughts* are speakable and consist in speaking.

Let us therefore not aspire to community, but to *one-sidedness.* Let us not seek the most comprehensive commune, "human society," but let us seek in others only means and organs which we may use as our property! As we do not see our equals in the tree, the beast, so the presupposition that others are *our equals* springs from a hypocrisy. No one is *my equal,* but I regard him, equally with all other beings, as my property. In opposition to this I am told that I should be a man among "fellow-men" (*Judenfrage,* p. 60); I should "respect" the fellow-man in them. For me no one is a person to be respected, not even the fellow-man, but solely, like other beings, an *object* in which I take an interest or else do not, an interesting or uninteresting object, a usable or unusable person.

And, if I can use him, I doubtless come to an understanding and make myself at one with him, in order, by the agreement, to strengthen *my power,* and by combined force to accomplish more than individual force could effect. In this combination I see nothing whatever but a multiplication of my force, and I retain it only so long as it is *my* multiplied force. But thus it is a—union.

Neither a natural ligature nor a spiritual one holds the union together, and it is not a natural, not a spiritual league. It is not brought about by one *blood,* not by one *faith* (spirit). In a natural league—like a family, a tribe, a nation, yes, mankind —the individuals have only the value of *specimens* of the same species or genus; in a spiritual league—like a commune, a church —the individual signifies only a *member* of the same spirit; what you are in both cases as a unique person must be—suppressed. Only in the union can you assert yourself as unique, because the union does not possess you, but you possess it or make it of use to you.

Property is recognized in the union, and only in the union, because one no longer holds what is his as a fief from any being. The Communists are only consistently carrying further what had already been long present during religious evolution, and especially in the State; to wit, propertylessness, the feudal system.

The State exerts itself to tame the desirous man; in other words, it seeks to direct his desire to it alone, and to *content* that desire with what it offers. To sate the desire for the desirous man's sake does not come into the mind: on the contrary, it stigmatizes as an "egoistic man" the man who breathes out unbridled desire, and the "egoistic man" is its enemy. He is this for it because the capacity to agree with him is wanting to the State; the egoist is precisely what it cannot "comprehend." Since the State (as nothing else is possible) has to do only for itself, it does not take care for my needs, but takes care only of how it make away with me, make out of me another ego, a good citizen. It takes measures for the "improvement of morals."— And with what does it win individuals for itself? With itself, with what is the State's, with *State property.* It will be unremittingly active in making all participants in its "goods," providing all with the "good things of culture"; it presents them its education, opens to them the access to its institutions of culture, capacitates them to come to property (as, to a fief) in the way of industry, etc. For all these *fiefs* it demands only the just rent of continual *thanks*. But the "unthankful" forget to pay these thanks.—Now, neither can "society" do essentially otherwise than the State.

You bring into a union your whole power, your competence, and *make yourself count;* in a society you are *employed,* with your working power; in the former you live egoistically, in the latter humanly, that is, religiously, as a "member in the body of this Lord"; to a society you owe what you have, and are in duty bound to it, are—possessed by "social duties"; a union you utilize, and give it up undutifully and unfaithfully when you see no way to use it further. If a society is more than you, then it is more to you than yourself; a union is only your instrument, or the sword with which you sharpen and increase your natural force; the union exists for you and through you, the society conversely lays claim to you for itself and exists even without you; in short, the society is *sacred,* the union your *own;* the society consumes *you, you* consume the union.

Nevertheless people will not be backward with the objection that the agreement which has been concluded may again become burdensome to us and limit our freedom; they will say, we too would at last come to this, that "every one must sacrifice a part of his freedom for the sake of the generality." But the sacrifice would not be made for the "generality's" sake a bit, as little as I concluded the agreement for the "generality's" or even for any other man's sake; rather I came into it only for the sake of my own benefit, from selfishness.[119] But, as regards the sacrificing, surely I "sacrifice" only that which does not stand in my power, that is, I "sacrifice" nothing at all.

To come back to property, the lord is proprietor. Choose then whether you want to be lord, or whether society shall be! On this depends whether you are to be an *owner* or a *ragamuffin!* The egoist is owner, the Socialist a ragamuffin. But ragamuffinism or propertylessness is the sense of feudalism, of the feudal system, which since the last century has only changed its overlord, putting "Man" in the place of God, and accepting as a fief from Man what

119. (Literally, "own-benefit.")

had before been a fief from the grace of God. That the raga-muffinism of Communism is carried out by the humane principle into the absolute or most ragamuffinly ragamuffinism has been shown above; but at the same time also, how ragamuffinism can only thus swing around into ownness. The *old* feudal system was so thoroughly trampled into the ground in the Revolution that since then all reactionary craft has remained fruitless, and will always remain fruitless, because the dead is—dead; but the resurrection too had to prove itself a truth in Christian history, and has so proved itself: for in another world feudalism is risen again with a glorified body, the *new* feudalism under the suzerainty of "Man."

Christianity is not annihilated, but the faithful are right in having hitherto trustfully assumed of every combat against it that this could serve only for the purgation and confirmation of Christianity; for it has really only been glorified, and "Christianity exposed" is the—*human Christianity*. We are still living entirely in the Christian age, and the very ones who feel worst about it are the most zealously contributing to "complete" it. The more human, the dearer has feudalism become to us; for we the less believe that it still is feudalism, we take it the more confidently for ownness and think we have found what is "most absolutely our own" when we discover "the human."

Liberalism wants to give me what is mine, but it thinks to procure it for me not under the title of mine, but under that of the "human." As if it were attainable under this mask! The rights of man, the precious work of the Revolution, have the meaning that the Man in me *entitles*[120] me to this and that; I as individual, as this man, am not entitled, but Man has the right and entitles me. Hence as man I may well be entitled; but, as I am more than man, to wit, a *special* man, it may be refused to this very me, the special one. If on the other hand you insist on the *value* of your gifts, keep up their price, do not let yourselves be forced to sell out below price, do not let yourselves be talked into the idea that your ware is not worth its price, do not

120. (Literally, furnishes me with a *right*.)

make yourself ridiculous by a "ridiculous price," but imitate the brave man who says, I will *sell* my life (property) dear, the enemy shall not have it at a cheap *bargain;* then you have recognized the reverse of Communism as the correct thing, and the word then is not "Give up your property!" but *"Get the value out of* your property!"

Over the portal of our time stands not that "Know thyself" of Apollo, but a *"Get the value out of thyself!"*

Proudhon calls property "robbery" (*le vol*). But alien property—and he is talking of this alone—is not less existent by renunciation, cession, and humility; it is a *present*. Why so sentimentally call for compassion as a poor victim of robbery, when one is just a foolish, cowardly giver of presents? Why here again put the fault on others as if they were robbing us, while we ourselves do bear the fault in leaving the others unrobbed? The poor are to blame for there being rich men.

Universally, no one grows indignant at *his,* but at *alien* property. They do not in truth attack property, but the alienation of property. They want to be able to call *more,* not less, *theirs;* they want to call everything *theirs.* They are fighting, therefore, against *alienness,* or, to form a word similar to property, against aliety. And how do they help themselves therein? Instead of transforming the alien into own, they play impartial and ask only that all property be left to a third party, such as human society. They revindicate the alien not in their own name but in a third party's. Now the "egoistic" coloring is wiped off, and everything is so clean and—human!

Propertylessness or ragamuffinism, this then is the "essence of Christianity," as it is essence of all religiousness (godliness, morality, humanity), and only announced itself most clearly, and, as glad tidings, became a gospel capable of development, in the "absolute religion." We have before us the most striking development in the present fight against property, a fight which is to bring "Man" to victory and make propertylessness complete: victorious humanity is the victory of—Christianity. But the "Christianity exposed" thus is feudalism completed, the most all-embracing feudal system, that is, perfect ragamuffinism.

Once more then, doubtless, a "revolution" against the feudal system?—

Revolution and insurrection must not be looked upon as synonymous. The former consists in an overturning of conditions, of the established condition or *status,* the State or society, and is accordingly a *political* or *social* act; the latter has indeed for its unavoidable consequence a transformation of circumstances, yet does not start from it but from men's discontent with themselves, is not an armed rising, but a rising of individuals, a getting up, without regard to the arrangements that spring from it. The Revolution aimed at new *arrangements;* insurrection leads us no longer to *let* ourselves be arranged, but to arrange ourselves, and sets no glittering hopes on "institutions." It is not a fight against the established, since, if it prospers, the established collapses of itself; it is only a working forth of me out of the established. If I leave the established, it is dead and passes into decay. Now, as my object is not the overthrow of an established order but my elevation above it, my purpose and deed are not a political or social but (as directed toward myself and my ownness alone) an *egoistic* purpose and deed.

The revolution commands one to make *arrangements,* the insurrection[121] demands that he *rise or exalt himself.*[122] What *constitution* was to be chosen, this question busied the revolutionary heads, and the whole political period foams with constitutional fights and constitutional questions, as the social talents too were uncommonly inventive in societary arrangements (phalansteries and the like). The insurgent[123] strives to become constitutionless.

While, to get greater clearness, I am thinking up a comparison, the founding of Christianity comes unexpectedly into my mind. On the liberal side it is noted as a bad point in the first

121. (*Empörung*)
122. (*sich auf-oder empörzurichten*)
123. To secure myself against a criminal charge I superfluously make the express remark that I choose the word "insurrection" on account of its *etymological sense,* and therefore am not using it in the limited sense which is disallowed by the penal code. [Another precautionary effort of Stirner's to avoid running afoul of the Saxon state press censorship laws.]

Christians that they preached obedience to the established heathen
civil order, enjoined recognition of the heathen authorities, and
confidently delivered a command, "Give to the emperor that which
is the emperor's." Yet how much disturbance arose at the same
time against the Roman supremacy, how mutinous did the Jews
and even the Romans show themselves against their own temporal
government! In short, how popular was "political discontent!"
Those Christians would hear nothing of it; would not side with the
"liberal tendencies." The time was politically so agitated that,
as is said in the gospels, people thought they could not accuse the
founder of Christianity more successfully than if they arraigned
him for "political intrigue," and yet the same gospels report that
he was precisely the one who took least part in these political
doings. But why was he not a revolutionist, not a demagogue,
as the Jews would gladly have seen him? Why was he not a
liberal? Because he expected no salvation from a change of
conditions, and this whole business was indifferent to him. He
was not a revolutionist, like Caesar, but an insurgent; not a
State-overturner, but one who straightened himself up. That was
why it was for him only a matter of "Be ye wise as serpents,"
which expresses the same sense as, in the special case, that "Give
to the emperor that which is the emperor's"; for he was not carrying
on any liberal or political fight against the established authorities,
but wanted to walk his own way, untroubled about, and undisturbed by, these authorities. Not less indifferent to him than
the government were its enemies, for neither understood what
he wanted, and he had only to keep them off from him with
the wisdom of the serpent. But, even though not a ringleader of
popular mutiny, not a demagogue or revolutionist, he (and every
one of the ancient Christians) was so much the more an *insurgent,*
who lifted himself above everything that seemed sublime to the
government and its opponents, and absolved himself from everything that they remained bound to, and who at the same time
cut off the sources of life of the whole heathen world, with which
the established State must wither away as a matter of course;
precisely because he put from him the upsetting of the established,
he was its deadly enemy and real annihilator; for he walled it

in, confidently and recklessly carrying up the building of *his* temple over it, without heeding the pains of the immured.

Now, as it happened to the heathen order of the world, will the Christian order fare likewise? A revolution certainly does not bring on the end if an insurrection is not consummated first!

My intercourse with the world, what does it aim at? I want to have the enjoyment of it, therefore it must be my property, and therefore I want to win it. I do not want the liberty of men, nor their equality; I want only *my* power over them, I want to make them my property, *material for enjoyment*. And, if I do not succeed in that, well, then I call even the power over life and death, which Church and State reserved to themselves—mine. Brand that officer's widow who, in the flight in Russia, after her leg has been shot away, takes the garter from it, strangles her child therewith, and then bleeds to death alongside the corpse— brand the memory of the—infanticide. Who knows, if this child had remained alive, how much it might have "been of use to the world!" The mother murdered it because she wanted to die *satisfied* and at rest. Perhaps this case still appeals to your senti-mentality, and you do not know how to read out of it anything further. Be it so; I on my part use it as an example for this, that *my* satisfaction decides about my relation to men, and that I do not renounce, from any access of humility, even the power over life and death.

As regards "social duties" in general, another does not give me my position toward others, therefore neither God nor humanity prescribes to me my relation to men, but I give myself this position. This is more strikingly said thus: I have no *duty* to others, as I have a duty even to myself (that of self-preservation, and therefore not suicide) only so long as I distinguish myself from myself (my immortal soul from my earthly existence, etc.).

I no longer *humble* myself before any power, and I recognize that all powers are only my power, which I have to subject at once when they threaten to become a power *against* or *above* me; each of them must be only one of *my means* to carry my point, as a hound is our power against game, but is killed by us if it should fall upon us ourselves. All powers that dominate me I then reduce to serving me. The idols exist through me; I need only refrain from creating them anew, then they exist no longer: "higher powers" exist only through my exalting them and abasing myself.

Consequently my relation to the world is this: I no longer do anything for it "for God's sake," I do nothing "for man's sake," but what I do I do "for my sake." Thus alone does the world satisfy me, while it is characteristic of the religious standpoint, in which I include the moral and humane also, that from it everything remains a pious wish (*pium desiderium*), an otherworld matter, something unattained. Thus the general salvation of men, the moral world of a general love, eternal peace, the cessation of egoism, etc. "Nothing in this world is perfect." With this miserable phrase the good part from it, and take flight into their closet to God, or into their proud "self-consciousness." But we remain in this "imperfect" world, because even so we can use it for our—self-enjoyment.

My intercourse with the world consists in my enjoying it, and so consuming it for myself-enjoyment. *Intercourse* is the *enjoyment of the world,* and belongs to my—self-enjoyment.

C. — MY SELF-ENJOYMENT

WE stand at the boundary of a period. The world hitherto took thought for nothing but the gain of life, took care for—*life.* For whether all activity is put on the stretch for the life of this world or of the other, for the temporal or for the eternal, whether one hankers for "daily bread" ("Give us our daily bread") or for "holy bread" ("the true bread from heaven"; "the bread of God, that comes from heaven and *gives life* to the world"; "the bread of life," John 6), whether one takes care for "dear life" or for "life to eternity"—this does not change the object of the strain and care, which in the one case as in the other shows itself to be *life.* Do the modern tendencies announce themselves otherwise? People now want nobody to be embarrassed for the most indispensable necessaries of life, but want every one to feel secure as to these; and on the other hand they teach that man has this life to attend to and the real world to adapt himself to, without vain care for another.

Let us take up the same thing from another side. When one is anxious only to live, he easily, in this solicitude, forgets the enjoyment of life. If his only concern is for life, and he thinks "if I only have my dear life," he does not apply his full strength to using, that is, enjoying, life. But how does one use life? In using it up, like the candle, which one uses in burning it up. One uses life, and consequently himself the living one, in *consuming* it and himself. *Enjoyment of life* is using life up.

Now—we are in search of the *enjoyment* of life! And what did the religious world do? It went in search of life. Wherein consists the true life, the blessed life, etc.? How is it to be attained? What must man do and become in order to becom a truly living man? How does he fulfill this calling? These and similar questions indicate that the askers were still seeking for *themselves*—to wit, themselves in the true sense, in the sense of true living. "What I am is foam and shadow; what I shall be is my true self." To chase after this self, to produce it, to realize it, constitutes the hard task of mortals, who die only to *rise again*, live only to die, live only to find the true life.

Not till I am certain of myself, and no longer seeking for myself, am I really my property; I have myself, therefore I use and enjoy myself. On the other hand, I can never take comfort in myself as long as I think that I have still to find my true self and that it must come to this, that not I but Christ or some other spiritual, ghostly, self (the true man, the essence of man, and the like) lives in me.

A vast interval separates the two views. In the old I go toward myself, in the new I start from myself; in the former I long for myself, in the latter I have myself and do with myself as one does with any other property—I enjoy myself at my pleasure. I am no longer afraid for my life, but "squander" it.

Henceforth, the question runs, not how one can acquire life, but how one can squander, enjoy it; or, not how one is to produce the true self in himself, but how one is to dissolve himself, to live himself out.

What else should the ideal be but the sought-for ever-distant

self? One seeks for himself, consequently one doth not yet have
himself; one aspires toward what one *ought* to be, consequently
one *is* not it. One lives in *longing* and has lived thousands of years
in it, in *hope*. Living is quite another thing in—*enjoyment!*

Does this perchance apply only to the so-called pious? No,
it applies to all who belong to the departing period of history,
even to its men of pleasure. For them too the work-days were
followed by a Sunday, and the rush of the world by the dream
of a better world, of a general happiness of humanity; in short,
by an ideal. But philosophers especially are contrasted with
the pious. Now, have they been thinking of anything else than
the ideal, been planning for anything else than the absolute self?
Longing and hope everywhere, and nothing but these. For me,
call it romanticism.

If the *enjoyment of life* is to triumph over the *longing for
life* or hope of life, it must vanquish this in its double significance,
which Schiller introduces in his "Ideal and Life"; it must crush
spiritual and secular poverty, exterminate the ideal and—the want
of daily bread. He who must expend his life to prolong life
cannot enjoy it, and he who is still seeking for his life does not
have it and can as as little enjoy it: both are poor, but "blessed
are the poor."

Those who are hungering for the true life have no power
over their present life, but must apply it for the purpose of
thereby gaining that true life, and must sacrifice it entirely to
this aspiration and this task. If in the case of those devotees
who hope for a life in the other world, and look upon that in
this world as merely a preparation for it, the tributariness of their
earthly existence, which they put solely into the service of the
hoped-for heavenly existence, is pretty distinctly apparent; one
would yet go far wrong if one wanted to consider the most
rationalistic and enlightened as less self-sacrificing. Oh, there
is to be found in the "true life" a much more comprehensive
significance than the "heavenly" is competent to express. Now,
is not—to introduce the liberal concept of it at once—the "human" and "truly human" life the true one? And is every one
already leading this truly human life from the start, or must he
first raise himself to it with hard toil? Does he already have

it as his present life, or must he struggle for it as his future life, which will become his part only when he "is no longer tainted with any egoism"? In this view life exists only to gain life, and one lives only to make the essence of man alive in oneself, one lives for the sake of this essence. One has his life only in order to procure by means of it the "true" life cleansed of all egoism. Hence one is afraid to make any use he likes of his life: it is to serve only for the "right use."

In short, one has a *calling in life,* a task in life; one has something to realize and produce by his life, a something for which our life is only means and implement, a something that is worth more than this life, a something to which one *owes* his life. One has a God who asks a *living sacrifice.* Only the rudeness of human sacrifice has been lost with time; human sacrifice itself has remained unabated, and criminals hourly fall sacrifices to justice, and we "poor sinners" slay our own selves as sacrifices for "the human essence," the "idea of mankind," "humanity," and whatever the idols or gods are called besides.

But, because we owe our life to that something, therefore —this is the next point—we have no right to take it from us.

The conservative tendency of Christianity does not permit thinking of death otherwise than with the purpose to take its sting from it and—live on and preserve oneself nicely. The Christian lets everything happen and come upon him if he—the arch-Jew —can only haggle and smuggle himself into heaven; he must not kill himself, he must only—preserve himself and work at the "preparation of a future abode." Conservatism or "conquest of death" lies at his heart; "the last enemy that is abolished is death."[124] "Christ has taken the power from death and brought life and *imperishable* being to light by the gospel."[125] "Imperishableness," stability.

The moral man wants the good, the right; and, if he takes to the means that lead to this goal, really lead to it, then these means are not *his* means, but those of the good, right, etc., itself. These means are never immoral, because the good end

124. 1 Cor. 15. 26.
125. 2 Tim. 1. 10.

itself mediates itself through them: the end sanctifies the means. They call this maxim jesuitical, but it is "moral" through and through. The moral man acts *in the service* of an end or an idea: he makes himself the *tool* of the idea of the good, as the pious man counts it his glory to be a tool or instrument of God. To await death is what the moral commandment postulates as the good; to give it to oneself is immoral and bad: *suicide* finds no excuse before the judgment-seat of morality. If the religious man forbids it because "you have not given yourself life, but God, who alone can also take it from you again" (as if, even taking in this conception, God did not take it from me just as much when I kill myself as when a tile from the roof, or a hostile bullet, fells me; for he would have aroused the resolution of death in me too!), the moral man forbids it because I owe my life to the fatherland, etc., "because I do not know whether I may not yet accomplish good by my life." Of course, for in me good loses a tool, as God does an instrument. If I am immoral, the good is served in my *amendment;* if I am "ungodly," God has joy in my *penitence.* Suicide, therefore, is ungodly as well as nefarious. If one whose standpoint is religiousness takes his own life, he acts in forgetfulness of God; but, if the suicide's standpoint is morality, he acts in forgetfulness of duty, immorally. People worried themselves much with the question whether Emilia Galotti's death can be justified before morality (they take it as if it were suicide, which it is too in substance). That she is so infatuated with chastity, this moral good, as to yield up even her life for it is certainly moral; but, again, that she fears the weakness of her flesh is immoral.[126] Such contradictions form the tragic

126. [See the next to the last scene of the tragedy:
ODOARDO: Under the pretext of a judicial investigation he tears you out of our arms and takes you to Grimaldi. . . .
EMILIA: Give me that dagger, father, me! . . .
ODOARDO: No, no! Reflect—You too have only one life to lose.
EMILIA: And only one innocence!
ODOARDO: Which is above the reach of any violence.—
EMILIA: But not above the reach of any seduction.—Violence! violence! Who cannot defy violence? What is called violence is nothing; seduction is the true violence.—I have blood, father; blood as youthful and warm as anybody's. My senses are senses.—I can warrant nothing.

conflict universally in the moral drama; and one must think and feel morally to be able to take an interest in it.

What holds good of piety and morality will necessarily apply to humanity also, because one owes his life likewise to man, mankind or the species. Only when I am under obligation to no being is the maintaining of life—my affair. "A leap from this bridge makes me free!"

But, if we owe the maintaining of our life to that being that we are to make alive in ourselves, it is not less our duty not to lead this life according to *our* pleasure, but to shape it in conformity to that being. All my feeling, thinking, and willing, all my doing and designing, belongs to—him.

What is in conformity to that being is to be inferred from his concept; and how differently has this concept been conceived! or how differently has that being been imagined! What demands the Supreme Being makes on the Mohammedan; what different ones the Christian, again, thinks he hears from him; how divergent, therefore, must the shaping of the lives of the two turn out! Only this do all hold fast, that the Supreme Being is to judge[127] our life.

But the pious who have their judge in God, and in his word a book of directions for their life, I everywhere pass by only reminiscently, because they belong to a period of development that has been lived through, and as petrifactions they may remain in their fixed place right along; in our time it is no longer the pious, but the liberals, who have the floor, and piety itself cannot keep from reddening its pale face with liberal coloring. But the

I am sure of nothing. I know Grimaldi's house. It is the house of pleasure. An hour there, under my mother's eyes—and there arose in my soul so much tumult as the strictest exercises of religion could hardly quiet in weeks.—Religion! And what religion?—To escape nothing worse, thousands sprang into the water and are saints.—Give me that dagger, father, give it to me. . . .

EMILIA: Once indeed there was a father who, to save his daughter from shame, drove into her heart whatever steel he could quickest find— gave life to her for the second time. But all such deeds are of the past! Of such fathers there are no more.

ODOARDO: Yes, daughter, yes! (*Stabs her.*)]

127. [Or, "regulate," (*richten*).]

liberals do not adore their judge in God, and do not unfold their life by the directions of the divine word, but regulate[128] themselves by man: they want to be not "divine" but "human," and to live so.

Man is the liberal's supreme being, man the *judge* of his life, humanity his *directions,* or catechism. God is spirit, but man is the "most perfect spirit," the final result of the long chase after the spirit or of the "searching in the depths of the Godhead," that is, in the depths of the spirit.

Every one of your traits is to be human; you yourself are to be so from top to toe, in the inward as in the outward; for humanity is your calling.

Calling—destiny—task!—

What one can become he does become. A born poet may well be hindered by the disfavor of circumstances from standing on the high level of his time, and, after the great studies that are indispensable for this, producing *consummate* works of art; but he will make poetry, be he a plowman or so lucky as to live at the court of Weimar. A born musician will make music, no matter whether on all instruments or only on an oaten pipe. A born philosophical head can give proof of itself as university philosopher or as village philosopher. Finally, a born dolt, who, as is very well compatible with this, may at the same time be a sly-boots, will (as probably every one who has visited schools is in a position to exemplify to himself by many instances of fellow-scholars) always remain a blockhead, let him have been drilled and trained into the chief of a bureau, or let him serve that same chief as bootblack. Nay, the born shallow-pates indisputably form the most numerous class of men. And why, indeed, should not the same distinctions show themselves in the human species that are unmistakable in every species of beasts? The more gifted and the less gifted are to be found everywhere.

Only a few, however, are so imbecile that one could not get ideas into them. Hence, people usually consider all men capable of having religion. In a certain degree they may be trained to other ideas too, to some musical intelligence, even some philosophy. At this point then the priesthood of religion, of morality,

128. (*richten*)

of culture, of science, etc., takes its start, and the Communists, for instance, want to make everything accessible to all by their "public school." There is heard a common assertion that this "great mass" cannot get along without religion; the Communists broaden it into the proposition that not only the "great mass," but absolutely all, are called to everything.

Not enough that the great mass has been trained to religion, now it is actually to have to occupy itself with "everything human." Training is growing ever more general and more comprehensive.

You poor beings who could live so happily if you might skip according to your mind, you are to dance to the pipe of schoolmasters and bear-leaders, in order to perform tricks that you yourselves would never use yourselves for. And you do not even kick out of the traces at last against being always taken otherwise than you want to give yourselves. No, you mechanically recite to yourselves the question that is recited to you: "What am I called to? What *ought* I to do?" You need only ask thus, to have yourselves *told* what you ought to do and *ordered* to do it, to have your *calling* marked out for you, or else to order yourselves and impose it on yourselves according to the spirit's prescription. Then in reference to the will the word is, I will to do what I *ought*.

A man is "called" to nothing, and has no "calling," no "destiny," as little as a plant or a beast has a "calling." The flower does not follow the calling to complete itself, but it spends all its forces to enjoy and consume the world as well as it can— it sucks in as much of the juices of the earth, as much air of the ether, as much light of the sun, as it can get and lodge. The bird lives up to no calling, but it uses its forces as much as is practicable; it catches beetles and sings to its heart's delight. But the forces of the flower and the bird are slight in comparison to those of a man, and a man who applies his forces will affect the world much more powerfully than flower and beast. A calling he has not, but he has forces that manifest themselves where they are because their being consists solely in their manifestation, and are as little able to abide inactive as life, which, if it "stood still" only a second, would no longer be life. Now,

one might call out to the man, "use your force." Yet to this
imperative would be given the meaning that it was man's task
to use his force. It is not so. Rather, each one really uses his
force without first looking upon this as his calling: at all times
every one uses as much force as he possesses. One does say of
a beaten man that he ought to have exerted his force more; but
one forgets that, if in the moment of succumbing he had had the
force to exert his forces (bodily forces), he would not have
failed to do it: even if it was only the discouragement of a minute,
this was yet a—destitution of force, a minute long. Forces may
assuredly be sharpened and redoubled, especially by hostile resistance or friendly assistance; but where one misses their application one may be sure of their absence too. One can strike
fire out of a stone, but without the blow none comes out; in
like manner a man too needs "impact."

Now, for this reason that forces always of themselves show
themselves operative, the command to use them would be superfluous and senseless. To use his forces is not man's *calling* and
task, but is his *act,* real and extant at all times. Force is only
a simpler word for manifestation of force.

Now, as this rose is a true rose to begin with, this nightingale
always a true nightingale, so I am not for the first time a true
man when I fulfill my calling, live up to my destiny, but I am
a "true man" from the start. My first babble is the token of
the life of a "true man," the struggles of my life are the outpour-
ings of his force, my last breath is the last exhalation of the force
of the "man."

The true man does not lie in the future, an object of longing,
but lies, existent and real, in the present. Whatever and whoever
I may be, joyous and suffering, a child or a graybeard, in confidence or doubt, in sleep or in waking, I am it, I am the true man.

But, if I am Man, and have really found in myself him whom
religious humanity designated as the distant goal, then everything
"truly human" is also *my own.* What was ascribed to the idea
of humanity belongs to me. That freedom of trade, for example,
which humanity has yet to attain—and which, like an enchanting
dream, people remove to humanity's golden future—I take by
anticipation as my property, and carry it on for the time in the

328 THE EGO AND HIS OWN

form of smuggling. There may indeed be but few smugglers who have sufficient understanding to thus account to themselves for their doings, but the instinct of egoism replaces their consciousness. Above I have shown the same thing about freedom of the press.

Everything is my own, therefore I bring back to myself what wants to withdraw from me; but above all I always bring myself back when I have slipped away from myself to any tributariness. But this too is not my calling, but my natural act.

Enough, there is a mighty difference whether I make myself the starting-point or the goal. As the latter I do not have myself, am consequently still alien to myself, am my *essence*, my "true essence," and this "true essence," alien to me, will mock me as a spook of a thousand different names. Because I am not yet I, another (like God, the true man, the truly pious man, the rational man, the freeman, etc.) is I, my ego.

Still far from myself, I separate myself into two halves, of which one, the one unattained and to be fulfilled, is the true one. The one, the untrue, must be brought as a sacrifice; to wit, the unspiritual one. The other, the true, is to be the whole man; to wit, the spirit. Then it is said, "The spirit is man's proper essence," or, "man exists as man only spiritually." Now, there is a greedy rush to catch the spirit, as if one would then have bagged *himself*; and so, in chasing after himself, one loses sight of himself, whom he is.

And, as one stormily pursues his own self, the never-attained, so one also despises shrewd people's rule to take men as they are, and prefers to take them as they should be; and, for this reason, hounds every one on after his should-be self and "endeavors to make all into equally entitled, equally respectable, equally moral or rational men."[129]

Yes, "if men were what they *should* be, *could* be, if all men were rational, all loved each other as brothers," then it would be a paradisaical life.[130]—All right, men are as they should be, can be. What should they be? Surely not more than they can

129. *Der Kommunismus in der Schweiz*, p. 24.
130. [*Above*] p. 63.

be! And what can they be? Not more, again, than they—can, than they have the competence, the force, to be. But this they really are, because what they are not they are *incapable* of being; for to be capable means—really to be. One is not capable for anything that one really is not; one is not capable of anything that one does not really do. Could a man blinded by cataract see? Oh, yes, if he had his cataract successfully removed. But now he cannot see because he does not see. Possibility and reality always coincide. One can do nothing that one does not, as one does nothing that one cannot.

The singularity of this assertion vanishes when one reflects that the words "it is possible that . . ." almost never contain another meaning than "I can imagine that . . . ," for instance, It is possible for all men to live rationally; that is, I can imagine that all, etc. Now—since my thinking cannot, and accordingly does not, cause all men to live rationally, but this must still be left to the men themselves—general reason is for me only think-able, a thinkableness, but as such in fact a *reality* that is called a possibility only in reference to what I *can* not bring to pass, to wit, the rationality of others. So far as depends on you, all men might be rational, for you have nothing against it; nay, so far as your thinking reaches, you perhaps cannot discover any hindrance either, and accordingly nothing does stand in the way of the thing in your thinking; it is thinkable to you.

As men are not all rational, though, it is probable that they—cannot be so.

If something which one imagines to be easily possible is not, or does not happen, then one may be assured that something stands in the way of the thing, and that it is—impossible. Our time has its art, science, etc,; the art may be bad in all conscience; but may one say that we deserved to have a better, and "could" have it if we only would? We have just as much art as we can have. Our art of to-day is the *only art possible,* and therefore real, at the time.

Even in the sense to which one might at last still reduce the word "possible," that it should mean "future," it retains the full force of the "real." If one says, "It is possible that the sun will rise to-morrow"—this means only, "for to-day to-morrow is the real future"; for I suppose there is hardly need of the suggestion that a future is real "future" only when it has not yet appeared.

Yet wherefore this dignifying of a word? If the most prolific misunderstanding of thousands of years were not in ambush behind it, if this single concept of the little word "possible" were not haunted by all the spooks of possessed men, its contemplation should trouble us little here.

The thought, it was just now shown, rules the possessed world. Well, then, possibility is nothing but thinkableness, and innumerable sacrifices have hitherto been made to hideous *thinkableness*. It was *thinkable* that men might become rational; thinkable, that they might know Christ; thinkable, that they might become moral and enthusiastic for the good; thinkable, that they might all take refuge in the Church's lap; thinkable, that they might meditate, speak, and do, nothing dangerous to the State; thinkable, that they *might* be obedient subjects; but, because it was thinkable, it was—so ran the inference—possible, and further, because it was possible to men (right here lies the deceptive point; because it is thinkable to me, it is possible to *men*), therefore they *ought* to be so, it was their *calling*; and finally— one is to take men only according to this calling, only as *called* men, "not as they are, but as they ought to be."

And the further inference? Man is not the individual, but man is a *thought,* an *ideal,* to which the individual is related not even as the child to the man, but as a chalk point to a point thought of, or as a—finite creature to the eternal Creator, or, according to modern views, as the specimen to the species. Here then comes to light the glorification of "humanity," the "eternal, immortal," for whose glory (*in majorem humanitatis gloriam*) the individual must devote himself and find his "immortal renown" in having done something for the "spirit of humanity."

Thus the *thinkers* rule in the world as long as the age of priests or of schoolmasters lasts, and what they think of is possible, but what is possible must be realized. They *think* an ideal of man, which for the time is real only in their thoughts; but they also think the possibility of carrying it out, and there is no chance for dispute, the carrying out is really—thinkable, it is an—idea.

But you and I, we may indeed be people of whom a Krummacher can *think* that we might yet become good Christians; if, however, he wanted to "labor with" us, we should soon make it palpable to him that our Christianity is only *thinkable,* but in other respects *impossible;* if he grinned on and on at us with his obtrusive *thoughts,* his "good belief," he would have to learn that we do not at all *need* to become what we do not like to become.

And so it goes on, far beyond the most pious of the pious. "If all men were rational, if all did right, if all were guided by philanthropy, etc."! Reason, right, philanthropy, are put before the eyes of men as their calling, as the goal of their aspiration. And what does being rational mean? Giving oneself a hearing?[131] No, reason is a book full of laws, which are all enacted against egoism.

History hitherto is the history of the *intellectual* man. After the period of sensuality, history proper begins; the period of intellectuality,[132] spirituality,[133] non-sensuality, supersensuality, nonsensicality. Man now begins to want to be and become *something.* What? Good, beautiful, true; more precisely, moral, pious, agreeable, etc. He wants to make of himself a "proper man," "something proper." *Man* is his goal, his ought, his destiny, calling, task, his—*ideal;* he is to himself a future, otherworldly he. And *what* makes a "proper fellow" of him? Being true, being good, being moral, and the like. Now he looks askance at every one who does not recognize the same "what," seek the same morality, have the same faith; he chases out "separatists, heretics, sects," etc.

No sheep, no dog, exerts itself to become a "proper sheep, a proper dog"; no beast has its essence appear to it as a task, as a concept that it has to realize. It realizes itself in living

131. (Cf. note 65, Chapter II.)
132. (*Geistigkeit*)
133. (*Geistlichkeit*)

itself out, in dissolving itself, passing away. It does not ask to be or to become anything *other* than it is.

Do I mean to advise you to be like the beasts? That you ought to become beasts is an exhortation which I certainly cannot give you, as that would again be a task, an ideal ("How doth the little busy bee improve each shining hour. . . . In works of labor or of skill I would be busy too, for Satan finds some mischief still for idle hands to do"). It would be the same, too, as if one wished for the beasts that they should become human beings. Your nature is, once for all, a human one; you are human natures, human beings. But, just because you already are so, you do not still need to become so. Beasts too are "trained," and a trained beast executes many unnatural things. But a trained dog is no better for itself than a natural one, and has no profit from it, even if it is more companionable for us.

Exertions to "form" all men into moral, rational, pious, human, "beings" (training) were in vogue from of yore. They are wrecked against the indomitable quality of I, against own nature, against egoism. Those who are trained never attain their ideal, and only profess with their *mouth* the sublime principles, or make a *profession,* a profession of faith. In face of this profession they must in *life* "acknowledge themselves sinners altogether," and they fall short of their ideal, are "weak men," and bear with them the consciousness of "human weakness."

It is different if you do not chase after an *ideal* as your "destiny," but dissolve yourself as time dissolves everything. The dissolution is not your "destiny," because it is present time.

Yet the *culture,* the religiousness, of men has assuredly made them free, but only free from one lord, to lead them to another. I have learned by religion to tame my appetite, I break the world's resistance by the cunning that is put in my hand by *science;* I even serve no man; "I am no man's lackey." But then it comes. You must obey God more than man. Just so I am indeed free from irrational determination by my impulses, but obedient to the master *Reason.* I have gained "spiritual freedom," "freedom of the spirit." But with that I have then become subject to that very *spirit.* The spirit gives me orders, reason guides me, they are my leaders and commanders. The "rational," the "servants of the spirit," rule. But, if *I* am not flesh, I am in truth not spirit either. Freedom of the spirit is servitude of me, because I am more than spirit or flesh.

Without doubt culture has made me *powerful*. It has given me power over all *motives,* over the impulses of my nature as well as over the exactions and violences of the world. I know, and have gained the force for it by culture, that I need not let myself be coerced by any of my appetites, pleasures, emotions, etc.; I am their—*master*; in like manner I become, through the sciences and arts, the *master* of the refractory world, whom sea and earth obey, and to whom even the stars must give an account of themselves. The spirit has made me *master.*—But I have no power over the spirit itself. From religion (culture) I do learn the means for the "vanquishing of the world," but not how I am to subdue *God* too and become master of him; for God "is the spirit." And this same spirit, of which I am unable to become master, may have the most manifold shapes; he may be called God or National Spirit, State, Family, Reason, also—Liberty, Humanity, Man.

I receive with thanks what the centuries of culture have acquired for me; I am not willing to throw away and give up anything of it: I have not lived in vain. The experience that I have *power* over my nature, and need not be the slave of my appetites, shall not be lost to me; the experience that I can subdue the world by culture's means is too dear-bought for me to be able to forget it. But I want still more.

People ask, what can man do? What can he accomplish? What goods procure, and put down the highest of everything as a calling. As if everything were possible to *me!*

If one sees somebody going to ruin in a mania, a passion, etc. (as in the huckster-spirit, in jealousy), the desire is stirred to deliver him out of this possession and to help him to "self-conquest." "We want to make a man of him!" That would be very fine if another possession were not immediately put in the place of the earlier one. But one frees from the love of money him who is a thrall to it, only to deliver him over to piety, humanity, or some principle else, and to transfer him to a *fixed standpoint* anew.

This transference from a narrow standpoint to a sublime one is declared in the words that the sense must not be directed to the perishable, but to the imperishable alone: not to the temporal, but to the eternal, absolute, divine, purely human, etc.— to the spiritual.

People very soon discerned that it was not indifferent what one set his affections on, or what one occupied himself with; they recognized the importance of the *object*. An object exalted above the individuality of things is the *essence* of things; yes, the essence is alone the thinkable in them, it is for the *thinking* man. Therefore direct no longer your *sense* to the *things*, but your *thoughts* to the *essence*. "Blessed are they who see not, and yet believe"; that is, blessed are the *thinkers,* for they have to do with the invisible and believe in it. Yet even an object of thought, that constituted an essential point of contention centuries long, comes at last to the point of being "No longer worth speaking of." This was discerned, but nevertheless people always kept before their eyes again a self-valid importance of the object, an absolute value of it, as if the doll were not the most important thing to the child, the Koran to the Turk. As long as I am not the sole important thing to myself, it is indifferent of what object I "make much," and only my greater or lesser *delinquency* against it is of value. The degree of my attachment and devotion marks the standpoint of my liability to service, the degree of my sinning shows the measure of my ownness.

But finally, and in general, one must know how to "put everything out of his mind," if only so as to be able to—go to sleep. Nothing may occupy us with which *we* do not occupy ourselves: the victim of ambition cannot run away from his ambitious plans, nor the God-fearing man from the thought of God; infatuation and possessedness coincide.

To want to realize his essence or live comfortably to his concept (which with believers in God signifies as much as to be "pious," and with believers in humanity means living "human-ly") is what only the sensual and sinful man can propose to himself, the man so long as he has the anxious choice between happiness of sense and peace of soul, so long as he is a "poor sinner." The Christian is nothing but a sensual man who, knowing of the sacred and being conscious that he violates it, sees in himself a poor sinner: sensualness, recognized as "sinfulness," is Christian consciousness, is the Christian himself. And if "sin" and "sinfulness" are now no longer taken into the mouths of moderns, but, instead of that, "egoism," "self-seeking," "selfishness," and the like, engage them; if the devil has been translated into the "unman" or "egoistic man"—is the Christian less present then than before? Is not the old discord between good and evil—is not a judge over us, man—is not a calling, the calling to make oneself man—left? If they no longer name it calling, but "task" or, very likely, "duty," the change of name is quite correct, because "man" is not, like God, a personal being that can "call"; but outside the name the thing remains as of old.

Every one has a relation to objects, and more, every one is differently related to them. Let us choose as an example that book to which millions of men had a relation for two thousand years, the Bible. What is it, what was it, to each? Absolutely, only what he *made out of it!* For him who makes to himself nothing at all out of it, it is nothing at all; for him who uses it as an amulet, it has solely the value, the significance, of a means of sorcery; for him who, like children, plays with it, it is nothing but a plaything, etc.

Now, Christianity asks that it shall *be the same for all*: say, the sacred book or the "sacred Scriptures." This means as much as that the Christian's view shall also be that of other men, and that no one may be otherwise related to that object. And with this the ownness of the relation is destroyed, and one mind, one disposition, is fixed as the *"true,"* the "only true" one. In the limitation of the freedom to make of the Bible what I will, the freedom of making in general is limited; and the coercion of a view or a judgment is put in its place. He who should pass the judgment that the Bible was a long error of mankind would judge —*criminally.*

In fact, the child who tears it to pieces or plays with it, the Inca Atahualpa[134] who lays his ear to it and throws it away

134. [The last native ruler of Peru, killed by the Spanish invaders in 1533.]

contemptuously when it remains dumb, judges just as correctly about the Bible as the priest who praises in it the "Word of God," or the critic who calls it a job of men's hands. For how we toss things about is the affair of our *option,* our *free will*: we use them according to our *heart's pleasure,* or, more clearly, we use them just as we *can.* Why, what do the parsons scream about when they see how Hegel and the speculative theologians make speculative thoughts out of the contents of the Bible? Precisely this, that they deal with it according to their heart's pleasure, or "proceed arbitrarily with it."

But, because we all show ourselves arbitrary in the handling of objects, that is, do with them as we *like* best, at our *liking* (the philosopher likes nothing so well as when he can trace out an "idea" in everything, as the God-fearing man likes to make God his friend by everything, and so, for example, by keeping the Bible sacred), therefore we nowhere meet such grievous arbitrariness, such a frightful tendency to violence, such stupid coercion, as in this very domain of our—*own free will*. If *we* proceed arbitrarily in taking the sacred objects thus or so, how is it then that we want to take it ill of the parson-spirits if they take us just as arbitrarily, *in their fashion,* and esteem us worthy of the heretic's fire or of another punishment, perhaps of the—censorship?

What a man is, he makes out of things; "as you look at the world, so it looks at you again." Then the wise advice makes itself heard again at once, You must only look at it "rightly, unbiasedly," etc. As if the child did not look at the Bible "rightly and unbiasedly" when it makes it a plaything. That shrewd precept is given us by Feuerbach. One does look at things rightly when one makes of them what one *will* (by things objects in general are here understood, such as God, our fellow-men, a sweetheart, a book, a beast, etc.). And therefore the things and the looking at them are not first, but I am, my will is. One *will* brings thoughts out of the things, *will* discover reason in the world, *will* have sacredness in it: therefore one shall find them. "Seek and ye shall find." *What* I will seek, I determine: I want, for example, to get edification from the Bible; it is to be found; I want to read and test the Bible thoroughly; my outcome will be a thorough instruction and criticism—to the extent of my powers. I elect for myself what I have a fancy for, and in electing I show myself—arbitrary.

Connected with this is the discernment that every judgment which I pass upon an object is the *creature* of my will; and that discernment again leads me to not losing myself in the *creature,* the judgment, but remaining the *creator,* the judger, who is ever creating anew. All predicates of objects are my statements, my judgments, my—creatures. If they want to tear themselves loose from me and be something for themselves, or acutally overawe me, then I have nothing more pressing to do than to take them back into their nothing, into me the creator. God, Christ, trinity, morality, the good, etc., are such creatures, of which I must not merely allow myself to say that they are truths, but also that they are deceptions. As I once willed and decreed their existence, so I want to have license to will their non-existence too; I must not let them grow over my head, must not have the weakness to let them become something "absolute," whereby they would be eternalized and withdrawn from my power and decision. With that I should fall a prey to the *principle of stability,* the proper life-principle of religion, which concerns itself with creating "sanctuaries that must not be touched," "eternal truths"—in short, that which shall be "sacred"—and depriving you of what is *yours.*

The object makes us into possessed men in its sacred form just as in its profane; as a supersensuous object, just as it does as a sensuous one. The appetite or mania refers to both, and avarice and longing for heaven stand on a level. When the rationalists wanted to win people for the sensuous world, Lavater[135] preached the longing for the invisible. The one party wanted to call forth *emotion,* the other *motion,* activity.

The conception of objects is altogether diverse, even as God, Christ, the world, were and are conceived of in the most manifold wise. In this every one is a "dissenter," and after bloody combats so much has at last been attained, that opposite

135. [Johann Kaspar Lavater (1741-1801), Swiss student of physiognomy, and the author of over 125 works published in Germany and Switzerland between 1770 and 1801; his *Aphorisms on Man* represents one of the small number of his writings translated into English.]

views about one and the same object are no longer condemned as heresies worthy of death. The "dissenters" reconcile themselves to each other. But why should I only dissent (think otherwise) about a thing? Why not push the thinking otherwise to its last extremity, that of no longer having any regard at all for the thing, and therefore thinking its nothingness, crushing it? Then the *conception* itself has an end, because there is no longer anything to conceive of. Why am I to say, let us suppose, "God is not Allah, not Brahma, not Jehovah, but—God"; but not, "God is nothing but a deception"? Why do people brand me if I am an "atheist?" Because they put the creature above the creator ("They honor and serve the creature more than the Creator")[136] and require a *ruling object,* that the subject may be right *submissive.* I am to bend *beneath* the absolute, I *ought* to.

By the "realm of thoughts" Christianity has completed itself; the thought is that inwardness in which all the world's lights go out, all existence becomes existenceless, the inward man (the heart, the head) is all in all. This realm of thoughts awaits its deliverance, awaits, like the Sphinx, Oedipus's key-word to the riddle, that it may enter in at last to its death. I am the annihilator of its continuance, for in the creator's realm it no longer forms a realm of its own, not a State in the State, but a creature of my creative—thoughtlessness. Only together and at the same time with the benumbed *thinking* world can the world of Christians, Christianity and religion itself, come to its downfall; only when thoughts run out are there no more believers. To the thinker his thinking is a "sublime labor, a sacred activity," and it rests on a firm *faith,* the faith in truth. At first praying is a sacred activity, then this sacred "devotion" passes over into a rational and reasoning "thinking," which, however, likewise retains in the "sacred truth" its underangeable basis of faith, and is only a marvelous machine that the spirit of truth winds up for its service. Free thinking and free science busy *me*—for it is not I that am free, not *I* that busy myself, but thinking is free and busies me—with heaven and the heavenly or "divine"; that is, properly, with the world and the worldly, not this world but

136. Rom. 1. 25.

"another" world; it is only the reversing and deranging of the world, a busying with the *essence* of the world, therefore a *derangement.* The thinker is blind to the immediateness of things, and incapable of mastering them: he does not eat, does not drink, does not enjoy; for the eater and drinker is never the thinker, nay, the latter forgets eating and drinking, his getting on in life, the cares of nourishment, etc., over his thinking; he forgets it as the praying man too forgets it. This is why he appears to the forceful son of nature as a queer Dick, a *fool*—even if he does look upon him as holy, just as lunatics appeared so to the ancients. Free thinking is lunacy, because it is *pure movement of the inwardness,* of the merely *inward man,* which guides and regulates the rest of the man. The shaman and the speculative philosopher mark the bottom and top rounds on the ladder of the *inward* man, the—Mongol. Shaman and philosopher fight with ghosts, demons, *spirits,* gods.

Totally different from this *free* thinking is *own* thinking, *my* thinking, a thinking which does not guide me, but is guided, continued, or broken off, by me at my pleasure. The distinction of this own thinking from free thinking is similar to that of own sensuality, which I satisfy at pleasure, from free, unruly sensuality to which I succumb.

Feuerbach, in the *Principles of the Philosophy of the Future,*[137] is always harping upon *being.* In this he too, with all his antagonism to Hegel and the absolute philosophy, is stuck fast in abstraction; for "being" is abstraction, as is even "the I." Only *I am* not abstraction alone: *I am* all in all, consequently even abstraction or nothing; I am all and nothing; I am not a mere thought, but at the same time I am full of thoughts, a thought-world. Hegel condemns the own, mine[138]—"opinion."[139] "Absolute thinking" is that which forgets that it is *my* thinking, that *I* think, and that it exists only through *me.* But I, as I, swallow up again what is mine, am its master; it is only my *opinion,* which

137. [Feuerbach's *Grundsätzen der Philosophie der Zukunft* was published in 1843.]
138. (*das Meinige*)
139. (*die—"Meinung"*)

I can at any moment *change,* annihilate, take back into myself, and consume. Feuerbach wants to smite Hegel's "absolute thinking" with *unconquered being.* But in me being is as much conquered as thinking is. It is *my* being, as the other is *my* thinking.

With this, of course, Feuerbach does not get further than to the proof, trivial in itself, that I require the *senses* for everything, or that I cannot entirely do without these organs. Certainly I cannot think if I do not exist sensuously. But for thinking as well as for feeling, and so for the abstract as well as for the sensuous, I need above all things *myself,* this quite particular myself, this *unique* myself. If I were not this one, for instance, Hegel, I should not look at the world as I do look at it, I should not pick out of it that philosophical system which just I as Hegel do, etc. I should indeed have senses, as do other people too, but I should not utilize them as I do.

Thus the reproach is brought up against Hegel by Feuerbach[140] that he misuses language, understanding by many words something else than what natural consciousness takes them for; and yet he too commits the same fault when he gives the "sensuous" a sense of unusual eminence. Thus it is said, p. 69, "the sensuous is not the profane, the destitute of thought, the obvious, that which is understood of itself." But, if it is the sacred, the full of thought, the recondite, that which can be understood only through mediation—well, then it is no longer what people call the sensuous. The sensuous is only that which exists for *the senses;* what, on the other hand, is enjoyable only to those who enjoy with *more* than the senses, who go beyond sense-enjoyment or sense-reception, is at most mediated or introduced by the senses, that is, the senses constitute a *condition* for obtaining it, but it is no longer anything sensuous. The sensuous, whatever it may be, when taken up into me becomes something non-sensuous, which, however, may again have sensuous effects, as by the stirring of my emotions and my blood.

It is well that Feuerbach brings sensuousness to honor, but the only thing he is able to do with it is to clothe the materialism of his "new philosophy" with what had hitherto been the property

140. Feuerbach, *Principles,* p. 47 ff.

of idealism, the "absolute philosophy." As little as people let
it be talked into them that one can live on the "spiritual" alone
without bread, so little will they believe his word that as a
sensuous being one is already everything, and so spiritual, full of
thoughts, etc.

Nothing at all is justified by *being*. What is thought of *is*
as well as what is not thought of; the stone in the street *is,* and
my notion of it *is* too. Both are only in different *spaces,* the former
in airy space, the latter in my head, in *me;* for I am space like
the street.

The professionals, the privileged, brook no freedom of
thought, no thoughts that do not come from the "Giver of all
good," be he called God, pope, church, or whatever else. If
anybody has such illegitimate thoughts, he must whisper them into
his confessor's ear, and have himself chastised by him till the
slave-whip becomes unendurable to the free thoughts. In other
ways too the professional spirit takes care that free thoughts shall
not come at all: first and foremost, by a wise education. He on
whom the principles of morality have been duly inculcated never
becomes free again from moralizing thoughts, and robbery, perjury, overreaching, and the like, remain to him fixed ideas against
which no freedom of thought protects him. He has his thoughts
"from above," and gets no further.

It is different with the holders of concessions or patents.
Every one must be able to have and form thoughts as he will.
If he has the patent, or the concession, of a capacity to think, he
needs no special *privilege*. But, as "all men are rational," it is
free to every one to put into his head any thoughts whatever, and,
to the extent of the patent of his natural endowment, to have a
greater or less wealth of thoughts. Now one hears the admonitions
that one "is to honor all opinions and convictions," that "every
conviction is authorized," that one must be "tolerant to the views
of others," etc.

But "your thoughts are not my thoughts, and your ways are
not my ways." Or rather, I mean the reverse: Your thoughts
are *my* thoughts, which I dispose of as I will, and which I strike
down unmercifully; they are my property, which I annihilate
as I list. I do not wait for authorization from you first, to decom-

pose and blow away your thoughts. It does not matter to me that you call these thoughts yours too, they remain mine nevertheless, and how I will proceed with them is *my affair,* not a usurpation. It may please me to leave you in your thoughts; then I keep still. Do you believe thoughts fly around free like birds, so that every one may get himself some which he may then make good against me as his inviolable property? What is flying around is all—*mine.*

Do you believe you have your thoughts for yourselves and need answer to no one for them, or as you do also say, you have to give an account of them to God only? No, your great and small thoughts belong to me, and I handle them at my pleasure.

The thought is my *own* only when I have no misgiving about bringing it in danger of death every moment, when I do not have to fear its loss as a *loss for me,* a loss of me. The thought is my own only when I can indeed subjugate it, but it never can subjugate me, never fanaticizes me, makes me the tool of its realization.

So freedom of thought exists when I can have all possible thoughts; but the thoughts become property only by not being able to become masters. In the time of freedom of thought, thoughts (ideas) *rule;* but, if I attain to property in thought, they stand as my creatures.

If the hierarchy had not so penetrated men to the innermost as to take from them all courage to pursue free thoughts, that is, thoughts perhaps displeasing to God, one would have to consider freedom of thought just as empty a word as, say, a freedom of digestion.

According to the professionals' opinion, the thought is *given* to me; according to the freethinkers', I *seek* the thought. There the *truth* is already found and extant, only I must—receive it from its Giver by grace; here the truth is to be sought and is my goal, lying in the future, toward which I have to run.

In both cases the truth (the true thought) lies outside me, and I aspire to *get* it, be it by presentation (grace), be it by earning (merit of my own). Therefore, (1) The truth is a *privilege;* (2) No, the way to it is patent to all, and neither the

Bible nor the holy fathers nor the church nor any one else is in possession of the truth; but one can come into possession of it by—speculating.

Both, one sees, are *propertyless* in relation to the truth: they have it either as a *fief* (for the "holy father," is not a unique person; as unique he is this Sixtus, Clement, but he does not have the truth as Sixtus, Clement, but as "holy father," that is, as a spirit) or as an *ideal*. As a fief, it is only for a few (the privileged); as an ideal, for *all* (the patentees).

Freedom of thought, then, has the meaning that we do indeed all walk in the dark and in the paths of error, but every one can on this path approach *the truth* and is accordingly on the right path ("All roads lead to Rome, to the world's end, etc."). Hence freedom of thought means this much, that the true thought is not my *own;* for, if it were this, how should people want to shut me off from it?

Thinking has become entirely free, and has laid down a lot of truths which I must accommodate myself to. It seeks to complete itself into a *system* and to bring itself to an absolute "constitution." In the State it seeks for the idea, say, till it has brought out the "rational State," in which I am then obliged to be suited; in man (anthropology), till it "has found man."

The thinker is distinguished from the believer only by believing much more than the latter, who on his part thinks of much less as signified by his faith (creed). The thinker has a thousand tenets of faith where the believer gets along with few; but the former brings *coherence* into his tenets, and takes the coherence in turn for the scale to estimate their worth by. If one or the other does not fit into his budget, he throws it out.

The thinkers run parallel to the believers in their pronouncements. Instead of "If it is from God you will not root it out," the word is "If it is from the *truth,* is true, etc."; instead of "Give God the glory"—"Give truth the glory." But it is very much the same to me whether God or the truth wins; first and foremost I want to win.

Aside from this, how is an "unlimited freedom" to be thinkable inside of the State or society? The State may well protect one against another, but yet it must not let itself be endangered by an unmeasured freedom, a so-called unbridleness. Thus in "freedom of instruction" the *State* declares only this— that it is suited with every one who instructs as the State (or, speaking more comprehensibly, the political power) would have it. The point for the competitors is this "as the State would have it." If the clergy, for example, does not will as the State does, then it itself excludes itself from *competition* (*vide* France). The limit that is necessarily drawn in the State for any and all competition is called "the oversight and superintendence of the State." In bidding freedom of instruction keep within the due bounds, the State at the same time fixes the scope of freedom of thought; because, as a rule, people do not think farther than their teachers have thought.

Hear Minister Guizot:[141] "The great difficulty of to-day is the *guiding and dominating of the mind.* Formerly the church fulfilled this mission; now it is not adequate to it. It is from the university that this great service must be expected, and the university will not fail to perform it. We, the *government,* have the duty of supporting it therein. The charter calls for the freedom of thought and that of conscience."[142] So, in favor of freedom of thought and conscience, the minister demands "the guiding and dominating of the mind."

Catholicism haled the examinee before the forum of ecclesiasticism, Protestantism before that of biblical Christianity. It would be but little bettered if one haled him before that of reason, as Ruge wants to.[143] Whether the church, the Bible, or reason (to which, moreover, Luther and Hus already appealed) is the *sacred authority* makes no difference in essentials.

The "question of our time" does not become soluble even when one puts it thus: Is anything general authorized, or only the individual? Is the generality (such as State, law, custom, morality, etc.) authorized, or individuality? It becomes soluble

141. [François Guizot (1787-1874), undoubtedly the dominant political figure in France between 1840 and 1847. Oddly enough, hardly more than a decade before the speech Stirner cites, Guizot had authored legislation which gave the Church control of French primary education.]

142. Chamber of peers, Apr. 25, 1844.

143. *Anekdota*, vol. 1, p. 120.

for the first time when one no longer asks after an "authorization" at all, and does not carry on a mere fight against "privileges."— A "rational" freedom of teaching, which recognizes only the conscience of reason,"[144] does not bring us to the goal; we require an *egoistic* freedom of teaching rather, a freedom of teaching for all ownness, wherein *I* become audible and can announce myself unchecked.   That I make myself *"audible,"*[145] this alone is "reason,"[146] be I ever so irrational; in my making myself heard, and so bearing myself, others as well as I myself enjoy me, and at the same time consume me.

What would be gained if, as formerly the orthodox I, the loyal I, the moral I, etc., was free, now the rational I should become free?   Would this be the freedom of me?

If I am free as "rational I," then the rational in me, or reason, is free; and this freedom of reason, or freedom of the thought, was the ideal of the Christian world from of old.   They wanted to make thinking—and, as aforesaid, faith is also thinking, as thinking is faith—free; the thinkers, the believers as well as the rational, were to be free; for the rest freedom was impossible.   But the freedom of thinkers is the "freedom of the children of God," and at the same time the most merciless— hierarchy or dominion of the thought; for *I* succumb to the thought.   If thoughts are free, I am their slave; I have no power over them, and am dominated by them.   But I want to have the thought, want to be full of thoughts, but at the same time I want to be thoughtless, and, instead of freedom of thought, I preserve for myself thoughtlessness.

If the point is to have myself understood and to make communications, then assuredly I can make use only of *human* means, which are at my command because I am at the same time man.   And really I have thoughts only as *man;* as I, I am at the same time *thoughtless.*[147]   He who cannot get rid of a thought is so far *only* man, is a thrall of *language,* this human

144. *Anekdota,* vol. 1, p. 127.
145. (*vernehmbar*)
146. (*Vernunft*)
147. (Literally "thought-rid.")

institution, this treasury of *human* thoughts. Language or "the word" tyrannizes hardest over us, because it brings up against us a whole army of *fixed ideas*. Just observe yourself in the act of reflection, right now, and you will find how you make progress only by becoming thoughtless and speechless every moment. You are not thoughtless and speechless merely in (say) sleep, but even in the deepest reflection; yes, precisely then most so. And only by this thoughtlessness, this unrecognized "freedom of thought" or freedom from the thought, are you your own. Only from it do you arrive at putting language to use as your *property*.

If thinking is not *my* thinking, it is merely a spun-out thought; it is slave work, or the work of a "servant obeying at the word." For not a thought, but I, am the beginning for my thinking, and therefore I am its goal too, even as its whole course is only a course of my self-enjoyment; for absolute or free thinking, on the other hand, thinking itself is the beginning, and it plagues itself with propounding this beginning as the extremest "abstraction" (such as being). This very abstraction, or this thought, is then spun out further.

Absolute thinking is the affair of the human spirit, and this is a holy spirit. Hence this thinking is an affair of the parsons, who have "a sense for it," a sense for the "highest interests of mankind," for "the spirit."

To the believer, truths are a *settled* thing, a fact; to the freethinker, a thing that is still to be *settled*. Be absolute thinking ever so unbelieving, its incredulity has its limits, and there does remain a belief in the truth, in the spirit, in the idea and its final victory: this thinking does not sin against the holy spirit. But all thinking that does not sin against the holy spirit is belief in spirits or ghosts.

I can as little renounce thinking as feeling, the spirit's activity as little as the activity of the senses. As feeling is our sense for things, so thinking is our sense for essences (thoughts). Essences have their existence in everything sensuous, especially in the word. The power of words follows that of things: first one is coerced by the rod, afterward by conviction. The might of things overcomes our courage, our spirit; against the power of a conviction, and so of the word, even the rack and the sword lose their overpoweringness and force. The men of conviction are the priestly men, who resist every enticement of Satan.

Christianity took away from the things of this world only their irresistibleness, made us independent of them. In like manner I raise myself above truths and their power: as I am supersensual, so I am supertrue. *Before me* truths are as common and as indifferent as things; they do not carry me away, and do not inspire me with enthusiasm. There exists not even one truth, not right, not freedom, humanity, etc., that has stability before me, and to which I subject myself. They are *words,* nothing but words, as all things are to the Christian nothing but "vain things." In words and truths (every word is a truth, as Hegel asserts that one cannot *tell* a lie) there is no salvation for me, as little as there is for the Christian in things and vanities. As the riches of this world do not make me happy, so neither do its truths. It is now no longer Satan, but the spirit, that plays the story of the temptation; and he does not seduce by the things of this world, but by its thoughts, by the "glitter of the idea."

Along with worldly goods, all sacred goods too must be put away as no longer valuable.

Truths are phrases, ways of speaking, words (λογος); brought into connection, or into an articulate series, they form logic, science, philosophy.

For thinking and speaking I need truths and words, as I do foods for eating; without them I cannot think nor speak. Truths are men's thoughts, set down in words and therefore just as extant as other things, although extant only for the mind or for thinking. They are human institutions and human creatures, and, even if they are given out for divine revelations, there still remains in them the quality of alienness for me; yes, as my own creatures they are already alienated from me after the act of creation.

The Christian man is the man with faith in thinking, who believes in the supreme dominion of thoughts and wants to bring thoughts, so-called "principles," to dominion. Many a one does indeed test the thoughts, and chooses none of them for his master without criticism, but in this he is like the dog who sniffs at people to smell out "his master"; he is always aiming at the *ruling* thought. The Christian may reform and revolt an infinite deal, may demolish the ruling concepts of centuries; he will always aspire to a new "principle" or new master again, always set up a higher or "deeper" truth again, always call forth a cult again, always proclaim a spirit called to dominion, lay down a *law* for all.

If there is even one truth only to which man has to devote his life and his powers because he is man, then he is subjected to a rule, dominion, law; he is a servingman. It is supposed that man, humanity, liberty, etc., are such truths.

On the other hand, one can say thus: Whether you will further occupy yourself with thinking depends on you; only know that, *if* in your thinking you would like to make out anything worthy of notice, many hard problems are to be solved, without vanquishing which you cannot get far. There exists, therefore, no duty and no calling for you to meddle with thoughts (ideas, truths); but, if you will do so, you will do well to utilize what the forces of others have already achieved toward clearing up these difficult subjects.

Thus, therefore, he who will think does assuredly have a task, which *he* consciously or unconsciously sets for himself in willing that; but no one has the task of thinking or of believing. In the former case it may be said, "You do not go far enough, you have a narrow and biased interest, you do not go to the bottom of the thing; in short, you do not completely subdue it. But, on the other hand, however far you may come at any time, you are still always at the end, you have no call to step farther, and you can have it as you will or as you are able. It stands with this as with any other piece of work, which you can give up when the humor for it wears off. Just so, if you can no longer *believe* a thing, you do not have to force yourself into faith or to busy yourself lastingly as if with a sacred truth of the faith, as theologians or philosophers do, but you can tranquilly draw back your interest from it and let it run. Priestly spirits will indeed expound this your lack of interest as "laziness, thoughtlessness, obduracy, self-deception," and the like. But do you just let the trumpery lie, notwithstanding. No thing,[148] no so-called "highest interest of mankind," no "sacred cause,"[149] is worth your serving it, and occupying yourself with it for *its sake*; you may seek its worth in this alone, whether it is worth anything to *you* for your sake. Become like children, the biblical saying admonishes us. But children have no sacred interest and know nothing of a "good cause." They know all the more accurately what they have a fancy for; and they think over, to the best of their powers, how they are to arrive at it.

Thinking will as little cease as feeling. But the power of thoughts and ideas, the dominion of theories and principles, the sovereignty of the spirit, in short the—*hierarchy,* lasts as long as the parsons, that is, theologians, philosophers, statesmen, philistines, liberals, schoolmasters, servants, parents, children, married couples, Proudhon, George Sand,[150] Blüntschli,[151] and others, have the floor; the hierarchy will endure as long as people believe in, think of, or even criticize, principles; for even the most inexorable criticism, which undermines all current principles, still does finally *believe in the principle.*

Every one criticizes, but the criterion is different. People run after the "right" criterion. The right criterion is the first presupposition. The critic starts from a proposition, a truth, a belief. This is not a creation of the critic, but of the dogmatist; nay, commonly it is actually taken up out of the culture of the time without further ceremony, like "liberty," "humanity," etc. The critic has not "discovered man," but this truth has been established as "man" by the dogmatist, and the critic (who, besides, may be the same person with him) believes in this truth,

148. (*Sache*)
149. (*Sache*)
150. [Pseudonym of Amantine Lucile Aurore Dupin (1804-1876), famous French novelist, whose stories were coming out in proliferation during Stirner's time; her works in the decade of the 1840s were deeply colored with contemporary socialist sentiments.]
151. [Johann Kaspar Blüntschli (1808-1881), Swiss historian and jurisconsult. The work of Blüntschli to which Stirner probably is referring is *Psychologische Studien über Staat und Kirche* (Zurich, 1844). This appeared in several German editions, the sixth being translated into English as *The Theory of the State* (Oxford, 1885.]

this article of faith. In this faith, and possessed by this faith, he criticizes.

The secret of criticism is some "truth" or other: this remains its energizing mystery.

But I distinguish between *servile* and *own* criticism. If I criticize under the presupposition of a supreme being, my criticism *serves* the being and is carried on for its sake: if I am possessed by the belief in a "free State," then everything that has a bearing on it I criticize from the standpoint of whether it is suitable to this State, for I *love* this State; if I criticize as a pious man, then for me everything falls into the classes of divine and diabolical, and before my criticism nature consists of traces of God or traces of the devil (hence names like Godsgift, Godmount, the Devil's Pulpit), men of believers and unbelievers; if I criticize while believing in man as the "true essence," then for me everything falls primarily into the classes of man and the un-man, etc.

Criticism has to this day remained a work of love: for at all times we exercised it for the love of some being. All servile criticism is a product of love, a possessedness, and proceeds according to that New Testament precept, "Test everything and hold fast the *good*."[152] "The good" is the touchstone, the criterion. The good, returning under a thousand names and forms, remained always the presupposition, remained the dogmatic fixed point for this criticism, remained the—fixed idea.

The critic, in setting to work, impartially presupposes the "truth," and seeks for the truth in the belief that it is to be found. He wants to ascertain the true, and has in it that very "good."

Presuppose means nothing else than put a *thought* in front, or think something before everything else and think the rest from the starting-point of this that has *been thought*, measure and criticize it by this. In other words, this is as much as to say that thinking is to begin with something already thought. If thinking began at all, instead of being begun, if thinking were a subject, an acting personality of its own, as even the plant is such, then indeed there would be no abandoning the principle

152. 1 Thess. 5. 21.

that thinking must begin with itself. But it is just the personification of thinking that brings to pass those innumerable errors. In the Hegelian system they always talk as if thinking or "the thinking spirit" (that is, personified thinking, thinking as a ghost) thought and acted; in critical liberalism it is always said that "criticism" does this and that, or else that "self-consciousness" finds this and that. But, if thinking ranks as the personal actor, thinking itself must be presupposed; if criticism ranks as such, a thought must likewise stand in front. Thinking and criticism could be active only starting from themselves, would have to be themselves the presupposition of their activity, as without being they could not be active. But thinking, as a thing presupposed, is a fixed thought, a *dogma*; thinking and criticism, therefore, can start only from a *dogma*, from a thought, a fixed idea, a presupposition.

With this we come back again to what was enunciated above, that Christianity consists in the development of a world of thoughts, or that it is the proper "freedom of thought," the "free thought," the "free spirit." The "true" criticism, which I called "servile," is therefore just as much "free" criticism, for it is not *my own*.

The case stands otherwise when what is yours is not made into something that is of itself, not personified, not made independent as a "spirit" to itself. *Your* thinking has for a presupposition not "thinking," but *you*. But thus you do presuppose yourself after all? Yes, but not for myself, but for my thinking. Before my thinking, there is—I. From this it follows that my thinking is not preceded by a *thought*, or that my thinking is without a "presupposition." For the presupposition which I am for my thinking is not one *made by thinking*, not one *thought of*, but it is *posited* thinking *itself*, it is the *owner* of the thought, and proves only that thinking is nothing more than—*property*, that an "independent" thinking, a "thinking spirit," does not exist at all.

This reversal of the usual way of regarding things might so resemble an empty playing with abstractions that even those against whom it is directed would acquiesce in the harmless aspect I give it, if practical consequences were not connected with it.

To bring these into a concise expression, the assertion now made is that man is not the measure of all things, but I am this measure. The servile critic has before his eyes another being, an idea, which he means to serve; therefore he only slays the false idols for his God. What is done for the love of this being, what else should it be but a—work of love? But I, when I criticize, do not even have myself before my eyes, but am only doing myself a pleasure, amusing myself according to my taste; according to my several needs I chew the thing up or only inhale its odor.

The distinction between the two attitudes will come out still more strikingly if one reflects that the servile critic, because love guides him, supposes he is serving the thing (cause) itself.

The truth, or "truth in general," people are bound not to give up, but to seek for. What else is it but the *être suprême,* the highest essence? Even "true criticism" would have to despair if it lost faith in the truth. And yet the truth is only a—*thought*; but it is not merely "a" thought, but the thought that is above all thoughts, the irrefragable thought; it is *the* thought itself, which gives the first hallowing to all others; it is the consecration of thoughts, the "absolute," the "sacred" thought. The truth wears longer than all the gods; for it is only in the truth's service, and for love of it, that people have overthrown the gods and at last God himself. "The truth" outlasts the downfall of the world of gods, for it is the immortal soul of this transitory world of gods, it is Deity itself.

I will answer Pilate's question, What is truth? Truth is the free thought, the free idea, the free spirit; truth is what is free from you, what is not your own, what is not in your power. But truth is also the completely unindependent, impersonal, unreal, and incorporeal; truth cannot step forward as you do, cannot move, change, develop; truth awaits and receives everything from you, and itself is only through you; for it exists only—in your head. You concede that the truth is a thought, but say that not every thought is a true one, or, as you are also likely to express it, not every thought is truly and really a thought. And by what do you measure and recognize the thought? By *your impotence,* to wit, by your being no longer able to make any successful assault on it! When it overpowers you, inspires you, and carries you away, then you hold it to be the true one. Its dominion over you certifies to you its truth; and, when it possesses you, and you are possessed by it, then you feel well with it, for then you have found your—*lord and master.* When you were seeking the truth, what did your heart then long for? For your master! You did not aspire to *your* might, but to a Mighty One, and wanted to exalt a Mighty One ("Exalt ye the Lord our God!"). The truth, my dear Pilate, is—the Lord, and all who seek the truth are seeking and praising the Lord. Where does the Lord exist? Where else but in your head? He is only spirit, and, wherever you believe you really see him, there he is a— ghost; for the Lord is merely something that is thought of, and it was only the Christian pains and agony to make the invisible visible, the spiritual corporeal, that generated the ghost and was the frightful misery of the belief in ghosts.

As long as you believe in the truth, you do not believe in yourself, and you are a—*servant,* a—*religious man.* You alone are the truth, or rather, you are more than the truth, which is nothing at all before you. You too do assuredly ask about the truth, you too do assuredly "criticize," but you do not ask about a "higher truth"—to wit, one that should be higher than you— nor criticize according to the criterion of such a truth. You address yourself to thoughts and notions, as you do to the appearances of things, only for the purpose of making them palatable to you, enjoyable to you, and your own: you want only to subdue them and become their *owner,* you want to orient yourself and feel at home in them, and you find them true, or see them in their true light, when they can no longer slip away from you, no longer have any unseized or uncomprehended place, or when they are *right for you,* when they are your *property.* If afterward they become heavier again, if they wriggle themselves out of your power again, then that is just their untruth—to wit, your impotence. Your impotence is their power, your humility their exaltation. Their truth, therefore, is you, or is the nothing which you are for them and in which they dissolve: their truth is their *nothingness*.

Only as the property of me do the spirits, the truths, get to rest; and they then for the first time really are, when they have been deprived of their sorry existence and made a property of mine, when it is no longer said "the truth develops itself, rules, asserts itself; history (also a concept) wins the victory," and the like. The truth never has won a victory, but was always my *means* to the victory, like the sword ("the sword of truth"). The truth is dead, a letter, a word, a material that I can use up. All truth by itself is dead, a corpse; it is alive only in the same way as my lungs are alive—to wit, in the measure of my own vitality. Truths are material, like vegetables and weeds; as to whether vegetable or weed, the decision lies in me.

Objects are to me only material that I use up. Wherever I put my hand I grasp a truth, which I trim for myself. The truth is certain to me, and I do not need to long after it. To do the truth a service is in no case my intent; it is to me only a nourishment for my thinking head, as potatoes are for my digesting stomach, or as a friend is for my social heart. As long as I have the humor and force for thinking, every truth serves me only for me to work it up according to my powers. As reality or worldliness is "vain and a thing of naught" for Christians, so is the truth for me. It exists, exactly as much as the things of this world go on existing although the Christian has proved their nothingness; but it is vain, because it has its *value* not *in itself* but *in me*. *Of itself* it is *valueless*. The truth is a—*creature*.

As you produce innumerable things by your activity, yes, shape the earth's surface anew and set up works of men everywhere, so too you may still ascertain numberless truths by your thinking, and we will gladly take delight in them. Nevertheless, as I do not please to hand myself over to serve your newly discovered machines mechanically, but only help to set them running for my benefit, so too I will only use your truths, without letting myself be used for their demands.

All truths *beneath* me are to my liking; a truth *above* me, a truth that I should have to *direct* myself by, I am not acquainted with. For me there is no truth, for nothing is more than I! Not even my essence, not even the essence of man, is more than I! than I, this "drop in the bucket," this "insignificant man"!

You believe that you have done the utmost when you boldly assert that, because every time has its own truth, there is no "absolute truth." Why, with this you nevertheless still leave to each time its truth, and thus you quite genuinely create an "absolute truth," a truth that no time lacks, because every time, however its truth may be, still has a "truth."

Is it meant only that people have been thinking in every time, and so have had thoughts or truths, and that in the subsequent time these were other than they were in the earlier? No, the word is to be that every time had its "truth of faith"; and in fact none has yet appeared in which a "higher truth" has not been recognized, a truth that people believed they must subject themselves to as "highness and majesty." Every truth of a time is its fixed idea, and, if people later found another truth, this always happened only because they sought for another; they only reformed the folly and put a modern dress on it. For they did want—who would dare doubt their justification for this?—they wanted to be "inspired by an idea." They wanted to be dominated—possessed, by a *thought*! The most modern ruler of this kind is "our essence," or "man."

For all free criticism a thought was the criterion; for own criticism I am, I the unspeakable, and so not the merely thought-of; for what is merely thought of is always speakable, because word and thought coincide. That is true which is mine, untrue that whose own I am; true, as in the union; untrue, the State and society. "Free and true" criticism takes care for the consistent dominion of a thought, an idea, a spirit; "own" criticism, for nothing but my *self-enjoyment*. But in this the latter is in fact—and we will not spare it this "ignominy"!—like the bestial criticism of instinct. I, like the criticizing beast, am concerned only for *myself*, not "for the cause." I am the criterion of truth, but I am not an idea, but more than idea, that is, unutterable.

My criticism is not a "free" criticism, not free from me, and not "servile," not in the service of an idea, but an *own* criticism.

True or human criticism makes out only whether something is *suitable* to man, to the true man; but by own criticism you ascertain whether it is suitable to *you.*

Free criticism busies itself with *ideas,* and therefore is always theoretical. However it may rage against ideas, it still does not get clear of them. It pitches into the ghosts, but it can do this only as it holds them to be ghosts. The ideas it has to do with do not fully disappear; the morning breeze of a new day does not scare them away.

The critic may indeed come to ataraxia before ideas, but he never gets *rid* of them; he will never comprehend that above the *bodily man* there does not exist something higher—to wit, liberty, his humanity, etc. He always has a "calling" of man still left, "humanity." And this idea of humanity remains unrealized, just because it is an "idea" and is to remain such.

If, on the other hand, I grasp the idea as *my* idea, then it is already realized, because I am its reality; its reality consists in the fact that I, the bodily, have it.

They say, the idea of liberty realizes itself in the history of the world. The reverse is the case; this idea is real as a man thinks it, and it is real in the measure in which it is idea, that is, in which I think it or *have* it. It is not the idea of liberty that develops itself, but men develop themselves, and, of course, in this self-development develop their thinking too.

In short, the critic is not yet *owner,* because he still fights with ideas as with powerful aliens—as the Christian is not owner of his "bad desires" so long as he has to combat them; for him who contends against vice, vice *exists.*

Criticism remains stuck fast in the "freedom of knowing," the freedom of the spirit, and the spirit gains its proper freedom when it fills itself with the pure, true idea; this is the freedom of thinking, which cannot be without thoughts.

Criticism smites one idea only by another, such as that of privilege by that of manhood, or that of egoism by that of unselfishness.

In general, the beginning of Christianity comes on the stage again in its critical end, egoism being combated here as there. I am not to make myself (the individual) count, but the idea, the general.

Why, warfare of the priesthood with *egoism,* of the spiritually-minded with the worldly-minded, constitutes the substance of all Christian history. In the newest criticism this war only becomes all-embracing, fanaticism complete. Indeed, neither can it pass away till it passes thus, after it has had its life and its rage out.

Whether what I think and do is Christian, what do I care? Whether it is human, liberal, humane, whether unhuman, illiberal, inhuman, what do I ask about that? If only it accomplishes what I want, if only I satisfy myself in it, then overlay it with predicates as you will; it is all alike to me.

Perhaps I too, in the very next moment, defend myself against my former thoughts; I too am likely to change suddenly my mode of action; but not on account of its not corresponding to Christianity, not on account of its running counter to the eternal rights of man, not on account of its affronting the idea of mankind, humanity, and humanitarianism, but—because I am no longer all in it, because it no longer furnishes me any full enjoyment, because I doubt the earlier thought or no longer please myself in the mode of action just now practiced.

As the world as property has become a *material* with which I undertake what I will, so the spirit too as property must sink down into a *material* before which I no longer entertain any sacred dread. Then, firstly, I shall shudder no more before a thought, let it appear as presumptuous and "devilish" as it will, because, if it threatens to become too inconvenient and unsatisfactory for *me,* its end lies in my power; but neither shall I recoil from any deed because there dwells in it a spirit of godlessness, immorality, wrongfulness, as little as St. Boniface pleased to desist, through religious scrupulousness, from cutting down the sacred oak of the heathens. If the *things* of the world have once become vain, the thoughts of the spirit must also become vain.

No thought is sacred, for let no thought rank as "devotions";[153] no feeling is sacred (no sacred feeling of friendship, mother's feelings, etc.), no belief is sacred. They are all *alienable,* my alienable property, and are annihilated, as they are created, by *me.*

The Christian can lose all *things* or objects, the most loved persons, these "objects" of his love, without giving up himself (that is, in the Christian sense, his spirit, his soul) as lost. The owner can cast from him all the *thoughts* that were dear to his heart and kindled his zeal, and will likewise "gain a thousandfold again," because he, their creator, remains.

Unconsciously and involuntarily we all strive toward ownness, and there will hardly be one among us who has not given up a sacred feeling, a sacred thought, a sacred belief; nay, we probably meet no one who could not still deliver himself from one or another of his sacred thoughts. All our contention against convictions starts from the opinion that maybe we are capable of driving our opponent out of his intrenchments of thought. But what I do unconsciously I half-do, and therefore after every victory over a faith I become again the *prisoner* (possessed) of a faith which then takes my whole self anew into its *service,* and makes me an enthusiast for reason after I have ceased to be enthusiastic for the Bible, or an enthusiast for the idea of humanity after I have fought long enough for that of Christianity.

Doubtless, as owner of thoughts, I shall cover my property with my shield, just as I do not, as owner of things, willingly let everybody help himself to them; but at the same time I shall look forward smilingly to the outcome of the battle, smilingly lay the shield on the corpses of my thoughts and my faith, smilingly triumph when I am beaten. That is the very humor of the thing. Every one who has "sublimer feelings" is able to vent his humor on the pettinesses of men; but to let it play with all "great thoughts, sublime feelings, noble inspiration, and sacred faith" presupposes that I am the owner of all.

153. (*Andacht,* a compound form of the word "thought.")

If religion has set up the proposition that we are sinners altogether, I set over against it the other: we are perfect altogether! For we are, every moment, all that we can be; and we never need be more. Since no defect cleaves to us, sin has no meaning either. Show me a sinner in the world still, if no one any longer needs to do what suits a superior! If I only need do what suits myself, I am no sinner if I do not do what suits myself, as I do not injure in myself a "holy one"; if, on the other hand, I am to be pious, then I must do what suits God; if I am to act humanly, I must do what suits the essence of man, the idea of mankind, etc. What religion calls the "sinner," humanitarianism calls the "egoist." But, once more: if I need not do what suits any other, is the "egoist," in whom humanitarianism has borne to itself a new-fangled devil, anything more than a piece of nonsense? The egoist, before whom the humane shudder, is a spook as much as the devil is: he exists only as a bogie and phantasm in their brain. If they were not unsophisticatedly drifting back and forth in the antediluvian opposition of good and evil, to which they have given the modern names of "human" and "egoistic," they would not have freshened up the hoary "sinner" into an "egoist" either, and put a new patch on an old garment. But they could not do otherwise, for they hold it for their task to be "men." They are rid of the Good One; good is left![154]

We are perfect altogether, and on the whole earth there is not one man who is a sinner! There are crazy people who imagine that they are God the Father, God the Son, or the man in the moon, and so too the world swarms with fools who seem to themselves to be sinners; but, as the former are not the man in the moon, so the latter are—not sinners. Their sin is imaginary.

Yet, it is insidiously objected, their craziness or their possessedness is at least their sin. Their possessedness is nothing but what they—could achieve, the result of their development, just as Luther's faith in the Bible was all that he was—competent to make out. The one brings himself into the madhouse with

154. (See note 84, second chapter.)

his development, the other brings himself therewith into the Pantheon and to the loss of—Valhalla.

There is no sinner and no sinful egoism!

Get away from me with your "philanthropy"! Creep in, you philanthropist, into the "dens of vice," linger awhile in the throng of the great city: will you not everywhere find sin, and sin, and again sin? Will you not wail over corrupt humanity, not lament at the monstrous egoism? Will you see a rich man without finding him pitiless and "egoistic?" Perhaps you already call yourself an atheist, but you remain true to the Christian feeling that a camel will sooner go through a needle's eye than a rich man not be an "un-man." How many do you see anyhow that you would not throw into the "egoistic mass"? What, therefore, has your philanthropy (love of man) found? Nothing but unlovable men! And where do they all come from? From you, from your philanthropy! You brought the sinner with you in your head, therefore you found him, therefore you inserted him everywhere. Do not call men sinners, and they are not: you alone are the creator of sinners; you, who fancy that you love men, are the very one to throw them into the mire of sin, the very one to divide them into vicious and virtuous, into men and un-men, the very one to befoul them with the slaver of your possessedness; for you love not *men*, but *man*. But I tell you, you have never seen a sinner, you have only—dreamed of him.

Self-enjoyment is embittered to me by my thinking I must serve another, by my fancying myself under obligation to him, by my holding myself called to "self-sacrifice," "resignation," "enthusiasm." All right: if I no longer serve any idea, any "higher essence," then it is clear of itself that I no longer serve any man either, but—under all circumstances—*myself*. But thus I am not merely in fact or in being, but also for my consciousness, the—unique.[155]

There pertains to *you* more than the divine, the human, etc.; *yours* pertains to you.

Look upon yourself as more powerful than they give you

155. (*Einzige*)

out for, and you have more power; look upon yourself as more, and you have more.

You are then not merely *called* to everything divine, *entitled* to everything human, but *owner* of what is yours, that is, of all that you possess the force to make your own;[156] you are *appropriate*[157] and capacitated for everything that is yours.

People have always supposed that they must give me a destiny lying outside myself, so that at last they demanded that I should lay claim to the human because I am—man. This is the Christian magic circle. Fichte's ego too is the same essence outside me, for every one is ego; and, if only this ego has rights, then it is "the ego," it is not I. But I am not an ego along with other egos, but the sole ego: I am unique. Hence my wants too are unique, and my deeds; in short, everything about me is unique. And it is only as this unique I that I take everything for my own, as I set myself to work, and develop myself, only as this. I do not develop men, nor as man, but, as I, I develop—myself.

This is the meaning of the—*unique one*.

156. (*eigen*)
157. (*geeignet*)

V

The Unique One

PRE-CHRISTIAN and Christian times pursue opposite goals; the former wants to idealize the real, the latter to realize the ideal; the former seeks the "holy spirit," the latter the "glorified body." Hence the former closes with insensitiveness to the real, with "contempt for the world"; the latter will end with the casting off of the ideal, with "contempt for the spirit."

The opposition of the real and the ideal is an irreconcilable one, and the one can never become the other: if the ideal became the real, it would no longer be the ideal; and, if the real became the ideal, the ideal alone would be, but not at all the real. The opposition of the two is not to be vanquished otherwise than if some one annihilates both. Only in this *"some one,"* the third party, does the opposition find its end; otherwise idea and reality will ever fail to coincide. The idea cannot be so realized as to remain idea, but is realized only when it dies as idea; and it is the same with the real.

But now we have before us in the ancients adherents of the idea, in the moderns adherents of reality. Neither can get clear of the opposition, and both pine only, the one party for the spirit, and, when this craving of the ancient world seemed to be satisfied and this spirit to have come, the others immediately for the secularization of this spirit again, which must forever remain a "pious wish."

The pious wish of the ancients was *sanctity*, the pious wish of the moderns is *corporeity*. But, as antiquity had to go down if its longing was to be satisfied (for it consisted only in the longing), so too corporeity can never be attained within the ring of Christianness. As the trait of sanctification or purification goes through the old world (the washings, etc.), so that of incorporation goes through the Christian world: God plunges down into this world, becomes flesh, and wants to redeem it, that is, fill it with himself; but, since he is "the idea" or "the spirit," people (Hegel, for example) in the end introduce the idea into everything, into the world, and prove "that the idea is, that reason is, in everything." "Man" corresponds in the culture of to-day to what the heathen Stoics set up as "the wise man"; the latter, like the former, a—*fleshless* being. The unreal "wise man," this bodiless "holy one" of the Stoics, became a real person, a bodily "Holy One," in God *made flesh;* the unreal "man," the bodiless ego, will become real in the *corporeal ego,* in me.

There winds its way through Christianity the question about the "existence of God," which, taken up ever and ever again, gives testimony that the craving for existence, corporeity, personality, reality, was incessantly busying the heart because it never found a satisfying solution. At last the question about the existence of God fell, but only to rise up again in the proposition that the "divine" had existence (Feuerbach). But this too has no existence, and neither will the last refuge, that the "purely human" is realizable, afford shelter much longer. No idea has existence, for none is capable of corporeity. The scholastic contention of realism and nominalism has the same content; in short, this spins itself out through all Christian history, and cannot end *in* it.

The world of Christians is working at *realizing ideas* in the individual relations of life, the institutions and laws of the Church and the State; but they make resistance, and always keep back something unembodied (unrealizable). Nevertheless this embodiment is restlessly rushed after, no matter in what degree *corporeity* constantly fails to result.

For realities matter little to the realizer, but it matters everything that they be realizations of the idea. Hence he is ever examining anew whether the realized does in truth have the idea, its kernel, dwelling in it; and in testing the real he at the same time tests the idea, whether it is realizable as he thinks it, or is only thought by him incorrectly, and for that reason unfeasibly.

The Christian is no longer to care for family, State, etc.,

as *existences;* Christians are not to sacrifice themselves for these "divine things" like the ancients, but these are only to be utilized to make the *spirit alive* in them. The *real* family has become indifferent, and there is to arise out of it an *ideal* one which would then be the "truly real," a sacred family, blessed by God, or, according to the liberal way of thinking, a "rational" family. With the ancients, family, State, fatherland, is divine as a thing *extant;* with the moderns it is still awaiting divinity, as extant it is only sinful, earthly, and has still to be "redeemed," that is, to become truly real. This has the following meaning: The family, etc., is not the extant and real, but the divine, the idea, is extant and real; whether *this* family will make itself real by taking up the truly real, the idea, is still unsetted. It is not the individual's task to serve the family as the divine, but, reversely, to serve the divine and to bring to it the still undivine family, to subject everything in the idea's name, to set up the idea's banner everywhere, to bring the idea to real efficacy.

But, since the concern of Christianity, as of antiquity, is for the *divine,* they always come out at this again on their opposite ways. At the end of heathenism the divine becomes the *extramundane,* at the end of Christianity the *intramundane.* Antiquity does not succeed in putting it entirely outside the world, and, when Christianity accomplishes this task, the divine instantly longs to get back into the world and wants to "redeem" the world. But within Christianity it does not and cannot come to this, that the divine as *intramundane* should really become the *mundane itself:* there is enough left that does and must maintain itself unpenetrated as the "bad," irrational, accidental, "egoistic," the "mundane" in the bad sense. Christianity begins with God's becoming man, and carries on its work of conversion and redemption through all time in order to prepare for God a reception in all men and in everything human, and to penetrate everything with the spirit: it sticks to preparing a place for the "spirit."

When the accent was at last laid on Man or mankind, it was again the idea that they *"pronounced eternal."* "Man does not die!" They thought they had now found the reality of the idea: *Man* is the I of history, of the world's history; it is he, this *ideal,* that really develops, *realizes,* himself. He is the really real and corporeal one, for history is his body, in which individuals are only members. Christ is the I of the world's history, even of the pre-Christian; in modern apprehension it is man, the figure of Christ has developed into the *figure of man:* man as such, man absolutely, is the "central point" of history. In "man" the imaginary beginning returns again; for "man" is as imaginary as Christ is. "Man," as the I of the world's history, closes the cycle of Christian apprehensions.

Christianity's magic circle would be broken if the strained relation between existence and calling, that is, between me as I am and me as I should be, ceased; it persists only as the longing of the idea for its bodiliness, and vanishes with the relaxing separation of the two: only when the idea remains—idea, as man or mankind is indeed a bodiless idea, is Christianity still extant. The corporeal idea, the corporeal or "completed" spirit, floats before the Christian as "the end of the days" or as the "goal of history"; it is not present time to him.

The individual can only have a part in the founding of the Kingdom of God, or, according to the modern notion of the same thing, in the development and history of humanity; and only so far as he has a part in it does a Christian, or according to the modern expression human, value pertain to him; for the rest he is dust and a worm-bag.

That the individual is of himself a world's history, and possesses his property in the rest of the world's history, goes beyond what is Christian. To the Christian the world's history is the higher thing, because it is the history of Christ or "man"; to the egoist only *his* history has value, because he wants to develop only *himself* not the mankind-idea, not God's plan, not the purposes of Providence, not liberty, and the like. He does not look upon himself as a tool of the idea or a vessel of God, he recognizes no calling, he does not fancy that he exists for the further development of mankind and that he must contribute his mite to it, but he lives himself out, careless of how well or ill humanity may fare thereby. If it were not open to confusion with the idea that a state of nature is to be praised, one might

recall Lenau's *Three Gypsies*.[1] What, am I in the world to realize
ideas? To do my part by my citizenship, say, toward the realization
of the idea "State," or by marriage, as husband and father, to
bring the idea of the family into an existence? What does such
a calling concern me! I live after a calling as little as the flower
grows and gives fragrance after a calling.

The ideal "Man" is *realized* when the Christian apprehension
turns about and becomes the proposition, "I, this unique one, am
man." The conceptual question, "what is man?"—has then
changed into the personal question, "who is man?" With "what"
the concept was sought for, in order to realize it; with "who" it is
no longer any question at all, but the answer is personally on
hand at once in the asker: the question answers itself.

They say of God, "Names name thee not." That holds good
of me: no *concept* expresses me, nothing that is designated as my
essence exhausts me; they are only names. Likewise they say of
God that he is perfect and has no calling to strive after perfection.
That too holds good of me alone.

I am *owner* of my might, and I am so when I know myself
as *unique*. In the *unique one* the owner himself returns into his
creative nothing, of which he is born. Every higher essence above
me, be it God, be it man, weakens the feeling of my uniqueness,
and pales only before the sun of this consciousness. If I concern
myself for myself,[2] the unique one, then my concern rests on its
transitory, mortal creator, who consumes himself, and I may say:

All things are nothing to me.[3]

1. [A story by Nicholaus Lenau, the pseudonym of Nicolaus Franz
Niembsch von Strehlenau (1802-1850). There is an immense volume of
comment and criticism pertaining to his poetry and stories.]

2. (*Stell' Ich auf Mich meine Sache.* Literally, "if I set my affair on
myself.")

3. (*"Ich hab' Mein' Sach' auf Nichts gestellt."* Literally, "I have set
my affair on nothing." See note on page 3.)

A CATALOG OF SELECTED DOVER
BOOKS IN ALL FIELDS OF INTEREST

CONCERNING THE SPIRITUAL IN ART, Wassily Kandinsky. Pioneering work by father of abstract art. Thoughts on color theory, nature of art. Analysis of earlier masters. 12 illustrations. 80pp. of text. 5⅜ x 8½. 23411-8

ANIMALS: 1,419 Copyright-Free Illustrations of Mammals, Birds, Fish, Insects, etc., Jim Harter (ed.). Clear wood engravings present, in extremely lifelike poses, over 1,000 species of animals. One of the most extensive pictorial sourcebooks of its kind. Captions. Index. 284pp. 9 x 12. 23766-4

CELTIC ART: The Methods of Construction, George Bain. Simple geometric techniques for making Celtic interlacements, spirals, Kells-type initials, animals, humans, etc. Over 500 illustrations. 160pp. 9 x 12. (Available in U.S. only.) 22923-8

AN ATLAS OF ANATOMY FOR ARTISTS, Fritz Schider. Most thorough reference work on art anatomy in the world. Hundreds of illustrations, including selections from works by Vesalius, Leonardo, Goya, Ingres, Michelangelo, others. 593 illustrations. 192pp. 7⅛ x 10¼. 20241-0

CELTIC HAND STROKE-BY-STROKE (Irish Half-Uncial from "The Book of Kells"): An Arthur Baker Calligraphy Manual, Arthur Baker. Complete guide to creating each letter of the alphabet in distinctive Celtic manner. Covers hand position, strokes, pens, inks, paper, more. Illustrated. 48pp. 8¼ x 11. 24336-2

EASY ORIGAMI, John Montroll. Charming collection of 32 projects (hat, cup, pelican, piano, swan, many more) specially designed for the novice origami hobbyist. Clearly illustrated easy-to-follow instructions insure that even beginning papercrafters will achieve successful results. 48pp. 8¼ x 11. 27298-2

THE COMPLETE BOOK OF BIRDHOUSE CONSTRUCTION FOR WOODWORKERS, Scott D. Campbell. Detailed instructions, illustrations, tables. Also data on bird habitat and instinct patterns. Bibliography. 3 tables. 63 illustrations in 15 figures. 48pp. 5¼ x 8½. 24407-5

BLOOMINGDALE'S ILLUSTRATED 1886 CATALOG: Fashions, Dry Goods and Housewares, Bloomingdale Brothers. Famed merchants' extremely rare catalog depicting about 1,700 products: clothing, housewares, firearms, dry goods, jewelry, more. Invaluable for dating, identifying vintage items. Also, copyright-free graphics for artists, designers. Co-published with Henry Ford Museum & Greenfield Village. 160pp. 8¼ x 11. 25780-0

HISTORIC COSTUME IN PICTURES, Braun & Schneider. Over 1,450 costumed figures in clearly detailed engravings–from dawn of civilization to end of 19th century. Captions. Many folk costumes. 256pp. 8⅜ x 11¾. 23150-X

STICKLEY CRAFTSMAN FURNITURE CATALOGS, Gustav Stickley and L. & J. G. Stickley. Beautiful, functional furniture in two authentic catalogs from 1910. 594 illustrations, including 277 photos, show settles, rockers, armchairs, reclining chairs, bookcases, desks, tables. 183pp. 6½ x 9¼.   23838-5

AMERICAN LOCOMOTIVES IN HISTORIC PHOTOGRAPHS: 1858 to 1949, Ron Ziel (ed.). A rare collection of 126 meticulously detailed official photographs, called "builder portraits," of American locomotives that majestically chronicle the rise of steam locomotive power in America. Introduction. Detailed captions. xi+ 129pp. 9 x 12.   27393-8

AMERICA'S LIGHTHOUSES: An Illustrated History, Francis Ross Holland, Jr. Delightfully written, profusely illustrated fact-filled survey of over 200 American light-houses since 1716. History, anecdotes, technological advances, more. 240pp. 8 x 10¾.
25576-X

TOWARDS A NEW ARCHITECTURE, Le Corbusier. Pioneering manifesto by founder of "International School." Technical and aesthetic theories, views of industry, eco-nomics, relation of form to function, "mass-production split" and much more. Profusely illustrated. 320pp. 6⅛ x 9¼. (Available in U.S. only.)   25023-7

HOW THE OTHER HALF LIVES, Jacob Riis. Famous journalistic record, expos-ing poverty and degradation of New York slums around 1900, by major social reformer. 100 striking and influential photographs. 233pp. 10 x 7⅞.   22012-5

FRUIT KEY AND TWIG KEY TO TREES AND SHRUBS, William M. Harlow. One of the handiest and most widely used identification aids. Fruit key covers 120 deciduous and evergreen species; twig key 160 deciduous species. Easily used. Over 300 photographs. 126pp. 5⅜ x 8½.   20511-8

COMMON BIRD SONGS, Dr. Donald J. Borror. Songs of 60 most common U.S. birds: robins, sparrows, cardinals, bluejays, finches, more—arranged in order of increasing complexity. Up to 9 variations of songs of each species.
Cassette and manual 99911-4

ORCHIDS AS HOUSE PLANTS, Rebecca Tyson Northen. Grow cattleyas and many other kinds of orchids—in a window, in a case, or under artificial light. 63 illus-trations. 148pp. 5⅜ x 8½.   23261-1

MONSTER MAZES, Dave Phillips. Masterful mazes at four levels of difficulty. Avoid deadly perils and evil creatures to find magical treasures. Solutions for all 32 exciting illustrated puzzles. 48pp. 8¼ x 11.   26005-4

MOZART'S DON GIOVANNI (DOVER OPERA LIBRETTO SERIES), Wolfgang Amadeus Mozart. Introduced and translated by Ellen H. Bleiler. Standard Italian libretto, with complete English translation. Convenient and thoroughly portable—an ideal companion for reading along with a recording or the performance itself. Introduction. List of characters. Plot summary. 121pp. 5¼ x 8½.   24944-1

TECHNICAL MANUAL AND DICTIONARY OF CLASSICAL BALLET, Gail Grant. Defines, explains, comments on steps, movements, poses and concepts. 15-page pictorial section. Basic book for student, viewer. 127pp. 5⅜ x 8½.   21843-0

CATALOG OF DOVER BOOKS

THE CLARINET AND CLARINET PLAYING, David Pino. Lively, comprehensive work features suggestions about technique, musicianship, and musical interpretation, as well as guidelines for teaching, making your own reeds, and preparing for public performance. Includes an intriguing look at clarinet history. "A godsend," *The Clarinet*, Journal of the International Clarinet Society. Appendixes. 7 illus. 320pp. 5⅜ x 8½. 40270-3

HOLLYWOOD GLAMOR PORTRAITS, John Kobal (ed.). 145 photos from 1926-49. Harlow, Gable, Bogart, Bacall; 94 stars in all. Full background on photographers, technical aspects. 160pp. 8⅜ x 11¼. 23352-9

THE ANNOTATED CASEY AT THE BAT: A Collection of Ballads about the Mighty Casey/Third, Revised Edition, Martin Gardner (ed.). Amusing sequels and parodies of one of America's best-loved poems: Casey's Revenge, Why Casey Whiffed, Casey's Sister at the Bat, others. 256pp. 5⅜ x 8½. 28598-7

THE RAVEN AND OTHER FAVORITE POEMS, Edgar Allan Poe. Over 40 of the author's most memorable poems: "The Bells," "Ulalume," "Israfel," "To Helen," "The Conqueror Worm," "Eldorado," "Annabel Lee," many more. Alphabetic lists of titles and first lines. 64pp. 5³⁄₁₆ x 8¼. 26685-0

PERSONAL MEMOIRS OF U. S. GRANT, Ulysses Simpson Grant. Intelligent, deeply moving firsthand account of Civil War campaigns, considered by many the finest military memoirs ever written. Includes letters, historic photographs, maps and more. 528pp. 6⅛ x 9¼. 28587-1

ANCIENT EGYPTIAN MATERIALS AND INDUSTRIES, A. Lucas and J. Harris. Fascinating, comprehensive, thoroughly documented text describes this ancient civilization's vast resources and the processes that incorporated them in daily life, including the use of animal products, building materials, cosmetics, perfumes and incense, fibers, glazed ware, glass and its manufacture, materials used in the mummification process, and much more. 544pp. 6⅛ x 9¼. (Available in U.S. only.) 40446-3

RUSSIAN STORIES/RUSSKIE RASSKAZY: A Dual-Language Book, edited by Gleb Struve. Twelve tales by such masters as Chekhov, Tolstoy, Dostoevsky, Pushkin, others. Excellent word-for-word English translations on facing pages, plus teaching and study aids, Russian/English vocabulary, biographical/critical introductions, more. 416pp. 5⅜ x 8½. 26244-8

PHILADELPHIA THEN AND NOW: 60 Sites Photographed in the Past and Present, Kenneth Finkel and Susan Oyama. Rare photographs of City Hall, Logan Square, Independence Hall, Betsy Ross House, other landmarks juxtaposed with contemporary views. Captures changing face of historic city. Introduction. Captions. 128pp. 8¼ x 11. 25790-8

AIA ARCHITECTURAL GUIDE TO NASSAU AND SUFFOLK COUNTIES, LONG ISLAND, The American Institute of Architects, Long Island Chapter, and the Society for the Preservation of Long Island Antiquities. Comprehensive, well-researched and generously illustrated volume brings to life over three centuries of Long Island's great architectural heritage. More than 240 photographs with authoritative, extensively detailed captions. 176pp. 8¼ x 11. 26946-9

NORTH AMERICAN INDIAN LIFE: Customs and Traditions of 23 Tribes, Elsie Clews Parsons (ed.). 27 fictionalized essays by noted anthropologists examine religion, customs, government, additional facets of life among the Winnebago, Crow, Zuni, Eskimo, other tribes. 480pp. 6⅛ x 9¼. 27377-6

FRANK LLOYD WRIGHT'S DANA HOUSE, Donald Hoffmann. Pictorial essay of residential masterpiece with over 160 interior and exterior photos, plans, elevations, sketches and studies. 128pp. 9¼ x 10¾.   29120-0

THE MALE AND FEMALE FIGURE IN MOTION: 60 Classic Photographic Sequences, Eadweard Muybridge. 60 true-action photographs of men and women walking, running, climbing, bending, turning, etc., reproduced from rare 19th-century masterpiece. vi + 121pp. 9 x 12.   24745-7

1001 QUESTIONS ANSWERED ABOUT THE SEASHORE, N. J. Berrill and Jacquelyn Berrill. Queries answered about dolphins, sea snails, sponges, starfish, fishes, shore birds, many others. Covers appearance, breeding, growth, feeding, much more. 305pp. 5¼ x 8¼.   23366-9

ATTRACTING BIRDS TO YOUR YARD, William J. Weber. Easy-to-follow guide offers advice on how to attract the greatest diversity of birds: birdhouses, feeders, water and waterers, much more. 96pp. 5³⁄₁₆ x 8¼.   28927-3

MEDICINAL AND OTHER USES OF NORTH AMERICAN PLANTS: A Historical Survey with Special Reference to the Eastern Indian Tribes, Charlotte Erichsen-Brown. Chronological historical citations document 500 years of usage of plants, trees, shrubs native to eastern Canada, northeastern U.S. Also complete identifying information. 343 illustrations. 544pp. 6½ x 9¼.   25951-X

STORYBOOK MAZES, Dave Phillips. 23 stories and mazes on two-page spreads: Wizard of Oz, Treasure Island, Robin Hood, etc. Solutions. 64pp. 8¼ x 11. 23628-5

AMERICAN NEGRO SONGS: 230 Folk Songs and Spirituals, Religious and Secular, John W. Work. This authoritative study traces the African influences of songs sung and played by black Americans at work, in church, and as entertainment. The author discusses the lyric significance of such songs as "Swing Low, Sweet Chariot," "John Henry," and others and offers the words and music for 230 songs. Bibliography. Index of Song Titles. 272pp. 6½ x 9¼.   40271-1

MOVIE-STAR PORTRAITS OF THE FORTIES, John Kobal (ed.). 163 glamor, studio photos of 106 stars of the 1940s: Rita Hayworth, Ava Gardner, Marlon Brando, Clark Gable, many more. 176pp. 8⅜ x 11¼.   23546-7

BENCHLEY LOST AND FOUND, Robert Benchley. Finest humor from early 30s, about pet peeves, child psychologists, post office and others. Mostly unavailable elsewhere. 73 illustrations by Peter Arno and others. 183pp. 5⅜ x 8½.   22410-4

YEKL and THE IMPORTED BRIDEGROOM AND OTHER STORIES OF YIDDISH NEW YORK, Abraham Cahan. Film Hester Street based on Yekl (1896). Novel, other stories among first about Jewish immigrants on N.Y.'s East Side. 240pp. 5⅜ x 8½.   22427-9

SELECTED POEMS, Walt Whitman. Generous sampling from Leaves of Grass. Twenty-four poems include "I Hear America Singing," "Song of the Open Road," "I Sing the Body Electric," "When Lilacs Last in the Dooryard Bloom'd," "O Captain! My Captain!"—all reprinted from an authoritative edition. Lists of titles and first lines. 128pp. 5³⁄₁₆ x 8¼.   26878-0

THE BEST TALES OF HOFFMANN, E. T. A. Hoffmann. 10 of Hoffmann's most important stories: "Nutcracker and the King of Mice," "The Golden Flowerpot," etc. 458pp. 5⅜ x 8½. 21793-0

FROM FETISH TO GOD IN ANCIENT EGYPT, E. A. Wallis Budge. Rich detailed survey of Egyptian conception of "God" and gods, magic, cult of animals, Osiris, more. Also, superb English translations of hymns and legends. 240 illustrations. 545pp. 5⅜ x 8½. 25803-3

FRENCH STORIES/CONTES FRANÇAIS: A Dual-Language Book, Wallace Fowlie. Ten stories by French masters, Voltaire to Camus: "Micromegas" by Voltaire; "The Atheist's Mass" by Balzac; "Minuet" by de Maupassant; "The Guest" by Camus, six more. Excellent English translations on facing pages. Also French-English vocabulary list, exercises, more. 352pp. 5⅜ x 8½. 26443-2

CHICAGO AT THE TURN OF THE CENTURY IN PHOTOGRAPHS: 122 Historic Views from the Collections of the Chicago Historical Society, Larry A. Viskochil. Rare large-format prints offer detailed views of City Hall, State Street, the Loop, Hull House, Union Station, many other landmarks, circa 1904-1913. Introduction. Captions. Maps. 144pp. 9⅜ x 12¼. 24656-6

OLD BROOKLYN IN EARLY PHOTOGRAPHS, 1865-1929, William Lee Younger. Luna Park, Gravesend race track, construction of Grand Army Plaza, moving of Hotel Brighton, etc. 157 previously unpublished photographs. 165pp. 8⅞ x 11¾. 23587-4

THE MYTHS OF THE NORTH AMERICAN INDIANS, Lewis Spence. Rich anthology of the myths and legends of the Algonquins, Iroquois, Pawnees and Sioux, prefaced by an extensive historical and ethnological commentary. 36 illustrations. 480pp. 5⅜ x 8½. 25967-6

AN ENCYCLOPEDIA OF BATTLES: Accounts of Over 1,560 Battles from 1479 B.C. to the Present, David Eggenberger. Essential details of every major battle in recorded history from the first battle of Megiddo in 1479 B.C. to Grenada in 1984. List of Battle Maps. New Appendix covering the years 1967-1984. Index. 99 illustrations. 544pp. 6½ x 9¼. 24913-1

SAILING ALONE AROUND THE WORLD, Captain Joshua Slocum. First man to sail around the world, alone, in small boat. One of great feats of seamanship told in delightful manner. 67 illustrations. 294pp. 5⅜ x 8½. 20326-3

ANARCHISM AND OTHER ESSAYS, Emma Goldman. Powerful, penetrating, prophetic essays on direct action, role of minorities, prison reform, puritan hypocrisy, violence, etc. 271pp. 5⅜ x 8½. 22484-8

MYTHS OF THE HINDUS AND BUDDHISTS, Ananda K. Coomaraswamy and Sister Nivedita. Great stories of the epics; deeds of Krishna, Shiva, taken from puranas, Vedas, folk tales; etc. 32 illustrations. 400pp. 5⅜ x 8½. 21759-0

THE TRAUMA OF BIRTH, Otto Rank. Rank's controversial thesis that anxiety neurosis is caused by profound psychological trauma which occurs at birth. 256pp. 5⅜ x 8½. 27974-X

A THEOLOGICO-POLITICAL TREATISE, Benedict Spinoza. Also contains unfinished Political Treatise. Great classic on religious liberty, theory of government on common consent. R. Elwes translation. Total of 421pp. 5⅜ x 8½. 20249-6

MY BONDAGE AND MY FREEDOM, Frederick Douglass. Born a slave, Douglass became outspoken force in antislavery movement. The best of Douglass' autobiographies. Graphic description of slave life. 464pp. 5⅜ x 8½.　　　22457-0

FOLLOWING THE EQUATOR: A Journey Around the World, Mark Twain. Fascinating humorous account of 1897 voyage to Hawaii, Australia, India, New Zealand, etc. Ironic, bemused reports on peoples, customs, climate, flora and fauna, politics, much more. 197 illustrations. 720pp. 5⅜ x 8½.　　　26113-1

THE PEOPLE CALLED SHAKERS, Edward D. Andrews. Definitive study of Shakers: origins, beliefs, practices, dances, social organization, furniture and crafts, etc. 33 illustrations. 351pp. 5⅜ x 8½.　　　21081-2

THE MYTHS OF GREECE AND ROME, H. A. Guerber. A classic of mythology, generously illustrated, long prized for its simple, graphic, accurate retelling of the principal myths of Greece and Rome, and for its commentary on their origins and significance. With 64 illustrations by Michelangelo, Raphael, Titian, Rubens, Canova, Bernini and others. 480pp. 5⅜ x 8½.　　　27584-1

PSYCHOLOGY OF MUSIC, Carl E. Seashore. Classic work discusses music as a medium from psychological viewpoint. Clear treatment of physical acoustics, auditory apparatus, sound perception, development of musical skills, nature of musical feeling, host of other topics. 88 figures. 408pp. 5⅜ x 8½.　　　21851-1

THE PHILOSOPHY OF HISTORY, Georg W. Hegel. Great classic of Western thought develops concept that history is not chance but rational process, the evolution of freedom. 457pp. 5⅜ x 8½.　　　20112-0

THE BOOK OF TEA, Kakuzo Okakura. Minor classic of the Orient: entertaining, charming explanation, interpretation of traditional Japanese culture in terms of tea ceremony. 94pp. 5⅜ x 8½.　　　20070-1

LIFE IN ANCIENT EGYPT, Adolf Erman. Fullest, most thorough, detailed older account with much not in more recent books, domestic life, religion, magic, medicine, commerce, much more. Many illustrations reproduce tomb paintings, carvings, hieroglyphs, etc. 597pp. 5⅜ x 8½.　　　22632-8

SUNDIALS, Their Theory and Construction, Albert Waugh. Far and away the best, most thorough coverage of ideas, mathematics concerned, types, construction, adjusting anywhere. Simple, nontechnical treatment allows even children to build several of these dials. Over 100 illustrations. 230pp. 5⅜ x 8½.　　　22947-5

THEORETICAL HYDRODYNAMICS, L. M. Milne-Thomson. Classic exposition of the mathematical theory of fluid motion, applicable to both hydrodynamics and aerodynamics. Over 600 exercises. 768pp. 6⅛ x 9¼.　　　68970-0

SONGS OF EXPERIENCE: Facsimile Reproduction with 26 Plates in Full Color, William Blake. 26 full-color plates from a rare 1826 edition. Includes "The Tyger," "London," "Holy Thursday," and other poems. Printed text of poems. 48pp. 5¼ x 7.
24636-1

OLD-TIME VIGNETTES IN FULL COLOR, Carol Belanger Grafton (ed.). Over 390 charming, often sentimental illustrations, selected from archives of Victorian graphics—pretty women posing, children playing, food, flowers, kittens and puppies, smiling cherubs, birds and butterflies, much more. All copyright-free. 48pp. 9¼ x 12¼.
27269-9

PERSPECTIVE FOR ARTISTS, Rex Vicat Cole. Depth, perspective of sky and sea, shadows, much more, not usually covered. 391 diagrams, 81 reproductions of drawings and paintings. 279pp. 5⅜ x 8½. 22487-2

DRAWING THE LIVING FIGURE, Joseph Sheppard. Innovative approach to artistic anatomy focuses on specifics of surface anatomy, rather than muscles and bones. Over 170 drawings of live models in front, back and side views, and in widely varying poses. Accompanying diagrams. 177 illustrations. Introduction. Index. 144pp. 8⅜ x11¼. 26723-7

GOTHIC AND OLD ENGLISH ALPHABETS: 100 Complete Fonts, Dan X. Solo. Add power, elegance to posters, signs, other graphics with 100 stunning copyright-free alphabets: Blackstone, Dolbey, Germania, 97 more–including many lower-case, numerals, punctuation marks. 104pp. 8⅛ x 11. 24695-7

HOW TO DO BEADWORK, Mary White. Fundamental book on craft from simple projects to five-bead chains and woven works. 106 illustrations. 142pp. 5⅜ x 8. 20697-1

THE BOOK OF WOOD CARVING, Charles Marshall Sayers. Finest book for beginners discusses fundamentals and offers 34 designs. "Absolutely first rate . . . well thought out and well executed."–E. J. Tangerman. 118pp. 7¾ x 10⅝. 23654-4

ILLUSTRATED CATALOG OF CIVIL WAR MILITARY GOODS: Union Army Weapons, Insignia, Uniform Accessories, and Other Equipment, Schuyler, Hartley, and Graham. Rare, profusely illustrated 1846 catalog includes Union Army uniform and dress regulations, arms and ammunition, coats, insignia, flags, swords, rifles, etc. 226 illustrations. 160pp. 9 x 12. 24939-5

WOMEN'S FASHIONS OF THE EARLY 1900s: An Unabridged Republication of "New York Fashions, 1909," National Cloak & Suit Co. Rare catalog of mail-order fashions documents women's and children's clothing styles shortly after the turn of the century. Captions offer full descriptions, prices. Invaluable resource for fashion, costume historians. Approximately 725 illustrations. 128pp. 8⅜ x 11¼. 27276-1

THE 1912 AND 1915 GUSTAV STICKLEY FURNITURE CATALOGS, Gustav Stickley. With over 200 detailed illustrations and descriptions, these two catalogs are essential reading and reference materials and identification guides for Stickley furniture. Captions cite materials, dimensions and prices. 112pp. 6½ x 9¼. 26676-1

EARLY AMERICAN LOCOMOTIVES, John H. White, Jr. Finest locomotive engravings from early 19th century: historical (1804–74), main-line (after 1870), special, foreign, etc. 147 plates. 142pp. 11⅜ x 8¼. 22772-3

THE TALL SHIPS OF TODAY IN PHOTOGRAPHS, Frank O. Braynard. Lavishly illustrated tribute to nearly 100 majestic contemporary sailing vessels: Amerigo Vespucci, Clearwater, Constitution, Eagle, Mayflower, Sea Cloud, Victory, many more. Authoritative captions provide statistics, background on each ship. 190 black-and-white photographs and illustrations. Introduction. 128pp. 8⅞ x 11¾. 27163-3

LITTLE BOOK OF EARLY AMERICAN CRAFTS AND TRADES, Peter Stockham (ed.). 1807 children's book explains crafts and trades: baker, hatter, cooper, potter, and many others. 23 copperplate illustrations. 140pp. 4⅝ x 6. 23336-7

VICTORIAN FASHIONS AND COSTUMES FROM HARPER'S BAZAR, 1867–1898, Stella Blum (ed.). Day costumes, evening wear, sports clothes, shoes, hats, other accessories in over 1,000 detailed engravings. 320pp. 9⅜ x 12¼. 22990-4

GUSTAV STICKLEY, THE CRAFTSMAN, Mary Ann Smith. Superb study surveys broad scope of Stickley's achievement, especially in architecture. Design philosophy, rise and fall of the Craftsman empire, descriptions and floor plans for many Craftsman houses, more. 86 black-and-white halftones. 31 line illustrations. Introduction 208pp. 6½ x 9¼. 27210-9

THE LONG ISLAND RAIL ROAD IN EARLY PHOTOGRAPHS, Ron Ziel. Over 220 rare photos, informative text document origin (1844) and development of rail service on Long Island. Vintage views of early trains, locomotives, stations, passengers, crews, much more. Captions. 8⅞ x 11¾. 26301-0

VOYAGE OF THE LIBERDADE, Joshua Slocum. Great 19th-century mariner's thrilling, first-hand account of the wreck of his ship off South America, the 35-foot boat he built from the wreckage, and its remarkable voyage home. 128pp. 5⅜ x 8½. 40022-0

TEN BOOKS ON ARCHITECTURE, Vitruvius. The most important book ever written on architecture. Early Roman aesthetics, technology, classical orders, site selection, all other aspects. Morgan translation. 331pp. 5⅜ x 8½. 20645-9

THE HUMAN FIGURE IN MOTION, Eadweard Muybridge. More than 4,500 stopped-action photos, in action series, showing undraped men, women, children jumping, lying down, throwing, sitting, wrestling, carrying, etc. 390pp. 7⅞ x 10⅝. 20204-6 Clothbd.

TREES OF THE EASTERN AND CENTRAL UNITED STATES AND CANADA, William M. Harlow. Best one-volume guide to 140 trees. Full descriptions, woodlore, range, etc. Over 600 illustrations. Handy size. 288pp. 4½ x 6⅜. 20395-6

SONGS OF WESTERN BIRDS, Dr. Donald J. Borror. Complete song and call repertoire of 60 western species, including flycatchers, juncoes, cactus wrens, many more–includes fully illustrated booklet. Cassette and manual 99913-0

GROWING AND USING HERBS AND SPICES, Milo Miloradovich. Versatile handbook provides all the information needed for cultivation and use of all the herbs and spices available in North America. 4 illustrations. Index. Glossary. 236pp. 5⅜ x 8½. 25058-X

BIG BOOK OF MAZES AND LABYRINTHS, Walter Shepherd. 50 mazes and labyrinths in all–classical, solid, ripple, and more–in one great volume. Perfect inexpensive puzzler for clever youngsters. Full solutions. 112pp. 8⅛ x 11. 22951-3

PIANO TUNING, J. Cree Fischer. Clearest, best book for beginner, amateur. Simple repairs, raising dropped notes, tuning by easy method of flattened fifths. No previous skills needed. 4 illustrations. 201pp. 5⅜ x 8½. 23267-0

HINTS TO SINGERS, Lillian Nordica. Selecting the right teacher, developing confidence, overcoming stage fright, and many other important skills receive thoughtful discussion in this indispensible guide, written by a world-famous diva of four decades' experience. 96pp. 5⅜ x 8½. 40094-8

THE COMPLETE NONSENSE OF EDWARD LEAR, Edward Lear. All nonsense limericks, zany alphabets, Owl and Pussycat, songs, nonsense botany, etc., illustrated by Lear. Total of 320pp. 5⅜ x 8½. (Available in U.S. only.) 20167-8

VICTORIAN PARLOUR POETRY: An Annotated Anthology, Michael R. Turner. 117 gems by Longfellow, Tennyson, Browning, many lesser-known poets. "The Village Blacksmith," "Curfew Must Not Ring Tonight," "Only a Baby Small," dozens more, often difficult to find elsewhere. Index of poets, titles, first lines. xxiii + 325pp. 5⅜ x 8¼. 27044-0

DUBLINERS, James Joyce. Fifteen stories offer vivid, tightly focused observations of the lives of Dublin's poorer classes. At least one, "The Dead," is considered a masterpiece. Reprinted complete and unabridged from standard edition. 160pp. 5$\frac{3}{16}$ x 8¼. 26870-5

GREAT WEIRD TALES: 14 Stories by Lovecraft, Blackwood, Machen and Others, S. T. Joshi (ed.). 14 spellbinding tales, including "The Sin Eater," by Fiona McLeod, "The Eye Above the Mantel," by Frank Belknap Long, as well as renowned works by R. H. Barlow, Lord Dunsany, Arthur Machen, W. C. Morrow and eight other masters of the genre. 256pp. 5⅜ x 8½. (Available in U.S. only.) 40436-6

THE BOOK OF THE SACRED MAGIC OF ABRAMELIN THE MAGE, translated by S. MacGregor Mathers. Medieval manuscript of ceremonial magic. Basic document in Aleister Crowley, Golden Dawn groups. 268pp. 5⅜ x 8½. 23211-5

NEW RUSSIAN-ENGLISH AND ENGLISH-RUSSIAN DICTIONARY, M. A. O'Brien. This is a remarkably handy Russian dictionary, containing a surprising amount of information, including over 70,000 entries. 366pp. 4½ x 6⅛. 20208-9

HISTORIC HOMES OF THE AMERICAN PRESIDENTS, Second, Revised Edition, Irvin Haas. A traveler's guide to American Presidential homes, most open to the public, depicting and describing homes occupied by every American President from George Washington to George Bush. With visiting hours, admission charges, travel routes. 175 photographs. Index. 160pp. 8¼ x 11. 26751-2

NEW YORK IN THE FORTIES, Andreas Feininger. 162 brilliant photographs by the well-known photographer, formerly with *Life* magazine. Commuters, shoppers, Times Square at night, much else from city at its peak. Captions by John von Hartz. 181pp. 9¼ x 10¾. 23585-8

INDIAN SIGN LANGUAGE, William Tomkins. Over 525 signs developed by Sioux and other tribes. Written instructions and diagrams. Also 290 pictographs. 111pp. 6⅛ x 9¼. 22029-X

ANATOMY: A Complete Guide for Artists, Joseph Sheppard. A master of figure drawing shows artists how to render human anatomy convincingly. Over 460 illustrations. 224pp. 8⅜ x 11¼. 27279-6

MEDIEVAL CALLIGRAPHY: Its History and Technique, Marc Drogin. Spirited history, comprehensive instruction manual covers 13 styles (ca. 4th century through 15th). Excellent photographs; directions for duplicating medieval techniques with modern tools. 224pp. 8⅜ x 11¼. 26142-5

DRIED FLOWERS: How to Prepare Them, Sarah Whitlock and Martha Rankin. Complete instructions on how to use silica gel, meal and borax, perlite aggregate, sand and borax, glycerine and water to create attractive permanent flower arrangements. 12 illustrations. 32pp. 5⅜ x 8½. 21802-3

EASY-TO-MAKE BIRD FEEDERS FOR WOODWORKERS, Scott D. Campbell. Detailed, simple-to-use guide for designing, constructing, caring for and using feeders. Text, illustrations for 12 classic and contemporary designs. 96pp. 5⅜ x 8½.
25847-5

SCOTTISH WONDER TALES FROM MYTH AND LEGEND, Donald A. Mackenzie. 16 lively tales tell of giants rumbling down mountainsides, of a magic wand that turns stone pillars into warriors, of gods and goddesses, evil hags, powerful forces and more. 240pp. 5⅜ x 8½. 29677-6

THE HISTORY OF UNDERCLOTHES, C. Willett Cunnington and Phyllis Cunnington. Fascinating, well-documented survey covering six centuries of English undergarments, enhanced with over 100 illustrations: 12th-century laced-up bodice, footed long drawers (1795), 19th-century bustles, l9th-century corsets for men, Victorian "bust improvers," much more. 272pp. 5⅜ x 8¼. 27124-2

ARTS AND CRAFTS FURNITURE: The Complete Brooks Catalog of 1912, Brooks Manufacturing Co. Photos and detailed descriptions of more than 150 now very collectible furniture designs from the Arts and Crafts movement depict davenports, settees, buffets, desks, tables, chairs, bedsteads, dressers and more, all built of solid, quarter-sawed oak. Invaluable for students and enthusiasts of antiques, Americana and the decorative arts. 80pp. 6½ x 9¼. 27471-3

WILBUR AND ORVILLE: A Biography of the Wright Brothers, Fred Howard. Definitive, crisply written study tells the full story of the brothers' lives and work. A vividly written biography, unparalleled in scope and color, that also captures the spirit of an extraordinary era. 560pp. 6⅛ x 9¼. 40297-5

THE ARTS OF THE SAILOR: Knotting, Splicing and Ropework, Hervey Garrett Smith. Indispensable shipboard reference covers tools, basic knots and useful hitches; handsewing and canvas work, more. Over 100 illustrations. Delightful reading for sea lovers. 256pp. 5⅜ x 8½. 26440-8

FRANK LLOYD WRIGHT'S FALLINGWATER: The House and Its History, Second, Revised Edition, Donald Hoffmann. A total revision—both in text and illustrations—of the standard document on Fallingwater, the boldest, most personal architectural statement of Wright's mature years, updated with valuable new material from the recently opened Frank Lloyd Wright Archives. "Fascinating"—*The New York Times.* 116 illustrations. 128pp. 9¼ x 10¾. 27430-6

CATALOG OF DOVER BOOKS

PHOTOGRAPHIC SKETCHBOOK OF THE CIVIL WAR, Alexander Gardner. 100 photos taken on field during the Civil War. Famous shots of Manassas Harper's Ferry, Lincoln, Richmond, slave pens, etc. 244pp. 10⅞ x 8¼.   22731-6

FIVE ACRES AND INDEPENDENCE, Maurice G. Kains. Great back-to-the-land classic explains basics of self-sufficient farming. The one book to get. 95 illustrations. 397pp. 5⅜ x 8½.   20974-1

SONGS OF EASTERN BIRDS, Dr. Donald J. Borror. Songs and calls of 60 species most common to eastern U.S.: warblers, woodpeckers, flycatchers, thrushes, larks, many more in high-quality recording.   Cassette and manual 99912-2

A MODERN HERBAL, Margaret Grieve. Much the fullest, most exact, most useful compilation of herbal material. Gigantic alphabetical encyclopedia, from aconite to zedoary, gives botanical information, medical properties, folklore, economic uses, much else. Indispensable to serious reader. 161 illustrations. 888pp. 6½ x 9¼. 2-vol. set. (Available in U.S. only.)   Vol. I: 22798-7
Vol. II: 22799-5

HIDDEN TREASURE MAZE BOOK, Dave Phillips. Solve 34 challenging mazes accompanied by heroic tales of adventure. Evil dragons, people-eating plants, blood-thirsty giants, many more dangerous adversaries lurk at every twist and turn. 34 mazes, stories, solutions. 48pp. 8¼ x 11.   24566-7

LETTERS OF W. A. MOZART, Wolfgang A. Mozart. Remarkable letters show bawdy wit, humor, imagination, musical insights, contemporary musical world; includes some letters from Leopold Mozart. 276pp. 5⅜ x 8½.   22859-2

BASIC PRINCIPLES OF CLASSICAL BALLET, Agrippina Vaganova. Great Russian theoretician, teacher explains methods for teaching classical ballet. 118 illustrations. 175pp. 5⅜ x 8½.   22036-2

THE JUMPING FROG, Mark Twain. Revenge edition. The original story of The Celebrated Jumping Frog of Calaveras County, a hapless French translation, and Twain's hilarious "retranslation" from the French. 12 illustrations. 66pp. 5⅜ x 8½.   22686-7

BEST REMEMBERED POEMS, Martin Gardner (ed.). The 126 poems in this superb collection of 19th- and 20th-century British and American verse range from Shelley's "To a Skylark" to the impassioned "Renascence" of Edna St. Vincent Millay and to Edward Lear's whimsical "The Owl and the Pussycat." 224pp. 5⅜ x 8½.   27165-X

COMPLETE SONNETS, William Shakespeare. Over 150 exquisite poems deal with love, friendship, the tyranny of time, beauty's evanescence, death and other themes in language of remarkable power, precision and beauty. Glossary of archaic terms. 80pp. 5³⁄₁₆ x 8¼.   26686-9

THE BATTLES THAT CHANGED HISTORY, Fletcher Pratt. Eminent historian profiles 16 crucial conflicts, ancient to modern, that changed the course of civilization. 352pp. 5⅜ x 8½.   41129-X

THE WIT AND HUMOR OF OSCAR WILDE, Alvin Redman (ed.). More than 1,000 ripostes, paradoxes, wisecracks: Work is the curse of the drinking classes; I can resist everything except temptation; etc. 258pp. 5⅜ x 8½. 20602-5

SHAKESPEARE LEXICON AND QUOTATION DICTIONARY, Alexander Schmidt. Full definitions, locations, shades of meaning in every word in plays and poems. More than 50,000 exact quotations. 1,485pp. 6½ x 9¼. 2-vol. set.
Vol. 1: 22726-X
Vol. 2: 22727-8

SELECTED POEMS, Emily Dickinson. Over 100 best-known, best-loved poems by one of America's foremost poets, reprinted from authoritative early editions. No comparable edition at this price. Index of first lines. 64pp. 5³⁄₁₆ x 8¼. 26466-1

THE INSIDIOUS DR. FU-MANCHU, Sax Rohmer. The first of the popular mystery series introduces a pair of English detectives to their archnemesis, the diabolical Dr. Fu-Manchu. Flavorful atmosphere, fast-paced action, and colorful characters enliven this classic of the genre. 208pp. 5³⁄₁₆ x 8¼. 29898-1

THE MALLEUS MALEFICARUM OF KRAMER AND SPRENGER, translated by Montague Summers. Full text of most important witchhunter's "bible," used by both Catholics and Protestants. 278pp. 6⅝ x 10. 22802-9

SPANISH STORIES/CUENTOS ESPAÑOLES: A Dual-Language Book, Angel Flores (ed.). Unique format offers 13 great stories in Spanish by Cervantes, Borges, others. Faithful English translations on facing pages. 352pp. 5⅜ x 8½. 25399-6

GARDEN CITY, LONG ISLAND, IN EARLY PHOTOGRAPHS, 1869–1919, Mildred H. Smith. Handsome treasury of 118 vintage pictures, accompanied by carefully researched captions, document the Garden City Hotel fire (1899), the Vanderbilt Cup Race (1908), the first airmail flight departing from the Nassau Boulevard Aerodrome (1911), and much more. 96pp. 8⅞ x 11¾. 40669-5

OLD QUEENS, N.Y., IN EARLY PHOTOGRAPHS, Vincent F. Seyfried and William Asadorian. Over 160 rare photographs of Maspeth, Jamaica, Jackson Heights, and other areas. Vintage views of DeWitt Clinton mansion, 1939 World's Fair and more. Captions. 192pp. 8⅞ x 11. 26358-4

CAPTURED BY THE INDIANS: 15 Firsthand Accounts, 1750-1870, Frederick Drimmer. Astounding true historical accounts of grisly torture, bloody conflicts, relentless pursuits, miraculous escapes and more, by people who lived to tell the tale. 384pp. 5⅜ x 8½. 24901-8

THE WORLD'S GREAT SPEECHES (Fourth Enlarged Edition), Lewis Copeland, Lawrence W. Lamm, and Stephen J. McKenna. Nearly 300 speeches provide public speakers with a wealth of updated quotes and inspiration–from Pericles' funeral oration and William Jennings Bryan's "Cross of Gold Speech" to Malcolm X's powerful words on the Black Revolution and Earl of Spenser's tribute to his sister, Diana, Princess of Wales. 944pp. 5⅜ x 8⅜. 40903-1

THE BOOK OF THE SWORD, Sir Richard F. Burton. Great Victorian scholar/adventurer's eloquent, erudite history of the "queen of weapons"–from prehistory to early Roman Empire. Evolution and development of early swords, variations (sabre, broadsword, cutlass, scimitar, etc.), much more. 336pp. 6⅛ x 9¼.
25434-8

AUTOBIOGRAPHY: The Story of My Experiments with Truth, Mohandas K. Gandhi. Boyhood, legal studies, purification, the growth of the Satyagraha (nonviolent protest) movement. Critical, inspiring work of the man responsible for the freedom of India. 480pp. 5⅜ x 8½. (Available in U.S. only.) 24593-4

CELTIC MYTHS AND LEGENDS, T. W. Rolleston. Masterful retelling of Irish and Welsh stories and tales. Cuchulain, King Arthur, Deirdre, the Grail, many more. First paperback edition. 58 full-page illustrations. 512pp. 5⅜ x 8½. 26507-2

THE PRINCIPLES OF PSYCHOLOGY, William James. Famous long course complete, unabridged. Stream of thought, time perception, memory, experimental methods; great work decades ahead of its time. 94 figures. 1,391pp. 5⅜ x 8½. 2-vol. set. Vol. I: 20381-6 Vol. II: 20382-4

THE WORLD AS WILL AND REPRESENTATION, Arthur Schopenhauer. Definitive English translation of Schopenhauer's life work, correcting more than 1,000 errors, omissions in earlier translations. Translated by E. F. J. Payne. Total of 1,269pp. 5⅜ x 8½. 2-vol. set. Vol. 1: 21761-2 Vol. 2: 21762-0

MAGIC AND MYSTERY IN TIBET, Madame Alexandra David-Neel. Experiences among lamas, magicians, sages, sorcerers, Bonpa wizards. A true psychic discovery. 32 illustrations. 321pp. 5⅜ x 8½. (Available in U.S. only.) 22682-4

THE EGYPTIAN BOOK OF THE DEAD, E. A. Wallis Budge. Complete reproduction of Ani's papyrus, finest ever found. Full hieroglyphic text, interlinear transliteration, word-for-word translation, smooth translation. 533pp. 6½ x 9¼. 21866-X

MATHEMATICS FOR THE NONMATHEMATICIAN, Morris Kline. Detailed, college-level treatment of mathematics in cultural and historical context, with numerous exercises. Recommended Reading Lists. Tables. Numerous figures. 641pp. 5⅜ x 8½. 24823-2

PROBABILISTIC METHODS IN THE THEORY OF STRUCTURES, Isaac Elishakoff. Well-written introduction covers the elements of the theory of probability from two or more random variables, the reliability of such multivariable structures, the theory of random function, Monte Carlo methods of treating problems incapable of exact solution, and more. Examples. 502pp. 5⅜ x 8½. 40691-1

THE RIME OF THE ANCIENT MARINER, Gustave Doré, S. T. Coleridge. Doré's finest work; 34 plates capture moods, subtleties of poem. Flawless full-size reproductions printed on facing pages with authoritative text of poem. "Beautiful. Simply beautiful."–*Publisher's Weekly*. 77pp. 9¼ x 12. 22305-1

NORTH AMERICAN INDIAN DESIGNS FOR ARTISTS AND CRAFTSPEOPLE, Eva Wilson. Over 360 authentic copyright-free designs adapted from Navajo blankets, Hopi pottery, Sioux buffalo hides, more. Geometrics, symbolic figures, plant and animal motifs, etc. 128pp. 8⅜ x 11. (Not for sale in the United Kingdom.) 25341-4

SCULPTURE: Principles and Practice, Louis Slobodkin. Step-by-step approach to clay, plaster, metals, stone; classical and modern. 253 drawings, photos. 255pp. 8⅛ x 11. 22960-2

THE INFLUENCE OF SEA POWER UPON HISTORY, 1660–1783, A. T. Mahan. Influential classic of naval history and tactics still used as text in war colleges. First paperback edition. 4 maps. 24 battle plans. 640pp. 5⅜ x 8½. 25509-3

CATALOG OF DOVER BOOKS

THE STORY OF THE TITANIC AS TOLD BY ITS SURVIVORS, Jack Winocour (ed.). What it was really like. Panic, despair, shocking inefficiency, and a little heroism. More thrilling than any fictional account. 26 illustrations. 320pp. 5⅜ x 8½.
20610-6

FAIRY AND FOLK TALES OF THE IRISH PEASANTRY, William Butler Yeats (ed.). Treasury of 64 tales from the twilight world of Celtic myth and legend: "The Soul Cages," "The Kildare Pooka," "King O'Toole and his Goose," many more. Introduction and Notes by W. B. Yeats. 352pp. 5⅜ x 8½.
26941-8

BUDDHIST MAHAYANA TEXTS, E. B. Cowell and others (eds.). Superb, accurate translations of basic documents in Mahayana Buddhism, highly important in history of religions. The Buddha-karita of Asvaghosha, Larger Sukhavativyuha, more. 448pp. 5⅜ x 8½.
25552-2

ONE TWO THREE . . . INFINITY: Facts and Speculations of Science, George Gamow. Great physicist's fascinating, readable overview of contemporary science: number theory, relativity, fourth dimension, entropy, genes, atomic structure, much more. 128 illustrations. Index. 352pp. 5⅜ x 8½.
25664-2

EXPERIMENTATION AND MEASUREMENT, W. J. Youden. Introductory manual explains laws of measurement in simple terms and offers tips for achieving accuracy and minimizing errors. Mathematics of measurement, use of instruments, experimenting with machines. 1994 edition. Foreword. Preface. Introduction. Epilogue. Selected Readings. Glossary. Index. Tables and figures. 128pp. 5⅜ x 8½.
40451-X

DALÍ ON MODERN ART: The Cuckolds of Antiquated Modern Art, Salvador Dalí. Influential painter skewers modern art and its practitioners. Outrageous evaluations of Picasso, Cézanne, Turner, more. 15 renderings of paintings discussed. 44 calligraphic decorations by Dalí. 96pp. 5⅜ x 8½. (Available in U.S. only.)
29220-7

ANTIQUE PLAYING CARDS: A Pictorial History, Henry René D'Allemagne. Over 900 elaborate, decorative images from rare playing cards (14th–20th centuries): Bacchus, death, dancing dogs, hunting scenes, royal coats of arms, players cheating, much more. 96pp. 9¼ x 12¼.
29265-7

MAKING FURNITURE MASTERPIECES: 30 Projects with Measured Drawings, Franklin H. Gottshall. Step-by-step instructions, illustrations for constructing handsome, useful pieces, among them a Sheraton desk, Chippendale chair, Spanish desk, Queen Anne table and a William and Mary dressing mirror. 224pp. 8⅛ x 11¼.
29338-6

THE FOSSIL BOOK: A Record of Prehistoric Life, Patricia V. Rich et al. Profusely illustrated definitive guide covers everything from single-celled organisms and dinosaurs to birds and mammals and the interplay between climate and man. Over 1,500 illustrations. 760pp. 7½ x 10⅛.
29371-8